# *Graphic Design Time Line*

# *Graphic Design Time Line*

## *A Century of Design Milestones*

*Steven Heller • Elinor Pettit*

ALLWORTH
P · R · E · S · S

05  04  03  02  01  00    5  4  3  2  1

Published by Allworth Press
An imprint of Allworth Communications
10 East 23rd Street, New York, NY 10010

Cover and interior design by James Victore, Beacon, NY
Page composition/typography by Sharp Des!gns, Lansing, MI

LIBRARY OF CONGRESS CATALOGING-IN-PUBLICATION DATA
Heller, Steven.
    Graphic design timeline: a century of design milestones/Steven Heller,
    Elinor Pettit.
        p.   cm.
    Includes bibliographical references and index.
    ISBN 1-58115-064-4
    1. Commercial art—History. 2. Graphic arts—History. I. Pettit, Elinor. II. Title.
NC998 .H455 2000
741.6'09'04—dc21
00-060559

Printed in Canada

# TABLE OF **CONTENTS**

Acknowledgments . . . . . . . . . . . . . . . . . . . . . . . . . . . . . . . . . . . . . . . . . . . . .vii

Signposts of History . . . . . . . . . . . . . . . . . . . . . . . . . . . . . . . . . . . . . . . . .viii

✦

Pre–1900 . . . . . . . . . . . . . . . . . . . . . . . . . . . . . . . . . . . . . . . . . . . . . . . . . .2

1900–1909 . . . . . . . . . . . . . . . . . . . . . . . . . . . . . . . . . . . . . . . . . . . . . . . .14

1910–1919 . . . . . . . . . . . . . . . . . . . . . . . . . . . . . . . . . . . . . . . . . . . . . . . .36

1920–1929 . . . . . . . . . . . . . . . . . . . . . . . . . . . . . . . . . . . . . . . . . . . . . . . .58

1930–1939 . . . . . . . . . . . . . . . . . . . . . . . . . . . . . . . . . . . . . . . . . . . . . . . .80

1940–1949 . . . . . . . . . . . . . . . . . . . . . . . . . . . . . . . . . . . . . . . . . . . . . . .102

1950–1959 . . . . . . . . . . . . . . . . . . . . . . . . . . . . . . . . . . . . . . . . . . . . . . .124

1960–1969 . . . . . . . . . . . . . . . . . . . . . . . . . . . . . . . . . . . . . . . . . . . . . . .146

1970–1979 . . . . . . . . . . . . . . . . . . . . . . . . . . . . . . . . . . . . . . . . . . . . . . .168

1980–1989 . . . . . . . . . . . . . . . . . . . . . . . . . . . . . . . . . . . . . . . . . . . . . . .190

1990–1999 . . . . . . . . . . . . . . . . . . . . . . . . . . . . . . . . . . . . . . . . . . . . . . .212

2000 Postscript . . . . . . . . . . . . . . . . . . . . . . . . . . . . . . . . . . . . . . . . . . . .234

✦

Appendices . . . . . . . . . . . . . . . . . . . . . . . . . . . . . . . . . . . . . . . . . . . . . . .238

Bibliography . . . . . . . . . . . . . . . . . . . . . . . . . . . . . . . . . . . . . . . . . . . . . .247

Index . . . . . . . . . . . . . . . . . . . . . . . . . . . . . . . . . . . . . . . . . . . . . . . . . . .250

# ACKNOWLEDGMENTS

Finding correct dates is not as easy as it might seem. We've found that different sources often list the same event on different dates. So it was necessary for us to employ the services of two dedicated graduate students, who helped track down what we hope are the correct chronologies. Thanks to Lisa M. Brown, who began this project as a graduate student in Communications/ Packaging at Pratt Institute, New York, and is currently an associate art director of *Yahoo* magazine; and Peter Buchanan-Smith, who is a graduate of the MFA/ Design program at the School of Visual Arts, New York, and is now the art director of the *New York Times* OpEd Page. Without their dogged devotion this book would have been impossible.

We are also indebted to the librarians at the Richland County Public Library, Columbia, South Carolina, and the Thomas Cooper Library, University of South Carolina—especially to Thomas F. McNally, the University of South Carolina Librarian for Public Service. We also extend our gratitude to Dr. James Fraser of Fairleigh Dickenson University Library, one of the finest art and design research libraries on the East Coast.

Thanks also to various individuals who provided bits and pieces of information when our scholarly sources ran dry: Phillip B. Meggs, Rick Poynor, Paul Shaw, Mike Salisbury, Sheila Levrant de Breteville, Dugald Stermer, Martin Fox, George Theophiles, and Lita Talarico.

Of course, this book would not have been possible if not for the efforts of our publishing house, Allworth Press. Thanks to Nicole Potter, editor; Jamie Kijowski, associate editor; Bob Porter, associate publisher; and Tad Crawford, publisher, for his continued support. Finally, we are grateful to James Victore for his splendid design.

SH & EP

# SIGNPOSTS OF HISTORY

*Steven Heller*

T he worst thing about elementary school was being forced to learn "important" dates. Ah, the tricks we students had to play to remember the blasted
things, such as the ditty: "In 1492 Columbus sailed the ocean blue."
Although this particular event is forever etched in my mind, I still can't remember
when the Magna Carta was signed (12-something, right?) or when the Gettysburg
Address was delivered (it wasn't 1865, was it? No, that was the year of Abe Lincoln's
assassination). Thanks to a popular song of my childhood I do know that "In 1814
we took a little trip, along with Colonel Jackson down the mighty Missisip . . ." but
I'm not certain why.

What was so important about knowing dates anyway? Isn't it more meaningful
to understand the reasons for the Magna Carta or the implications of the Gettysburg Address? Which, incidentally, I didn't grasp at the time because I was too busy
trying to memorize dates. Learning these numerals was a mechanical function of
rote education. Sure, dates were necessary in placing historical events in chronologi-
cal context, but memorizing them as an end in and of itself did precious little to
encourage one's concern for or pleasure in the relevancy of the past. What's more,
not all the dates that I was given to memorize were accurate anyway. Come on,
Jesus wasn't really born on December 25, was he?

Nonetheless, dates are indeed the signposts of history. In fact, too many young
students today do not know which came first, the American Revolution or the Civil
War—unlike the two twentieth century world wars (or Super Bowls), they are not
followed by numbers. But even with these numerical designations, many pupils falter
when asked exactly during which timeframe the wars were fought. Or, for that matter, what year the Russian Revolution began, the United States dropped the first A-
bomb on Japan, John Glenn first orbited the earth, or President Kennedy and
Martin Luther King Jr. were assassinated. Of course, knowing dates alone is not
going to increase intellectual rigor, but at least dates provide grounding.

Nonetheless, by high school I was so turned off by the way dates were force-fed that I simply ignored them (just as I reflexively skipped over *italicized* passages of texts because I believed whatever was set in italic was extraneous). But at a certain point (though the date escapes me) I had something of a revelation. It came in the form of a book called *Flight*, one of those American Heritage tomes published in the mid-1960s, which, like comparable Time-Life books on eras and events, were the Ken and Ric Burns documentaries of their day. In *Flight* I was first introduced to a "timeline" which juxtaposed dates in relation to other dates. But these were not mere numbers detached from meaning, rather they were markers along a continuum of time and place. In fact, under each year there were brief texts that gave a concise narrative about the legacy of flight. Although to thoroughly understand how manned flight evolved from biplanes to supersonic aircraft required a closer reading, the timeline summarily covered many milestones in less than half the reading time. The timeline also was the glue that bonded the raw data together. From that moment on I became something of a timeline junkie.

A timeline is an index of facts. Yet it can be much richer than a terse summary. Although timelines filter out most verbiage leaving only the salient points behind, this veritable mainline of pure information can be quite pleasurable to read, particularly in the age of information overload. A timeline is indeed viable for detailed narratives, as in museum or gallery exhibitions where lengthy copy challenges a reader's tolerance. Of course, a timeline is, by definition, economical, but not all timelines need be reduced to a few pages. Obviously, the one you are about to read is rather extensive.

The idea to publish a book-length timeline comes from what I perceive is a lack in graphic design history courses of a simple tool which would succinctly outline the events that have shaped the broad field of visual communication. In recent years, although there has been a marked increase in design history curricula, owing to limited budgets and time constraints, these have mostly been general surveys that last a semester or less. However, even the skimpiest overview of movements, styles, and personalities require considerable time to impart and absorb. So this timeline is designed to complement the survey class by highlighting significant (and sometimes forgotten) events, works, and people and enabling students to view them as components of a great continuum. The timeline does not replace broader anecdotal or critical narratives, but rather serves as a study guide that supplements the organization of history into accessible units.

Another motive for developing this book is that in writing graphic design history, referencing dates is an invariably arduous yet necessary task. Perhaps this compilation will help the neophyte scholar, as well as the casual student, find his or her way through the morass of historical detail by providing an "at-a-glance" sketch of the intersection between graphic design, mass media, popular culture, technology, and world events. Indeed, the entries on this timeline are both related and disparate, but when read in conjunction with more detailed historical analyses, they provide insight into graphic design's cultural role.

This timeline ostensibly examines the nexus where the graphic design legacy parallels and intersects kindred arts and other cultural manifestations throughout the twentieth century. Although the first section addresses developments prior to this timeframe (1890–1899), graphic design came of age as a discrete commercial art during the 1900s. It further was adapted by other visual arts during this time and split off into numerous subsets and genres. This timeline is, therefore, based on an admittedly catholic view of graphic design that extends beyond typography and layout into visual and textual communications of numerous kinds.

For example, advertising, which is tainted by hucksterism, has long been at odds with so-called pure graphic design. However, graphic design has played an important role in the arts of persuasion throughout the century, especially in the United States. Hence included are many entries about the development of advertising campaigns, slogans, trademarks, and agencies. Modern art movements, particularly in Europe, have borrowed from advertising design and, in turn, influenced typography; hence, the abundance of entries on this subject.

The timeline is admittedly centered on Western developments (although the formation of the commercial arts in China and Japan are accounted for). It is important to focus on the wellsprings of Western graphic design and advertising, owing to the birth of industrialization and commercialization in these regions, and yet it is imperative to cover events and individuals that held sway in other cultures.

Not only is this a straightforward directory of facts—births, deaths, premieres, foundings, closings, etc.—this timeline is also a miscellany of curious arcana, small blips that have nonetheless had impact on the design legacy. There is no attempt, however, to distinguish between acknowledged major events and presumably minor occurrences because each has its own inherent significance. Juxtaposing the origin of a major typeface, for example, next to a lesser alphabet does not diminish the importance of the latter but reveals the level of creative production at a particular time. And who can argue with the contention that, seen in the context of the past and the future, minor inventions or events can prove to be the precursors of major developments in history? This book aspires to be more than a record, it should be a stimulus for further discovery.

The timeline does not endeavor to sum up each and every decade as though every ten years is a clearly defined package. Graphic design is influenced and characterized, in part, by certain consequential events, such as war, economic depression, technological progression, etc., but these are not neatly confined to five or ten year categories. During war there may be a surge in propaganda (which is reflected herein), but this endeavor continues long afterward. The Modern movement, for example, emerged over a period of time beginning in the early twentieth century, but it did not precipitously cease the instant the term "Postmodernism" was coined. Entries, therefore, address the overlapping nature of visual communications as a way of showing that history is not as neatly organized as the history books make it appear.

Yet in a field that did not earnestly begin to chronicle its own history until fairly recently, providing an accurate picture has not been easy. While every attempt has been made to track down viable data and unambiguous dates, accuracy is allusive. Paradoxically, many of the most common graphic design signposts point in different directions. While dates are clearly written on numerous artifacts, there are also many undated relics that lead researchers to countless inconsistencies. Individual memories are often fuzzy as well, and even presumably definitive resources are sometimes suspect. For this book, determining dates involved referencing primary and secondary sources—respectively, the individuals who made history and the history books, archives, and Web sites that have chronicled them. The most profound realization was finding that miscalculations could come from the horses' own mouths. Sometimes the experts and creators can be one or many years off. So we apologize in advance for any mistakes and welcome rectification.

This timeline is a record in the making, a starting point for an even more inclusive compilation. Additional suggestions are indeed welcome. For now, this is but a basic guide; through future revisions, however, it will become a definitive one.

# Graphic Design Time Line

18'90

# Radio has no future.

*Lord Kelvin, 1897*

# <sup>18</sup>**90**

## GRAPHIC ARTS

✴ Art Nouveau movement begins
and continues through 1910. Primarily
an architectural, decorative, and
graphic arts style, Art Nouveau is
noted for its use of flowing,
curvilinear lines, organic shapes, and
sensuous female figures. Influences of
the style are felt in architecture,
furniture, product and apparel design,
and in graphics and typography.

✴ Charles R. Ashbee forms the Essex
House Press. Editorial cartoons
become regular features in American
newspapers and continue to grow in
popularity throughout the decade.

✴ Walt McDougall fathers the
editorial cartoon as a regular feature
for the *New York World*.

✴ William Pickering becomes the
publisher of the Chiswick Press,
England. Chiswick concentrates on
composition and illustration of books
rather than printing process, and
begins the transformation of the visual
communications field by
distinguishing between printer and
designer.

## CONSUMABLES

🍴 Henry John Heinz distributes a
line of ready-to-serve foods. He
installs a ten-foot-high concrete sign
of the number 57, the symbol for the
company's range of products, and
builds one of the first large electric
signs in New York—a six-story
billboard at the corner of Fifth
Avenue and Twenty-third Street,
which includes a forty-foot pickle.

## ARTS AND CULTURE

🕯 Louis C. Tiffany begins producing
decorative glass.

🕯 Ty Tolbert Lanston invents the
Monotype machine, which controls
typesetting by means of a perforated
pattern.

Advertisement for Bing's L'Art Nouveau store in Paris

# 18**91**

## GRAPHIC ARTS

✦ William Morris founds Kelmscott Press and has a profound influence on several prominent members of the graphic arts community in turn-of-the-century Boston, including Daniel Berkeley Updike, Frederic W. Goudy, and W. A. Dwiggins. Though Morris's medievalism dies out as a style, his insistence on the integrity of materials and workmanship continues to be of great interest, as does his use of historical models for book design.

## ADVERTISING

❧ George Batten (1854–1918) opens George Batten Newspaper Advertising Agency (the first *B* in the later-formed BBD&O).
❧ Kate F. Griswold becomes the editor of *Profitable Advertising* journal (published through 1910), one of the earliest journals devoted to the business of advertising.

## ARTS AND CULTURE

♣ *Ladies' Home Journal* bans patent-medicine advertising.

## TECHNOLOGY

⚡ In France, Rene Panhard and Emile Lavassor invent the first true automobile.
⚡ The zipper is invented by W. L. Judson (United States).

## TYPE

✦ Peter Behrens designs the type specimen Initials.

William Morris, Kelmscott Press

Fraktur initials by Peter Behrens

# ¹⁸**92**

## ADVERTISING

⚓ N. W. Ayer & Son hires its first full-time copywriter.

## ARTS AND CULTURE

♟ Henri de Toulouse-Lautrec paints at the Moulin Rouge.

## TECHNOLOGY

♟ Escalator is invented by Jesse Reno.
♟ First car is produced by Henry Ford.

Henri de Toulouse-Lautrec, poster

# 18**93**

## GRAPHIC ARTS

✦ George P. Rowell founds *Printer's Ink*, a trade magazine devoted to advertising and its design (Boston).

✦ Talwin Morris becomes the art director for Blackie's publishing firm, London, and applies geometrical spatial division and lyrical organic forms of the Glasgow Group to mass communication. His work is a major factor in introducing Art Nouveau to the English public.

## ADVERTISING

❧ Asa Briggs Candler registers Coca-Cola as a trademark.

❧ Aunt Jemima trade character, created by Chris Rutt/Davis Milling Co., is introduced.

❧ Frank Munsey drops the cover and subscription price of *Munsey's Magazine*, marking the first attempt at keeping a magazine afloat through advertising revenue.

## TECHNOLOGY

⚡ Thomas A. Edison conducts his first experiment in the development of moving pictures, employing his Kinetoscope and George Eastman's roll film.

Advertisement for Aunt Jemima flour

## Graphic Arts

✦ *Chap Book* begins publishing in Chicago.

✦ Elbert Hubbard establishes arts-and-crafts workshop and commune called the Roycrofters in East Aurora, New York (it lasts through 1938).

✦ February 4 marks the beginning of Sunday comics in color. On that day the *New York World* printed Mark Fenderson's nine-panel pantomime "On the Tramp: A Song Without Words."

✦ Frederic W. Goudy, American book/type designer, starts Camelot Press.

## Type

✦ Theodore Lowe De Vinne, printer of the *Century* magazine, commissions Lynn B. Benton to design Century typeface.

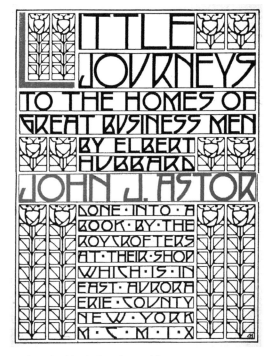

Books produced for the Roycrofters workshop

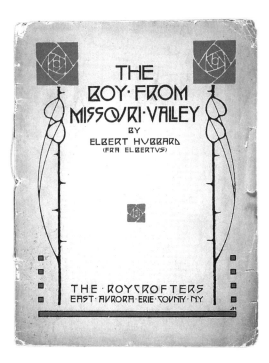

# <sup>18</sup>95

### GRAPHIC ARTS

✦ Ethel Reed designs poster *Folly or Saintliness*. Reed becomes the first American woman to achieve national prominence as a graphic designer and illustrator.

✦ *Field and Stream* publishes its first issue.

✦ Frederic W. Goudy starts Booklet Press.

### CONSUMABLES

☛ Safety razor is mass-produced by King C. Gillette.

### ARTS AND CULTURE

♠ Josef Sattler publishes *Pan* magazine, providing a forum for literature (until 1931).

### TECHNOLOGY

⚡ First practical system of wireless telegraphy is developed by Guglielmo Marconi, Italy.

⚡ X ray is discovered by Wilhelm Conrad Roëntgen.

# 18**96**

## GRAPHIC ARTS

✦ Albert Bruce Rogers (American) becomes designer for Riverside Press of the Houghton Mifflin Co. until 1912.

✦ *Argosy* magazine publishes its first issue.

✦ Art Nouveau becomes the popular style in Germany, where it is christened *Jugendstil* (Young Style), after the Munich arts and cultural periodical *Jugend*.

✦ Parsons School of Design is founded in New York.

✦ *Simplicissimus*, a magazine of modern caricature and cartoon, is started in Munich and edited by Albert Langen.

## ARTS AND CULTURE

♠ First modern Olympic Games open in Athens.

♠ Klondike gold rush begins.

## TYPE

♣ Bertram Goodhue designs typeface Cheltenham.

♣ Frederic W. Goudy designs Camelot, the first of more than 199 typefaces in his lifetime.

Cover of *Jugend*

Cover of *Simplicissimus*

# 18**97**

## GRAPHIC ARTS

✦ Henry Lewis Johnson, pioneer in graphic design journalism, helps found the Society of Arts and Crafts of Boston.

✦ *International Studio*, an art and applied art magazine, launches its first issue (published through 1921).

✦ Pratt Institute is founded in Brooklyn, New York.

✦ Rudolph Dirks creates the comic strip "The Katzenjammer Kids."

✦ *Sezessionstil* (a.k.a. Vienna Secession) is founded in Vienna. This countermovement to the floral excesses of Art Nouveau emphasizes geometric shapes, especially the square and rectangle. The painter Gustav Klimt is *Sezessionstil*'s first president, and key members are architects Joseph Maria Olbrich and Josef Hoffmann, and graphic artist Koloman Moser.

## ARTS AND CULTURE

♣ Cooper Hewitt (National Museum of Design) is founded in New York.

♣ Marcus and Sam Samuels found the Shell Transport and Trading Company in London, naming the company after their late father's trade—decorative seashells. In 1903, the company merged with the Royal Dutch Company (brand name, Crown Oil) to form the Asiatic Petroleum Co.

## TECHNOLOGY

♠ The electron discovered by Sir J. J. Thomson.

# 18**98**

## GRAPHIC ARTS

✦ *Outdoor Life* publishes first issue.

✦ *Ver Sacrum* (Sacred Spring) magazine of the Austrian Secession publishes its first issue, allowing designers to experiment with innovative graphic design, merging text, illustration, and ornament into lively formats, usually square. The publication makes unprecedented use of white space and coated stock, color plates are tipped in, etchings and lithographs are bound into volumes.

## ADVERTISING

❧ N. W. Ayer & Son is the first advertising agency to establish a separate design department to create its advertising.

❧ N. W. Ayer & Son helps National Biscuit Co. launch the first prepackaged biscuit, Uneeda.

❧ The Michelin Man (Bibendum) is conceived by the Michelin brothers, Edouard and Andre, and designed as a logo by publicist O'Galop.

❧ Uneeda biscuit introduces slogan "Lest you forget, we say it yet, Uneeda Biscuit."

## POLITICS

⚚ Spanish-American War begins.

## TECHNOLOGY

⚑ Diesel engine invented by Rudolf Diesel.

## TYPE

♣ Berthold Foundry produces the typeface Akzidenz Grotesks (refinements continue through 1906).

Bibendum, the Michelin Man

Page from *Ver Sacrum*

# 18**99**

## GRAPHIC ARTS

✦ *Die Insel,* literary journal in Munich, is the first magazine to establish uniform typographic layouts.

✦ Frederic W. Goudy becomes a freelance designer in Chicago.

✦ Frederick Burr Opper's comic strip "Happy Hooligan" debuts in the *New York Journal.*

✦ Hans Christiansen's cover design for *Jugend,* predates Fauve movement of the early twentieth century in its use of sans-serif letterforms and flat planes of bright color.

✦ Koloman Moser designs white-on-white embossed graphic design for *Ver Sacrum* (Sacred Spring) magazine.

## ADVERTISING

❧ Campbell Soup Co. makes its first advertising buy in national magazines.

❧ J. Walter Thompson Company becomes the first American advertising agency to open an office in the United Kingdom.

❧ National Biscuit Co. adopts Boy in Boots (created by N. W. Ayer & Son) as trade character for Uneeda Biscuit.

❧ The Association of American Advertisers, predecessor to the Association of National Advertisers, is formed.

## CONSUMABLES

➤ First stoppered-bottled of Coca-Cola is distributed. (Asa Briggs Candler had started the Coca-Cola Company with Charles Pemberton, Woolfork Walker, and Mrs. M. C. Bozier of Atlanta, but he bought out his partners in 1888).

## POLITICS

⚔ The Boer War begins. The British create the first "concentration camps" to imprison Boer fighters and civilians.

The Uneeda Biscuit boy

Poster for *Die Insel*

# 1900

# *Everything that can be invented has been invented.*

*Charles H. Duell, U.S. Commissioner of Patents, 1899*

# 19**00**

## GRAPHIC ARTS

✦ Bruno Seuchter designs *Die Fläche,* Austrian design magazine.

✦ Charles Dana Gibson creates his Gibson Girls.

✦ Cornell Greening creates "Prince Errant," one of the first comic strips to use legends and no "balloons" (phylacteries). His "Percy the Robot" is one of the first pictorial science fictions; and "Adam's Troubles Raising Cain" opens door to history and prehistory themes.

✦ Lou Rogers is the first American woman to do cartoons on suffrage.

✦ *Pan,* the arts and literary magazine founded in Berlin in 1895, ceases publication.

✦ Peter Behrens publishes *Celebration of Life and Art: A Consideration of the Theater as the Highest Symbol of a Culture.* It is considered to be the first use of sans-serif type as running text.

✦ *Sie,* album of drawings by Eduard von Reznicek, one of the exemplars of German *Jugendstil* illustration, is published by Albert Langen (Munich).

✦ Sports cartooning begins in San Francisco with Tad Dorgan, Rube Goldberg, Hype Igoe, and Robert Ripley; on the East Coast with Bob Edgren and Edward Windsor Kemble.

✦ T. J. Cobden-Sanderson, with Emery Walker, establish Doves Press at Hammersmith, England.

✦ The Seglitz Studio in Berlin is founded by Fritz Helmuth Ehmcke, Georg Belew, and Friedrich Wilhelm Kleukens. Germany's first comprehensive design studio, it becomes the standard bearer for the new graphic design and exists until 1903.

✦ Walter Crane publishes *Line and Form.*

✦ Will Bradley is commissioned to design eight full pages of house interiors for *Ladies' Home Journal.*

✦ Alphonse Mucha with Georges Auriol and Maurice Verneuil create *Combinaisons OrnAmentales,* which exemplify the fashionable use of art nouveau ornament in books.

## ADVERTISING

❧ Abott Graves designs "After all, no ink like Carter's" ad for the Carter Ink Co.

❧ Cecil Aldin Cadbury designs cocoa ad "Our Grandfathers Drank It" for Cadbury Bros. Ltd.

❧ Experimental advertising art in visual perception and market research appear in trade journals.

❧ Georges Auriol designs Otto Gotha advertisements.

❧ John E. Powers, the New York independent ad writer, is called "advertising's most influential copywriter."

❧ N. W. Ayer & Son advertising agency in Philadelphia establishes its "Business-Getting Department."

❧ Palmer Cox designs "Snag-Proof" boots ad for Lambertville Rubber Co.

❧ Publishers earn $95,861,127 from advertising in the United States.

❧ The first shell trademark for Shell Transport and Trading Company introduced is a mussel. However, in 1904, realizing that the mussel was too plain, the company chooses a scallop (pecten) as the official trademark.

## BIRTHS AND DEATHS

Beatrice Warde is born.
Georgy Stenberg is born.
Gerd Arntz is born.
Herbert Bayer is born.
Jean Carlu is born.
John Atherton is born.
Karel Teige is born.
Rudolph Belarski is born.
Vladimir Stenberg is born.
Yves Tanguy is born.
Ham (Hammond) Fisher is born
Chester Gould is born
Otto Soglow is born

Page from *Die Fläche*

## CONSUMABLES

☛ First hamburger is served at Louis Lunch, New Haven, Connecticut.

☛ First metal-capped bottled Coca-Cola distributed.

☛ Ground Vacuum Packed Coffee is introduced by Hills Bros.

☛ Hershey's Chocolate Bars are introduced.

## ARTS AND CULTURE

♠ Circulation of *Ladies' Home Journal* (Curtis Publishing Co.) passes 1 million.

♠ Hattie E. Wilcox creates arts-and-craft pottery.

♠ Number of U.S. magazines reaches 5,500.

♠ Paul Gauguin's *Noa-Noa* is published as a book.

♠ The Eiffel Tower and the Metro celebrate openings at the World Exposition, Paris.

♠ The Tenement House Exhibition is produced by New York's Charity Organization Society.

## TECHNOLOGY

⚡ Brownie Box camera is introduced by Eastman Kodak.

⚡ Charles D. Seeberger designs the first public escalator with steps, built by the Otis Elevator Company for the Paris Exposition.

⚡ Count Zeppelin flies his namesake airship.

⚡ Johann Vaaler, Norwegian, invents the paper clip.

## TYPE

✦ Arnold Böcklin designs Böcklin alphabet.

✦ Otto Eckmann designs Eckmannschrift typeface for the Klingspor foundry, the first German type foundry to commission new fonts from artists.

✦ Peter Behrens designs *Feste des Legens*, the first book to be set in all sans-serif type.

✦ Wilhelm Woellmer designs Siegfried alphabet.

Caricature by Eduard von Reznicek

# ¹⁹01

♪ Victor Talking Machine Company introduces the dog as Victrola trademark. Francis Barraud designs Victor Talking Machine Company ad "His master's voice."

## GRAPHIC ARTS

✦ Alphonse Mucha designs *Lisee, Princess de Tripoli* poster.

✦ The first issue of Gustav Stickley's art journal *Craftsman* is published in Eastwood, New York, and produced until 1916.

✦ *L'Assiette au Beurre (The Butter Dish)*, satiric illustrated journal published in Paris, includes the work of French painters Juan Gris, Felix Vallaton, and others.

✦ The Society of Illustrators is founded in New York.

✦ Elbert Hubbard publishes *Little Journeys to the Homes of English Authors*, first in a series of Roycrofters books.

## EDUCATION

✦ Henry van de Velde takes over the Weimar Academy of Arts and Crafts, later integrated into the Bauhaus.

## BIRTHS AND DEATHS

A. M. Cassandre (Adolphe Jean-Marie Mouron) is born.
Adriano Olivetti is born.
Henri de Toulouse-Lautrec dies.
Queen Victoria dies.
Theodore L. Bates is born.
Walt Disney is born.
William Paley is born.
André Malraux is born

## CONSUMABLES

✦ First instant coffee by Japanese-American Sartori Kato is presented at the Pan-American Exposition in Buffalo.

✦ Ransome E. Olds sells a staggering six hundred Oldsmobiles.

## ARTS AND CULTURE

♠ Frank Lloyd Wright publishes *The Art and Craft of the Machine*.

♠ Pablo Picasso begins his Blue Period.

♠ Wassily Kandinsky establishes the Phalanx association and art school in Munich.

# "HIS MASTER'S VOICE"
### REG. U.S. PAT. OFF.

Victor Talking Machine logo

## TECHNOLOGY

♠ First electric vacuum cleaner is developed by Hubert Cecil Booth.
♠ First peanut vending machine, from the Mills Novelty Co., debuts at the Pan-American Exposition in Buffalo, New York.
♠ Marconi transmits first transatlantic radio message.

## TYPE

♣ Bruce Rogers designs his first typeface, Montaigne, for Riverside Press's publication of *The Essays of Montaigne.*
♣ Frederic W. Goudy designs Copperplate Gothic typeface.
♣ Peter Behrens designs Behrensscript typeface, issued by Klingspor foundry.

Cover of *L'Assiette au Beurre*

## GRAPHIC ARTS

✦ Art Young, editorial cartoonist, goes to Wisconsin to lend his pen to Republican Progressive Robert La Follette's campaign to be reelected governor.

✦ British and American Tobacco Company (BAT) is founded and establishes design studio in Shanghai.

✦ Charles R. Ashbee's Guild of Handicraft in London moves to Chipping Campden in the Cotswolds.

✦ Charles R. Ashbee prints *The Psalter.*

✦ Cliff Sterret creates comic strip "For This We Have Daughters." It first appears in the *New York Evening Telegram.*

✦ Cracow School, Poland, is founded.

✦ Gödölo Workshops, Budapest, Hungary, is founded.

✦ *Handicraft* art journal in Boston founded and published until 1904, and again between 1910 and 1912.

✦ John T. McCutcheon creates first human-interest editorial cartoon, "The Boy in Springtime," for the *Chicago Tribune.*

✦ Koloman Moser designs the thirteenth Vienna Secession Exhibition poster.

✦ Richard Outcault creates comic strip "Buster Brown," which debuts in the *New York Herald.*

✦ Stile Liberty, the Italian version of Art Nouveau, reaches zenith at Turin International Exhibition.

✦ *Monotype Recorder* founded as the journal of the Lanston Monotype Corporation (ceases publication in 1970).

Poster by Koloman Moser

Arne Jacobsen is born.

Jan Tschichold is born.

Marcel Breuer is born.

Nikolaus Pevsner is born.

Otto Eckmann dies.

Ray Kroc is born.

Richard P. Lohse is born.

Théo Ballmer is born.

Thomas Nast, pioneer American cartoonist and caricaturist, creator of such symbols as Democratic Donkey, Republican Elephant, and the robust, jolly Santa Claus, dies.

Ben Duffy is born

## CONSUMABLES

🍗 Barnum's Animal Crackers are introduced by Nabisco.

## ARTS AND CULTURE

♠ Beatrix Potter publishes *The Tale of Peter Rabbit*.

♠ P. G. Konody publishes *The Art of Walter Crane*.

♠ The British Engineering Standards Association is founded.

## TECHNOLOGY

♠ Willis H. Carrier invents air conditioning for Sackett-Wilhelms Lithographing and Publishing Co. in Brooklyn, New York, to prevent contraction and expansion of coated paper.

## TYPE

♣ T. M. Cleland designs Della Robbia and Westminster Old Style typefaces.

## ADVERTISING

🦌 Earnest Elmo Calkins opens Calkins & Holden advertising agency in New York.

🦌 Shanghai advertising agencies begin using outdoor sources, transforming urban landscape.

🦌 Walter Dill Scott, advertising psychologist, writes about the psychological implications of persuasion for *Mahin's Magazine*, Chicago, until 1904.

## ARCHITECTURE

🦌 Frank Lloyd Wright designs the Ward Willitts House, Highland Park, Illinois.

🦌 The Flatiron Building, the first cast-iron structure, is completed in New York.

# 19**03**

## GRAPHIC DESIGN

✦ Charles W. Kahles creates comic strip "Sandy Highflyer" for the *Philadelphia North American*. (This is year the Wright brothers first fly.)

✦ Doves Press at Hammersmith, England, publishes *Doves Press Bible*.

✦ Edward Johnston designs initial caps for the *Doves Press Bible*.

✦ Gustave Verbeck creates the comic-strip series "The Upside Downs."

✦ Lucien and Esther Bensusan Pissarro design *Ishtar's Descent to the Nether World*.

✦ Peter Behrens becomes director of the Düsseldorf School of Arts and Crafts (until 1907), and changes the floral and decorative style of the nineteenth century to functional geometric form of the twentieth century.

✦ *Printing Art*, a graphic design journal, is founded in Cambridge and published until 1941. Henry Lewis Johnson, a pioneer in graphic design journalism, is the editor.

✦ *Ver Sacrum* (Silent Spring), the journal of the Vienna Secession founded in 1898, ceases publication.

✦ Walt McDougall creates comic strip "Fatty Felix."

✦ Wiener Werkstätte (Vienna Workshops), an outgrowth of *Sezessionstil*, are founded by Josef Hoffmann and Koloman Moser (last until 1932).

✦ Winsor "Silas" McCay creates the comic strip "Hired Hand," which predates his pioneering "Little Nemo in Slumberland."

## BIRTHS AND DEATHS

Adolph Gottlieb is born.
Al Hirschfeld is born.
Aram Khachaturian is born.
Ashley Haviden is born.
Camille Pissarro dies.
Fairfax Cone is born.
Fré Cohen is born.
Henry C. Beck is born.
Lester Beall is born.
Lu Shao-fei is born.
Paul Gauguin dies.
Bill (William) Holman is born.

## CONSUMABLES

➤ First decaffeinated coffee is introduced by German coffee wholesaler, Ludwig Roselius, in the United States in 1923.

➤ Pepsi-Cola is introduced.

➤ The first ice-cream cone is sold by Italian ice-cream salesman Italo Marcioni of New Jersey.

➤ The safety razor is invented by William Painter, employee of King C. Gillette, and the "disposable" era begins.

## ARTS AND CULTURE

♣ The New York Yankees are founded.

Marks for the Vienna Workshops

❀IT WAS THE TERRACE OF
God's house
That she was standing on,—
By God built over the sheer depth
In which Space is begun;
So high, that looking downward

Village Type specimen

## BIG BUSINESS

🏛 Ford Motor Company is founded by Henry Ford.

🏛 Shell Transport and Trading Company merges with the Royal Dutch Company (brand name, Crown Oil) to form the Asiatic Petroleum Co. in 1907. The company extends its trade worldwide and changes its name to Royal/Dutch Shell Group of Companies. The two parent companies keep their own separate logos (pecten and crown).

## TECHNOLOGY

⚡ Arthur Korn transmits images by telegraph.

⚡ Electrocardiograph is invented by Wilhelm Einthoven.

⚡ First outdoor telephone booth is erected by the Great Central Railway, London.

⚡ First powered flight is accomplished by Orville and Wilbur Wright at Kitty Hawk, North Carolina.

⚡ President Theodore Roosevelt sends telegram message around the world in nine minutes.

## TYPE

❧ Childe Harold Wills, Ford's first chief engineer and designer, develops Ford logotype from Heavy Script No. 9.

❧ Arthur Eric Rowton Gill becomes an independent letter cutter.

❧ Frederic W. Goudy designs the first Village Type.

❧ Morris Fuller Benton becomes type designer for American Type Founders Company (until 1912).

❧ Will Bradley spearheads campaign of type display and publicity for American Type Founders.

Marks for the Vienna Workshops

# ¹⁹04

## GRAPHIC ARTS

✦ C. R. Mackintosh designs the Willows Tea Room decorations in Glasgow.

✦ Clare Briggs creates "A. Piker Clerk," the first comic strip to appear across the top of a page in the sports section for the *Chicago American*. It's a hit, but Hearst cancels it because he finds it vulgar.

✦ Ferdinand Hodler designs poster for the XIX Exhibition of the Secession, Vienna.

✦ Herman Muthesius, cofounder of the German Workshop, publishes *Das Englische Haus.*

✦ J. L. Mathieu Lauweriks teaches geometric grid composition in Germany.

✦ Walt McDougall creates comic strip "Strange Visitors from the Land of Oz."

✦ Will Bradley designs for the American Chap-Book for American Type Founders published through 1905.

## ADVERTISING

✦ Buster Brown trademark is designed.

✦ Campbell's Soup Kid is adopted as trademark for Campbell's Soup until 1999).

✦ The Associated Advertising Clubs of America are formed.

C. R. Mackintosh cabinet for Willows Tea Room

## Arts and Culture

♠ J. M. Barrie publishes *Peter Pan*.

♠ Puccini's *Madame Butterfly* opens in Milan.

## Technology

♣ First electric milk shaker introduced by George Schmidt and Fred Osius of Racine, Wisconsin.

♣ First thermos flask is invented by James Dewar, Scottish scientist.

## Births and Deaths

Hans Neuburg is born.

Henry Dreyfus is born.

Neil McElroy is born.

Peter Arno is born.

Rudolf Arnheim is born.

Salvador Dali is born.

Theodor Seuss Geisel is born.

Walter M. Baumhofer is born.

Warren Chappell is born.

Xanti (Alexander) Schawinsky is born.

## Consumables

🍗 Campbell's Pork and Beans is introduced.

🍗 Dr. Pepper is introduced.

🍗 French's Mustard is introduced.

🍗 Rolls-Royce founded by Henry Royce and C. S. Rolls.

# ¹⁹**05**

## Graphic Arts

✦ E. P. Kinsella designs *The Blue Moon* musical-play postcard for the Lyric Theatre, London.

✦ Emmanuel Orazi designs *La Maison Moderne* poster, utilizing art nouveau letterforms to create a trademark design.

✦ F. T. Marinetti publishes *Poesia* magazine, a journal of poetry and prose, launching the literary concept of *parole in liberte* or words in freedom.

✦ Georg Jensen Workshop, Copenhagen, is founded.

✦ Jean Francois van Royen joins Dutch PTT (postal telephone and telegraph company) as designer.

✦ Jean-Pierre Pinchon creates the comic strip "Bécassine" for *La Semaine de Suzette* magazine.

✦ Lucian Bernhard designs Priester matches poster which launches the style called *Sachplakat* or object poster because its content is reduced to all but the company name and the object (matches) being advertised.

✦ Emmanuel Orazi designs *L'Hippodrome*, equestrian spectacle poster for L'Hippodrome, Paris.

✦ Massias designs poster for Cycles Gladiator, Paris.

✦ Maurice Leloir Chérubin designs musical-comedy poster for Théatre National de L'Opéra Comique, Paris.

✦ National Tuberculosis Association (NTA) sponsors the first traveling information graphics show designed to educate the public about tuberculosis.

✦ Sir Emery Walker designs series of German classics for Insel-Verlag, Berlin.

✦ The Society of Printers is founded in New York. The society is run by printers/publishers Henry Turner Bailey, George French, Carl H. Heintzemann, Henry Lewis Johnson, Frederick D. Nichols, William Dana Orcutt, Bruce Rogers, Daniel Berkeley Updike, and C. Howard Walker, all of whom actively support the founding of the American Institute of Graphic Arts (AIGA).

✦ Winsor McCay's comic strip "Little Nemo" debuts in the *New York Herald.*

## Advertising

❧ Aunt Jemima trademark is created.

❧ *Colliers Weekly* magazine begins using color in advertising.

❧ Rolls-Royce double red "R" trademark is introduced.

## Architecture

✝ Frank Lloyd Wright makes first trip to Japan.

✝ Josef Hoffmann designs and builds Palais Stoclet, Brussels.

## Births and Deaths

Berthold Wolpe is born.
Edward Rondthaler is born.
Jean-Paul Sartre is born.
Ernie (Ernest ) Bushmiller is born.

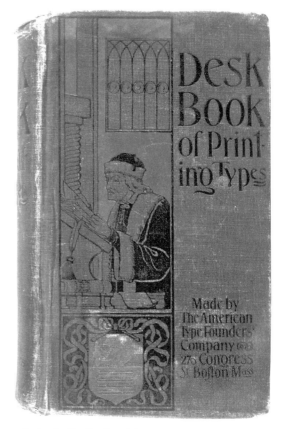

The American Type Founders catalog

## CONSUMABLES

⊤ First pizzeria is established by Gennaro Lombardi at 53$^{1}/_{2}$ Spring Street in New York's Little Italy.

⊤ Ovaltine is introduced.

## ARTS AND CULTURE

♠ Erich Heckel, Ernst Ludwig Kirchner, and Karl Schmidt-Rottluff found *Die Brücke* (the Bridge), association of expressionist artists, in Dresden.

♠ F. T. Marinetti lays foundation for Futurism, an activist art movement.

♠ Nickelodeon movie houses open in the United States.

♠ Number of magazines published in the United States reaches six thousand.

♠ Otto Wagner completes the modernist Vienna Post Office Savings Bank.

## INDUSTRIAL DESIGN

⊼ Gustav Stickley opens furniture design workshop in Eastwood, New York. His work is also displayed in his showroom/restaurant in New York City.

## TECHNOLOGY

♠ Albert Einstein formulates his special theory of relativity.

## TYPE

♣ American Type Founders Co. publishes *Desk Book* type specimen catalog.

♣ Ira Rubel invents offset lithography. Morris F. Benton designs Franklin Gothic typeface.

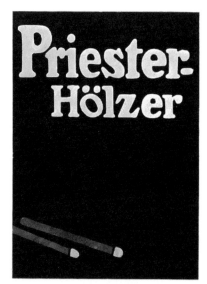

Priester match poster by Lucian Bernhard

*Poesia* magazine cover

# ¹⁹**06**

## GRAPHIC ARTS

✦ Adolf Loos condemns the excessive decoration of *Sezessionstil*, calling for functional simplicity.

✦ Alphonse Mucha designs *Weiner Chic* magazine cover.

✦ Charles W. Kahles creates the comic strip "Hairbreadth Harry" for the *Philadelphia Press*.

✦ Dmitrii Stakhievich Moor publishes his first satirical cartoons at an underground print shop in Russia to protest Czarist authority.

✦ J. C. Leyendecker designs U. of P. poster for the University of Pennsylvania.

✦ Lyonel Feininger creates comic strips "The Kin-der-Kids" and "Wee Willie Winkie's World," drawn in a *Jugendstil* (Art Nouveau) style, for the *Chicago Tribune*.

✦ New York's Charity Organization Society presents "Charities and Commons," a show that displays studies of urban life using photographs, diagrams, innovative maps, and graphic interpretations.

✦ Walt McDougall creates comic strip "Peck's Bad Boy."

## ADVERTISING

♣ Corn Flakes first advertisements, placed by W. K. Kellogg, run in six Midwestern newspapers.

♣ Daniel Starch, Daniel Starch & Staff, New York, publishes *Advertising: Its Principles, Practices & Techniques*.

## ARCHITECTURE

♰ Adolf Loos designs his Villa Karma, a vacation home in Switzerland. This design influences the geometric forms of the 1920s avant-garde. Loos blastsed the nineteenth-century love of useless decoration.

## BIRTHS AND DEATHS

Alec Issigonis is born.
Anton Stankowski is born.
Emerson Foote is born.
Eva Zeisel is born.
Gyorgy Kepes is born.
Jack Tinker is born.
Philip Johnson is born.
Qian Jun-tao is born.

"Wee Willie Winkie's World"

Rudolph Modley is born.
Samuel Beckett is born.
Phil (Philip) Davis is born.
Zack (Zachery) Mosley is born.

## CONSUMABLES
➤ First hot dog "hot dachshund sausages" are sold at Harry Mosley Stevens's concession stand at the Polo Grounds, home of the New York Giants.
➤ First soap flakes, Lux, are introduced by Lever Brothers, England.
➤ Kellogg's Corn Flakes are introduced.
➤ Milk cartons, rather than bottles, are introduced by G. W. Maxwell, San Francisco.
➤ Pure Food & Drug Act passed by Congress, forcing product labels to list active ingredients.

## ARTS AND CULTURE
♣ Ruth St. Denis introduces modern dance.
♣ Viktor Nikolaevich Deni is the first artist to exhibit at the Association of Independent Artists.

## TECHNOLOGY
♠ First radio is broadcast off the coast of Massachusetts, Christmas Eve, by Reginald Aubrey Fessenden, Canadian pioneer of radio telephony.

## TYPE
✦ Morris F. Benton designs Alternate Gothic typeface.

## ACT OF GOD
★ San Francisco earthquake.

San Francisco earthquake

# 19**07**

## GRAPHIC ARTS

✦ Berthold Löffler designs *Fledermaus* poster.

✦ Bud Fisher creates the first genuine daily comic strip "Mr. A. Mutt" for the *San Francisco Chronicle*.

✦ Dan Hoeksema designs Arnhem poster in Dutch art nouveau style.

✦ Everyman Library designed by Reginald L. Knowles, London.

✦ Herman Muthesius, architect, advocates unity of artists and craftsmen with industry.

✦ Hermann Muthesius founds Deutsche Werkbund with Peter Behrens. Walter Gropius begins a three-year assistantship with Behrens.

✦ Peter Behrens is appointed as design problem solver for Allgemeine Elektricitats-Gesellschaft (AEG), one of the world's largest electrical manufacturing corporations. He develops first cohesive corporate design program (until 1914).

✦ Rube Goldberg creates sports comics "Foolish Questions" for the *New York Evening Mail*.

✦ Will Bradley becomes art editor for *Collier's* magazine.

## ADVERTISING

❧ Advertising revenue at the *Saturday Evening Post* (Curtis Publishing Co.) surpasses $1 million.

❧ Claude C. Hopkins is hired as copywriter at Lord & Thomas, Chicago.

❧ *Country Life* magazine begins using color in advertising.

❧ The term "blurb" is coined by artist Gelett Burgess to describe a brief advertisement or announcement.

## BIRTHS AND DEATHS

Alberto Moravia is born.
Art Nelson is born.
Charles Eames is born.
Nicholas Bentley is born.
Norman Saunders is born.
Milton Caniff is born.

## CONSUMABLES

➤ Canned tuna introduced by A. P. Halfhill, San Francisco.

➤ Hershey's Kisses are introduced.

## ARTS AND CULTURE

♠ Pablo Picasso paints *Les Demoiselles d'Avignon*.

## INDUSTRIAL DESIGN

✦ Harry Peach founds Dryad, manufacturer of cane furniture.

## TECHNOLOGY

⚡ Color photography invented by the Lumière brothers.

⚡ Facsimile machine invented by Arthur Korn.

⚡ The first plastic, Bakelite, is invented by Belgian scientist Leo Hendrik Baekeland.

## TYPE

♣ Morris F. Benton designs Clearface typeface.

♣ Peter Behrens designs typeface Behrens-Kursiv, italic version.

Poster by Dan Hoeksema

# 19**08**

## GRAPHIC ARTS

✦ Bud Fisher's comic strip "Mr. A. Mutt" becomes "Mutt and Jeff."

✦ Henry van de Velde designs *Ecce Homo* by Friedrich Nietzsche.

✦ Ludwig Hohlwein designs his first PKZ poster for a popular department store.

✦ Otto Elsner publishes Maximilian Bern's *Die zehnte Muse*, set in Eckmann-Schmuck.

✦ Peter Newell produces one of the earliest examples of "interactive" publication design, *The Hole Book*, the first in a series of such novelties.

✦ Pirelli logotype is designed, and the image conveys its tire product's quality and elasticity.

✦ Robert J. Wildhack designs *Century* magazine cover for the Century Magazine Co.

## ADVERTISING

❧ Frank Pick, director of publicity for the London Underground, raises level of advertising and brings it to the forefront of graphic design.

❧ *Ladies' Home Journal* magazine begins using color in advertising.

❧ National Arts Club, New York, sponsors the first annual exhibition of advertising art, demonstrating that advertising art can be both effective advertising and of artistic merit.

❧ Stanley Resor with his wife, Helen Lansdowne Resor, open J. Walter Thompson Co. office in Cincinnati.

## ARCHITECTURE

⸕ Frank Lloyd Wright designs the Robie House, Chicago.

⸕ Gamble House, Pasadena, is designed by Greene & Greene, architects.

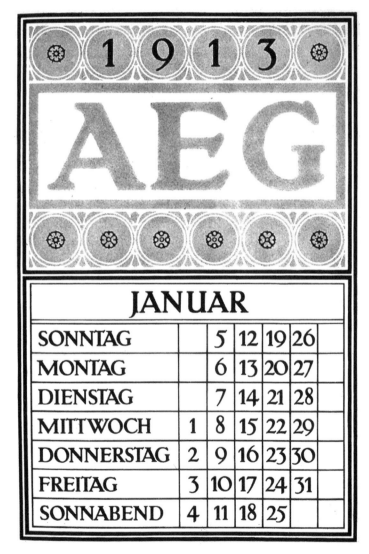

Calendar by Peter Behrens

## BIRTHS AND DEATHS

Erik Nitsche is born.
Frank Stanton is born.
George Giusti is born.
Joseph Maria Olbrich dies.
Max Bill is born.
Shirley Polykoff is born.
Sylvester L. Weaver is born.
Walter Herdeg is born.
Will Burtin is born.
Dave Berger is born.

## ARTS AND CULTURE

♣ Robert Baden-Powell creates the Boy Scout movement and develops its iconography.

♣ The Eight is founded in New York. These painters, who created images of real, gritty urban life, are later known as members of the Ashcan School (it is said that people of taste would throw their paintings in the ash can).

## BIG BUSINESS

🏛 Olivetti Corporation, Italian typewriter and business machines company, is founded by Camillo Olivetti.

## INDUSTRIAL DESIGN

✦ Peter Behrens designs electric table fan for AEG.

## TECHNOLOGY

♠ First Model T Ford is introduced.

♠ Geiger counter invented by Hans Geiger and W. Müller at Manchester University, England.

## TYPE

♣ Frederic W. Goudy begins association with Lanston Monotype Company, designs 122 typefaces.

♣ Frederic W. Goudy publishes *The Alphabet*.

♣ Fritz Helmuth Ehmcke designs Ehmcke typeface.

♣ Morris F. Benton designs News Gothic typeface.

♣ Peter Behrens designs Behrens-Antiqua typeface.

*Ecce Homo* by Henry van de Velde

# 19**09**

## GRAPHIC ARTS

✦ F. (Filippo) T. Marinetti publishes *Manifesto of Futurism* in Paris, *Le Figaró* and inaugurates Futurism, a revolutionary movement in all arts that includes experimentation with typographic form and syntax.

✦ Fritz Helmuth Ehmcke designs *Insel-Almanach* cover.

✦ Italian comic-strip production begins with "Attilio Mussino's Bilbolbul" for the *Corriere dei Piccoli.*

✦ Strobridge, artist for Barnum & Bailey Circus, designs the *Greatest Show on Earth* poster.

✦ Winsor McCay creates the first animated cartoon, "Gertie the Dinosaur," which includes a live action segment of McCay himself.

✦ *Der Sturm* founded by Herwarth Walden as a German avant-garde culture and art journal (ceases publication in 1932)

## ADVERTISING

❦ Publishers earn $202,527,925 from advertising in the United States.

❦ Royal/Dutch Shell Group of Companies abandons the Crown Oil trade name and adopts the name Shell for their petrol and the pecten for their logo.

## ARCHITECTURE

🕇 Frank Lloyd Wright completes the Robie House in Chicago.

## BIRTHS AND DEATHS

Al (Alfred )Capp is born.
Dick Dooijes is born.
Frederick Remington dies.
Herbert L. Block is born.
Reynolds Stone is born.
Alexander Raymond is born.

## ARTS AND CULTURE

♣ Diaghilev Ballet gives its first performance at the Châtelet Theatre in Paris.

♣ Georges Braque paints *Pitcher and Violin.*

♣ Wassily Kandinsky founds the *Neue Kunstlervereinigung* (New Artists' Society) in Munich.

♣ Pablo Picasso and Georges Braque develop Analytical Cubism.

♣ Robert Peary reaches North Pole.

♣ Sergei Diaghilev founds Ballets Russes.

Royal/Dutch Shell Group logo

## BIG BUSINESS

🏛 Alfa Romeo is founded in Milan.

🏛 Condé Nast of Condé Nast
Publications, New York, purchases
Paris *Vogue*.

## INDUSTRIAL DESIGN

✈ Peter Behrens completes the
modernist steel and glass AEG
Turbine Factory and designs electric
kettles for AEG.

MARINETTI
declama
un'areopoesia

F. T. Marinetti

# 19'10

*That the automobile has practically reached the limit of its development is suggested by the fact that during the past year no improvements of a radical nature have been introduced.*

*Scientific American, Jan. 2, 1909*

# 19**10**

## GRAPHIC ARTS

✦ Carl Moll designs *Beethoven Hauser* catalog cover.

✦ Harry Hirshfield creates comic strip "Abie the Agent."

✦ Harry Hirshfield satirizes the serial movies of the day in comic strip "Desperate Desmond."

✦ Lucian Bernhard designs GEG posters (through c. 1912), for German power company.

✦ Maxfield Parrish designs *Collier's* magazine cover (the Idiot or the Booklover) for P. F. Collier & Son.

✦ Gap closes between nineteenth-century Art Nouveau and twentieth-century Geometric Formalism.

✦ Peter Behrens designs AEG Lamp poster.

✦ Symbol for London Transport based on the wheel of an engine appears, original designer unknown.

✦ *The Masses* publishes first issue. Art Young, John Sloan, Robert Minor, and George Bellows are among the artists who create cartoons and graphic commentary.

✦ Will Bradley becomes art director for *Good Housekeeping, Century,* and *Metropolitan* magazines simultaneously and continues through 1915. He also revises the typographic makeup of the *Christian Science Monitor.*

## ADVERTISING

❧ Cyrus H. K. Curtis of Curtis Publishing Co., Philadelphia, develops the Advertising Code, which presages the "truth in advertising" doctrine that calls for honest claims of product viability.

❧ J. V. Cissarz designs Restaurant Bahnhof ad.

❧ *Das Plakat,* the journal of the Society of the Friends of the Poster, is founded in Berlin by Hans Sachs.

## BIRTHS AND DEATHS

Allen Hurlburt is born.

Eero Saarinen is born.

Jean Genet is born.

Leo Lionni is born.

Roger Excoffon is born.

Rosser Reeves is born.

C. C. (Charles Clarence) Beck is born.

Misha Black is born.

## ARTS AND CULTURE

♠ Antonio Sant'Elia publishes the *Manifesto of Futurist Architecture.*

♠ F. T. Marinetti publishes *Manifesto of the Futurist Painters* with five Italian artists: Umberto Boccioni, Carlo Carrá, Luigi Russolo, Giacomo Balla, and Gino Severini.

♠ Herwarth Walden founds the journal *Der Sturm* to explore and promote expressionist art.

♠ Max Pechstein founds the Neue Secession in Berlin, a collective of expressionist artists.

♠ Piet Mondrian introduced to Cubism.

♠ Wassily Kandinsky publishes *Concerning the Spiritual in Art,* which leads the way to nonobjective art.

Cover of *Good Housekeeping*

## TECHNOLOGY

⚘ Neon light invented by Georges
Claude for the Grand Palais in Paris.
⚘ Tubular steel used in Fokker Spider
Mark 1 aeroplane.

## TYPE

♣ Sol Hess designs Hess Bold
typeface.
♣ Rudolf Koch designs Condensed
German Script (he continues to refine
it through 1913).

## ACT OF GOD

★ Halley's Comet sweeps across the
sky.

Cover of *Das Plakat*

Cover of *The Masses*

# 19**11**

## GRAPHIC ARTS

✦ Fortunato Depero writes *Ruptures (Impressions-Signs-Rhythms)*.

✦ George Herriman creates comic strip "Krazy Kat and Ignatz."

✦ Hans Rudi Erdt designs Opel Motorcar poster.

✦ Harrison Fisher, illustrator of fashionable women, designs the *Ladies' Home Journal* magazine cover "A Romance and Social Number."

✦ Henry Lewis Johnson edits *Graphic Arts*, Boston until 1915.

✦ Jean Cocteau and Sergei Diaghilev design Ballets Russes *Le Spectre de la Rose* poster for Théâtre de Monte Carlo.

✦ Kwan Wai Nung, dubbed the "King of Calendar Art" in Hong Kong, becomes art director of the *South China Morning Post*.

✦ Lucian Bernhard designs trademark for Manoli cigarettes.

✦ Ludwig Hohlwein designs Herman Scherrer Tailored Clothes poster for his friend Hermann Scherrer.

✦ Margaret Macdonald, founding member of the Glasgow School, designs menu for Miss Cranston's Exhibition Cafés using the lines and squares that characterize her style of Art Nouveau.

✦ Peter Newell publishes *The Silent Book*, second in a series of "interactive" publications.

✦ *The Masses* magazine contributors reject notion of "official" left-wing imagery and journalism.

✦ Walt McDougall creates comic strip "Hank the Hermit."

✦ Willy Wiegand founds the Bremer Press in Germany.

## ADVERTISING

❧ Advertising Clubs of America (formed in 1904) becomes the Associated Advertising Clubs of America.

❧ Association of New York Agents, predecessor to the American Association of Advertising Agencies, is formed.

❧ Harrison K. McCann becomes ad manager for Standard Oil Co.

❧ Morton Salt Girl trademark is introduced.

❧ Procter & Gamble becomes the first company in history to pay an outside advertising agency, J. Walter Thompson, to launch its product, Crisco.

❧ Vacuum Oil Co., South Africa, adopts white Pegasus for its trademark.

❧ Woodbury Soap launches "The skin you love to touch" campaign in the *Ladies' Home Journal*. It's the first time overt sex appeal is used in advertising.

## ARCHITECTURE

🕆 Walter Gropius designs Fagus Shoe Factory, at Alfeld an der Leine, Germany, one of the first modern buildings to incorporate glass-curtain walls.

## Births and Deaths

Bradbury Thompson is born.
Cipe Pineles is born.
David Ogilvy is born.
Giancarlo Menotti is born.
Marshall McLuhan is born.
Morton Goldsholl is born.
Nicolette Gray is born.
Qin Wei is born.
Talwin Morris dies.
William Bernbach is born.
William Golden is born.
Otto Binder is born.
Burne Hogarth is born.

## Arts and Culture

♣ Franz Pfemfert founds *Die Aktion*, expressionist literary and political journal.
♣ Czech Cubism begins.
♣ *Der Bluer Reiter* is founded in Munich. This Expressionist movement includes such members as Wassily Kandinsky, Franz Marc, Paul Klee, August Macke, and Gabrielle Munter.
♣ Hollywood's first film studio, Nestor Film Co., begins production.
♣ Madame Curie receives the Nobel Prize.
♣ Marcel Duchamp paints the first version of *Nude Descending a Staircase*.

## Type

♣ Frederic W. Goudy designs Kennerly and Deepdene typefaces.
♣ Rudolf Koch designs Halfwide German Script (refinements continue through 1913).

Manoli posters by Lucian Bernhard

# 19**12**

## GRAPHIC ARTS

✦ Cliff Sterret creates comic strip "Polly and Her Pals" (ends in 1958).

✦ E. McKnight Kauffer emigrates from the United States to Europe and lives in Munich and Paris.

✦ George Kenngott publishes *The Record of a City*, a social survey of Lowell, Massachusetts, with colored maps by Chester Wheeler.

✦ George McManus creates comic strips "Their Only Child," "Rosie's Beau," and "Bringing Up Father" (a.k.a. "Maggie and Jiggs").

✦ John Sloan becomes art editor for *The Masses*.

✦ Lucian Bernhard designs Bernhard Block type specimen, Stiller Shoes poster, and trademark for Hommel Micrometers.

✦ Peter Newell publishes *The Rocket Book*, third in a series of "interactive" publications.

✦ William Randolph Hearst establishes the first genuine comic-strip syndicate, the International News Service.

## ADVERTISING

✦ Ford adds the oval to its distinctive logo.

✦ Harrison K. McCann forms H. K. McCann, introduces the "total marketing" concept in advertising.

✦ James Webb Young joins J. Walter Thompson, Cincinnati, as copywriter.

✦ Morton Salt ad "When It Rains It Pours" is created by N. W. Ayer & Son.

✦ World's first neon advertising sign CINZANO is erected on the Boulevard Haussmann in Paris.

## EDUCATION

✦ Liu Hai-su, Jiangsu Province, introduces first formalized art and design curriculum in China, based on Western methodology. This same year he founds the Shanghai Institute of Fine Art.

## BIRTHS AND DEATHS

Alexander Liberman is born.
Cai Zhen-hau is born.
Carl Dair is born.
Finn Juhl is born.
Giovanni Pintori is born.
Jackson Pollock is born.
Li Qun is born.
Morris Louis is born.
Ollie Harrington is born.
Ray Eames is born.
Alfred Andriola born.
John Cheever is born.
Ray Eames is born.

Hommel poster by Lucian Bernhard

♣ Vladimir Vladimirovich Mayakovsky collaborates on the futurist manifesto *A Slap in the Face of Public Taste.*
♣ *Der Blaue Reiter Almanach* is published.
♣ F. T. Marinetti publishes *Technical Manifesto of Futurist Literature.*
♣ Frank Lloyd Wright designs Clooney house in Riverside, Illinois, with geometric stained-glass windows.
♣ Herwarth Walden opens Der Sturm gallery.
♣ Juan Gris paints *Portrait of Picasso.*
♣ Mikhail Larionov and Natalia Goncharova establish Rayonism in Russia.
♣ Tarzan makes his first appearance in the *All-Story* magazine.
♣ Vaslav Nijinsky appears as the Blue God in *Le Dieu Bleu*, Ballets Russes, costume design by Léon N. Bakst.

## CONSUMABLES

🍴 Manhattan deli proprietor Richard Hellman introduces ready-made mayonnaise, Hellman's Blue Ribbon Mayonnaise.
🍴 Oreo cookies are introduced.

## ARTS AND CULTURE

♣ Aleksei Kruchenykh publishes *Old-time Love*, first Russian futurist poetry book, with ornamentation by Mikhail Larionov.
♣ El Lissitzky's (Lazar Markovich Lissitzky) first exhibition takes place at the Union of Artists, St. Petersburg.

## TECHNOLOGY

♠ David Sarnoff provides *Titanic* survivor lists to newspapers via Morse code.
♠ Plate tectonics hypothesis originated by Alfred Wegener, Germany (continues through 1915).

## TYPE

♣ Imprint typeface is designed, the first typeface created specifically for the Monotype type foundry and named for the typographic journal *The Imprint.*
♣ Louis Oppenheim designs Lo Kursiv, Die Lo Schriften, and Lo Schrift typefaces.

## ACT OF GOD

★ *Titanic* sinks, 1,513 drown.

Ford Motor Company logo

Type specimen by Louis Oppenheim

# ¹⁹13

## GRAPHIC ARTS

✦ Daniel R. Fitzpatrick, editorial cartoonist, succeeds Robert Minor at the *St. Louis Dispatch*, to become a power in the Mississippi Valley.

✦ Elizabeth Colwell becomes the only woman ever featured in the *Graphic Arts* magazine.

✦ George Herriman's comic strip, "Krazy Kat and Ignatz" becomes "Krazy Kat."

✦ Giovanni Papini publishes *Lacerba* in Florence. The new graphic method called "free typography" and "words in freedom" continues.

✦ Harry Graf Kessler starts Cranach Press in Weimar, Germany.

✦ Martin Munkacsi, Hungarian photographer, goes to work for *Harper's Bazaar* using a new miniature camera.

✦ P. E. Vibert creates woodcuts for *Le Nouveau Monde*.

✦ Rudolph Dirks loses rights to the title and original characters of his comic strip "The Katzenjammer Kids," but retains the right to draw same characters under a new title creating "The Captain and the Kids."

✦ William Randolph Hearst purchases *Harper's Bazaar*.

## ADVERTISING

✤ *American Magazine* begins using color in advertising.

✤ J. C. Leyendecker illustrates "Arrow Collars and Shirts for Dress" ad (man/woman dancing) for Cluett, Peabody & Co, Inc.

✤ R. J. Reynolds adopts a one-humped dromedary for the Camel cigarettes pack after a photograph of "Old Joe," a camel from the Barnum & Bailey Circus.

## BIRTHS AND DEATHS

Ad Reinhardt is born.

Albe Steiner is born.

Ferdinand de Saussure, Swiss founder of modern linguistics, dies.

Otto Storch is born.

Tolbert Lanston dies.

Walter Landor is born.

Albert Camus born.

Walt (Walter) Kelly born.

## CONSUMABLES

➤ 92,000 telephones in Paris, 500,000 in New York.

➤ Peppermint Life Savers are introduced.

## ARTS AND CULTURE

♠ Alvin Langdon Coburn, photographer, focuses on patterns and structures rather than objects.

♠ Walter Benjamin publishes *The Renaissance of the Irrational.*

♠ Charlie Chaplin makes his first movie, *Making a Living.*

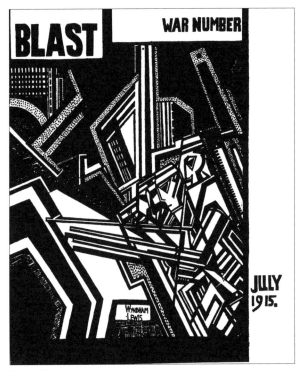

Cover of *Blast*

- Ebbets Field, home of the Brooklyn Dodgers, opens.
- The vorticist group forms in London, and is the first to explore avant-garde typography in its 1914–1915 journal, *Blast*.
- F. T. Marinetti publishes manifesto *Destruction of Syntax—Imagination without Strings—Words-in-Freedom.*
- Grand Central Station, New York, then the largest railroad station in the world, is completed.
- Kazimir Malevich paints *Black Square on White*, furthering the development of nonobjective art and ushering in the Russian Suprematist movement.
- Marcel Duchamp's *Nude Descending the Staircase* creates furor at the New York Armory Show.
- Stieglitz 291 gallery, New York, shows Marius de Zayas's abstract caricatures, considered among first abstract portraits in twentieth-century Western art.
- Synthetic Cubism is introduced.
- The New York Armory Show of European modernist art, the first major exhibition of avant-garde work, erupts in controversy.
- The Omega Workshop is founded by artists of London's Bloomsbury Group.

## POLITICS
- First Federal Income Tax is introduced.

## TECHNOLOGY
- Stainless steel is developed by Harry Brearley.
- 35mm camera is invented by an employee of Leitz Company in Germany.
- First moving assembly line is launched by Henry Ford.
- *The Imperator*, Hamburg-Amerika liner, the largest ship in the world, is launched.
- Citroën is founded by André Citroën.

## TYPE
- Emil Rudolf Weiss designs Weiss Fraktur typeface.
- Morris F. Benton designs Cloister Bold typeface.
- Peter Behrens designs Behrens-Medieval typeface.
- The Packard Series of Type is designed by Oswald Cooper and Morris Fuller Benton.

Packard type specimen sheet

# ¹⁹14

★ Léon Bakst and Valentine Gross design *Scheherazade* souvenir programme cover for performances of the Russian Opera and Ballet at the Royal Theatre, London.
★ Ludwig Holwein designs Red Cross fund-raising poster.

## GRAPHIC ARTS

★ American Institute of Graphic Arts is founded in New York by founding members F. G. Cooper, Frederic W. Goudy, Hal Marchbanks, William Comfort Tiffany, William Edwin Rudge, and Cyril Nast. The AIGA, named by Charles McKay, elects William H. Howland, publisher and editor of the *Outlook*, its first president.
★ *Deutsche Werkbund* embraces Muthesius's rationalism.
★ Dmitrii Stakhievich Moor produces political cartoons in the *lubki* style.
★ E. McKnight Kauffer moves to London and applies principles of modern art to visual communications.
★ Fortunato Depero exhibits in *Esposizione Libera Futurista Internazionale* at the Sprovieri Gallery in Rome. He also experiments in plastic dynamism in an exhibition at the Circolo Sociale defined as "polemical." Depero further creates first Motorumoristic Plastic Complexes, and publishes *Plastic Complexity—The Free Futurist Game—The Artificial Living Being*.
★ Germany and Austria-Hungary poster designs of the Vienna Secession become major means of communication, particularly for propaganda, through 1918.
★ H. S. Foxwell creates comic strip "The Bruin Boys" for the illustrated magazine the *Rainbow* in England.
★ Hy Mayer becomes editor-in-chief of *Puck*, America's leading illustrated satirical magazine.
★ King Features Syndicate is established.

## ADVERTISING

❧ Associated Advertising Clubs of America (formerly the Advertising Clubs of America) becomes the Associated Advertising Clubs of the World.
❧ Painted Display Advertising Association becomes Outdoor Advertising Association.
❧ The Association of National Advertisers is formed.

## ARCHITECTURE

✝ Construction of the Fagus Factory is completed.

## EDUCATION

✦ Willard C. Brinton publishes *Graphic Methods for Presenting Facts*, first textbook on graphic techniques.
✦ Henry van de Velde, art nouveau architect, resigns as director of the Weimar Arts and Crafts School and returns to Belgium.

Exhibition at the AIGA, New York

Cover of *Zang Tumb Tumb*

important collections of modern art in America (before 1919).

♣ Russian Constructivism begins, ultimately splits into several factions at the end of the teens.

♣ Wyndham Lewis publishes *Blast*, a journal of Vorticism, the English variant of Futurism.

## BIRTHS AND DEATHS

Abram Games is born.

Alphonese Bertillon, inventor of fingerprinting, dies.

August Macke dies.

Emil Ruder is born.

F. H. K. Henrion is born.

Georges Peignot dies.

Henryk Tomaszewski is born.

Jack Cole is born.

Josef Müller-Brockmann is born.

Paul Rand is born.

Saul Steinberg is born.

Tadeusz Trepkowski is born.

Thomas J. Watson Jr. is born.

Tom Eckersley is born.

Vance Packard is born.

Virgil Finlay is born.

Walter Tracy is born.

Jim Flora is born.

Jerry (Jerome) Siegel is born.

## ARTS AND CULTURE

♣ Arthur Cravan attacks modern art in a review of the *Salon des Indépendants*.

♣ Clarence H. White School of Photography, New York, is founded by Clarence H. White and Max Weber.

♣ Edgar Rice Burroughs publishes *Tarzan of the Apes*.

♣ F. T. Marinetti publishes *Zang Tumb Tumb*, theory of "words-in-freedom."

♣ First exhibition of so-called primitive art, "African Savage Art," opens in New York.

♣ Giorgio de Chirico, Italian leader in the Metaphysical Movement, prepares the way for the Surrealists.

♣ Giorgio de Chirico paints *Premonitory Portrait of Apollinaire* and publishes *Departure of the Poet*.

♣ Jean Arp meets Max Ernst at Werbund exhibition, Cologne.

♣ Louise and Walter Arensberg assemble one of the earliest and most

## BIG BUSINESS

🏛 International Business Machines (IBM) is founded.

## INDUSTRIAL DESIGN

✦ Alfred Grenander designs tram interior for Berlin's elevated tramway.

✦ Walter Gropius designs the Mitropa carriage sleeping compartment, influences apartment design.

## POLITICS

✗ Austrian Archduke Francis Ferdinand and his wife, Duchess of Hohenberg, are assassinated by Gavrillo Princip.

✗ Federal Trade Commission Act is passed, and Joseph E. Davis is named first FTC chairman. Section 5 of the Act allows the FTC to issue cease-and-desist orders against dishonest advertising.

✗ The Audit Bureau of Circulations is formed and standardizes auditing procedures which tighten up the definition of paid magazine circulation.

✗ World War I begins.

## TECHNOLOGY

♠ Robert Goddard experiments with rockets.

## TYPE

✦ Albert Bruce Rogers designs Centaur typeface.

✦ Edward Johnston designs sans-serif type for the London Transport System.

✦ Morris F. Benton designs Souvenir typeface.

# THE AMERICAN INSTITUTE OF GRAPHIC ARTS

AS PREPARATIONS WERE BEING made in all parts of the World to send exhibits to the International Exposition at Leipzig for Book Industries and Graphic Arts, there was brought very sharply into notice the lack of an organization in the United States which looks after the interests of those connected with the Graphic Arts.

We have an extraordinary number of printers and publishers, etchers and engravers, men engaged in the paper and ink industries, artists and men of business who care for the graphic arts, but they have had no society, club or institute for a place of meeting, or an exchange where their several interests might be discussed.

Realization of this gap in our art societies led a number of gentlemen to plan the founding of an Institute of the Graphic Arts at once. Messrs Wm. B. Howland, Alexander W. Drake, John G. Agar, John Clyde Oswald and Charles de Kay were the first movers to this end. The Institute was incorporated and the following officers elected:

Honorary President, ALEX. W. DRAKE, of the Century Company, New York. President, WM. B. HOWLAND, Publisher the Independent, New York. Vice-President, JOHN CLYDE

Founding charter of the AIGA, New York

# <sup>19</sup>**15**

## GRAPHIC ARTS

✦ Alfred A. Knopf founds publishing company, encourages fine book design.

✦ Alfred Leete designs *Your Country Needs You* recruitment poster for the British Army, the prototype of James Montgomery Flagg's *I Want You.*

✦ Charles Dana Gibson becomes editor of *Life*, then a nationally renowned humor magazine.

✦ Design and Industries Association is founded in England.

✦ First issue of *291* is edited by Marius de Zayas and Paul Haviland.

✦ Fortunato Depero with Giacomo Balla publish *Futurist Reconstruction of the Universe.*

✦ Lajos Kassák founds the Hungarian Avant-Garde (until 1926) and publishes *A Tett* (Action) journal.

✦ Lucian Bernhard designs German Seventh War Loan poster and *Das Groshere Deutschland* periodical cover.

✦ *Rogue* begins publication, edited by Allen Norton.

✦ Street & Smith publishes the first all-crime pulp *Detective Story* magazine.

✦ Will Bradley works exclusively for William Randolph Hearst's enterprises, supervises the art for motion picture serials, including *Patria.*

## ADVERTISING

❧ Ira L. Hill designs Heatherbloom Petticoats ad (Ethel Barrymore) for A. G. Hyde & Sons.

❧ Theodore F. MacManus designs "The Penalty of Leadership" ad for General Motors' Cadillac (voted "The Greatest Ad of All Time" in 1945).

## EDUCATION

✐ Boardman Robinson, editorial cartoonist, leaves the *New York Tribune* and teaches at the Art Students League in New York.

✐ Frederic W. Goudy teaches lettering at the Art Students League, New York through 1924.

## BIRTHS AND DEATHS

Ai Zhong-xin is born.
Alvin Lustig is born.
Elbert Hubbard dies.
Robert Motherwell is born.
Silas Rhodes is born.
Tapio Wirkkala is born.
Walter Crane dies.
Yusaku Kamekura is born.
George Baker is born.

## CONSUMABLES

🌱 Kellogg's 40% Bran Flakes introduced.

*Das Grösere Deutschland* by Lucian Bernhard

## ARTS AND CULTURE

♣ D. W. Griffith directs *Birth of a Nation*.

♣ F. T. Marinetti publishes *Mountains + Valleys + Streets = Jaffre*.

♣ Fortunato Depero joins futurist group of painters and sculptors.

♣ Man Ray's (Emanuel Rabinovitch) first exhibition at Daniel Gallery, New York.

♣ The Circle of Hungarian Activists, avant-garde artists group, is founded.

## TYPE

♣ Albert Bruce Rogers refines his typeface, Montaigne, resulting in Centaur for Maurice de Guerin's *Centaur*, the typeface praised as the most elegant version of the much copied Jenson.

♣ Frederic W. Goudy designs Goudy Old Style typeface.

Cover of *Life* magazine

Borzoi Books logo

## GRAPHIC ARTS

✦ Bart van der Leck designs Batavier Line poster.

✦ *Deutsche Warenkunde* is launched, first publication to define and publicize standards of design.

✦ Edwina Dumm, one of the first women editorial cartoonists, creates cartoons for the *Columbus Monitor*, Ohio.

✦ Emile Cardinaux designs Palace Hotel poster for Palace Hotel, St. Moritz, Switzerland.

✦ Hans Rudi Erdt designs *U-boats Out* poster.

✦ Jay N. Darling accepts a syndication deal with the *New York Herald Tribune*, becoming the first editorial cartoonist to be nationally distributed.

✦ József Nemes Lampérth rejoins *MA* (Today) circle.

✦ *MA* (Today), a Hungarian radical arts journal edited by Lajos Kassák, is published in Budapest until 1919 and later in Vienna (1920–1925).

✦ Norman Rockwell illustrates his first cover for the *Saturday Evening Post*.

✦ The Malik Verlag publishes the left-wing *Neue Jugend* until 1917, with format and montages by John Heartfield and George Grosz.

## ADVERTISING

🦃 Antonio Gentile, age thirteen, designs the original Mr. Peanut for Planters Nut company trademark contest, the hat and cane are added later.

🦃 Coles Phillips creates Overland's "Never Before Such an Instantaneous Success" ad for the Willys-Overland Company.

🦃 Edward V. Brewer creates Cream of Wheat Breakfast Food ad for Cream of Wheat Co.

🦃 J. Walter Thompson coins the phrase "It pays to advertise."

🦃 J. Walter Thompson retires.

🦃 National Outdoor Advertising Bureau formed.

🦃 Stanley Resor buys J. Walter Thompson's agency for $500,000 and establishes the marketing and research department.

## BIRTHS AND DEATHS

Alex Steinweiss is born.
Antonio Sant'Elia dies.
David Stone Martin is born.
Franz Marc dies.
Marion Harper Jr. is born.
Max Caflisch is born.
Umberto Boccioni dies.
Bob Kane is born.
Jerome Snyder is born.
Marco Zanini is born.
Marco Zanuso is born.

Front page of *Neue Jugend*

## CONSUMABLES

✝ First fortune cookies are baked by George Jung of Hong Kong Noodle Company, Los Angeles.

## ARTS AND CULTURE

♠ BMW (Bayerische Motoren Werke) is founded in Bavaria.

♠ Cabaret Voltaire, founded by Hugo Ball, opens and closes in six months.

♠ Frank Lloyd Wright begins work on the Imperial Hotel in Tokyo.

♠ J. Allen St. John illustrates *The Beasts of Tarzan*, Edgar Rice Burroughs's first Tarzan book.

♠ The name "dada" is chosen in Zurich at Hugo Ball's Cabaret Voltaire when a group of young artists stick a knife into a French-German dictionary pointing to the word "dada," which means "hobby-horse" in French. This way of choosing an identity reflects the true level of meaninglessness that these artists saw in the world.

♠ Tristan Tzara and Jean Arp establish the Dada movement in Zurich, with Cabaret Voltaire as headquarters.

♠ Tzara publishes *La première aventure céleste de Monsieur Antipyrine* (the First Celestial Adventure of Mr. Fire Extinguisher), color woodcuts by Marcel Janco, defines Dada.

## INDUSTRIAL DESIGN

✦ Gispen workshops are founded by industrial designer, Willem H. Gispen, in Rotterdam.

## POLITICS

✗ Grigory Rasputin is assassinated.

## TECHNOLOGY

♠ Frank and Lillian Gilbreth release their Industrialization Fatigue Study.

♠ The Deutsche Normen Ausschuss begins national technical standardization in Germany.

♠ The loudspeaker, using the Audion triode developed by the radio pioneer Lee De Forest, is first used at the annual convention of the National Educational Association held at Madison Square Garden, New York.

## TYPE

✦ Edward Johnston designs Cranach Press Italic typeface.

✦ Elizabeth Colwell designs Colwell's Handletter and Colwell's Handletter Italic typefaces for the American Type Founders.

✦ Frederic W. Goudy designs Goudy typeface.

A B C D E F G H I J K L M N O P Q R S T U V W X Y Z a b c d e f g h i j k l m n o p q r s t u v w x y z $ & . : ; , - ! ? ' 1 2 3 4 5 6 7 8 9 0

Goudy type

Batavier Lun poster by Bart van der Leck

## GRAPHIC ARTS

✦ Committee on Public Information (CPI) is founded, with Charles Dana Gibson as the art director to the division of Pictorial Publicity.

✦ Dada artists produce periodicals and books that influence the New Typography.

✦ J. Allen St. John illustrates for *The Son of Tarzan.*

✦ James Montgomery Flagg designs *I Want You* poster.

✦ Joseph Leyendecker designs USA Bonds, Third Liberty Campaign poster.

✦ Julius Gipkens designs *Deutsche Luftfriegsbeute Ausstellung* poster for an exhibition of captured airplanes, example of German anti-Allies poster.

✦ Julius Klinger designs Eighth Bond Drive campaign poster.

✦ Marcel Duchamp publishes one issue of *Rongwrong*, with contributions by Carl Van Vechten, Allen Norton, and Helen Freeman.

✦ Oskar Kokoschka designs *Kunstschau* poster.

✦ Raoul Hausmann and Hannah Höch experiment with photomontage.

✦ Italian-born Sergio Tofano creates comic strip "Bonaventura."

✦ *The Blind Man, No.1* is published by Marcel Duchamp, Henri-Pierre Roché, and Beatrice Wood.

✦ *The Blind Man, No. 2* is published by Beatrice Wood.

✦ The *De Stijl* movement begins in the Netherlands. Founded by Théo van Doesburg, joined by painters Piet Mondrian and Bart van der Leck, and architect J. J. P. Oud, it ushers in objectivity and collectivism.

✦ Tristan Tzara, Hungarian poet, edits the periodical *Dada*, poets separate "the word" from its language context, using it as a purely visual form.

✦ Vilmos Huszar, founding member of *De Stijl* magazine, designs first issue cover.

## ADVERTISING

♣ American Association of Advertising Agencies, the first agency trade association, is established with 111 charter members.

♣ Josef Popp designs BMW trademark, Germany.

♣ Victor O. Schwab is hailed as "the greatest mail-order copywriter of all time."

## BIRTHS AND DEATHS

Armando Testa is born.
Ettore Sottsass Jr. is born.
Freeman Godfrey Craw is born.
Howard Luck Gossage is born.
Irving Penn is born.
Jock Kinneir is born.
Robert Lowell is born.
William F. "Buffalo Bill" Cody, who killed Indians, dies.
Hy Mayer is born.

## CONSUMABLES

➤ Marshmallow Fluff is introduced.

➤ Moon Pie is introduced.

➤ The Clark Bar is introduced.

## ARTS AND CULTURE

♠ Alexander Rodchenko, with others, founds the Union of Artists in Russia.

♠ Alvin Langdon Coburn develops first nonobjective photographic images, vortographs.

♠ Bart van der Leck publishes essay "The Place of Modern Painting and Architecture" for *De Stijl.*

♠ John Heartfield and his brother, Weiland Herzfeld, start the Malik Verlag (a left-wing publishing house) primarily set up for the publication of George Grosz's lithographs.

♠ Carlo Carrà and Giorgio de Chirico found the Scuola Metafisica (School of Metaphysical Painting).

Cover of *Dada*

♠ Marcel Duchamp displays his snow shovel and urinal as art at Society of Independent Artists' exhibition, New York.

♠ Piet Mondrian develops plastic art, reducing paintings from traditional to pure color and form.

♠ Stieglitz 291 gallery mounts Georgia O'Keeffe's first one-artist exhibition (and the gallery's last).

♠ The First Annual Exhibition of the Society of Independent Artists opens.

♠ Charles Sheeler, photographer, has his first show at the Modern Gallery, New York.

♠ First Dada exhibition at Galerie Corray, Zurich.

♠ Gerrit Rietveld designs his *Red and Blue Chair* using elementary forms and colors.

♠ Guillaume Apollinaire uses the expression "surreal drama" in reviewing a play in Paris, thus introducing the term to the Surreal movement.

♠ Hugo Ball writes Dada sound poems.

♠ Man Ray with Marcel Duchamp and Francis Picabia found the New York Dada movement.

**Lenin**

## POLITICS

↗ *The Masses*, edited by Max Eastman, is found "unmailable" under the Espionage Act of June 15, 1917, by the U.S. Post Office.

↗ Mata Hari is found guilty of espionage and executed in France. Nicholas II, the Russian czar, abdicates.

↗ The Progressive movement begins in China and continues through the 1930s.

↗ The Russian Revolution begins.

↗ The United States enter World War I.

## TYPE

♣ Morris F. Benton and T. M. Cleland collaborate on the revival of Garamond typeface for the American Type Founders Company.

♣ Morris Fuller Benton designs Century Schoolbook typeface for American Type Foundry.

**Red and Blue Chair**

*I Want You . . .* by James Montgomery Flagg

# {}^{19}\mathbf{18} 19**18**

## GRAPHIC ARTS

✦ Guillaume Apollinaire publishes *Calligrammes*, a book of poems, introducing the concept of simultaneity, a presentation of different views in the same work of art. Apollinaire dies of influenza later that same year.

✦ Charles Buckles Falls designs *Books Wanted for Our Men* poster for the American Library Association.

✦ E. McKnight Kauffer designs *Daily Herald* poster in a Vorticist manner.

✦ Ernst Ludwig Kirchner designs KG Brücke catalog cover.

✦ El Lissitzky joins IZO Narkompros.

✦ Ernst Keller joins Zurich *Kunstgewerbeschule*.

✦ Howard Chandler Christy designs *Gee!! I Wish I Were a Man* recruitment poster for the U.S. Navy.

✦ *Iskusstvo kommuny* (Art of the Commune), Russian radical arts newspaper designed by Natan Altman, begins publication and continues until 1919.

✦ János Kmetty joins *MA*.

✦ London Underground symbol is redesigned by Edward Johnston (refined again in 1972).

✦ *Rote Hand* (Red Hand), the left-wing German newspaper, begins publication and continues until 1921.

✦ Russ Westover, artist for comic strip "Betty," which debuts in the *New York Herald Tribune*, turns his work over to Charles A. Voight, the illustrator who will give Betty her real glamour.

✦ Will Bradley writes and directs motion pictures independently. He directs *Moongold*, a Pierrot pantomime shot against black velvet.

✦ Théo van Doesburg creates *Composition XI*.

✦ Viktor Nikolaevich Deni creates nearly fifty posters for the Revolutionary and Military Council of the Republic through 1921.

✦ Vladimir Vladimirovich Mayakovsky designs posters for ROSTA (Russian Telegraph Agency) through 1922.

## ADVERTISING

⚜ Bruce Barton, with Roy Durstine and Alex Osborn, opens an advertising agency in New York (destined for greatness).

⚜ Coles Phillips designs Luxite Hosiery ad for Luxite Textiles, Inc.

⚜ Edward A. Wilson designs Armand's Complexion Powder ad "In the Little Pink & White Box" for the Armand Company.

⚜ Gilbert Prilibert designs Michelin's tires *Bibendum* poster for the Michelin Company launching the trade character that exists today.

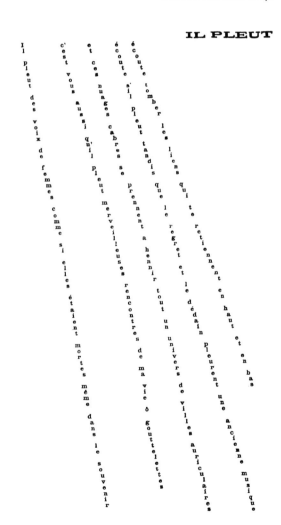

Apollinaire's *Il Pleut*

## Births and Deaths

Clifford Baldowski is born.
Gene Federico is born.
Guillaume Apollinaire dies.
Gundrun Zapf von Hesse is born.
Gustav Klimt dies.
Hans Rudi Erdt dies.
Herb Lubalin is born.
Hermann Zapf is born.
Koloman Moser dies.
Lou Dorfsman is born.
Morton Livingston Schamberg dies.
Wells Lawrence is born.
John H. Johnson is born.
Christian Schad is born.
Aleksandr Solzhenitsyn is born.

## Arts and Culture

♣ *After Cubism,* manifesto on Purism by Le Corbusier and Amédée Ozenfant, is published.
♣ America adopts Daylight Saving Time.
♣ *Arbeitsrat für Kunst* artists' group is established by Bruno Taut. Members include Walter Gropius, Ludwig Meidner, Lyonel Feininger, and Erich Mendelsohn.
♣ Bart van der Leck publishes essay "On Painting and Building" in *De Stijl.*
♣ Berlin Dada is founded by Richard Huelsenbeck, John Heartfield, George Grosz, and others.
♣ Christian Schad develops schadographs: bits of fabric, paper, and small objects on photographic paper composed in the darkroom.
♣ Club Dada, Berlin, is founded.
♣ Wassily Kandinsky joins the Soviet Commissariat for Popular Culture.
♣ Marcel Duchamp makes a miniature version of *Nude Descending a Staircase* for Carrie Stettheimer's doll house.
♣ Marcel Duchamp produces his final oil painting, *Tu m'*.
♣ Russian avant garde, taking its first steps toward developing the new "agitational media," creates large-scale public propaganda spectacles.
♣ The Modern Gallery, New York, closes.
♣ The *Novembergruppe*, a union of artists, architects, and writers, is initiated by Max Pechstein and César Klein.
♣ Vladimir Vladimirovich Mayakovsky writes play *Mystery-Bouffe*, directed in Petrograd by Vsevolod Meyerhold with theatrical designs by Kazimir Malevich.

## Big Business

🏛 Matsushita, largest manufacturer of electrical consumer goods in the world, is founded.

## Politics

🏹 284,114 women register to vote in New York City.
🏹 American Standards Association is founded, responsible for overseeing industrial manufacturing standardization.
🏹 Art Young and other *Masses* contributors are charged under the Espionage Act with "conspiracy to obstruct the [Army's] recruiting and enlistment" by objecting to the war.
🏹 Communist Workers' Party is founded in Germany by Rosa Luxemburg and Karl Liebknecht.
🏹 Manfred von Richtofen, the "Red Baron," is shot down.
🏹 President Wilson announces his "Fourteen Points" proposal for peace.
🏹 World War I armistice is signed on November 11.

## Type

♣ Frederic W. Goudy designs Goudy Modern and Goudy Open typefaces.
♣ Will Ransom designs Parsons typeface.

## Act of God

★ Worldwide influenza epidemic.

# 19**19**

## Graphic Arts

✦ Billy De Beck creates comic strip "Barney Google."

✦ Captain Joseph Patterson begins the *New York Illustrated Daily News* (soon shortened to the *Daily News*). It contains one comic strip, "The Gumps," by artist Sidney Smith.

✦ El Lissitzky designs *Beat the Whites with the Red Wedge* poster.

✦ El Lissitzky establishes, with others, Kultur Lige Yiddish publishing house, the Society for the Encouragement of Jewish Art, and the Exhibition of Paintings and Sculpture by Jewish Artists.

✦ Elzie Segar creates comic strip "Thimble Theatre."

✦ *Litterature* inaugural issue is edited by Louis Aragon, André Breton, and Soupault (published until 1924).

✦ Man Ray publishes sole issue of the pseudo-anarchist periodical, *TNT*, featuring Ilya Arenberg's poem *Vacuum Tires: A Formula for the Digestion of Figments.*

✦ Walt Wallet creates comic strip "Gasoline Alley" for the *Chicago Tribune.*

## Advertising

✦ Publishers earn $528,299,378 from advertising in the United States.

## Education

✦ El Lissitzky joins faculty at the Vitebsk Institute of Art and Practical Work, adopts Suprematism.

✦ First international and private exhibition of Bauhaus students' work in July.

✦ Lyonel Feininger teaches at Bauhaus.

✦ Walter Gropius becomes director of the Weimar Arts and Crafts School and Weimar Art Academy. He names the merger of the two schools *Das Staatliches Bauhaus* (the State Home for Building). The school opens on April 12 and exists through 1924. Gropius publishes the Bauhaus Manifesto and establishes philosophy of the Bauhaus.

## Births and Deaths

James K. Fogleman born

Gene Frederico born

Max Huber born

John Cullen Murphy born

John E. Powers dies

Carlo L. Vivarelli born

Gu Yuan born

## Consumables

➤ Citroën's Type A is created, Europe's first mass-produced car.

➤ Fiat Lingotto factory begins production.

## Arts and Culture

♠ El Lissitzky joins Kazimir Malevich's UNOVIS group.

♠ El Lissitzky and Alexander Rodchenko found Constructivist movement; they draw on the abstract paintings of Malevich and concrete typography of Futurism and Dada.

♠ El Lissitzky develops PROUN (Project for the Affirmation of the New).

♠ Fernand Léger creates *La Fin du Monde.*

♠ For the first time Census Bureau distinguishes between newspapers and periodicals.

*Beat the Whites With the Red Wedge* by El Lizzitsky

♣ Georgy and Vladimir Stenberg help found OBMOKHU (Society of Young Artists).
♣ Hannah Höch joins Berlin Dada group.
♣ Kurt Schwitters has his first Merz exhibition.
♣ May Fourth Movement in China (student demonstrations) is responsible for new explorations in artistic and literary circles.
♣ Bernáth Aurél joins *MA* group.
♣ Vladimir Vladimirovich Mayakovsky becomes a founding member of the Komfut group (Communist-Futurist) in Petrograd.
♣ *Walter's Room*, poem about Arensberg's salon, is published in the *Quill,* a Greenwich Village, New York, literary journal.

### INDUSTRIAL DESIGN
✦ Lloyd Loom, American furniture-manufacturing company is founded. It is first to use imitation cane work made of twisted paper.

### POLITICS
⚔ American Communist Party is founded in Chicago.
⚔ Peace Conference in Paris recognizes need for League of Nations.
⚔ Treaty of Versailles is signed by the Allies and Germany on June 28.

### TECHNOLOGY
♠ Albert Einstein's theory of relativity is verified through observations of a total eclipse of the sun.
♠ First daily airmail service begins between New York and Chicago.

### TYPE
✦ Frederic W. Goudy designs Goudy Antique typeface.
✦ Oswald B. Cooper becomes a partner in design firm Bertsch and Cooper, Chicago. He designs Cooper Old Style typeface for Barnhart Brothers and Spindler Foundry of Chicago.

Art department at Barnhard Brothers and Spindler

# 36 Point COOPER Oldstyle
# ABCDEFGHIJKLMNOPQRS
# TUVWXYZ&
## abcdefghijklmnopqrstuvwxyz
## $12457890!?

Cooper Old Style by Oswald B. Cooper

# 19'20

*The . . . artist will . . . occupy an independent, responsible position both in the factory and in the trade and sale aparatus. We may predict that not a single production shop will be able to function without him, but he will have to make significant changes in the way he works. He will have to become more of an artist-technician, and his creative work will be rationalized along with the factory itself.*

*Varvara Stepanova, 1929*

# ¹⁹20

## GRAPHIC ARTS

✦ Francis Picabia and Tristan Tzara publish first issue of *Cannibale.*

✦ Alexander Rodchenko and Varvara Stepanova publish *Production Manifesto*, addressing the new responsibility of artists and designers.

✦ Art Directors Club of New York is founded, with fifty-three charter members and Pierce Johnson as president.

✦ El Lissitzky designs *What Did You Do for the Front* poster in a constructivist manner.

✦ Fang Yun, textile pattern designer, becomes the only woman designer to have work selected for the cover of China's *Contribution* magazine.

✦ Frederic W. Goudy becomes the art director for Lanston Monotype Co., New York.

✦ Karel Teige, typographer, designer, and photographer, joins *Devetsil* group and publishes *Orfeo* magazine.

✦ Ke Lian-hui, chief designer at Shanghai's Oriental Press, founds Lian-hui Art Association with sons Ke Dao-zhong, Ke Ting, and Ke Luo, and edits *Models for the English Alphabet.* He is the first to address graphic needs of a foreign clientele.

✦ *L'Esprit Nouveau* journal, which espouses theories on Purism, is founded by Amédée Ozenfant and Le Corbusier and is published until 1926.

✦ Lajos Kassák emigrates to Vienna from Hungary, becomes editor of *MA* (until 1926).

✦ Mary Tourtel creates comic strip "The Adventures of the Little Lost Bear."

✦ National Tuberculosis Association (NTA) adopts the Christmas Seal and uses the double-barred cross as its trademark.

✦ Oskar Schlemmer is appointed Bauhaus Master of Form.

✦ Oswald B. Cooper publishes *HiLite* (until 1926).

✦ Paul Schuitema, Dutch painter, turns to graphic design, uses over printing and objective photography through the 1920s.

✦ Paul Terry creates comic strip "Aesop's Fables."

✦ Percy Lee Crosby creates comic strip "Skippy," which is to become one of the best-loved and most influential strips of the 1920s and 1930s.

✦ Russell Patterson creates the Patterson Girl, responsible for bringing the raccoon coat and galoshes to the United States (popular throughout the 1920s).

✦ Shanghai Style develops in China with roots in European Art Deco (throughout 1920s).

✦ Tao Yuan-qing becomes one of the most influential Chinese graphic designers of the twentieth century.

✦ The Society of Illustrators (est. 1901) allows women memberships. The first four are Elizabeth Shippen Green, Violet Oakley, May Wilson Preston, and Jessie Wilcox Smith.

✦ Will Bradley, having failed at filmmaking, returns to Hearst as typography supervisor and helps launch the format for *Cosmopolitan* magazine.

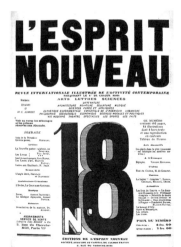

Cover of *L'Esprit Nouveau*

Illuminated Nazi Swastika

## ADVERTISING

❧ AT&T's station WEAF in New York offers ten minutes of radio time to anyone who will pay $200. The Queensboro Corp., a Long Island real estate firm, buys the first commercials in advertising history: four fifteen-second spots at $50 apiece.

❧ Following the ads extolling Hawthorne Court, a new tenant-owned apartment complex in Jackson Heights, sales total thousands of dollars.

❧ C. F. Neagle designs Djer-Kiss talc ad "The Warm Summer Through" for the Alfred H. Smith Company.

❧ Fred L. Packer Mavis creates talcum and eau de toilette ad "Irresistible!" for Vivaudou Parfumeurs Inc.

❧ Grace Gebbie Drayton designs first Campbell's Condensed Vegetable Soup ad (Campbell Kid) for Campbell Company.

❧ Lord & Thomas create "Shot from Guns," Quaker Puffed Wheat ads.

❧ Lucky Strike cigarettes ads "Reach for a Lucky Instead of a Sweet" are introduced.

❧ Neysa McMein Adams creates California Fruit Gum ad "Join the Big Parade . . . Beech-Nut Gum and Candies" for American Chicle Co.

❧ O. W. Hadank, German advertising artist, designs Räritat Cigarette poster.

❧ René Lalique designs Cinq Chevaux mascot (frosted-glass figurines, e.g., Jaguar, attached to the front-center of the hood, and lit from inside).

🥢 Roy S. Durstine, American adman, publishes *Making Advertisements and Making Them Pay,* an early tract on advertising strategies.

## ARCHITECTURE
🕇 *Architectural Digest* publishes first issue.
🕇 Mendelsohn's visionary Einstein Tower built in Potsdam, Germany.

## EDUCATION
🌿 Alréd Forbáth works with Walter Gropius at the Bauhaus Weimar through 1922.
🌿 Bauhaus pottery workshop is set up in stables of the Dornbury Castle.
🌿 Josef Albers enrolls in the Bauhaus.
🌿 Marcel Breuer arrives from Hungary to study at the Bauhaus.
🌿 VKHUTEMAS (Higher State Artistic and Technical Workshops), INKHUK (Institute of Artistic Culture), and OBMOKHU (Society of Young Artists) are founded in Moscow.

## BIRTHS AND DEATHS
Anthony Froshaug is born.
Armin Hofmann is born.
Georg Olden is born.
Jay Doblin is born.
Lester Wunderman is born.
Saul Bass is born.
Hank (Henry) Ketchum is born.
Brant Parker is born.

## CONSUMABLES
🌱 Baby Ruth candy bar is introduced in the United States.
🌱 First ice cream on a stick, Good Humor Bar, is created by Harry Burt in the United States.
🌱 Wonder Bread introduced in the United States.

## ARTS AND CULTURE
♠ Alexander Rodchenko heads the First Working Group of Constructivists.
♠ *Devetsil* group is founded in Prague, Czechoslovakia.
♠ Bart van der Leck leaves *De Stijl*, to work in textiles and ceramics.
♠ International Dada Fair is held in Berlin.
♠ József Nemes Lampérth exhibits at Galerie Gurlitt with László Moholy-Nagy.
♠ KDKA, Pittsburgh, becomes the first radio station in the United States and is the first to broadcast results of 1920 presidential election.
♠ Lu Xun, China's reformer of literature, art, and design, brings design to the middle class, with an emphasis on German Expressionism.
♠ Olympic Games are held at Antwerp after an eight-year hiatus.
♠ Paul Klee, painter and a founding member of Der Blaue Reiter (the Blue Rider) expressionist group in Munich, joins the faculty at the Bauhaus at Weimar.
♠ Société Anonyme is founded by Marcel Duchamp, Man Ray, and Katherine Dreier, in New York.
♠ Tatlin's Monument to Third International is unveiled in Moscow.

## INDUSTRIAL DESIGN
✦ Kem Weber, a German interior and furniture designer, opens firm in Los Angeles. (In 1934 he designs the Airline Chair).
✦ Paul T. Frankl designs Skyscraper furniture.
✦ Productivism is established in Russia to bring beauty and functionality to everyday products.

## POLITICS
🕉 Adolf Hitler proclaims his twenty-five-point program for the transformation of Germany at the Hofbrauhaus in Munich.
🕉 The National Workers Party, Germany, changes its name to the National Socialist Workers Party

Rarität designed by O. W. Hadank

(NSDAP–Nazi), adopts the ancient swastika, previously the symbol of German racialist and nationalist organizations, as its official symbol.
🕉 The New Economic Policy sponsored by Lenin's government, endorses a partial return to free enterprise (through the 1920s). This partial return to free enterprise is responsible for new developments in advertising design.
🕉 Women's suffrage granted in the United States.

## TECHNOLOGY
⚓ Rotor ship is invented by Anton Flettner.

## TYPE
♣ J. Van Krimpen, Dutch type designer, designs the Palladium book series and Lutetia typeface.
♣ J. L. Frazier writes *Modern Type Display,* an early look at typographic progress.
♣ Morris F. Benton designs Century Schoolbook typeface.
♣ Sol Hess designs Hess Old Style typeface (refinements continue until 1923).

# 19**21**

✦ Théo van Doesburg explores Dada typography and poetry, is published in *De Stijl* under pseudonym I. K. Bonset.

## GRAPHIC ARTS

✦ Alexander Rodchenko, painter, turns to graphic design and photo-journalism. Together with his wife, Varvara Stepanova, and Aleksei Gan, he publishes *Program of the First Working Group of Constructivists* at INKHUK.

✦ *Arbieter Illustriete Zeitung* (A-I-Z) founded by Willi Münzenberg at Neuer Deutscher Verlag in Berlin.

✦ Marcel Duchamp and Man Ray publish first and only issue of *New York Dada.*

✦ El Lissitzky and Ilya Ehrenburg create the multilingual journal *Veshch* (Russian*)*, *Gegenstand* (German), *Objet* (French), *Object* (English), a forum for new art and design of different nations (published through 1922).

✦ First issue of *Zenit,* the journal of Zenitism's free verse and avant-garde art, is published in Zagreb, Yugoslavia (continues until 1926).

✦ Frederic W. Goudy publishes *Elements of Lettering.*

✦ H. Willoughby designs the *Peep Show Revue* programme cover for London Hippodrome.

✦ L. Vallee designs *La Vie Parisienne* magazine cover.

✦ Pat Sullivan creates comic strip "Felix the Cat."

✦ Russ Westover creates comic strip "Tillie the Toiler."

✦ The first daily comic strip in Europe is J. Millar Watt's "Pop," in England's *Daily Sketch.*

✦ The Malik Verlag, German Publishing House known for anti-government publications, is incorporated by John Heartfield, George Grosz, and Weiland Herzfeld. With Heartfield as art director the press publishes books and periodicals on left-wing politics and culture.

## ADVERTISING

❧ "Betty Crocker," General Mills' first lady of food, is introduced in advertising campaigns developed by Washburn Crosby Co. In 1947, she becomes a brand name.

❧ Bozell & Jacobs, advertising and public relations agency, opens in Omaha, Nebraska.

❧ Camel cigarette ad "I'd Walk a Mile for a Camel" is created by N. W. Ayer & Son.

❧ Coles Phillips designs Holeproof Hosiery (woman/peacock) ad for Holeproof Hosiery Company.

❧ John B. Watson, the father of behavioral research, is hired by J. Walter Thompson, New York, to help agency plumb consumers' minds. He develops blindfold tests in advertising. *Reichskuration für Wirtschaftlichkeit* (State Efficiency Board), founded by the German government, has an impact on the quality of advertising.

## ARCHITECTURE

✝ Walter Gropius and Adolf Meyer design Berlin villa for timber merchant Adolf Sommerfeld.

## EDUCATION

✷ Herbert Bayer begins his studies at the Bauhaus.

✷ László Moholy-Nagy becomes Master of Form at the Bauhaus.

## BIRTHS AND DEATHS

Bill Mauldin is born.
Bob Gage is born.
Phyllis K. Robinson is born.
Günter Gerhard is born.

Covers of Malik Verlag books

**CONSUMABLES**

☞ Chocolate-covered ice-cream bar, I-Scream, later changed to Eskimo Pie, is introduced by Christian K. Nelson who coins the slogan, "I scream, you scream, we all scream for ice cream."

☞ Wise Potato Chips introduced.

**ARTS AND CULTURE**

♣ André Breton, poet, founds Surrealism in Paris, believing Dada has lost its relevance.

♣ De Zayas Gallery, a wellspring of progressive art in New York, closes.

♣ El Lissitzky moves to Berlin, and is responsible for spreading suprematist and constructivist ideas in Western Europe.

♣ Farkas Molnar with László Moholy-Nagy and Oskar Schlemmer develop concept of "total theatre."

♣ Last major Dada exhibition is shown at Salon Dada Exposition Internationals at Galerie Montaigne, Paris.

♣ Man Ray creates "Rayogramme," photographs that look like x rays.

♣ Man Ray moves to Paris and joins André Breton. During the 1920s he works as a professional photographer while applying Dada and Surrealism to photography, and is the first photographer to explore the creative potential of solarization.

♣ Max Ernst's first Paris exhibition, *Exposition Dada, Max Ernst,* opens.

♣ Piet Zwart, Dutch designer, combines Dada with *De Stijl,* conceiving of space as a "field of tension."

♣ Vladimir Tatlin and Alexander Rodchenko lead twenty-five artists in renouncing "art for art's sake." They devote their work to industrial design, visual communications, and applied arts.

**POLITICS**

🎋 Chinese Communist Party is founded.

**TYPE**

♣ Oswald B. Cooper designs Cooper Black typeface family.

**COOPER BLACK**

PATENT PENDING

48 Point     3 A 4 a

# SCORE PUNCH
## Bold Ideas Goal

36 Point     3 A 4 a

# CRITICS HONORED
## Vigorous & Original

30 Point     4 A 7 a

# SUCH STRONG DESIGN
## Inspires Absolute Belief

24 Point     5 A 9 a

# ꝗ MAKING METHODS PUBLIC
## Startle Foes—Convince Friend

18 Point    6 A 13 a

**MAIL ORDER HOUSE Desires Strong Virile Figures $1234567890**

10 Point    14 A 28 a

**THIS FACE TAKES HEAVY INK Because of this fact a spotlight [so to speak] may be directed to the strong points one may wish emphasized in sales arguments**

14 Point    10 A 20 a

**SHOWING UNIFORM SIZES By Using More Cooper Black Modern Ideas Are Produced**

8 Point    16 A 32 a

**COOPER DESIGN BY LETTER EXPERT Oswald Cooper who has originated this letter of character occupies an enviable place among advertising profession and has added great deal to its advancement**

12 Point    13 A 26 a

**LETTERS ARE MADE CLOSE SET Making Possible Designs of Massed Arrangement Like Hand Lettering**

6 Point    18 A 36 a

**DESIGNS WITH THE PROPER KNOWLEDGE He understands the anatomy of letters—their bones as he calls them—the result of which is structure and form with strength and beauty giving design intrinsic worth of enduring art**

All Fonts contain **ꝗ ❦ — { }** special characters

Cooper Black

# 19**22**

## GRAPHIC ARTS

✦ "Fritzi Ritz" makes her debut in the *New York World*, a comic strip about the poor little rich girl.

✦ Alexander Rodchenko designs brochure *Konstruktivism* by Aleksei Gan.

✦ American caricature emerges in the art deco style. Alfred Frueh publishes a collection called "Stage Folk" in both *Vanity Fair* and the *New Yorker*. Other caricaturists of note are Eva Herrmann, Peggy Bacon, William Auerbah-Levy, Miguel Covarrubias, Irma Selz, and Al Hirschfeld.

✦ *Better Homes & Gardens* produces its first issue.

✦ El Lissitzky publishes *Story of Two Squares*, a children's book illustrated in the constructivist manner.

✦ El Lissitzky designs a cover for *Broom*, an international avant-garde arts journal, with isometric perspective letterforms.

✦ *Esység*, founded as an alternative to *MA*, is designed by Béla Uitz who was influenced by Russian Suprematism and Constructivism.

✦ F. X. Leyendecker designs *Life* (the humor magazine) cover for Life Publishing Co.

✦ First Comic Strip Exhibition is held at the Waldorf Astoria Hotel, New York.

✦ Georgy and Vladimir Stenberg, Russian graphic artists known for their film posters, exhibit spatial paintings and nonobjective constructions at the Kafe Poetov, Moscow. Later they show at First Exhibition of Russian Art, Berlin, and create sets and costumes for Alexander Tairov's Kamernyi Teatr (until 1931).

✦ Lajos Kassák publishes his portfolio, *Graphik*.

✦ László Péri publishes album of linocuts and joins the expressionist group Der Sturm.

✦ Lucian Bernhard opens a studio in New York, leaving his studio in Berlin in the hands of his partner Fritz Rosen.

✦ Maxfield Parrish designs Mazda Lamps calendar for Edison Lamp Works.

✦ Oskar Schlemmer designs the Bauhaus seal.

✦ *Reader's Digest* publishes its first issue.

✦ Rudolph Ruzicka designs a trademark for Borzoi Books, a division of Alfred A. Knopf (many other artists and designers, including W. A. Dwiggins, Warren Chappell, and Paul Rand subsequently design other versions of the Borzoi).

✦ Sidney Smith, artist for the comic strip "The Gumps," signs contract with the *Chicago Tribune* for $100,000 for ten years, one of the highest fees paid.

✦ Théo van Doesburg designs *Mecano* periodical cover, type, and collage in an ad hoc manner.

✦ *Transbordeur Dada* puts out its first issue, edited by Serge Charcoline, Paris (published until 1949).

✦ W. A. Dwiggins coins the term "graphic design" in his article "New Kind of Printing Calls for New Design," published in the *Boston Evening Transcript* (August 29), to describe the encompassing work of a type, typography, page, and ad designer.

## ADVERTISING

✦ Alfred P. Sloan Jr., General Motors president, chairs company's first advertising committee.

✦ Andrew Loomis Gainsborough creates Genuine Hair Net ad for the Western Company.

✦ Norman Price creates Victrola ad "Christmas Morning—and in Come the Greatest Artists!" for Victor Talking Machine Company.

## EDUCATION

✦ Dmitrii Stakhievich Moor, political

**Pages from *Fascist* magazine**

caricaturist and poster artist, cofounds *Krokodil*, the satirical magazine, and joins faculty at VKHUTEMAS, where he teaches until 1930.

✧ Wassily Kandinsky, painter and a founding member of Der Blaue Reiter (the Blue Rider) expressionist group in Munich, joins the faculty at the Bauhaus at Weimar.

## BIRTHS AND DEATHS

Aaron Burns is born.
Charles Schulz is born.
Madsuda Tadashi is born.
Otl Aicher is born.
Ralph Eckerstrom is born.
T. J. Cobden-Sanderson dies.
Harvey Kurtzman is born.

## ARTS AND CULTURE

♠ Dada more or less ends in Europe with advent of Surrealism.

♠ First radio sound effects on WGY, Schenectady, New York.

♠ George Gallup founds Gallup & Robinson, public relations and polling agency, Princeton, New Jersey.

♠ Grauman's Egyptian Theater opens in Los Angeles. Its design is directly influenced by the discovery of Tutankhamen's Tomb.

♠ Henryk Berlewi, a Polish designer working in Germany (until 1923), introduces an avant-garde philosophy called Mechano-faktura.

♠ Howard Carter discovers Tutankhamen's tomb, triggers reappreciation of Egyptian style, particularly in architecture and graphic design.

♠ Lyubov Popova founds constructivist stage design with her first

installation for Vsevolod Meyerhold's production of Fernand Crommelynck's *Magnanimous Cuckold*.

♠ *Nosferatu*, a film by F. W. Murnau, premieres.

♠ Oskar Schlemmer's production of Triadic Ballet is performed in Stuttgart.

♠ Walt Disney and his brother Roy found the Disney Company in Los Angeles.

## INDUSTRIAL DESIGN

✦ Eileen Gray, furniture designer, founds Jean Desert in Paris.

✦ Körting and Mathisen, Leipzig, Germany, design industrial and commercial functional lighting equipment.

## POLITICS

↗ Benito Mussolini and his Fascist party stalwarts "march" on Rome. In fact, fearing violence, King Victor Emmanuel appoints Mussolini prime minister before the march begins.

## TYPE

✦ Douglas Crawford McMurtrie designs McMurtrie Title typeface.

✦ Jakob Erbar designs Lucina, Lumina, Lux, and Phosphor typefaces (through 1930).

✦ Rudolf Koch designs Neuland typeface (through 1923), a bold sans serif with an expressionist sensibility.

✦ Stanley Morison, type designer and typographer, joins Monotype Corporation in England.

*Of Two Squares*

# 19**23**

## GRAPHIC ARTS

✦ A. J. Knorr designs *Theatre* magazine cover "Why It Costs So Much to Amuse You" for the Theatre Magazine Company.

✦ Alexander Rodchenko creates photomontages for *Pro Eto*.

✦ Austin Cooper, British graphic artist, designs London Underground posters.

✦ El Lissitzky designs Merz Matinee flyer.

✦ El Lissitzky publishes *Topography of Typography*.

✦ Elena Semenova and Varvara Stepanova design for *Lef* (through 1925).

✦ Francis Meynell founds the Pelican Press in London.

✦ Frank Williard creates comic strip "Moon Mullins" for the *Chicago Tribune*, New York News Syndicate.

✦ Herbert Bayer designs symbol for Kraus stained-glass workshop, which is meant to convey harmony of proportion.

✦ John Heartfield designs for *Der Knüppel* (until 1927), a journal of left-wing politics.

✦ Joost Schmidt designs *Staatliches Bauhaus* in Weimar exhibition poster, introducing a constructivist sensibility to the Bauhaus.

✦ Joseph Binder, poster artist known for his unique streamline airbrush style, designs posters in Vienna.

✦ Karel Teige publishes *Ziot 2* (Life), edits *Starba* (Building), and designs typophoto alphabet for Vitezslav Nezval's book *Abeceda*.

✦ Kurt Schwitters, German artist, poet, and typographer, publishes *Merz*, a journal that explores the nexus between avant-garde art and functional design.

✦ László Moholy-Nagy publishes the essays "The New Typography" and "Typophoto," which address advances in form and technique.

✦ László Moholy-Nagy, Hungarian Constructivist, experiments with photograms and photoplastics.

✦ *Staatliches Bauhaus in Weimar 1919–1923* is published by the Bauhaus in Weimar, with Walter Gropius and László Moholy-Nagy as editors. Herbert Bayer creates the cover design, and Moholy-Nagy, the interior design.

✦ Vladimir Vladimirovich Mayakovsky and El Lissitzky publish *For the Voice*, a book of poetry designed to be read out loud in groups. The graphics, composed from type-case materials, serve as icons. The book is also unique in its tabular organizing system wherein each spread is introduced by a tab with a symbolic device.

✦ Vladimir Mayakovsky helps founds *Lef*, a Russian journal of progressive art and culture.

✦ Jan Tschichold, typographer who codified the New Typography, attends his first Bauhaus exhibition.

✦ Hendrik N. Werkman designs the first issue of *Next Call*, a journal of typographic experimentation.

## ADVERTISING

⚞ Russian-born A. M. Cassandre (Adolphe Jean-Marie Mouron) emigrates to Paris, through 1936 designs posters that will revitalize French advertising art.

⚞ A. C. Nielsen Sr. introduces marketing's share-of-market concept.

⚞ Esso (Standard Oil Company) oval trademark is introduced.

⚞ First poster for the Olivetti Company, showing a typewriter on railroad tracks, is designed by A. Bresciani.

⚞ John Orr Young and Raymond Rubicam form Young & Rubicam in Philadelphia.

⚞ Jordan Motor Car Co. ad "Somewhere West of Laramie" is created by Edward S. (Ned) Jordan.

⚞ Listerine ad "Always a Bridesmaid, Never a Bride" is created by Lambert & Feasley.

⚞ Theodore F. MacManus, ad man, helps Walter Chrysler launch his new car, the Chrysler Six.

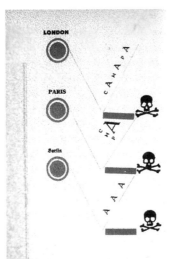

*For the Voice*

## EDUCATION

✒ Bauhaus hosts first full-scale exhibition (August 15–September 30). The exhibition garners international acclaim.

✒ László Moholy-Nagy is appointed by Walter Gropius as head of the preliminary course at the Bauhaus at Weimar, replacing Johannes Itten.

✒ Oskar Schlemmer appointed to head the Bauhaus theatre workshop by Walter Gropius.

✒ Walter Gropius changes Bauhaus slogan from "A Unity of Art and Handicraft" to "Art and Technology, a New Unity."

## BIRTHS AND DEATHS

Ellsworth Kelly is born.
Alexandre Gustave Eiffel, engineer of the Eiffel Tower, dies at 91.
Louis Danziger is born.
Richard Avedon is born.
Ralph Coburn is born.
Jane Trahey is born.
Fred Woodward is born.

## CONSUMABLES

🍭 Popsicle is introduced by Joe Lower, a food processing company.

🍭 Reese's Peanut Butter Cup is introduced in the United States.

🍭 Welch's Grape Jelly is introduced in the United States.

🍭 Yoo-Hoo Chocolate Drink is introduced in the United States.

## ARTS AND CULTURE

♠ Abstract painting appears in Poland.

♠ Albert Schweitzer publishes *Philosophy of Civilization*.

♠ Dada's death notice appears in the February 8th issue of the *Freeman*, New York, written by critic Vincent O'Sullivan.

♠ Felix Salten publishes *Bambi*.

♠ First Triennale of progressive art is held in Monza, Italy.

♠ Giorgio de Chirico is declared first surrealist painter by Surrealists André Breton, Louis Aragon, and Paul Eluard.

♠ Gustav Gustavovich Klutsis with Sergei Sen'kin establish the *Masterskaia revoliutsii* (Workshop of the Revolution) in Moscow.

♠ Henry Luce publishes the first issue of *Time* magazine, America's first weekly newsmagazine.

♠ Jacob Henneberger publishes the first issue of *Weird Tales*, a pulp science fiction magazine.

♠ National Carbon Co. launches "Eveready Hour," the first regular series of broadcast entertainment and music sponsored by an advertiser.

♠ Sigmund Freud publishes *Das Ich und das Es* (the Ego and the Id).

## POLITICS

🏹 Adolf Hitler's beer-hall putsch in Munich fails. He is sentenced to prison, during which time he writes his memoir/manifesto *Mein Kampf*.

## TECHNOLOGY

⚡ 16mm home movie camera is introduced by Kodak.

⚡ Charles Francis Jenkins transmits television pictures of President Harding from Washington to Philadelphia.

⚡ John Baird transmits silhouettes by television.

## TYPE

♣ Douglas Crawford McMurtrie designs Vanity Fair Capitals typefaces.

♣ Frederic W. Goudy establishes Village Letter Foundry on the Hudson, New York.

♣ Jakob Erbar designs Erbar typeface.

Staatliches Bauhaus catalog

## GRAPHIC ARTS

✦ Alexander Rodchenko designs ten covers in the *Mess Mend* book series written by the Soviet author Jim Dollar (pseudonym for Marietta Shaginian). Using a standardized format, each cover, unique to its content, was illustrated as a photo-montage and printed in black and a second color.

✦ Anton Grut designs *The Thief of Baghdad* motion picture poster for United Artists Corp.

✦ Austin Cooper designs collage-like London Electric Railway posters.

✦ Benjamin Péret and Pierre Naville found and edit the review *La Révolution Surréaliste*.

✦ *Blok* magazine is published in Warsaw by Praeseno, a group of writers under Henryk Stazéwski and Szymon Syrkus, champions modern art and architecture.

✦ *Bund Deutscher Gebrauchsgraphiker* (Alliance of German Graphic Artists) is formed. Its membership comprises four hundred of the best designers in the field.

✦ Daniel Berkeley Updike publishes *In a Day's Work*.

✦ Edgar Martin launches his comic strip "Bootsy," one of the most frankly feminine of the "flapper" girls of the twenties.

✦ Edward McKnight Kauffer publishes *The Art of the Poster*.

✦ Erté (pseudonym for Roman de Tirtoff), Russian art deco fashion illustrator and set designer, designs covers for *Harper's Bazaar* magazine (until 1937).

✦ F. G. Cooper, typographer and poster artist, designs Prince George Hotel (New York) poster. He later becomes known for creating the Consolidated Edison trade character, a comic drawing of Old Knickerbocker.

✦ Fortunato Depero takes part in the First Futurist Congress in Milan, making a gift of one of his famous paintings, *Psychological Portrait*, to F. T. Marinetti.

✦ H. M. Bateman, cartoonist, produces a series of lorry bills for Shell, illustrating single words, such as "Concentration," "Appreciation," and "Recommendation."

✦ Harold Gray introduces his comic strip "Little Orphan Annie" to the world in the *Chicago Tribune*.

✦ Kurt Schwitters and Theo van Doesburg design *Merz 8/9*.

✦ French-born Louis Forton creates comic strip "Bibi Fricotin" that appears in *Le Petit Illustré*.

✦ Norman Rockwell illustrates "Time to Retire?" ad for the Fisk Tire Co., Inc.

✦ Théo van Doesberg develops the theory of Elementarism, declaring the diagonal more dynamic than horizontal or vertical construction. This becomes one of the dominant directions of graphic design in the twentieth century.

## ADVERTISING

❧ Henryk Berlewi establishes the advertising company Reklama Mechano, with futurist poets Aleksander Wat and Stanley Brucz in Warsaw. Reklama Mechano introduces modern art forms in commercial print advertising.

❧ Joost Schmidt designs YKO advertisement.

❧ Max Burchartz designs *Die Gute Reklame* (Good Advertising) as a guideline for the practice of progressive advertising.

❧ Stanley Resor buys out Commodore Thompson at J. Walter Thompson advertising agency in New York.

*Merz*

## ARCHITECTURE

🕆 Gerrit Rietveld builds Schröder House in Utrecht, Holland. It quickly becomes an architectural landmark.

🕆 The Wilhelm Marx House, one of Germany's first skyscrapers, is completed in Düsseldorf.

## EDUCATION

🕊 The Bauhaus is informed by the Minister of Education that it will receive only half of its necessary funding. Walter Gropius and the Council of Masters announce that the Bauhaus will close by the end of March 1925.

## BIRTHS AND DEATHS

Bertram G. Goodhue dies.
Carl Fisher is born.
George Segal is born.
George Tscherny is born.
Herbert Spencer is born.
József Nemes Lampérth dies.
Kenneth Noland is born.
Léon N. Bakst dies.
Peter Newell dies.
Rudolf De Harak is born.
Vladimir Ilyich Lenin dies.
Carl Ally is born.
Paul Conrad is born
Lee Iacocca is born.

## CONSUMABLES

🌱 Wheaties are introduced.

## ARTS AND CULTURE

♣ Anatoly Lunacharsky, the Soviet commissar of culture and benefactor of the avant-garde, publishes *Theater and Revolution.*

♣ André Breton publishes *Manifesto du Surréalisme*, influenced by writings of Sigmund Freud.

♣ Bruce Barton, adman, of Batton, Barton, Durstine & Osborn publishes *The Man Nobody Knows.*

♣ Chen Zhi-fo teaches at Shanghai Eastern Art School, Shanghai Institute of Fine Art, and Guangzhou State School of Fine Art.

♣ Konstantin Stanislavsky publishes *My Life in Art.*

♣ El Lissitzky publishes *The Isms of Art.*

♣ First surrealist group exhibition, *Exposition la peinture surréaliste*, opens in Paris.

♣ Francis Picabia's ballet, Relâche, performs in Paris, with music by Erik Satie.

♣ Goodrich Tires sponsors the first hour-long show over a network of nine radio stations.

♣ Henryk Berlewi, Polish Constructivist, returns to Warsaw from Berlin, publishes *Mechano Faktura* (Mechano-texture), and founds the Group of Abstract Constructive Art.

♣ J. J. P. Oud designs the Rotterdam Cafe (Cafe de Unie).

♣ Paul Klee's first one-person exhibition opens in Paris.

♣ Stravinsky's New York debut at the New York Philharmonic.

♣ Surrealism comes to Paris.

♣ Thomas Mann publishes *Der Zauberberg* (the Magic Mountain).

## BIG BUSINESS

🏛 Last phase of formation is completed for International Business Machines (IBM). The company was incorporated in 1911 as Computing-Tabulating-Recording Company in a merger of three smaller companies. After further acquisitions, it absorbs the International Business Machines Corporation in 1924 and assumes that company's name.

## INDUSTRIAL DESIGN

✈ Mart Stam designs tubular steel cantilever chair.

## POLITICS

🏹 Germany's New Reichsmark is introduced.

🏹 J. Edgar Hoover is appointed director of the FBI.

🏹 Native Americans are granted full U.S. citizenship.

## TECHNOLOGY

🔥 Masonite invented by William Mason.

## TYPE

♣ Frederic W. Goudy designs Frenchwood Ronde/Italian Old Style typeface.

♣ Robert Hunter Middleton designs Ludlow Black typeface.

Consolidated Edison mascot by F. G. Cooper

# 19**25**

## GRAPHIC ARTS

✦ A. M. Cassandre designs *L'Intransiegeant* poster, introducing cubist method to advertising art.

✦ Alain Saint-Organ creates "Zig et Puce," the first genuine comic strip in France.

✦ El Lissitzky predicts that photo-mechanical processes will replace metal type.

✦ Fortunato Depero creates "Futurist" advertisements for the Campari liquor and aperitif distillery (through 1933).

✦ Fred Pegram designs *Take a Kodak with You* poster for Eastman Kodak Company.

✦ Herbert Bayer designs Bauhaus Printing posters and postcards (through 1928).

✦ Jan Tschichold edits "*Elementare Typographie*" issue of *Typographische Miteilungen*.

✦ Kurt Schwitters and Théo van Doesburg design *Die Scheuche* (the Scarecrow), a constructivist children's book that uses letterforms as characters.

✦ Louis Lozowick, American printmaker and painter, designs cover for Modern Russian Art catalog for the Museum of Modern Art, New York.

✦ Otto Neurath creates a graphic system for presenting statistical information using pictorial symbols or Isotypes (International System of Typographic Picture Education). He works with Marie Reidemeister, who was the "transformer," responsible for translating collected data into visual terms.

✦ Paul Colin begins career as graphic designer and set designer. He is the most prolific designer using an art deco or pictorial modernism approach to graphic design.

✦ The *New Yorker* magazine launches, declaring itself "not for the old lady from Dubuque." The first generation of artists include Miguel Covarrubias, John Held Jr., Helen Hokinson, Ralph Barton, Rea Irvin, Gluyas Williams, Otto Soglow, Carl Rose, Alfred Frueh, Bruce Bairns-father, James Thurber, Gilbert Bundy, Mary Petty, Percy Barlow, and Reginald Marsh. Rea Irvin, a cartoonist, becomes the art director for the *New Yorker* (until 1951) and designs its distinctive format and typeface.

✦ Walter M. Baumhofer begins career as pulp artist with *Adventure* magazine.

✦ Will Bradley, graphic designer, illustrator, typographer, printer, retires.

✦ *Die Form* founded as the official journal of the Deutscher Werkbund (ceases publication in 1934).

## ADVERTISING

♦ Neil McElroy, adman, begins work at Procter & Gamble Co. in Cincinnati as mail clerk.

♦ Outdoor Advertising Association (previously Painted Display Advertising Association) merges with Poster Advertising Association to form Outdoor Advertising Association of America.

♦ Standard Oil Company, New York, adopts the Pegasus trademark designed by Ray Nash.

♦ The Jolly Green Giant trademark first introduced by the Minnesota Valley Canning Co. in LeSueur, Minnesota.

♦ U.S. School of Music ad "They Laughed When I Sat Down at the Piano, but When I Started to Play!" is created by Ruthrauff & Ryan.

## ARCHITECTURE

✝ Walter Gropius designs Student Apartment Block at the Dessau Bauhaus.

## EDUCATION

✐ Cranbrook Academy is founded in Bloomfield Hills, Michigan, by George C. Booth.

✐ Herbert Bayer becomes master of the department of typography at the Bauhaus.

✐ El Lissitzky joins the faculty at the Moscow VKHUTEMAS and remains there until 1930.

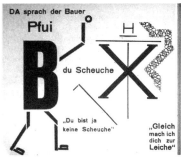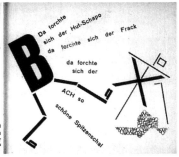

**Pages from *Die Scheuche* (the Scarecrow)**

Universal Alphabet

- László Moholy-Nagy joins Bauhaus at Dessau.
- Sun Fu-Xi founds China's West Lake College of Fine Art, begins magazines *Art Air* and *Literature Tea Party.*
- The Bauhaus moves to new Dessau quarters, designed by Walter Gropius, where it remains until 1932. In Dessau the Bauhaus philosophy comes to fruition.

## BIRTHS AND DEATHS

Al Achenbaum is born.
Art Kane is born.
Art Paul is born.
Charles W. Moore is born.
Edward Gorey is born.
Ha Qiong-wen is born.
Muriel Cooper is born.
Pierre Boulat is born.
Robert Brownjohn is born.
Robert Massin is born.
Robert Rauschenberg is born.
Roger de La Fresnaye dies.
Seymour Cray is born.
Theo Crosby is born.
Victor Papanek is born.
Willy Fleckhaus is born.
Robert Ventury is born.
Henry Wolf is born.

Cover of *Typographische Mitteilungen*

## ARTS AND CULTURE

- George Gershwin's *Rhapsody in Blue* is performed for the first time.
- In the painting *Addition*, Spanish surrealist Joan Miró explores the notion of metamorphosis.
- Sandor Bortnyik, typographer and graphic designer, founds Zöld Szamár (Green Donkey) theatre, in Budapest.
- Sergei Eisenstein's film masterpiece, *Battleship Potemkin,* premieres.

## INDUSTRIAL DESIGN

- Alexander Rodchenko designs a model workers' club for the *Exposition Internationale des Arts Décoratifs et Industriels Modernes.*
- Dmitrii Stakhievich Moor's works are represented at the *Exposition Internationale des Arts Décoratifs et Industriels Modernes.*
- Emile-Jacques Ruhlmann designs *Hôtel d'un Collectionneur* at the *Exposition Internationale des Arts Décoratifs et Industriels Modernes*, Paris, Pierre Patout, architect.
- Georgy and Vladimir Stenberg receive Gold Medal for stage design at the *Exposition Internationale des Arts Décoratifs et Industriels Modernes.*
- Le Corbusier builds *Pavillon de l'Esprit Nouveau* for the *Exposition Internationale des Arts Décoratifs et Industriels Modernes.*
- Marcel Breuer designs the first tubular chair, the "Wassily Chair."
- Melnikov designs the Soviet Pavilion for the Paris *Exposition Internationale des Arts Décoratifs et Industriels Modernes.*
- The *Exposition Internationale des Arts Décoratifs et Industriels Modernes*, opens along the banks of the Seine in Paris. This marks the formal introduction of the art moderne style (later known as Art Deco) as practiced by fashion, industrial, architectural, and graphic designers.

## TECHNOLOGY

- Chromium is made commercially available.

## TYPE

- Arthur Eric Rowton Gill designs Golden Cockerel typeface for the *Four Gospels*, combining Old Style and Transitional qualities.
- Frederic Warde designs Arrighi typeface.
- Herbert Bayer designs the Universal Alphabet, an experiment in reducing the alphabet to one set of geometrically constructed characters.
- Herbert Bayer omits capital letters, experiments with flush left–ragged right typesetting, uses extreme contrasts of type size and weight, bars, rules, points, and squares to subdivide space and unify elements to emphasize importance.
- Jan Van Krimpen designs Lutetia typeface.
- Joost Schmidt designs lowercase bold condensed typeface.
- Victor Hammer designs Hammer Uncial (Hammerschrift) typeface.

Mobilgas logo

# <sup>19</sup>**26**

## GRAPHIC ARTS

✦ *Bauhaus* magazine begins publication, with Klee, van Doesburg, Mondrian, Gropius, and Moholy-Nagy as editors.

✦ Carl Anderson creates a gag-driven comic strip "Henry," the mute, bald, expressionless kid who always wins.

✦ El Lissitzky publishes the essay "Our Book," addressing progressive ideas about book design and production.

✦ Frances Atwater, typographer at the *New York Times*, and Florence N. Levy, director of the Baltimore Museum of Art, become the first women to be admitted to the American Institute of Graphic Arts.

✦ Fred Taylor designs *Mr. Pickwick Passing the Ancient House* poster for London & North-Eastern Railway Company.

✦ Herbert Bayer designs the Dessau Bauhaus building opening party invitation and a poster commemorating the celebration of Wassily Kandinsky's sixtieth birthday. Both are exemplars of Bauhaus economy.

✦ Hugo Gernsback publishes *Amazing Stories,* the first American science fiction magazine.

✦ Frank R. Paul provides all the art for *Amazing Stories* until 1929.

✦ Jan Tschichold designs *Lusts of Mankind* film poster.

✦ Jan Tschichold designs *Phoebus-Palast* movie poster in the minimalist style of the New Typography.

✦ Joost Schmidt designs format for *Die Form*, architectural review.

✦ Karel Teige designs covers and interiors for *ReD*, a left-wing architectural magazine.

✦ Lajos Kassák returns to Hungary from Vienna to edit *Dokumentum* (until 1927), an avant-garde arts journal.

✦ Maurice Thireau recommends Egyptian ornament in his book *Modern Typography*.

✦ László Moholy-Nagy in *Offset, Book and Commercial Art* (a Bauhaus book, *Bauhausbücher*) advocates the use of greatly contrasting typefaces within a text to denote the hierarchy of information.

✦ *Parents* magazine is launched.

✦ Roger Broders designs Vichy Festival poster for *Vichy Comité des Fêtes*.

✦ Schulz-Neudamm designs *Metropolis* movie poster showing a futuristic, robotic woman.

✦ *UjFöld* (New Land) magazine and Muhely graphic and advertising studio in Hungary are founded.

✦ Wassily Kandinsky publishes *Point and Line to Plane*, a *Bauhausbücher*, in which he identifies the vocabulary of simple graphic elements underlying all pictorial expression.

## ADVERTISING

❧ Barton, Durstine & Osborn establishes the first self-contained radio program production department in an advertising agency. Arthur Pryor Jr. heads the radio department.

❧ Young & Rubicam, Philadelphia, move to New York at the request of General Foods, their largest client.

## EDUCATION

❧ Anni Albers designs at the Bauhaus weaving workshop in Dessau.

❧ Bauhaus adds *Hochschule für Gestaltung* (High School for Form) to its title.

❧ Masters are appointed at the Bauhaus Dessau. Josef Albers takes on a preliminary course investigating constructive qualities of materials, Marcel Breuer teaches the furniture workshop, and Herbert Bayer is in charge of the typography and graphic design workshop.

⚔ Walter Gropius agrees to establish the Bauhaus GmbH, a limited company, to protect the Bauhaus school's interests.

## BIRTHS AND DEATHS
Antonio Gaudi dies.
Arnold Varga is born.
Bill Backer is born.
David Levine is born.
Jacob Jensen is born.
Louis Rhead dies.
Mary Cassatt dies.
Richard Lord is born.
Sam Vitt is born.
Siegfried Odermatt is born.
Stan Freberg is born.
Tomás Gonda is born.
Jane Trahey is born.
Carl Ally is born.
George Melly is born.

## CONSUMABLES
⊤ Dannone prepackaged yogurt is introduced by Isaac Carasso in Paris.
⊤ Model A Ford is introduced.

## ARTS AND CULTURE
♠ A. A. Milne publishes *Winnie-the-Pooh*.
♠ The *New Masses*, a Communist politics, art, and culture magazine, begins publishing in New York.
♠ Eileen Gray and Jean Badovici build their house, E. 1027.
♠ El Lissitzky designs Abstract Room for the *Internationale Kunstausstellung*, Dresden.
♠ Karel Teige founds *Osvobozene divadlo* (Liberated Theatre) in Prague, with J. Frejka and J. Honzl as artistic directors.
♠ Praesens, an avant-guard art group, is founded in Warsaw, Poland.

## BIG BUSINESS
🏛 Deutsche Lufthansa airline is founded.
🏛 Radio Corp. of America buys New York radio station WEAF from AT&T and renames it WNBC. Together, this and eighteen other stations become the National Broadcasting Co., the first American radio network, founded by David Sarnoff.
🏛 Victor O. Schwab, with Robert Beatty, buys Sackheim & Scherman, and founds Book-of-the-Month Club in New York.

## INDUSTRIAL DESIGN
⚒ The Container Corporation develops the first cardboard packaging.
⚒ Walter P. Paepke founds Container Corporation of America (CCA) in Chicago, recognizing design as business function and contribution to society.

## TECHNOLOGY
⚡ First motion picture with synchronized musical score, *Don Juan*, is produced.
⚡ Television (mechanical disk-scanning method) successfully demonstrated by J. K. Baird in England and C. F. Jenkins in the United States.

## TYPE
✦ Josef Albers designs stenciled letter alphabet.
✦ Emil Rudolf Weiss designs Weiss Roman typeface (continues to refine type through 1931).
✦ Frederic W. Goudy designs Goudy Extra Bold typeface.

Cover of the *Bauhaus* magazine

## GRAPHIC ARTS

✦ A. M. Cassandre designs *Etoile du Nord* poster.

✦ *Arbeiter Illustrierte Zeitung* (Workers' Illustrated News) shortens its name to *A-I-Z*. It has its cover redesigned and uses photomontages by John Heartfield.

✦ Arthur Lehning, editor for *i10*, a progressive art journal, embraces *De Stijl* and the Bauhaus ideals. The first issue is designed by László Moholy-Nagy.

✦ Osip Brik and Vladimir Mayakovsky found *Novyi Lef*, successor to *Lef* (publishes until 1928).

✦ Douglas C. McMurtrie publishes *The Golden Book* on the history of book production and design.

✦ El Lissitzky designs Russian Typographical Exhibition, Moscow. Elena Semenova and Varvara Stepanova design for *Novyi Lef* (until 1928).

✦ First issue of *Tank*, designed by August Cernigoj, published in Ljubljana, Slovenia.

✦ Fortunato Depero publishes *Depero Futurista*, one of the key works of Futurist self-promotion and graphic design. Known as the "bolted book" because it is bound by two stainless industrial screws, it is a catalog of his fine and applied art.

✦ Frederic W. Goudy designs and, briefly, edits *Typographica*, a periodical devoted to printing and typography.

✦ Frederic W. Goudy publishes the essay "I Am Type," about his inextricable relationship with fine type.

✦ John Howard Benson takes over the John Steves Shop, a lettercutters in Newport, Rhode Island.

✦ Max Bill attends the Bauhaus in Dessau, Germany, through 1929.

✦ Walter Dexel, a Frankfurt-based designer and typographer, publishes the essay "What is New Typography?" which describes the contrasts between conventional and progressive typography.

✦ *Commercial Art* magazine, later known as *Art and Industry*, is founded as England's most prominent design magazine (ceases publication in 1959).

## ADVERTISING

✦ Fortunato Depero designs his first work of advertising architecture for *Bestetti Treves*.

✦ Frank Hummert joins Blackett & Sample to become Blackett-Sample-Hummert, Chicago. The company creates, writes, and produces fifteen-minute daily radio soap operas.

✦ Theodore F. MacManus founds Theodore F. MacManus Inc., Detroit.

## ARCHITECTURE

✝ *Domus*, Italian architecture magazine, begins publication.

✝ Le Corbusier publishes *Vers une Architecture*.

✝ *Tuminelli* is built for the *La Mostra Internazionale delle Arti Decorative* in Monza.

Babe Ruth

## EDUCATION

✦ VKHUTEMAS (Higher State Artistic and Technical Workshops) becomes VKHUTEIN (Higher State Artistic and Technical Institute).

## BIRTHS AND DEATHS

Baroness Elsa von Freytag-Loringhoven dies.

Hugo Ball dies.

Ira Herbert is born.

Jacqueline S. Casey is born.

John Smale is born.

Juan Gris dies.

Reid Miles is born.

Hugh Haynie is born.

## CONSUMABLES

➤ Hostess Cakes are introduced in the United States.

➤ Kool-Aid is introduced in the United States.

*New Lef* by Alexander Rodchenko

## ARTS AND CULTURE

♣ Babe Ruth hits sixty home runs.

♣ Columbia Broadcasting System, second major radio station, launched.

♣ Grauman's Chinese restaurant opens in Los Angeles.

♣ The American Union of Decorative Artists and Craftsmen is formed.

## INDUSTRIAL DESIGN

✠ Thonet catalog is the first to offer a complete line of tubular furniture.

## POLITICS

⚔ Gottfried Feder publishes the *Program of the NSDAP* (Nazi Party).

⚔ Nicola Sacco and Bartolomeo Vanzetti, anarchist sympathizers accused of murder and memorialized in a painting and drawings by Ben Shahn, are executed in Massachusetts.

⚔ The Federal Radio Commission is established.

## TECHNOLOGY

⚒ Charles Lindbergh flies nonstop from New York to Paris, first one-man crossing of the Atlantic by air.

⚒ First motion picture with spoken dialogue, *The Jazz Singer* starring Al Jolson, is produced by Warner Bros.

⚒ First transatlantic telephone calls between Bell Telephone in the United States and General Post Office in the United Kingdom are made at a cost of $75 for three minutes.

⚒ Henri Chrétien invents anamorphic lens, precursor to wide-screen cinematography.

⚒ W. H. Gispen, a lighting firm in Holland, begins manufacture of Giso lamp.

## TYPE

♣ Imre Reiner designs Meridian typeface (through 1930).

♣ J. Erbar designs Erbar typeface for Ludwig & Mayer Foundry (through 1930).

♣ Kurt Schwitters designs Single alphabet phonetic type.

♣ Paul Renner designs Futura typeface and font family (through 1930). Renner believed that each generation should create a contemporary form that is true to its own time.

♣ Robert Hunter Middleton designs Record Gothic typeface, a successful version of early German Gothic faces.

♣ The Society of Typographic Arts is established in Chicago.

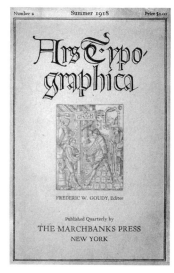

Cover of *Ars Typographica*

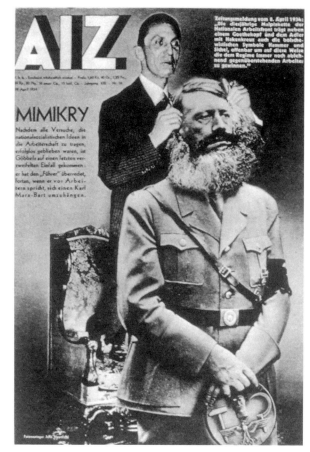

Cover of *AIZ* by John Heartfield

# ¹⁹28

## GRAPHIC ARTS

✦ Aldous Huxley publishes introduction to *Printing of Today*, a survey of international book design, in which the author of *Brave New World* (1932) addresses contemporary design trends.

✦ Albert Bruce Rogers designs the *Oxford Lectern Bible* (through 1932).

✦ Buckminster Fuller develops his Dymaxion Projection, a map that shows the globe in two dimensions without distortion.

✦ *Contribution*, a Chinese bimonthly magazine, is a pioneer of European-style Modern design in both theory and practice.

✦ Fortunato Depero moves to New York and establishes a studio, works exclusively in advertising graphics and stage design, for clients such as *Vogue* and the *New York Daily News*.

✦ Joost Schmidt becomes master of typography and design at Bauhaus at Dessau, develops the grid-system organization.

✦ Karel Teige illustrates Konstantin Biebl's book *Zlom* (the Break).

✦ Lajos Kassák edits *Munka*, an avant-garde arts journal.

✦ Max Burchartz designs a poster for Schubert Festival in Essen.

✦ Mehemed Fehmy (M. F.) Agha, who had been the art director of Condé Nast's *Vanity Fair*, becomes art director of *Vogue* until 1943. At *Vanity Fair* he pioneered the use of sans-serif typefaces (Futura) and innovative photography and illustration.

✦ Norman Saunders, a pulp magazine artist, begins work as cover illustrator for Fawcett Publications until 1934.

✦ Solomon Benediktovich Telingater with Gustav Klutsis cofound the *Oktiabr'* (October) group in Moscow.

✦ *VU*, the French photo magazine, is founded by Lucien Vogel. (Alexander Liberman later becomes art editor/director, 1933–1936.)

✦ Jan Tschichold publishes *Die Neue Typographie*, codifying and explaining new ideals of Modern typography to tradesmen typesetters in practical terms. It becomes the handbook of dynamic, asymmetrical typographic endeavor.

## ADVERTISING

❧ Barton, Durstine & Osborn merges with George Batten Co., forming Batten, Barton, Durstine & Osborn, located at 383 Madison Avenue, New York. With billings of $32 million, it becomes one of the biggest shops.

❧ Lintas, Lever International Advertising Services, is formed as the house agency for Unilever in England, Holland, and Germany.

❧ *Ring neuer Werbegestaler* (Circle of New Advertising Designers) exhibition takes place at the Cologne *Kunstgewerbemuseum*.

❧ T. M. Cleland designs the Cadillac ad "There Is a Double Reason Why the Vast Majority of Women . . ." for General Motors Inc.

❧ The *Advertising Business* magazine launches.

❧ The Jolly Green Giant trade character makes its first appearance in print advertising.

**Josef Stalin**

## ARCHITECTURE

☫ El Lissitzky designs interior of apartments in Moisei Ginzburg and Ignatii Milinis's House for the Employees of the Commissariat of France in Moscow.

☫ First CIAM (*Congrés Internationaux le d'Architecture Moderne*) is held in Paris.

## EDUCATION

☇ László Moholy-Nagy and Herbert Bayer leave Bauhaus.

☇ Walter Dexel is appointed director of the commercial art program at *Kunstgewerbeschule* (School of Arts and Crafts) in Frankfurt, Germany.

☇ Walter Gropius resigns as director of the Bauhaus. Swiss architect Hannes Meyer becomes director of Bauhaus at Dessau, resigns in 1930.

☇ Walter Peterhans becomes director of the new Bauhaus photography department.

**Advertisement by Depero**

## BIRTHS AND DEATHS

Adrian Frutiger is born.
Andy Warhol is born.
Colin Forbes is born.
George Sadek is born.
Hermann Muthesius dies.
J. Walter Thompson dies.
Jan Lenica is born.
N. W. Ayer dies.
Robert Jacoby is born.
Wim Crouwel is born.
John E. Kennedy dies.
Richard Outcault dies.

## CONSUMABLES

➤ BMW produces its first automobile.
➤ Peter Pan Peanut Butter is introduced.
➤ Scotch tape, first cellulose self-adhesive tape, goes on sale, developed by the 3M Company.
➤ Velveeta Cheese is introduced.

## ARTS AND CULTURE

♣ Georgy and Vladimir Stenberg design celebratory decorations for hanging in Red Square.
♣ Mickey Mouse debuts in Walt Disney's animated cartoon *Steamboat Willie*.
♣ Paul Terry begins animated film production company Terrytoons, eventually creating such characters as Mighty Mouse, Tom Terrific, Mighty Manfred, and Heckle and Jeckle.
♣ Walter Lantz creates Woody Woodpecker and Max Fleischer creates Betty Boop.
♣ The *Lucky Strike Dance Orchestra* show, later renamed *Your Hit Parade*, premieres on over thirty-nine radio stations.

## BIG BUSINESS

🏛 *Family Party* inaugurates NBC's coast-to-coast network, sponsored by General Motors.

## POLITICS

↗ Joseph Stalin initiates USSR's first Five-Year-Plan.

## INDUSTRIAL DESIGN

✦ Eileen Gray designs tubular ceiling light.
✦ Le Corbusier designs his Grand Comfort armchair.
✦ Marcel Breuer develops the folding chair.
✦ Otto Frederick invents the slicing machine, and consumers get their first taste of presliced bread.

## TECHNOLOGY

♠ Alexander Fleming discovers penicillin.
♠ Amelia Earhart flies across the Atlantic.

## TYPE

♣ A. M. Cassandre designs Bifur typeface for Deberny & Peignot, Paris.
♣ Arthur Eric Rowton Gill designs Gill Sans series, inspired by the typeface Railway, designed by Edward Johnston.
♣ Douglas C. McMurtrie designs Ultra-Modern typeface with Aaron Borad and Leslie Sprunger (they continue to refine it until 1930).
♣ Frederic W. Goudy designs Goudy Text & Lombardic Capitals.
♣ Lucian Bernhard designs typefaces for American Type Founders.
♣ Oswald B. Cooper designs Cooper Fullface typeface.
♣ Rudolf Koch designs Kabel typeface.
♣ Walter Cyliax designs Europa typeface.

Cover of *Vanity Fair* by Paolo Garretto

# 19**29**

## GRAPHIC ARTS

✦ *Business Week* begins publication.

✦ Douglas C. McMurtrie publishes *The Philosophy of Modernism in Typography.*

✦ El Lissitzky designs USSR *Russische Ausstellung* exhibition poster for the *Kunstgewerbemuseum*, Zurich.

✦ Elzie Segar introduces comic strip "Popeye."

✦ Erik Nitsche, Swiss designer, starts career with Maximilian Vox printing firm in Paris.

✦ European comic strip "Tintin," created by the Belgian Georges "Herge" Remi debuts in *Le Vingtième Siècle* weekly news.

✦ First genuinely modern comic strip begins with Harold Foster's "Tarzan," the same day Dick Calkins introduces his comic strip "Buck Rogers," the first strip to handle science fiction themes in an interesting manner.

✦ George Massiot Brown designs Porto Sanderman poster for George G. Sanderman & Sons, Co., Ltd.

✦ Gustav Klutsis becomes vice president of the Association of Revolutionary Poster Artists until 1932.

✦ John Newton Howitt, portrait and landscape artist, starts to paint for the pulps and becomes known as the "Dean of Weird Menace Cover Art."

✦ Michel Bouchaud designs *La Plage de Monte Carlo* poster for Monte Carlo Publicité Vox.

✦ Paul Chesney designs *The Five O'clock Girl* musical comedy programme cover for London Hippodrome.

✦ Philipp Albinus publishes *Grundsätzliches zur neuen Typographie.*

## ADVERTISING

❧ Advertising spending plummets after stock market crash, from $3.5 billion to $1.5 billion by 1933.

❧ American Tobacco Co. spends $12.3 million to advertise Lucky Strikes, the most ever spent on single-product advertising.

❧ Coca-Cola ad "The Pause That Refreshes" is created by D'Arcy Co.

❧ Fairfax Cone, later of Foote Cone Belding, joins Lord & Thomas San Francisco as copywriter.

❧ Fortunato Depero publishes *Outline of the Art of Advertising Manifesto.*

❧ Kellogg introduces the Rice Krispies slogan, "Snap, Crackle, and Pop."

❧ The first advertising jingle ever aired on radio is "Have You Tried Wheaties?" which General Mills placed on the Jack Armstrong radio program.

❧ William Benton and Chester Bowles open Benton & Bowles.

## ARCHITECTURE

ⵟ Chanin Building, New York, is fitted with radiator grille designed by Jacques Delamarre.

ⵟ Hugh Ferris, an architectural renderer, publishes *The Metropolis of Tomorrow*, predicting massive interconnected skyscrapers in the megalopolises of the future.

## BIRTHS AND DEATHS

Arno Holz dies.
Bert Stern is born.
Bruce Crawford is born.
Claes Oldenberg is born.
Jules Feiffer is born.
Kazumasa Nagai is born.
Ken Garland is born.
Mike Parker is born.
Milton Glaser is born.
R. D. E. Oxenaar is born.
Sergei Diaghilev dies.
Tad (Thomas Aloysious) dorgan dies.

W. A. Dwiggins

## CONSUMABLES

❧ 7-Up (named for its seven-ounce bottle) is introduced by C. L. Grigg.

❧ First frozen food, created by Charles Birdseye, is "Fresh Ice Fillets," introduced in Toronto, Canada.

## ARTS AND CULTURE

♠ "Westinghouse Salutes" debuts, one of the first dramatic radio productions to use historical anecdote and pastiche to underscore the prospects of industrial progress.

♠ Alexander Rodchenko designs sets for the film *Bedbug*.

♠ El Lissitzky designs Soviet sections at *Film und Foto*, Stuttgart.

♠ Man Ray creates *Sleeping Woman*, an example of his solarization technique as applied to a surreal image.

♠ Museum of Modern Art, New York, is founded by Alfred Barr. Its primary focus is on painting and sculpture.

♠ The first Academy Award Oscar is designed by sculptor George Stanley.

## BIG BUSINESS

🏛 Victor Talking Machine Company is taken over by the Radio Corporation of America (RCA).

## POLITICS

🏃 Leon Trotsky is exiled from the USSR.

## INDUSTRIAL DESIGN

🕂 Alvar Aalto designs stacking chairs.

## TECHNOLOGY

🔌 Car radio is invented by William Lear and Elmer Wavering, United States.

🔌 Hoover vacuum cleaner is introduced.

## TYPE

❦ Arthur Eric Rowton Gill designs Perpetua typeface (through 1930).

❦ Bruce Rogers designs Centaur typeface for Monotype.

❦ Emil Rudolf Weiss designs Memphis typeface.

❦ Frederic W. Goudy designs Deepdene typeface (refinements continue until 1934).

❦ Morris F. Benton designs Broadway typeface.

❦ Robert Hunter Middleton designs Garamond typeface.

❦ Stanley Morison publishes *First Principles of Typography*.

❦ W. A. Dwiggins designs Metroblack typeface for Mergenthaler (he continues to refine it through 1930).

## ACT OF GOD

★ New York stock market crashes on Black Friday, October 28.

The Oscar

## Memphis

die Stadt der „weißen Mauer", die älteste ägyptische Hauptstadt, südlich von Gizeh am Nil gelegen. Sie war einstens Hauptkulturort des „Ptah", wurde von Menes erbaut und gleichzeitig zur Residenz des alten Reiches erhoben, bis Theben ihre Stelle einnahm.

## Memphis

die Zigarette aus erstklassigen Orient-Tabaken mit all ihren erlesenen Eigenschaften, die Zigarette mit einem herrlichen und vorzüglichen Aroma und von höchstem Genuß, die Zigarette für den anspruchsvollen und auch für den verwöhntesten Raucher!

## Memphis

die neue zeitgemäße Schrift, die aus dem Geist und den Bedürfnissen der Zeit entstanden ist. Mit ihrer Einfachheit und Klarheit ist sie der Formenwelt der Technik wesensverwandt. Geschnitten von der Schriftgießerei D. Stempel A.-G., Frankfurt am Main.

Memphis type specimen

1930

*We shall escape the absurdity of growing a whole chicken in order to eat the breast or the wing, by growing these parts separately, under a suitable medium.*

*Winston Churchill, 1932*

# ¹⁹30

## GRAPHIC ARTS

✦ Alexey Brodovitch, an advertising and publication designer, immigrates to the United States from France.

✦ Chen Zhi-fo designs book and magazine covers based on traditional Chinese architecture and handicrafts throughout the 1930s.

✦ Dmitrii Stakhievich Moor creates posters at the Exhibition of Graphic Arts, Poster, and Book Design, Danzig, and joins *Oktiabr'* (October) group.

✦ El Lissitzky designs for the *Internationale Hygiene-Ausstellung*, Dresden, and the *Internationale Pelz-Ausstellung*, Leipzig.

✦ First Tintin comic book, *Tintin au Pays des Soviets* (Tintin in the Land of the Soviets) is published in Belgium.

✦ Ham Fisher, a comic-strip artist, introduces "Joe Palooka," a boxer with iron fists and a heart of gold.

✦ Henry Luce starts *Fortune* magazine, the most lavish (and expensive) mainstream publication in America, known for its illustrated posterlike covers and lengthy graphic and photographic essays. Eleanor Teacy becomes the magazine's first art editor. Thomas M. Cleland, known as an advertising designer and typographer, designs the first issue cover and format of the magazine.

✦ Herbert Bayer designs *Section Allemande* (German Section) exhibition poster and catalog (with embossed plastic cover) for the Society of Decorative Artists in Paris.

✦ Jan Van Krimpen designs the book *De Pen op Papier* by M. Nijhoff.

✦ Jean Carlu, French poster designer, designs *Vanity Fair* cover, combining telegraphic copy, strong geometric forms, natural forms, pictographs, and symbols.

✦ John Reynolds designs Shell petroleum poster *That's Shell—That Was!* for Shell-Mex Ltd.

✦ Lu Shao-fei, caricaturist for *Shen Bao* newspaper, launches the satirical magazine *Modern Sketch*, the longest-running and most influential caricature magazine in China.

✦ M. F. Agha publishes the essay, "What Makes a Magazine 'Modern?'" Murat "Chic" Young introduces comic strip "Blondie."

✦ Otto Storch, who in the 1950s becomes an influential magazine art director, begins his career as art director for Dell Publishing.

✦ Qian Jun-tao becomes a major influence in China's Progressive movement, and a major force in the evolution toward graphic functionalism. He is influenced by Hannah Höch and Raoul Hausmann.

✦ Solomon Telingater, Russian typographic designer, designs *The Word Belongs to Kirsano,* a poem in the constructivist typographic style.

✦ *The Savoy Cocktail Book*, published by Richard R. Smith, New York, featuring cocktail recipes from London's Savoy Hotel, is designed by Gilbert Rumbold with decorative illustrations that epitomize Jazz Age Art Deco.

**Cover of *Advertising Arts***

✦ Victor Hammer establishes the *Stamperia del Santuccio*, a hand press at Corbignano, Italy.

✦ Walter Herdeg, Swiss graphic designer and later the founder of *Graphis* magazine, is responsible for early use of collage in Swiss tourism posters.

✦ USSR in Construction, founded by Maxim Gorky, and whose designers include El Lissitzky and Alexander Rodchenko, begins publishing in five languages (continues until 1940).

## ADVERTISING

✦ *Advertising Age* magazine is launched in Chicago by C. D. Crain Jr. of Crain Communications Inc.

✦ *Advertising Arts* magazine, the weekly supplement of *Advertising and Selling* magazine, introduces "modernistic" design to American advertising.

✦ Austin Cooper designs Austin Reed's men's clothing shop ad campaign for Austin Reed Ltd., London.

**Cover of *USSR in Construction***

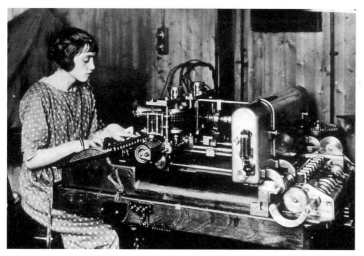
Early phototypesetting machine

🍴 Campbell Soup ads "Mmmm mmm good!" are created by BBD&O.

🍴 Harrison K. McCann merges with Albert Erickson to form McCann Erickson advertising agency.

🍴 Wheaties ads "Breakfast of Champions" are created by Blackett-Sample-Hummert.

## Architecture

🕊 Greystone Hotel, Miami Beach, Florida, is built. It is an archetype of South Beach art deco architecture, underscored by its resemblance to an ocean liner.

🕊 The Chrysler Building opens in New York City. The building, designed in a geometric art deco style, is the creation of architect William van Alen.

## Education

✂ Art Center College of Design, Pasadena, California, is founded.

✂ Hannes Meyer resigns as director of Bauhaus at Dessau.

✂ Mies van der Rohe, Berlin architect, becomes director of the Bauhaus. His theory that "less is more" becomes the attitude of twentieth-century architecture. He moves Bauhaus to Berlin.

## Births and Deaths

Edward Sorel is born.
Franciszek Starowicjski is born.
Günther Kieser is born.
Ikko Tanaka is born.
Jerzy Flisak is born.
Karl Gerstner is born.
Reynolds Ruffins is born.
Vladimir Mayakovsky commits suicide, his body lies in state in a catafalque built at VKHUTEIN.
Clare Briggs dies.
Ken Hiebert is born.

## Consumables

🍗 Hostess Twinkies are introduced.

🍗 Snickers Candy Bar is introduced.

## Arts and Culture

♟ F. T. Marinetti publishes *Parole in Libertà Futuriste, olfattive, tattili, termiche,* the definitive book of futurist poetry.

♟ Grant Wood paints *American Gothic.*

♟ Prometheus's statue, mounted at the RCA Building, Rockefeller Center, New York, is designed by Paul Manship.

♟ Théo van Doesburg publishes *Manifesto of Art Concret.*

## Industrial Design

✈ Pininfarina, automobile design firm, is founded in Turin by Battista "Pinin" Farina.

✈ Roneo pressed metal modular office furniture is introduced.

✈ The Thonet No. 14 chair production reaches 50 million.

✈ Walter Dorwin Teague creates the "No. 1A Gift Kodak" camera with lacquered wood and chrome box.

## Technology

⚡ J. Walter Reppe invents artificial fabrics from acetylene base.

⚡ Philips 930A wireless is one of the first local receivers to incorporate speaker and radio in one tabletop cabinet.

⚡ An early attempt is made in Great Britain at setting type photo-graphically

## Type

✦ Ashley Havinden designs Ashley Crawford typeface.

✦ Frederic W. Goudy designs Goudy Sans Serif typeface (revisions go into 1931).

✦ Georg Trump designs City Medium typeface.

✦ Henrich Jost designs Beton Extra Bold typeface for Bauer (continues through 1936).

✦ Jan Tschichold designs Transito typeface.

✦ Joseph Blumenthal designs Spiral/Emerson typeface (italic designed in 1936).

✦ Morris F. Benton designs Stymie Medium typeface.

✦ Robert Hunter Middleton designs Tempo typeface, modeled on the newer geometric sans serifs such as Futura (refinements made through 1942).

# 19**31**

## Graphic Arts

✦ A. M. Cassandre (Adolphe Jean-Marie Mouron) designs *L'Atlantique* poster, which becomes the quintessential graphic travel poster.

✦ Alfred Tolmer's *Mise en Page: The Theory and Practice of Layout,* published in Paris, is a compilation of modern and modernistic techniques and ornamental styles for book and magazine design.

✦ C. D. Russell's comic strip "Pete the Tramp" premieres in full color on the Sunday page of the *New York Mirror.*

✦ Chicago Tribune Syndicate gets Chester Gould to create the police-adventure comic strip "Dick Tracy" with comment directed at the laxity of the police and largely against authorities who collude with racketeers.

✦ Dmitrii Stakhievich Moor is named "Honored Art Worker" of the Russian Federation, elected to the presidium of the Union of Revolutionary Poster Workers.

✦ Eric Gill publishes influential "Essay on Typography," advocating text typesetting that is "unjustified" or "ragged left/ragged right," a style that will not be common until forty years later.

✦ First English translation of Jan Tschichold's *Die Neue Typographie,* is published.

✦ Fortunato Depero publishes a book with a recorded soundtrack, *New York. A Film that Was Lived.*

✦ Fortunato Depero publishes *Campari Futurist,* a publication devoted to his advertising campaigns for Campari liquors.

✦ Ladislav Sutnar art-directs and designs *Zijeme,* Czech culture magazine, in the manner of the New Typography.

✦ Max Bill designs poster for *Negerkunst* exhibition.

✦ Walt Disney's "Mickey Mouse" appears as a comic strip.

## Advertising

✦ F. S. May designs Schweppes Table Waters ad for Schweppes Co. Ltd.

✦ Liggett & Myers Tobacco Co. creates a Chesterfield Cigarettes ad featuring Adele and Fred Astaire.

## Architecture

✦ BBC Broadcasting House, London, is completed. Val Myers is its designer, Wells Coates and Serge Chermayeff design the interior fittings.

✦ Empire State Building, New York, is completed; Shreve, Lamb, and Harmon are the architects.

Campari advertisement

## Births and Deaths

Alan Fletcher is born.
Bob Gill is born.
Deborah Sussman is born.
George Lois is born.
Grace Gebbie Drayton dies.
Jay Chiat is born.
John Massey is born.
Josef Sattler dies.
Massimo Vignelli is born.
Mitsuo Katsui is born.
Ralph Barton, cartoonist and book illustrator known for his satirical works in the *New Yorker,* commits suicide.
Rupert Murdoch is born.
Seymour Chwast is born.
Steve Frankfurt is born.
Théo van Doesburg dies, *De Stijl* journal ceases publication.
Thomas Geismar is born.
Waldemar Swierzy is born.
Roone Arledge is born.

Cao Jie is born.
Johnny Hart is born.
Charles W. Kahles dies.
Al Williamson is born.

## Arts and Culture

♠ "The Star-Spangled Banner" officially becomes U.S. national anthem.

♠ *Circle: The International Survey of Constructivist Art* disseminates information about European modernist graphic design.

♠ Salvador Dali paints *The Persistence of Memory*.

♠ Shanghai presents the first exhibition of modern Chinese woodcuts, focusing extensively on contemporary social and political issues.

## Big Business

🏛 Airstream company is founded.

🏛 Neil McElroy fosters brand manager system at Procter & Gamble Co., Cincinnati, which leads to the intra-P&G brand rivalries.

🏛 Vacuum Oil Company and Standard Oil Company of New York (Socony) join forces to create the Socony-Vacuum Corporation. To commemorate the merger, a redesigned Pegasus logo is commissioned to represent the strength and vitality of the united company worldwide.

## Industrial Design

✦ Gustav B. Jensen, Danish-born graphic and industrial designer working in New York, designs a stainless-steel sink for International Nickel Co., which becomes the standard for industrial sinks.

✦ PEL (Practical Equipment Limited) is founded.

## Politics

↗ Nazi party gains majority in Dessau.

## Technology

⚡ Electronic flash photography invented by Harold Edgerton at MIT.

## Type

♣ Berthold Wolpe designs Hyperion typeface.

♣ Jan Tschichold designs Zeus typeface.

♣ Jan Van Krimpen designs Romulus typeface.

♣ Robert Hunter Middleton designs Karnak typeface (through 1942).

Cover of *Zijeme* by Ladislav Sutnar

# ¹⁹**32**

## GRAPHIC ARTS

✦ "Adolf, the Superman: Swallows Gold and Talks Garbage" is an A-I-Z cover designed by John Heartfield. The satiric photo-montage shows the x-ray of interior organs of the German leader digesting gold coins.

✦ A. M. Cassandre designs *DUBO . . . DUBON . . . DUBONNET* poster for Dubonnet. The three-panel sequence shows a seated man wearing a derby and eyeing the beverage in his glass with uncertainty, DUBO (doubt), he tastes the beverage, DUBON (of some good), he refills the glass and the product name is identified, DUBONNET.

✦ Albatross Library, paperback publishers, is founded by J. Holroyd-Reese, Kurt Enoch, and Max Christian Wegner in Hamburg.

✦ Alexeieff designs the "Night Scotsman" for London & North-eastern Railway.

✦ American comic strips arrive in Italy.

✦ Beatrice Warde publishes "The Crystal Goblet or Printing Should Be Invisible," a virtual manifesto about the benefit of clarity and, by extension, subordination of typo-graphy to meaning.

✦ Cipe Pineles is hired as assistant to M. F. Agha, art director of Condé Nast Publications, New York City (through 1938). She will later become the first woman admitted into the New York Art Directors Club.

✦ First issue of *De 8 en opbouw,* an architectural journal in the style of the New Typography, Amsterdam, launches and continues until 1943.

✦ George Jerome Rozen produces covers for *Shadow,* a pulp magazine, through 1939.

✦ German election poster for the Nazi Party shows photograph of Hitler as a silhouette against black with sans-serif line of type pro-claiming "Hitler" below his head, a decidedly modern design for the otherwise avowedly antimodern Nazi Party.

✦ Jean Carlu designs *Disarmament* poster for Propaganda Office for Peace, Paris.

✦ Ladislav Sutnar designs the book jacket for *Obraceni Kapitana Brassbounda* by George Bernard Shaw in constructivist style.

✦ Martha Orr creates "Apple Mary," the comic strip reflecting the climate of the Great Depression.

✦ Otis Shepard, Chicago-based designer, designs Wrigley's Gum poster in flat, airbrush style, influenced by the Viennese designer Joseph Binder.

✦ Paul Colin, French graphic designer, designs poster for dancer Georges Pomies.

✦ Solomon Telingater designs title page for the *In Full Voice* book.

## ADVERTISING

❧ George W. Gallup joins Young & Rubicam as director of research, develops a widely syndicated opinion poll.

❧ William Esty leaves J. Walter Thompson to start his own agency.

## ARCHITECTURE

⟁ MARS (Modern Architectural Research Group) is founded.

⟁ Modern Architecture: International Exhibition at the Museum of Modern Art, New York, sets forth a restricted model of "true" Modernism.

⟁ Viktor Nikolaevich Deni, architect and designer, is named "Honored Art Worker" of the Russian Federation.

Advertising fan with design by A. M. Cassandre

## BIRTHS AND DEATHS

Alice Barber Stephens dies.
Barbara Stauffacher Solomon is born.
Claude C. Hopkins dies.
Hal Riney is born.
Ivan Chermayeff is born.
J. L. Mathieu Lauweriks dies.
John Berg is born.
John Updike is born.
Len Sirowitz is born.
Linn Boyd Benton dies.
Shigeo Fukuda is born.
Sylvia Plath is born.

## CONSUMABLES

✝ Frito's Corn Chips are introduced in the United States.
✝ The 3 Musketeers candy bar is introduced in the United States.
✝ Zippo Lighter is introduced in the United States.

## ARTS AND CULTURE

♣ Aldous Huxley publishes *Brave New World*.
♣ Herbert Matter returns to Switzerland from Paris after studying under Fernand Léger, and becomes interested in photography and design.
♣ Museum of Modern Art, New York, adds architectural, industrial, and graphic design to painting and sculpture.
♣ The Museum of Modern Art, New York, presents the International Style exhibition.

## INDUSTRIAL DESIGN

✈ Audi, German automobile company, trademark is designed by Horch.
✈ Norman Bel Geddes publishes *Horizons*, a book about the future of American industrial design.
✈ Pye Model K wireless receiver, "sunray" motif becomes the 1930s classic icon.
✈ The Oriole stove is designed by Norman Bel Geddes of Standard Gas Equipment Corp., New York.

## POLITICS

⚔ Adolf Hitler becomes a German citizen.

## TECHNOLOGY

⚑ First stereo recording is made by Arthur Keller of Bell Telephone Laboratories of the Philadelphia Orchestra performing under Leopold Stokowski.
⚑ Ford V8 is introduced.

## TYPE

✦ Berthold Wolpe designs Albertus typeface (through 1940).
✦ Jan Tschichold designs Saskia typeface.
✦ Stanley Morison, graphic designer for Cambridge University and British Monotype Corporation, designs Times New Roman for the *Times of London*. It becomes one of the most widely used typefaces of the twentieth century.

# 19**33**

## GRAPHIC ARTS

✦ A Century of Progress, the first modern world's fair, opens in Chicago, logo is designed by Joseph P. Birren.

✦ E. McKnight Kauffer designs the poster, *Actors Prefer Shell.*

✦ Eddie Sullivan and Charlie Schmidt create comic strip "Pinkerton, Jr." for the *Boston Daily Record.* It becomes "Radio Patrol" in 1934 under King Features Syndicate.

✦ *Esquire* magazine begins publication in Chicago and adopts the comically haughty "Eskie" as its mascot.

✦ Henry C. Beck designs new subway system map sponsored by London Underground.

✦ *Jugend*, which began as the first *Jugendstil* journal in 1897 but continued as a mass culture magazine, ceases publication.

✦ Leo Lionni, Dutch-born designer living in Italy, becomes art director for Motta, an Italian food supplier.

✦ Lester Beall designs *Chicago Tribune* advertising campaign in a manner that incorporates European Modernism with American vernacular forms.

✦ Jan Tschichold resigns from the Meisterschule für Deutschland Buchdrucker (Master School for German Book Printing) in Munich.

✦ *Newsweek* begins publication.

✦ Street & Smith publishes the first "Doc Savage, Man of Bronze." Walter M. Baumhofer produces forty-three covers for Street & Smith's *Doc Savage* magazine through 1936 and becomes known as the "King of the Pulps."

✦ Studio Boggeri, a graphic design firm specializing in posters, is founded in Milan, Italy.

✦ The New BMW poster by Hemberger brings the *Ring Neuer Werbegestaler*, modern design principles, to advertising.

✦ Xanti (Alexander) Schawinsky immigrates to Milan from Berlin, designs for Olivetti and Motta.

✦ Zack Mosley's "Smilin' Jack" aviation comic strip makes its debut.

## ADVERTISING

⚓ The first Volkswagen logo shows the VW in a circle framed by a swirling swastika in the shape of an engine fan.

## ARCHITECTURE

⚑ Fortunato Depero designs a glass façade for the Post Office Palace in Trento, Italy.

⚑ Karel Teige cofounds the *Svaz socialistickych architektu* (Association of Socialist Architects).

⚑ The Hover Factory, London, is designed by Wallis, Gilbert, and partners using Art Deco and Egyptian motifs.

Cover of *Esquire* (Eskie in the corner)

## BIRTHS AND DEATHS

Adolf Loos dies.
Alfred Leete dies.
Amil Gargano is born.
Cyrus H. K. Curtis dies.
Georgy Stenberg dies.
James Rosenquist is born.
Joe Sedelmaier is born.
Louis Comfort Tiffany dies.
Susan Sontag is born.
Pat (Patrick) Sullivan dies.
Emery Walker dies.

## CONSUMABLES

☛ Campbell's Chicken Noodle Soup is introduced.

☛ Duesenberg SJ convertible is introduced by Fred Duesenberg, at $15,000, one of the most expensive cars produced in the United States in the 1920s and 1930s.

☛ The first chocolate-chip cookies are baked by Ruth Wakefield, owner of the Toll House Inn in Whitman, Massachusetts.

## ARTS AND CULTURE

♠ *Footlight Parade* set design by Busby Berkeley is released.

♠ *Gold Diggers of 1933* is released, with choreography by Busby Berkeley.

♠ King Kong abducts Faye Wray.

♠ Lajos Tihanyi, one of the founders of *Nyolcak* (the Eight), joins Abstraction-Création group.

## POLITICS

⚔ Adolf Hitler becomes Chancellor of Germany on January 30. He is given dictatorial power through the Enabling Law.

⚔ Anti-Semitic Day is designated in Germany on April 1.

⚔ Nazis cancel Bauhaus faculty contracts, the Gestapo removes the "Cultural Bolsheviks" to replace faculty with Nazi sympathizers.

⚔ Eugen Hadamovsky publishes *Radio as a Means of Political Leadership*, presaging the method that Adolf Hitler will use to capture the hearts and minds of his constituency.

⚔ First concentration camps are being constructed in Germany.

⚔ Jan Tschichold is arrested in Munich by Nazis for creating "un-German" typography. He is released soon after and moves to Basel, Switzerland.

⚔ Mussolini proposes the Four Power Pact between Italy, Germany, France, and Britain.

⚔ Nazis officially close the Bauhaus.

⚔ Nazis raid John Heartfield's apartment.

⚔ United States abandons the gold standard.

## TECHNOLOGY

⚓ Italian ocean liner, *Rex*, takes the Blue Ribbon from the German liner, *Bremen*, for crossing the Atlantic in the shortest length of time.

## TYPE

✦ Howard Allen Trafton designs Trafton Script.

**21 kinds**

Asparagus
Beef
Bouillon
Celery
Chicken
Chicken-Gumbo (Okra)
Clam Bouillon
Clam Chowder
Consommé
Julienne
Mock Turtle
Mulligatawny
Mutton
Ox Tail
Pea
Pepper Pot
Printanier
Tomato
Tomato-Okra
Vegetable
Vermicelli-Tomato

**10c a can**

*Campbell's* SOUPS

Campbell's Soup mascot

# 19**34**

## GRAPHIC ARTS

✦ A. M. Cassandre designs *Angleterre: Horses and Elm Trees at High Noon* poster for British Railway Companies.

✦ Al Capp creates comic strip "Li'l Abner," a satire of all aspects of American society.

✦ Alexander Raymond creates three new comics for King Features Syndicate: "Secret Agent X-9," a police adventure; "Jungle Jim," an exotic adventure; and "Flash Gordon," a space adventure.

✦ Alexey Brodovitch is hired as art director for *Harper's Bazaar* where he transforms the genre of fashion photography until 1958.

✦ Anthony Velonis joins the Civil Works Administration (CWA) and implements silk-screen printing of posters in a small workshop on an upper floor of the GE Building at 51st Street and Lexington Avenue in New York.

✦ Bruno Munari illustrates F. T. Marinetti's book *L'anguria lirica.*

✦ Cipe Pineles receives Art Directors Club award (with M. F. Agha) for a *Vanity Fair* cover.

✦ Erik Nitsche, Swiss designer and illustrator, moves to New York City where he begins a long career as graphic designer in fashion, advertising, recording, book jacket, and corporate design.

✦ Harry Donenfield and Frank Armer start Culture Productions, publishing the pulps *Spicy Adventure Stories*, *Spicy Western Stories*, *Spicy Detective Stories*, and *Mystery Detective Stories.*

✦ Herbert Matter designs posters for the Swiss National Tourist Office. He pioneers the use of extreme contrasts of scale, and the integration of color and black-and-white photography.

✦ Herbert Read, British art historian and critic, publishes *Art and Industry,* on the marriage of fine and applied arts.

✦ John Heartfield designs "Yuletide" anti-Nazi poster and cover for A-I-Z, with the headline "Oh German Evergreen, How Crooked Are Your Branches."

✦ Max Ernst, German dadaist, creates surreal collages in his pictorial novel, *Une Semaine De Bonté* (A Week of Kindness), the technique influences illustration, painting, and print-making.

✦ Milton Caniff introduces his comic strip "Terry and the Pirates" with imaginative cinematographic style.

✦ Phil Davis creates comic strip "Mandrake the Magician," scripted by Lee Falk.

✦ *PM* (Production Manager), a house organ of the Composing Room, New York, and America's foremost graphic arts journal, begins publishing. It is the first in the United States to publish articles by Herbert Bayer and on Paul Rand and other modernists. The publisher is Dr. Robert Leslie, the editor, Percy Seitlin. The *PM* is changed to *AD* (Art Director) in 1940 and folds in 1942.

✦ Solomon Telingater designs Ilya Feinberg's book *1914*, exemplifying the new use of word and image with typography and montage.

✦ The first commercial comic book, *Famous Funnies*, is edited by Harry Chessler, and produced by Eastern Color Printing Co. It comprises reproductions of strips from newspapers.

✦ The Shanghai journals *Anti-war Caricature* and *China Sketch* become vehicles of resistance and reform through 1937.

✦ Vincent Hamlin introduces the comic strip "Alley Oop," about the caveman who brings order to the Kingdom of Moo, a prehistoric version of Mac Sennett's *Bathing Beauties.*

✦ Walter Gropius moves to Britain from Germany.

Shirley Temple

## ADVERTISING

⚜ Ford V8 is advertised as "a symbol of progress and the newest, latest developments in automobile building."

⚜ Theodore F. MacManus Inc., Detroit, becomes MacManus, John & Adams advertising agency, later becomes D'Arcy, MacManus, Benton & Bowles.

## EDUCATION

✎ Georg Trump becomes head of the School for Master Book Printers in Munich until 1953.

## BIRTHS AND DEATHS

Emmanuel Orazi dies.
Gui Bonsiepe is born.
Hans Hollein is born.
James McMullan is born.
Michael Graves is born.
Richard Hess is born.
Rudolf Koch dies.

## CONSUMABLES

🌱 Ritz Crackers are introduced.

## ARTS AND CULTURE

♠ First sailing of the S.S. *Normandie*, French cruise ship.

♠ *Art Front*, a politically activist though nonsectarian monthly addressing artist concerns, begins publication and continues until 1937.

♠ Peggy Bacon, the gritty realist painter and etcher, publishes her book of caricatures, *Off with Their Heads.*

♠ Shirley Temple stars in her first movie, *Stand Up and Cheer.*

## INDUSTRIAL DESIGN

✦ Chrysler's "Airflow" hits the road.

✦ George Cawardine designs the Terry "Anglepoise" lamp for Terry and Co., England.

✦ Gerrit Rietveld designs Zig Zag Chair.

✦ The A4 Pacific locomotive, designed by Sir Nigel Gresley, is launched.

✦ Raymond Loewy designs office exhibit at the Metropolitan Museum of Art, New York.

✦ The Ford "810" automobile is modernity incarnate.

## POLITICS

↗ Joseph Stalin begins the first bloody purge of Communist Party.

↗ USSR is admitted to the League of Nations.

## TECHNOLOGY

⚐ First crystalline-made hormone, androsterone, is isolated by Adolf Butenandt.

⚐ First practical radio and ranging radar is invented by Sir Robert Watson-Watt, England (through 1935).

## TYPE

♣ Jan Van Krimpen designs Van Dijck typeface.

a journal for art directors and production people

Cover of *PM* magazine

# ¹⁹**35**

## GRAPHIC ARTS

✦ *Keeps London Going* poster is designed by Man Ray.

✦ A. M. Cassandre designs *Normandie* poster for French Lines, another archetype of the travel advertising genre.

✦ Bill Holman begins contract with syndicate *Chicago Tribune–New York Daily News* to create memorable comic strips including "Smokey Stover," "Spooky the Cat," "Foo," and seven daily cartoons.

✦ Herbert Bayer publishes "Towards a Universal Type" essay in *PM* (Production Manager) magazine.

✦ Herbert Matter designs *Pontresina* poster using photomontage.

✦ J. Wiertz designs *South America in 3 Days and Nights!* poster for *Deutsche Zeppelin-Reederei*.

✦ Jan Tschichold publishes *Typographische Gestaltung*, a manual for typographers in which the codifier of the New Typography reverses many of his positions, calls for a return to the traditions of formal typography, and advocates the golden section.

✦ Jerome George Rozen creates covers for the pulp magazine *Mysterious Wu Fang* through 1936.

✦ Joseph Binder moves to the United States from Austria. He develops a stylized naturalism in posters, using airbrush techniques to refine and simplify forms. His style, which had already been introduced to America in the work of Otis Shephard, becomes representative of the streamline graphic approach.

✦ Karel Teige illustrates Jan Tschichold's *Typographische Gestaltung* in Czechoslovakia.

✦ Lester Beall moves his studio to New York City from Chicago.

✦ *Mademoiselle* magazine begins publication in New York.

✦ Norman Saunders, illustrator, produces two covers a week for the pulp magazine *Mystery Adventures* through 1942.

✦ Ollie Harrington introduces "Dark Laughter" panel cartoon.

✦ Paul Rand designs *Industrial Arts Exposition* poster—one of his first—in the modernistic/baroque drawing style of industrial designer Gustav B. Jensen.

✦ Penguin Books, one of the first paperback publishers, opens in Great Britain, founded by Sir Allen Lane.

✦ Tom Purvis designs *BP Ethyl Petroleum for Snappy Engines* poster for British Petroleum Co., Ltd.

✦ Xanti (Alexander) Schawinsky designs his first photomontage poster for Olivetti.

✦ *Yankee* magazine, celebrating the virtues of New England, begins publication.

## ADVERTISING

✦ Leo Burnett leaves Erwin-Wasey, and starts his own advertising agency, Leo Burnett Co., Chicago.

✦ Martin Mankacsi, art director and photographer, creates "Airflow De Soto" ad for Chrysler Corporation.

✦ Theodore L. Bates joins Benton & Bowles.

## ARCHITECTURE

✦ Charles Eames opens architectural firm and designs two churches in Arkansas.

## BIRTHS AND DEATHS

Alfred Roller dies.
Charles Demuth dies.
Charlotte Beers is born.
Kazimir Malevich dies.
Margaret Calvert is born (c. 1935)
Philip Geier is born.
Keith Reinhard is born.
Sidney Smith dies.
Leonard Starr is born.

## CONSUMABLES

✦ First canned beer, Cream Ale, is produced by Krueger Brewing Company of Newark, New Jersey.

## ARTS AND CULTURE

✦ AA (Alcoholics Anonymous) is founded.

✦ First *Surrealismus v CSR* (Surrealism in Czechoslovakia) is shown at a gallery in Mánes, Prague.

## INDUSTRIAL DESIGN

✦ First Coldspot refrigerator is produced by Raymond Loewy Studio.

✦ Industrial Design Partnership, formerly Basset-Gray Group of Artists and Writers, Britain's first multidisciplinary design studio, opens until 1940.

✦ Marcel Breuer designs a chaise lounge in plywood for Isokon.

✦ Piet Zwart designs a modular kitchen system for Bruynzeel Co., Netherlands (manufactured in 1938).

## POLITICS

✗ Federal Project Number One, a section of the Works Progress Administration's Division of Professional Service Projects, is established. "Federal One" administers four projects: the Federal Theatre Project, the Federal Music Project, the Federal Writers Project, and the Federal Art Project.

✗ President Roosevelt signs the Social Security Act.

✗ The swastika is declared the national emblem and flag of Germany. Jews are forbidden from flying the national flag.

✗ The Works Progress Administration is established. The WPA hires artists and designers to create graphics and murals for public works projects through 1943.

## TECHNOLOGY

✦ Douglas DC3 is introduced.

✦ First fluorescent lamp is exhibited by GEC at the Illuminating Engineering Society convention in Cincinnati.

✦ First successful three-color roll film, Kodachrome, is developed by Leopold Mannes and Leopold Godowsky.

✦ First sulfa drug, Prontosil, is discovered by Gerhard Domagk. It is used for treating streptococcal infections.

✦ The parking meter is invented by Carlton C. Magee.

✦ Tricolor is introduced in filmmaking.

✦ Wells Coates designs Ekco Model AD26 wireless.

## TYPE

✦ Offenbach typeface, designed by Rudolf Koch, is released posthumously.

✦ Walter Huxley designs Huxley Vertical typeface.

✦ W. A. Dwiggins designs Electra typeface.

*Pontresina* by Herbert Matter

# <sup>19</sup>**36**

## GRAPHIC ARTS

✦ A photolettering firm is established in New York, headed by Edward Rondthaler, who was responsible for perfecting the Rutherford Photo-lettering Machine.

✦ Burne Hogarth, comic-strip artist, takes over "Tarzan," replacing Harold Foster.

✦ Charles E. Brown designs *I'm Taking an Early Holiday . . .* poster for Southern Railway Company, England.

✦ Charles T. Coiner designs the National Recovery Act's "blue eagle," the graphic symbol of the New Deal.

✦ *Consumer Reports,* America's first consumer advocacy magazine, publishes its first issue.

✦ Gustav B. Jensen designs labels for Morrell Meats and Golden Blossom Honey (the latter is the basis for the product's labels used through the twentieth century).

✦ Heindrik Willem van Loon and Frederic W. Goudy publish *Observations on the Mystery of Print.*

✦ Henry Luce publishes the first edition of *Life* as a magazine of photojournalism (he buys the name "Life" from America's leading humor magazine). The cover photograph, of the Fort Peck Dam, is taken by Margaret Bourke-White.

✦ Herbert Matter moves to the United States from Switzerland.

✦ James H. McGraw Sr., chairman of McGraw-Hill Publishing Company, retires. At the time of his departure, McGraw-Hill owns twenty-four national trade publications.

✦ Ludwig Hohlwein designs propaganda posters for the Nazi government ministries and organizations through 1943.

✦ Nikolaus Pevsner publishes *Pioneers of the Modern Design.*

✦ Otto Neurath, founder of the "Vienna method" of pictorial statistics, publishes *International Picture Language,* which contains a comprehensive description of his statistical methods.

✦ Paul Rand designs cover for *Glass Packer* magazine, for A. A. Knight & Son Corporation.

✦ Ray Moore creates the comic strip "Phantom," scripted by Lee Falk.

✦ Richard Floethe becomes administrator of the WPA's New York City poster division.

## ADVERTISING

✦ Earnest Elmo Calkins publishes *Advertising Art in the United States,* a survey of the new developments in the form. He proposes the concept of "Styling the Goods," the restyling of products to increase consumer demand—the precursor of "forced obsolescence."

**Package by Justav Jensen**

## EDUCATION

✦ Xanti (Alexander) Schawinsky immigrates to the United States and is hired by Josef Albers to teach at Black Mountain College in North Carolina.

## BIRTHS AND DEATHS

Alan E. Cober is born.
Dugald Stermer is born.
Harry Peach dies.
Jerry Della Femina is born.
Lu Xun dies.
Phil Dusenberry is born.
Richard Saul Wurman is born.
Tadanori Yokoo is born.
Victor Moscoso is born.
Winsor "Silas" McCay dies.

**Poster by Ludwig Hohlwein**

## ARTS AND CULTURE

♣ Alexander Korda produces H. G. Wells's *Things to Come* for London Film Productions.

♣ *Modern Times*, starring Charlie Chaplin, is released.

♣ Salvador Dali, Spanish surrealist, paints *La Grand Paranoiac* (the Great Paranoid).

## INDUSTRIAL DESIGN

✦ Egbert Jacobson becomes the first director of Container Corporation of America's department of design.

✦ Giovanni Pintori joins the Olivetti Corporation to oversee all aspects of design.

✦ Lincoln Zepher is introduced.

✦ Hoover Dam, on the border of Nevada and Arizona, is completed. A massive engineering project, it is 726 feet high and 1,244 feet long.

## POLITICS

✶ Germany and Japan sign a pact against USSR's Communist International Party, the Comintern.

✶ Jessie Owens wins four gold medals at Berlin Olympic Games. Adolf Hitler snubs Owens because he is an African-American.

✶ Spanish Civil War begins.

✶ Three thousand WPA workers from twenty-four states march on the Capitol and White House for expansion of government work-relief programs.

## TECHNOLOGY

⚑ First transmission of regularly scheduled TV programs from London.

⚑ Helicopter (double rotor) is invented by Heinrich Focke, Germany.

⚑ The *Wupperthal*, Germany's diesel-electric vessel, is launched.

## TYPE

♣ A. M. Cassandre designs Acier Noir typeface.

♣ Frederic W. Goudy designs Goudy Village typeface.

♣ Howard Allen Trafton designs Cartoon typeface.

♣ Robert Hunter Middleton designs Bodoni typeface.

First issue of *Life*

# 19**37**

## GRAPHIC ARTS

✦ Russian-born Alexander Liberman wins the gold medal for magazine design at the Paris International Exhibition.

✦ Anthony Velonis publishes *Technical Problems of the Artist: Technique of the Silk Screen Process,* predicting "The silk-screen process . . . will undoubtedly play an important role in the future of fine arts."

✦ China's "propaganda teams" are founded. Their aim is to help the rural population understand the meaning of "Anti-Japanese" and "Rescue China" through the use of large-scale posters and murals.

✦ Christian Berard designs Ballets Russes programme cover for Théâtre des Champs-Elysées.

✦ *Detective Comics,* the first comic book to devote an entire issue to the adventures of a single hero, is published by D. C. Comics.

✦ Douglas C. McMurtrie publishes *The Book: The Story of Printing and Bookmaking.*

✦ Dronsfield designs National Benzole mixture poster *"Oh, Mr. Mercury, You Did Give Me a Start!"* for National Benzole Co., Ltd.

✦ E. McKnight Kauffer designs *Air Mail Routes* poster for London's General Post Office.

✦ Edwin Calligan designs Watney's Brown Ale display card for Watney, Combe, Reid & Co., Ltd.

✦ Frederic Pedrocchi writes two epochal science-fiction comic strips, *"Saturno Contro la Terra"* (Saturn Versus Earth) with artist Giovanni Scolari, and *"Virus il Mago della Foresta Morta"* (Virus the Magician of the Dead Forest) with artist Walter Molino, published in Italy.

✦ Gyorgy Kepes, a Bauhaus student and teacher, moves to the United States.

✦ Lester Beall begins designing posters for the Rural Electrification Administration using flat colors and simple graphic forms.

✦ Natan Isaevich Altman, Russian graphic designer and architect, wins the gold medal at the International Exposition in Paris.

✦ Otto Neurath moves to Holland, where his "Vienna Method" of visual data symbol system is renamed Isotype (International System of Typographic Picture Education). The Isotype team is headed by Marie Reidemeister, mathematician and scientist who suggested changing the name to Isotype, and Gerd Arntz, designer of pictographs. The same year Neurath visits the United States where his work is financially supported by the National Tuberculosis Association of America and the Oberlaender Trust.

✦ Paul Rand becomes art director of special sections for *Esquire* and *Apparel Arts* magazines, creating a series of now-classic covers that reveals his genius for adapting the ideas of modern art to his own creative concepts.

✦ Rene Pellos creates the comic strip "Futuropolis," a completely adult series and a milestone in the French comic strip. Pellos is the first European artist to apply his knowledge of anatomical drawing to the comic strip.

✦ Rino Albertarelli creates the Western comic strip "Kit Carson."

✦ Stefan Lorant, an author and photo editor, is founding editor of *Lilliput,* "the Pocket Magazine for Everyone," in England.

✦ The *Cosmopolitan,* a Shanghai magazine, makes significant advances in the representation of women with themes of independence and rejection of traditional courtship and marriage practices.

✦ Harold Foster creates the comic strip "Prince Valiant."

✦ William Golden joins the CBS Radio Network as art director.

✦ *Woman's Day* magazine begins publication.

Cover of *Apparel Arts*
by Paul Rand

🕊 SPAM is introduced (acronym for Shoulder Pork and hAM) by Hormel. It feeds millions of GIs in World War II, helps Britain during rationing, and sustains the Russian front.

## ADVERTISING
🎣 Frank Hummert becomes the highest paid advertising executive in the industry.
🎣 Marcel Vertes designs "Shocking de Schiaparelli" ad for Parfums Schiaparelli, Inc.

## ARCHITECTURE
🏛 Albert Speer is named Hitler's chief architect.

## EDUCATION
🖋 László Moholy-Nagy moves to the United States from Hungary and establishes the New Bauhaus: the American School of Design (now the Institute of Design in Chicago). Walter Paepcke, founder of the Container Corporations of America (CCA) and advocate of the Bauhaus, provides moral and financial support for the new institute.
🖋 Walter Gropius and Herbert Bayer move to the United States. Both take posts at Harvard University.

## BIRTHS AND DEATHS
Henry Lewis Johnson dies.
Lance Wyman is born.
Matthew Carter is born.
Maurice Ravel dies.
Peter Max is born.
Robert Wesley "Wes" Wilson is born.
Rosemarie Tissi is born.
Shiro Karamata is born.
Frederic Burr Opper dies.
Gustave Verbeck dies.

## CONSUMABLES
🕊 M&Ms are named after their "inventors," Forest E. Mars and Bruce Murie.
🕊 Regularly scheduled TV programming begins in France.
🕊 Kraft Macaroni and Cheese Dinner is introduced.

## ARTS AND CULTURE
🏺 *Entarte Kunst* (Degenerate Art) exhibition is presented by the Nazis in Munich. The show, which features paintings, drawings, and sculptures by avant-garde artists, is mounted for the purpose of defaming Modern art, Modern artists, and Modernist aesthetics.
🏺 *Exposition Internationale des Arts et Techniques* held in Paris.
🏺 Pablo Picasso paints *Guernica*, a memorial to the savage attack on a Basque town by Nazi bombers.
🏺 Piet Mondrian completes *Composition with Red, Yellow, and Blue*.
🏺 Walt Disney releases *Snow White and the Seven Dwarfs* in Technicolor.

## INDUSTRIAL DESIGN
✈ Harley Earle, leading automobile stylist, designs Buick "Y."
✈ Henry Dreyfuss designs model "302" desk-set telephone with Bell Telephone Lab's engineering staff.
✈ LMS Pacific locomotive designed by Oliver Vaughan Snell Bulleid.
✈ Paris Exposition Universelle opens in Paris and introduces Europe to the latest trends in Modern design.

A_A B_b C_c D_d E_E F_f G_G
H_H I_i J_j K_k L_l M_M N_N
O_O P_p Q_q R_R S_S T_T U_U
V_V W_W X_x Y_y Z_z

1234567890
1234567890

Peignot type specimen

## POLITICS
🏹 Rally protesting the cutback of WPA programs (January) takes place in Madison Square Garden, New York.
🏹 Washington adds new regulation to the Works Progress Administration (WPA), stating that noncitizens cannot be employed, leading to a significant drop in the number of Federal Art Project (FAP) artists.

## TECHNOLOGY
🔥 Polyurethane is developed.
🔥 The first turbo jet is launched.

## TYPE
✦ A. M. Cassandre designs Peignot typeface, naming it in honor of type foundry owner Charles Peignot.
✦ George Salter designs Flex typeface.

Albert Einstein

97

## GRAPHIC ARTS

✦ Adriano Olivetti, son of Camillo Olivetti, the founder of the international typewriter and business machine company, becomes president of the Olivetti Corporation. Adriano is responsible for the concept of the corporate design program.

✦ Alice Bronsch designs *Die Dame* magazine circular for Ullstein Verlag, Berlin.

✦ *Art & Architecture* publishes its first issue and continues through 1967.

✦ *Entarete Musik* (Degenerate Music) poster and book jacket show a ludicrous caricature of a black man playing the saxophone with a Jewish star on his collar, a prime example of racist Nazi propaganda.

✦ Ernie Bushmiller launches the "Nancy" comic strip, wherein the curly-headed tyke is cared for by her Aunt Fritzi and paired with little boy friend "Sluggo."

✦ F. Laskoff designs *Cordial Compari* poster (polar bear) for Davide Campari & Co.

✦ Harry Gottlieb, original member of the FAP, designs the *Strike is Won* poster.

✦ Herbert Bayer moves to the United States from Germany.

✦ John Gilroy designs *My Goodness, My Guinness* poster for Arthur Guinness, Son & Co., Ltd.

✦ June issue of *Action Comics* introduces the comic strip "Superman," created by author Jerry Siegel and artist Joe Shuster.

✦ Nicolette Gray publishes *XIXth Century Types and Title Pages.*

✦ Oskar Kokoschka immigrates to England from Germany.

✦ Paul Rand designs *Direction* magazine covers through 1944.

✦ *Picture Post*, English version of *Life* magazine, premieres.

✦ Richard Floethe designs WPA Poster Exhibition poster.

✦ Shell Poster exhibition takes place in London.

✦ Will Burtin moves to the United States from Germany, and works as a freelance designer for the U.S. Army and Air Force.

## ADVERTISING

♣ Elsie the Cow, the Borden trade character, is introduced, the creation of Stuart Peabody, Borden's director of advertising.

♣ Joyce Hall of Kansas City, Missouri, uses radio advertising to establish her greeting card business— Hallmark Cards.

♣ Radio surpasses magazines as a source of advertising revenue.

♣ Volkswagen (VW) trademark design (without the swastika) is introduced in Germany.

## BIRTHS AND DEATHS

Andrea Branzi is born.
Bea Feitler is born.
Dietmar Winkler is born.
Edward Fella is born.
Elzie Segar dies.
Ernst Ludwig Kirchner dies.
Gunter Rambow is born.
Lajos Tihanyi dies.
Mary Hallock Foote dies.
Paul Davis is born.
Ruth Ansel is born.
Ted Turner is born.

Cover of *Picture Post*

## CONSUMABLES

⟐ Lay's Potato Chips are introduced.

## ARTS AND CULTURE

♣ "Flat Foot Floogie with a Floy Floy" becomes hit song.

♣ Hogie Carmichael composes "Heart and Soul."

♣ Orson Welles's radio broadcast of H. G. Wells's *War of the Worlds* convinces thousands that the earth is under attack.

♣ Qin Wei, Chinese film set designer and woodcut artist, aids in founding Shanghai Artists and Writers Association.

♣ The Museum of Modern Art, New York, exhibits the first American survey of work from the defunct Bauhaus, along with publicity and publications, thereby positioning itself as the judge of modern design and opponent of Art Deco as imitation or streamlining. MoMA defines what constitutes "good design."

## INDUSTRIAL DESIGN

⚒ Hudson 4-6-4 locomotive is designed by Henry Dreyfuss.

## POLITICS

⚔ American comic strips are banned in Italy.

⚔ Arthur Neville Chamberlain seeks peace with Hitler at Munich.

⚔ Gustav Gustavovich Klutsis is deported to a concentration camp. Although he is thought to have been executed shortly after this point, some sources say he died there in 1944.

⚔ Nazi Germany occupies Sudetenland.

⚔ President Roosevelt recalls American ambassador to Germany, Germany recalls its ambassador to the United States.

⚔ The Federal Art Project (FAP) now exists in all forty-eight U.S. states, making it possible for artists to work. Some of the artists nurtured by the FAP who would go on to achieve prominence are Lee Krasner, Will Barnet, Stuart Davis, Alice Neel, Louise Nevelson, Jackson Pollock, and Willem de Kooning.

## TECHNOLOGY

⚡ Albert Einstein and Leopold Infeld publish *The Evolution of Physics*.

⚡ Ballpoint pen is invented by László and Georg Biró.

⚡ Sir Nigel Gresley's fastest steam locomotive ever built, the Mallard A4, sets the speed record at 126 mph (202.7 km/h).

⚡ Nylon is invented by Wallace Carrothers.

⚡ Xerography is invented by Chester Carlson.

## TYPE

✦ Berthold Wolpe designs Pegasus typeface.

✦ Warren Chappell designs Lydian typeface.

✦ W. A. Dwiggins designs Caledonia typeface based on the nineteenth-century Scottish faces for Mergenthaler Linotype Company.

✦ W. A. Dwiggins designs Cordelia typeface.

Cover of *Direction* magazine by Paul Rand

# 19**39**

## GRAPHIC ARTS

✦ A. M. Cassandre designs various covers for *Harper's Bazaar*.

✦ A. M. Cassandre returns to Paris from New York.

✦ Alois Carigiet designs *Aroso* poster for the Swiss Travel Bureau.

✦ Bradbury Thompson becomes designer for West Virginia Pulp and Paper Company arts magazine, *Westvaco Inspirations*, a four-color publication showing the advantages of the company's papers. Thompson uses the forum to foster an appreciation for progressive design techniques until 1961.

✦ Bradbury Thompson designs a cover for the official program for the New York World's Fair.

✦ *Glamour* magazine begins publication.

✦ Cipe Pineles becomes art director at *Glamour* through 1946.

✦ Joseph Binder designs streamlined New York World's Fair poster.

✦ Leo Lionni moves permanently to the United States from Italy.

✦ Lou Dorfsman begins his career, designing posters for the World's Fair and art-directing training films for the U.S. Navy.

✦ Pocket Books is founded by Robert de Graaf in the United States in association with Simon and Schuster, one of the first paperback publishers.

✦ Village Letter Foundry on the Hudson, New York, established by Frederick W. Goudy in 1908, is destroyed by fire.

✦ Vrest Orton publishes *Goudy, Master of Letters*.

## ADVERTISING

✦ First "national" TV broadcast originates from the New York World's Fair.

## ARCHITECTURE

✝ General Motors' "Highways and Horizons" exhibition at the New York World's Fair is designed by Norman Bel Geddes.

✝ George Giusti, Italian graphic designer, collaborates with Herbert Matter on the design of the Swiss Pavilion for the New York World's Fair.

✝ Harrison and Fouiloux design the Trylon and Perisphere as the architectural centerpiece and graphic symbol of the 1939 New York World's Fair.

✝ Ladislav Sutnar designs Czechoslovakian Pavilion for the New York World's Fair, which summarily closes after the Nazi invasion of Czechoslovakia. Against orders, Sutnar remains in New York and refuses to return materials from the closed pavilion.

✝ Walter Dorwin Teague designs the National Cash Register Building and Du Pont Building for the New York World's Fair.

✝ Xanti (Alexander) Schawinsky designs North Carolina Pavilion at the New York World's Fair.

## BIRTHS AND DEATHS

Alphonse Mucha, Czech poster artist, dies.

Barry Zaid is born.

Charles Jencks is born.

Georges Auriol dies.

Jayme Odgers is born.

John McConnell is born.

Jules Cheret dies.

R. O. Blechman is born.

Sigmund Freud dies.

Thomas J. Burrell is born.

Tom Carnase is born.

Allen Rosenshine is born.

## CONSUMABLES

✝ Birds Eye precooks the first frozen meal, offering a harbinger of the TV dinner.

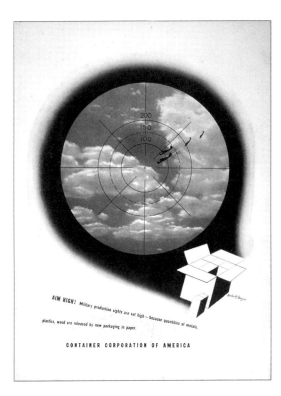

CONTAINER CORPORATION OF AMERICA

Left and opposite:
Advertisements for the
Container Corporation
of America

**♣ The New York World's Fair "The World of Tomorrow"** opens in Flushing Meadows, Queens (through 1940), introducing the marvels of industrial design in the streamline style (features the work of Norman Bel Geddes, Raymond Loewy, Henry Dreyfuss, and others).

## ARTS AND CULTURE
♠ "Indian Head" television test pattern is originated by RCA.
♠ NBC experiments with the first baseball game TV telecast, Princeton vs. Columbia.
♠ The FAP-sponsored New Horizons in American Art exhibition is on display at M. H. DeYoung Museum, San Francisco.
♠ The first science fiction convention is held in New York City.
♠ *The Wizard of Oz* film debuts.

## BIG BUSINESS
🏛 Hewlett Packard is founded.

## INDUSTRIAL DESIGN
♣ CCA (Container Corporation of America) commissions Herbert Bayer, Fernand Léger, Man Ray, Herbert Matter, and Jean Carlu to work on advertising campaigns.
♣ Citroën 2CV is introduced in France.
♣ Paul Fuller designs the Wurlitzer 950, jukebox-as-architecture.

## POLITICS
⚔ France and Britain declare war on Germany on September 3. World War II begins.
⚔ Hitler signs nonaggression pact with Stalin.
⚔ The House Un-American Activities Committee (HUAC), headed by Texas Democratic representative Martin Dies Jr., a precursor to the Army-McCarthy hearings in 1954, persuades Congress to kill America's first and only national theater, the Federal Theatre Project, by arguing that it is Communist-dominated.
⚔ USSR army invades Poland.

⚔ WPA art projects are closing all over the United States. New York's FAP remains alive through Mayor LaGuardia's New York City sponsorship.

## TECHNOLOGY
⚡ A-bomb is developed by Otto Frisch, Niels Bohr, and Rudolf Peierls.
⚡ FM broadcasting is developed by Edwin Armstrong.
⚡ Otto Hahn and Fritz Strasman bombard uranium with neutrons and obtain isotopes.

## TYPE
❦ Imre Reiner designs Floride typeface.
❦ Rudolph Ruzicka designs Fairfield typeface (through 1949).

Poster for the 1939 World's Fair

DIVERSIFICATION

Folding cartons, corrugated and solid fibre shipping cases for every industry.

CONTAINER CORPORATION OF AMERICA

# 1940

# I think there is a world market for maybe five computers.

Thomas Watson, chairman of IBM, 1943

# <sup>19</sup>**40**

## GRAPHIC ARTS

✦ Alvin Lustig designs *The Ghost in the Underblows* book and book jacket, one of his earliest experiments with typecase materials as decorative design elements.

✦ Alvin Lustig is commissioned to design book and jacket designs by publisher James Laughton of New Directions in New York.

✦ C. C. (Charles Clarence) Beck creates the comic strips "Captain Marvel" (originally "Captain Thunder") and "Billy Batson," both scripted by Otto Binder.

✦ Cyril Kenneth Bird designs defense posters, including *Careless Talk Costs Lives*, for Ministry of Home Security, London.

✦ E. McKnight Kauffer designs "Outposts of Britain" poster for General Post Office, London.

✦ Frederic W. Goudy publishes *Typologia*.

✦ Joseph Binder designs A&P Coffee poster, using his emblematic, stream-lined airbrush style.

✦ Li Qun, teacher at Lu Zun Academy in China, creates the *People's Illustrated* newspaper.

✦ Martha Orr abandons the comic strip "Apple Mary," and revives it as "Mary Worth's Family," with Dale Connor as artist and Allen Saunders as scriptwriter.

✦ Otto Neurath and Marie Reidmeister (now married) move to England and, in 1941, start the Isotype Institute, which continues until Neurath's death in 1945.

✦ *Print* magazine, founded by William Edwin Rudge, produces its first issue.

✦ Raymond Loewy redesigns the Lucky Strike cigarette package, creating the emblematic bullseye logo.

✦ T. M. Cleland gives some "Harsh Words" in the form of a lecture to the AIGA, attacking the novelty of contemporary modern design and typography. His lecture is seen as an attack on those who mindlessly follow Bauhaus principles, as well as those who seriously extend those ideas into newer realms.

✦ *View*, an arts magazine devoted to Europe's most important painters and writers, many of whom fled war-torn Europe (Man Ray and René Magritte, for example), is founded by Charles Henri Ford. *View* becomes known for its modern covers by Marcel Duchamp, Fernand Léger, and others and is published until 1947.

✦ William Golden becomes art director for the CBS corporation.

## ADVERTISING

✦ Herb Lubalin and Lou Dorfsman begin their careers with Reiss Advertising.

✦ Carling Black Label beer "Hey, Mabel! Black Label!" ads are created by Lang, Fisher & Stashower.

✦ George Petty designs Old Golds ad "Buzzing with News about Cigarettes!" for P. Lorillard & Co. Petty, a master of the stylish pinup, injects sex appeal into cigarette advertising.

✦ Gillette ads with the slogan "Look Sharp, Feel Sharp" are created by BBD&O.

✦ Rosser Reeves and Theodore L. Bates form Ted Bates & Co., New York, and launch a "hard sell" approach.

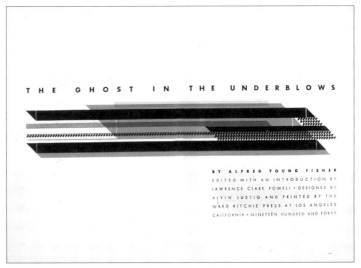

THE GHOST IN THE UNDERBLOWS

BY ALFRED YOUNG FISHER
EDITED WITH AN INTRODUCTION BY
LAWRENCE CLARK POWELL · DESIGNED BY
ALVIN LUSTIG AND PRINTED BY THE
WARD RITCHIE PRESS AT LOS ANGELES
CALIFORNIA · NINETEEN HUNDRED AND FORTY

Title page by Alvin Lustig

♦ Ted Bates leaves Benton & Bowles to start his own agency, taking Wonder Bread and Colgate dental cream with him.

♦ Texaco's "You Can Trust Your Car to the Men Who Wear the Star" ad campaign begins, created by Benton & Bowles.

## Births and Deaths

Anthon Beeke is born.
Arthur Eric Rowton Gill dies.
Chuck Close is born.
David Kennedy is born.
Gert Dumbar is born.
Sheila Levrant de Bretteville is born.
Oswald B. Cooper, typographer, dies.
Paul Klee dies.
Peter Behrens dies.
Peter Murdoch is born.
Theodore F. MacManus dies.
Thomas Ockerse is born.
Gordon Salchow is born.

## Arts and Culture

♣ Charlie Chaplin's *Great Dictator* parodies the swastika with the sign of the Double Cross.

♣ Walt Disney releases *Fantasia*.

## Industrial Design

✛ "Organic Design in Home Furnishings Competition" is exhibited at the Museum of Modern Art.

✛ Hungarian-born Albert Kner moves to the United States and is hired as a package designer for CCA. He creates the prototype for the six-pack.

✛ Container Corporation of America (CCA), Chicago, establishes a design laboratory.

✛ Eliot Noyes is appointed first director of the Museum of Modern Art's department of industrial design (New York City).

✛ Henry Dreyfuss designs the round Honeywell thermostat, arguably his most enduring design.

## Politics

✗ Evacuation of Dunkirk. Battle of Britain begins.

✗ Leon Trotsky, cofounder of the Bolshevik movement, organizer of the Red Army, is assassinated by Jaime Ramón Mercader in México City.

✗ Winston Churchill becomes prime minister of England.

## Technology

⚲ Prehistoric wall drawings are discovered at the Lascaux caves in France.

⚲ PVC, polystyrene, Perspex, and polythene are developed.

## Type

♣ Robert Hunter Middleton designs Radiant typeface.

♣ Warren Chappell designs Trajanus typeface.

Cover of *Verve* magazine

# 19**41**

## GRAPHIC ARTS

✦ *Deserve Victory* poster (Winston Churchill pointing finger) illustrated by "Little."

✦ A. Brener designs *Save for the Brave!* poster for National Savings Committee.

✦ Ai Zhong-xin exhibits his work in an anti-Japanese caricature exhibition in Shanghai, which later becomes part of a permanent collection of the Central Library, Nanjing.

✦ Alexander Liberman comes to the United States to work for *Vogue*.

✦ Alexey Brodovitch becomes art director of Saks Fifth Avenue, New York, until 1943.

✦ Boris Efimov, Russian cartoonist, designs *What Is an "Aryan"? He Is Handsome as Goebbels* poster, produced for Russian War Relief Inc., London, showing a caricature of Dr. Josef Goebbels as a rat with his tail twisted into a swastika.

✦ Charles and Ray Eames marry.

✦ Jack Cole creates the comic strip "Plastic Man."

✦ Jean Carlu receives top award from the New York Art Directors Club.

✦ Joseph Binder designs a recruitment poster for the U.S. Army Air Corps, a masterpiece of graphic simplicity.

✦ Ladislav Sutnar becomes the art director for the Sweet's Catalog Service until 1960. He popularizes the grid for organizing complex technical information reflecting the Bauhaus philosophy. He designs Sweet's Catalog Service logo and reworks Sweet Files, a set of annually updated catalogs of industrial and architectural products.

✦ W. A. Dwiggins publishes essay "A Technique for Dealing With Artists," a satirical commentary on how to optimize the talents of artists in graphic and advertising art.

## ADVERTISING

✦ James Thurber designs Talon Fasteners ad for Talon, Inc.

✦ Landor Associates, founded by Walter Landor, becomes one of the leading graphic identity firms in the United States.

✦ Paul Rand becomes the art director of William Weintraub Advertising agency until 1954, and designs the Coronet Brandy trademark and advertising campaign.

✦ René Prinet designs "Tabu, the Forbidden Fragrance" ad for Dana Perfumes Corp.

## ARCHITECTURE

✦ Ludwig Mies Van Der Rohe designs modern apartments on Lake Shore Drive, Chicago.

## EDUCATION

✦ Alexey Brodovitch starts the Brodovitch Design Laboratory at the New School for Social Research (until 1949), attended by many future leaders in the fields of graphic design and photography.

Logo for Sweets Catalog Service

## BIRTHS AND DEATHS

Alexei von Jawlensky dies.
Christopher Pullman is born.
Daniel Berkeley Updike dies.
El Lissitzky dies.
Frank Pick dies.
Henri Bergson dies.
Masanori Umeda is born.
Mike Salisbury is born.
Richard Eckersey is born.
Robert Delaunay dies.
Wolfgang Weingart is born.
Cliff Freeman is born.

## ARTS AND CULTURE

♨ *Citizen Kane*, one of the first films noir, premieres.

♨ With 7,500 TV sets in New York City, NBC's WNBT begins telecasting July 1. The first TV spots air featuring a Bulova watch that ticks for sixty seconds as open-and-close-time signals for the day's schedule.

## POLITICS

⚔ Germany invades the Soviet Union.
⚔ Japanese bomb Pearl Harbor.

## TECHNOLOGY

⚑ Dacron is invented.

Advertisement for Coronet brandy

# <sup>19</sup>42

## GRAPHIC ARTS

✦ Abram Games designs *Emergency Blood Transfusion Service* poster in England.

✦ Abram Games designs *Your Talk May Kill Your Comrades*, surrealistic propaganda poster, England.

✦ Bradbury Thompson becomes an art director of Office of War Information (OWI).

✦ Cipe Pineles becomes art director for *Glamour*.

✦ Crockett Johnson creates comic strip "Barnaby," combining the fantasy of Little Nemo with humor of Krazy Kat.

✦ Jean Carlu designs *America's Answer! Production* poster for Office for Emergency Management. The stark image of a gloved fist holding a wrench as if tightening a bolt (the "o" in the word production) is the paradigm of the graphic pun, in which a letterform substitutes for another object or image.

✦ John H. Johnson, writer, editor, and publisher of the Johnson Publishing Co. of Chicago, founds *Negro Digest*.

✦ Max Bill designs book cover for *Moderne Schweizer Architektur* (Modern Swiss Architecture), an example of his use of mathematical proportions to create harmony and order in an asymmetrical layout.

✦ *Organic Gardening* begins publication in New York.

✦ Saul Steinberg draws his first cartoon for *Fortune* magazine.

✦ World War II gives birth to three comic strips: "G. I. Joe" by Dave Breger, "The Sad Sack" by Sergeant George Baker, and "Male Call" by Milton Caniff.

*Production* by Jean Carlu

## CONSUMABLES

✝ Zoot suit is popular among jitterbuggers.

## ARTS AND CULTURE

♣ Jackson Pollock has his first one-man show in New York.

## INDUSTRIAL DESIGN

✈ Charles and Ray Eames begin experiments with molded plywood, which they use to make arm and leg splints for the Army. Mass production of molded plywood chairs begins in Venice, California, in the summer of 1946. Herbert Matter works as designer in Eames office until 1945.

✈ Misha Black founds Design Research Unit (DRU), with Milner Gray, a design consultancy devoted to modernizing British industrial products.

## POLITICS

🏹 Mussolini is stripped of his rank of prime minister, imprisoned, then freed by Nazi commandos. Hitler installs Mussolini as the head of the Republic of Saló, Italian Social Republic.

🏹 WPA projects are phased out.

## TECHNOLOGY

♠ Penicillin is introduced as an antibiotic.

## TYPE

♣ Victor Hammer designs American Uncial Typeface.

Poster by Ben Shahn

# 19**44**

## GRAPHIC ARTS

✦ Alexander Liberman becomes art director for *Vogue* magazine, succeeding M. F. Agha.

✦ Bradbury Thompson becomes art director of *Mademoiselle* magazine until 1959 and art director of *Art News* until 1972.

✦ *Graphis* magazine is founded by Walter Herdeg in Zurich, Switzerland, and becomes the leading showcase for an international array of design and designers.

✦ Joseph Binder designs *Time Is Short* poster for the Emergency Management Office, Washington, D.C., showing a stylized sword of Damocles dangling over a surreal landscape.

✦ Ladislav Sutnar designs *Catalog Design*, a handbook for the rational design of trade catalogs using constructivist principles.

✦ Lester Beall designs for the Upjohn Pharmaceutical Company until 1952, becomes art director for its in-house magazine, *Scope*, until 1948 when Will Burtin succeeds him.

✦ *Seventeen* magazine begins publication.

## ADVERTISING

✦ Bobri designs "Toujours Moi" perfume ad for Parfums Corday, Inc.

✦ Carl Erickson designs Air-Spun Makeup ads for Coty, Inc.

✦ Joyce Hall of Hallmark Cards, Kansas City, Missouri, unveils the slogan "When You Care Enough to Send the Very Best."

✦ U.S. Forest Service Smokey the Bear "Only You Can Prevent Forest Fires" ad is created for the Advertising Council by Foote, Cone & Belding.

✦ William Steig illustrates Lifebuoy soap ad "So Long, Junior. I Warned You . . ." for Lever Bros. Company.

## EDUCATION

✦ Basel School of Design, Switzerland, becomes the Institute of Design.

Cover for *Catalog Design*

## BIRTHS AND DEATHS

Carol Devine Carson is born.
Charles Dana Gibson dies.
Douglas C. McMurtrie dies.
Edward Johnston dies.
F. T. Marinetti dies.
Florine Stettheimer dies.
Gilbert Rhode dies.
Koichi Sato is born.
Lucien Pissaro dies.
Piet Mondrian dies.
Rick Griffin is born.
Rose O'Neill dies.
Stafan Schlesinger dies.
Takenobu Igarashi is born.
Wassily Kandinsky dies.
George Herriman dies.

๙ Allies invade Europe on D-Day, June 6.

๙ Franklin D. Roosevelt is elected to a fourth term.

๙ Germans hit London with V-2 rockets.

## CONSUMABLES

๙ First ballpoint pens, patented by Hungarian László Biró in 1943, are manufactured solely for the Royal Air Force, England. (They are made available to the public in 1945, distributed by Eterpen Co., Buenos Aires.)

## INDUSTRIAL DESIGN

๙ Paul Rand designs bottle for Coty perfume.

Cover for *Graphis* magazine

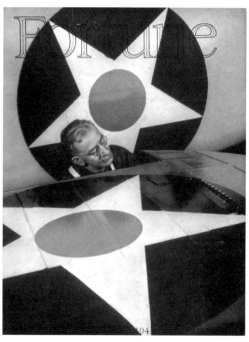

Cover of *Fortune* magazine

# ¹⁹**45**

## GRAPHIC ARTS

★ Alvin Lustig becomes visual design research director at *Look* magazine until 1946, designs magazine covers for *Art Digest* and book jackets for New Direction Books and Noonday Press.

★ Georg Olden, one of the first prominent African-American designers, is hired by CBS to establish a graphics department for its new television division. Later in his fifteen-year tenure he plays a major role in developing on-air visuals.

★ George McManus receives honors at a Congressional dinner in Washington on the twenty-fifth anniversary of "Maggie and Jiggs." He is the first cartoonist to receive this honor.

★ John H. Johnson, of Johnson Publishing Co., Chicago, founds *Ebony*, a general-interest magazine for African-Americans.

★ Paul Rand designs book jackets for Alfred A. Knopf through 1968 and book covers for Vintage Books through 1962.

★ Richard Avedon works as staff photographer for *Harper's Bazaar* until 1965.

★ Saul Steinberg publishes his first anthology, *All in Line*, with cartoons previously published in *PM* (the daily newspaper) and other sources. The anthology includes satires on the Axis leaders.

★ Will Burtin becomes art director for *Fortune* magazine (through 1949).

## ADVERTISING

⚓ Container Corporation of America (CCA) begins its "Allied Nations" advertisements.

⚓ Frederick Hollander illustrates the Studebaker cars and Wright Cyclone Engines ad "To the Few to Whom So Many Owe So Much!" for the Studebaker Corporation, which emphasizes appreciation for U.S. soldiers.

## EDUCATION

✎ Gyorgy Kepes, designer and instructor at the Institute of Design, Chicago, becomes professor of Visual Design at the Massachusetts Institute of Technology (MIT).

## BIRTHS AND DEATHS

Charles Bigelow is born.
Dan Friedman is born.
Dan Wieden is born.
David Lance Goines is born.
F.D.R. dies.
Farkas Molnar dies.
Francis Bruguiere dies.
Hans Christiansen dies.
Katherine McCoy is born.
Martin Sorrell is born.
Otto Neurath dies.
Samuel Rosenstock dies.
Sumner Stone is born.
Theodore Dreiser dies.
Hartmut Esslinger is born.
Hendrik N. Werkman dies.

Cover for *Fortune* magazine by Ladislav Sutnar

## ARTS AND CULTURE

♠ Pierre Boulat, photographer, begins career at the Paris magazine *Samedi Soir*.

♠ Vannevar Bush develops the theory of hypermedia, a theory that in the 1980s becomes the cornerstone of interactive media.

## INDUSTRIAL DESIGN

⊀ Contemporary Style, also known as the Festival Style, the South Bank Style, or the New English Style, begins in Britain and continues until 1956.

⊀ George Nelson begins to design for Herman Miller (Irving Harper in Nelson's office designs the Miller "M").

*The Next Call* by H. N. Werkman

## POLITICS

↗ A-bomb is dropped on Hiroshima, August 6.

↗ Hendrik N. Werkman, editor/designer of the *Next Call*, is murdered by the Nazis, much of his work is destroyed.

↗ Nuremberg war crimes trials begin and continue through 1946.

↗ United Nations is founded.

↗ VE Day, May 8, the war ends in Europe.

↗ VJ Day, August 14, the war ends in the Pacific.

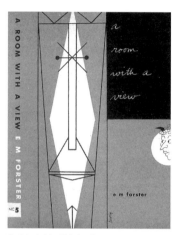

Book jacket by Alvin Lustig

## TECHNOLOGY

⚡ ENIAC (Electronic Numerical Integrator and Calculator) is invented by J. Presper Eckert and John W. Mauchly, marking the beginning of the first generation of modern computers. This was the first all-purpose electronic digital computer.

⚡ Microwave oven is invented by Percy Le Baron Spencer.

## TYPE

✤ Bradbury Thompson designs Monalphabet, a simplified alphabet developed to increase the ease of reading.

# 19**46**

## GRAPHIC ARTS

✦ Allen Hurlburt becomes art director for NBC.

✦ *Design Quarterly*, the magazine of the Walker Art Center, publishes first of fifty years worth of issues.

✦ Edgar P. Jacobs, Belgian comic-strip artist, introduces science fiction characters Professor Mortimer, Francis Blake of the Intelligence Service, and Colonel Olrik in "Le Rayon 'U'" (the first U-Ray).

✦ Frederic W. Goudy publishes *A Half-Century of Type Design and Typography*.

✦ *Highlights for Children* begins publication.

✦ Lou Dorfsman becomes art director for CBS Radio.

✦ French-born Maurice De Bevere launches comic strip "Lucky Luke," about a very humorous cowboy.

✦ Paul Rand designs *Jazzways* yearbook cover in a witty cubistic manner and Ohrbachs ads with simple line drawings (Bill Bernbach, copywriter).

✦ Paul Rand publishes *Thoughts on Design*, a monograph cum Modern design manifesto.

✦ Saul Bass moves to Los Angeles to work on film promotion and movie titles.

## ADVERTISING

❧ Ben Duffy becomes president of Batten, Barton, Durstine & Osborn, New York.

❧ Don Bender creates PM whiskey ad "For Pleasant Moments . . ." for National Distillers Products Corporation.

❧ E. V. Johnson creates Borden's dairy products ad "But, Dear, Mothers-in-Law Are Harmless!" for the Borden Company.

❧ Gene Federico works as an assistant designer at *Fortune* magazine.

❧ James Webb Young, with Ted Repplier, transforms the War Advertising Council into the Advertising Council. Young becomes the Council's postwar chairman.

❧ Paul Rand designs Disney Hats ads through 1948, introducing elements of modern art to mainstream advertising.

## BIRTHS AND DEATHS

Arthur G. Dove dies.
Dmitrii Stakhievich Moor dies.
Howard Allen Trafton dies.
John Steuart Curry dies.
Joseph Stella dies.
László Moholy-Nagy dies.
Maurice Saatchi is born.
Michael Ovitz is born.
Viktor Nikolaevich Deni dies.

## CONSUMABLES

➤ Slinky, developed by Richard James, a marine engineer, is launched at Gimbel's, New York. Four hundred sell out in ninety minutes.

➤ Minute Maid Frozen Orange Juice is introduced.

➤ Piaggio launches Vespa motor scooter.

Book Jacket by Paul Rand

Cover of *Jazzways*

## ARTS AND CULTURE

♣ "Britain Can Make It" exhibition is mounted in London.

♣ "Zip-a-dee-doo-da" becomes hit song.

♣ Dr. Benjamin Spock publishes *Baby and Child Care*.

♣ Eugene O'Neill publishes *The Iceman Cometh*.

♣ First bikini swimsuit is modeled by Micheline Bernardini of Paris on July 11. It is named in honor of Bikini Atoll, site of atomic testing.

♣ Herbert Matter becomes staff photographer for Condé Nast publications until 1957.

♣ Salvador Dali paints *La tentation de Saint Antoine* (the Temptation of St. Anthony).

## BIG BUSINESS

🏛 Tupperware Corporation is founded.

## INDUSTRIAL DESIGN

✦ Herbert Bayer becomes design consultant for Container Corporation of America (CCA).

## TYPE

♣ Frederic W. Goudy designs Goudy Thirty typeface.

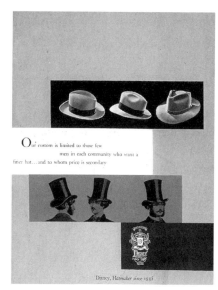

Disney Hats advertisement

Goudy Thirty type

# 19**47**

## GRAPHIC ARTS

✦ Armin Hofmann, Swiss graphic designer, opens studio with wife Dorothea in Zurich, and begins teaching at the Basel School of Design, Switzerland.

✦ British design magazine *Alphabet and Image*, edited by Robert Harling, is launched.

✦ Cipe Pineles becomes art director for *Seventeen* until 1950.

✦ Jan Tschichold joins Penguin Books, London, until 1949. He leads the revival of classical typography after having rejected the New Typography for its rigid rules.

✦ *Kiplinger's Personal Finance* magazine begins publication.

✦ Lee Garmes designs *The Secret Life of Walter Mitty* motion picture ad for Samuel Goldwyn Productions.

✦ Leo Lionni moves to New York from Philadelphia, where he worked at N. W. Ayer & Son, Inc.

✦ Milton Caniff introduces his comic strip "Steve Canyon," about a former World War II air force captain and hero who becomes director of an airline company.

✦ Noel Martin joins the Cincinnati Museum as its designer.

✦ Paul Rand designs the New York Subways Advertising Co. poster, *Subway Posters Score*.

✦ *Skiing* magazine begins publication.

## ADVERTISING

✦ Albert Schneck designs Suchard chocolates box label for Suchard, Neuchâtel.

✦ Bernard Lamotte designs "Bond Street by Yardley" ad for Yardley of London, Inc.

✦ Betty Crocker becomes a brand name with the introduction of Betty Crocker Ginger Cake Mix.

✦ Constantin Alajalov illustrates Naturalizer shoes ad "The Shoe with the Beautiful Fit" for Brown Shoe Company.

✦ Gene Federico becomes art director for Grey Advertising.

✦ Lester Wunderman (b. 1920) is hired as a copywriter by Maxwell Sackheim at Maxwell Sackheim & Co. and introduces the "direct marketing" concept.

✦ Lucian Bernhard designs the Cats Paw logo for the shoe company of the same name.

✦ Matthew Leibowitz designs pharmaceuticals display for Sharp & Dohme.

✦ Pepsi-Cola "Pepsi-Cola Hits the Spot" ads are created by the Newell-Emmett Co.

## ARCHITECTURE

✦ Le Corbusier's Marseille Apartment Block is built.

## EDUCATION

✦ Emil Ruder and Armin Hoffman join the Basel School of Design.

✦ Silas Rhodes founds the Cartoonist and Illustrators School in New York City. The name changes to School of Visual Arts in 1956.

Cats Paw logo by Lucian Bernhard

## Births and Deaths

Erik Spiekermann is born.
Frederic W. Goudy dies.
Henk Elenga is born.
Henry Ford dies.
Jack McGregor (Jamie) Reid is born.
Jeff MacNelly is born.
Joseph Michael Essex is born.
Luigi Russolo dies.
Michael Vanderbyl is born.
Pat Gorman is born.
Peter Shire is born.
Pierre Bonnard dies.
Richard Greenberg is born.
William Longhauser is born.
Dan Boyarski is born.
Douglass G. A. Scott is born.
Charles A. Voight dies.

## Consumables

➤ Reddi Whip whipped cream, first food product in an aerosol can, is introduced.

## Arts and Culture

♣ Dead Sea Scrolls are discovered.
♣ Jackie Robinson becomes the first African-American in major league baseball.
♣ *The Diary of Anne Frank* is published.

## Technology

♣ First supersonic flight is accomplished.
♣ Holograph is invented by Dennis Gabor, England.

This number **6** of ALPHABET AND IMAGE contains copiously illustrated articles on:

(1) 'artistic' Victorian printing   (2) the type designs of Eric Gill

# ALPHABET

(3) changes in news presentation in the English provincial press

# AND

(4) pre-Raphaelite drawings   (5) architectural drawings by Hugh Casson

# IMAGE

Published by ART AND TECHNICS LTD 58 Frith Street, Soho, London W1

Subscription: 7s 6d a copy, or 25s a year post free through your bookseller or direct

Cover of *Alphabet and Image* magazine

# 19**48**

## GRAPHIC ARTS

✦ Cipe Pineles is the first woman to be admitted to the Art Directors Club of New York because her husband, William Golden, refuses to be a member without her.

✦ Festival of Britain logo is designed by Abram Games.

✦ Frank Edgington creates "Rex Morgan, M.D." with psychiatrist-turned-scriptwriter Dr. Nicholas Dallis. It is one of the first "soap opera" comic strips.

✦ Henri Matisse designs *Nice* poster for French National Tourist Office.

✦ Herbert Bayer begins work on *World Geo-Graphic Atlas,* a massive survey of maps and data on the world's geography and resources.

✦ *Hot Rod* magazine begins publication.

✦ Max Huber designs *Gran premio dell' Autodrome* (Grand Prix in the Autodrome) automobile racing poster, a complex layering of shapes, typography, and transparent inks creating order within chaos.

## ADVERTISING

⚜ Carl Paulson and Fred Siebel design Ballantine's Ale ad "Purity, Body and Flavor . . ."

⚜ Clayton Underhill creates Stetson hats ad "Can't Both be Bing Crosby!" for John B. Stetson Company.

⚜ DeBeers "A Diamond Is Forever" ad is created by N. W. Ayer & Son.

⚜ Hewitt, Ogilvy, Benson & Mather is launched.

⚜ Jean Balet illustrates Lees's Carpets ad "Those Heavenly Carpets by Lees" for James Lees & Sons Company.

⚜ John Cullen Murphy creates Lastex Yarn ad "Lastex—for the Players Too" (football) for the United States Rubber Company.

⚜ Leon Gregori creates Sanforized Preshrunk Fabrics ad "The Thinker" for Cluett, Peabody & Co., Inc.

⚜ Salvador Dali illustrates ad for Bryan Nylons, "Beauty Is Rather a Light That Plays . . ." for Bryan Fall Fashion Mills, Inc.

## ARCHITECTURE

✝ Le Corbusier publishes *Modular I* and *Modular II.*

## BIRTHS AND DEATHS

April Greiman is born.
James H. McGraw Sr. dies.
Joost Schmidt dies.
Kurt Schwitters dies.
Morris Fuller (M. F.) Benton dies.
Paula Scher is born.
Carl Anderson dies.

## CONSUMABLES

🍴 33¹/₃ LP record is invented by Peter Goldmark and marketed to the public. (RCA developed a long-playing record in the 1930s, but it did not succeed.) Alex Steinweiss invents the paperboard record cover.

🍴 Cheetos are introduced.

🍴 Edwin Land introduces the first instant camera.

🍴 Richard and Maurice McDonald convert their drive-in restaurant in San Bernardino, California, to self-service, offering fast food (hamburgers, fries, shakes).

🍴 V8 Juice is introduced.

## ARTS AND CULTURE

♨ Kinsey report is published.

♨ Sigfried Giedion publishes *Mechanization Takes Command.*

## BIG BUSINESS

🏛 Neil McElroy becomes president of Procter & Gamble Co., Cincinnati.

## INDUSTRIAL DESIGN

✦ "International Competition for Low-cost Furniture Design" is held at MoMA.

✦ Alvin Lustig designs office interiors and furniture for Reporter publications, and architectural projects for Beverly Carlton Hotel and Landau apartment buildings.

✦ Herbert Matter designs Knoll chair ads.

✦ Xerox Model A, first dry copier, is unveiled by the Haloid Company and nicknamed "the Ox Box."

## POLITICS

↗ Israel is established.

↗ Mahatma Gandhi is assassinated.

↗ United States inaugurates the Marshall Plan.

## TECHNOLOGY

⚡ Transistor is invented by William Shockley, John Bardeen, and Walter Brattain for Bell Labs.

## TYPE

❧ Dick Dooijes and Stafan Schlesinger design Rondo typeface.

❧ Hermann Zapf designs Palatino typeface (through 1950).

## ACT OF GOD

★ First batch of baby boom babies are born (through 1963).

Album cover by Alex Steinweiss

# 19**49**

## GRAPHIC ARTS

✦ Alvin Lustig designs covers for Federico Garcia Lorca's *3 Tragedies* and Tennessee Williams's *27 Wagons Full of Cotton*, which integrate lettering and photography.

✦ Ben Shahn designs posters for CBS until early 1950s. Although he is branded a Communist by a congressional committee, CBS refuses to boycott his work, which was often the situation for other blacklisted artists at other companies.

✦ British design magazine *Typographica*, edited by Herbert Spencer, is launched.

✦ Carlo L. Vivarelli designs *For the Elderly* poster, an exemplary use of minimal type and stark photography in the Swiss style.

✦ *Design* magazine is published by the Council for Industrial Design, with art direction by Ken Garland.

✦ George Jerome Rozen produces covers for the pulp magazine *Shadow*.

✦ Leo Lionni becomes art director at *Fortune* magazine. He reduces the magazine to just two typefaces—Century and Franklin—and commissions numerous visual essays.

✦ Louis Danziger, modernist designer, begins his freelance career in Los Angeles.

✦ *Modern Bride* magazine begins publication.

✦ *Motor Trend* magazine begins publication.

✦ Netherlands Postal and Telecommunications Service (PPT), established in 1919, institutes an Aesthetic Design Department.

✦ Penguin Books trademark is redesigned by Jan Tschichold.

✦ *Portfolio* magazine, a cultural design journal, publishes the first of three issues. Frank Zachary is the editor and Alexey Brodovitch is the art director until 1951.

✦ Walt Kelly, formerly of the Walt Disney studios, creates "Pogo," revolutionizing the style and content of the American comic strip.

✦ Will Burtin publishes "Integration, the New Discipline in Design," in *Graphis* magazine, advocating a multidisciplinary approach that is inclusive of every phase of design, from the sketch on paper to the final exhibition.

## ADVERTISING

✦ Bill Bernbach and Ned Doyle found Doyle Dane Bernbach in New York City. They institute "creative teams" of copywriter and art director and launch the "Creative Revolution" in American advertising.

✦ Helen E. Hokinson illustrates Maxwell House Coffee ad "Everybody Knows the Sign of Good Coffee" for General Foods Corp.

✦ Maidenform ad "I Dreamed I Went Shopping in My Maidenform Bra" is created by Norman, Craig & Kummel.

✦ Phyllis K. Robinson joins Doyle Dane Bernbach as a copywriter, with Bob Gage as art director. Together they change the look and "sound" of advertising by focusing on a photographic image of the product with brief, memorable copy.

## ARCHITECTURE

✦ Buckminster Fuller develops his first Geodesic dome.

## BIRTHS AND DEATHS

Ed Cleary, fontographer, is born.
Harold H. Knerr, artist who replaced Rudolph Dirks for the comic strip "The Katzenjammer Kids," dies.
Joe Duffy is born.
John T. McCutcheon dies.
José Orozco dies.
Ludwig Hohlwein dies.
Tibor Kalman is born.
William Nicholson (half of the Beggarstaff Brothers) dies.

In this issue: Industrial India

Cover by Leo Lionni

## CONSUMABLES

☛ Pillsbury and General Mills cake mixes are introduced.

☛ Sara Lee Cheesecake is introduced.

☛ Silly Putty, discovered by General Electric engineer James Wright during World War II, is introduced by Peter Hodgson of New Haven, Connecticut, and sold through Doubleday bookshops.

## ARTS AND CULTURE

♣ "Rudolph, the Red-Nosed Reindeer" becomes a hit.

♣ George Orwell publishes *1984*.

♣ MoMA mounts exhibitions entitled "Good Design" through 1955.

♣ MoMA presents the exhibition *Modern Art in Your Life*.

♣ Soviet Socialist Realism is imposed on art throughout Eastern Europe.

## INDUSTRIAL DESIGN

✦ Finn Juhl designs the Chieftain chair.

Cover of *Portfolio* magazine

## POLITICS

✗ Apartheid is established in South Africa.

✗ Mao Tse-tung's Communist forces capture China (Chinese Revolution).

✗ Mao Tse-tung's slogan "More, Faster, Better, and Cheaper" is the basis of the most extensive Chinese propaganda campaign to date.

✗ NATO is established.

✗ People's Republic of China established.

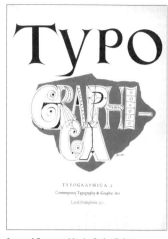

Cover of *Typographica* by Emire Reiner

Buckminster Fuller and Geodesic Dome

# 1950

*How can man get into harmony with his surroundings when he is constantly altering them? The future of our race is, in this direction, more unpleasant than we care to admit, and it has sometimes seemed to me that its best chance lies through apathy, uninventiveness, and inertia.*

*E. M. Forster, 1949*

# 19**50**

## GRAPHIC ARTS

✦ Alvin Lustig designs the signs and graphics for one of America's first shopping malls, Northland Shopping Center, Detroit.

✦ Charles M. Schulz's "Peanuts" first strip premieres and runs until 2000, the quintessential baby-boomer comic strip.

✦ China rejects Western influence in design, embraces Soviet Socialist Realism. Style remains unchanged until long after Mao Tse-tung's death in 1976.

✦ Cipe Pineles becomes the art director of *Charm* until 1959.

✦ *Flair* magazine's first issue is published by Fleur Cowles as a fashion and lifestyle book. It is set apart from other grand magazines by its ambitious production values, including die-cuts, tip-ins, and foldouts.

✦ Giovanni Pintori, the art director for Olivetti until 1968, raises the bar for corporate graphic communications with advertisements, posters, brochures, books, and exhibitions featuring work by Paul Rand, Leo Lionni, Milton Glaser, R. O. Blechman, and others.

✦ Henryk Tomaszewski, Polish designer and teacher, creates *Cryk* and other posters that wed abstract art, anarchic shapes, and robust colors (influencing two generations of artists in Poland and abroad).

✦ Herbert L. Block, editorial cartoonist for the *Washington Post*, sets the standard for this genre of cartooning, coins the term "McCarthyism," and eventually creates memorable caricatures of McCarthy, as well as the A- and H-bombs.

✦ International graphic or Swiss typographic style takes hold through the 1950s, its roots are in *De Stijl* and the Bauhaus.

✦ Ladislav Sutnar coauthors with Knud Lonberg-Holm and designs *Catalog Design Progress* for the Sweet's Catalog Service, exhibiting ways that common information (i.e., plumbing supplies) can be both logically and aesthetically designed for quick access (prefigures the interest in information architecture).

✦ Leo Lionni, coeditor of *Print* magazine until 1951, writes a regular feature of design miscellany called "The Lion's Tail."

✦ Max Huber, Swiss designer based in Italy, creates covers for the magazines *Arbiter* and *Jazztime*, combining photomontage and layering type, which prefigures Postmodern approaches.

✦ Mort Walker, comic-strip artist, creates "Beetle Bailey," a satire of military life.

✦ Morton Goldsholl, Chicago designer, designs books for Paul Theobald and the Martin-Senour Paint Company. He also develops the corporate identity program for Kimberly-Clarke Paper Company and H.U.H. Hoffman Company through the 1950s.

✦ Otl Aicher, German designer and typographer, cofounds the Institute of Design in Ulm, Germany, which proffers a rational and scientific approach to graphic, product, and industrial design.

Cover of *Flair* magazine

✦ *Prevention* magazine begins publication in the United States.

✦ Saul Steinberg illustrates *American Fabrics* magazine cover for Reporter Publications, Inc., introduces a surrealist cartoon sensibility to American illustration.

✦ Siegfried Odermatt, Swiss designer, opens studio in Zurich and helps define the International Typographic Style applied to the design of communications for business and industry.

✦ Theodor Seuss Geisel (Dr. Seuss) publishes *If I Ran the Zoo*, in which, according to the *American Heritage Dictionary*, he coins the word "nerd."

✦ Yusaku Kamekura, Japanese designer, creates posters for Nikon.

Cover of *Catalog Design Progress*

## ADVERTISING

♦ Armando Testa, Italian designer, creates ad campaigns for Pirelli tires.

♦ Chesterfield cigarettes ad features spokesperson Ronald Reagan for Liggett & Myers Tobacco Company.

♦ Chevrolet ads "See the USA in Your Chevrolet" are launched, courtesy of Campbell-Ewald.

♦ Container Corporation of America (CCA) "Great Ideas" ads are launched in February. They involve over a score of influential designers and artists.

♦ Hamm Beer "From the Land of Sky Blue Waters" ad campaign is created by Campbell-Mithun.

♦ Lucky Strikes cigarette ad for the American Tobacco Company features Marlene Dietrich.

♦ Paul Rand designs El Producto Cigar ad campaign for GHP Cigar Co. through 1957, using his witty line drawings, and the *No Way Out* billboard for 20th Century Fox, using geometric shapes and close-cropped photographs.

♦ René Gruau creates "Sans Héisiter" lipstick ad for Paul Baudecroux.

♦ Timex "Takes a Licking and Keeps on Ticking" ads are introduced, created by W. B. Doner & Co.

♦ Will Burtin becomes consultant for Upjohn.

## EDUCATION

✎ Massachusetts Institute of Technology (MIT) establishes a comprehensive graphic design program that is based on a commitment to the grid and sans-serif typography, lead by Jacqueline S. Casey and Ralph Coburn.

✎ The graphic design graduate department, School of Art, is instituted at Yale University. Josef Albers is named as director.

## BIRTHS AND DEATHS

Frank Olinsky is born.
Javier Mariscal is born.
Julius Klinger dies.
Karel Teige dies.
Kris Holmes is born.
Max Beckman dies.
Rick Vermeulen is born.
Rob Schroder is born.
Terry Koppel is born.
Steven Heller is born.
Cliff Freeman is born.

## CONSUMABLES

🌱 Minute Rice is introduced.

🌱 Sugar Pops breakfast cereal is introduced.

## ARTS AND CULTURE

♣ *Betty Crocker's Picture Cookbook* is among the top-selling nonfiction books of the 1950s.

♣ Fortunato Depero, still active long after the demise of Futurism, publishes a manifesto on "nuclear plastic painting."

♣ Paul Terry introduces *Gerald McBoing-Boing* and *Mister Magoo* for UPA Pictures, Inc. (Alvin Lustig designs opening typographic sequence for *Mister Magoo*).

♣ *Rashomon*, the first major Japanese film, debuts in the United States.

♣ Street Style cinematography is exemplified by *Young Man with a Horn*.

## BIG BUSINESS

🏛 The first copying machine is introduced by an upstate New York company that soon changes its name to Xerox.

## INDUSTRIAL DESIGN

✦ Charles and Ray Eames design and develop one of the first one-piece fiberglass-reinforced plastic chairs in collaboration with Zenith Plastics of Gardena, California. Zenith mass-produces the armchair versions for Herman Miller.

✦ Ernest Race designs Antelope and Springbok chairs in England.

✦ Hans Wegner designs "The Chair," a wood frame, with white leather upholstery.

Cover of *Print* magazine by Leo Lionni

## POLITICS

↗ Communist North Korea invades South Korea, the Korean War begins.

↗ Ollie Harrington, editorial cartoonist, leaves the United States for Paris, fearing that he would be caught up in the anti-communist nets of McCarthyism.

## TECHNOLOGY

⚑ Development of CAD, Computer-Aided Design program for architecture, begins at MIT.

⚑ Gas-turbine powered car is introduced by Rover Motor Co.

⚑ Lucian Bernhard develops a process called "Magnetype," which involves placing magnified piece of type together on a board to form words or headlines that are then photographed. Unfortunately, the almost simultaneous introduction of phototypesetting renders this process obsolete.

⚑ Lumitype/Photon typesetting machine, developed through Deberny & Peignot in Paris, is the first viable phototypesetting equipment. Charles Peignot hires type designers to adapt existing types and create new ones for this revolutionary advancement in type technology.

## TYPE

✦ Bradbury Thompson designs "Alphabet 26," a typeface with combined caps and lowercase letters, continuing the work he did with the earlier "Monalphabet" to make reading more efficient.

## GRAPHIC ARTS

✦ Allen Hurlburt becomes a designer, works for Paul Rand at the Weintraub Agency.

✦ Art Kane becomes art director for *Seventeen* magazine, helps make a magazine for teenage girls into a wellspring of inventive design, photography, and illustration.

✦ Ashley Havinden designs Liberty Department Store poster for Liberty & Co., Ltd., London.

✦ Aspen conference introduces the theme of "Design as a Function of Management."

✦ Cecil Beaton illustrates the International Silk Congress ad for Silk & Rayon Users Association.

✦ E. McKnight Kauffer designs travel poster *To England* for American Airlines, Inc.

✦ *Gentry* magazine, a fashion magazine for men, is launched and is published through 1957. It is notable for its ambitious production tricks and inventive covers.

✦ George Krikorian, promotion art director, designs *Good Books* poster for the *New York Times.*

✦ Hank Ketcham creates the comic strip "Dennis the Menace."

✦ Supported by Walter Paepke of Container Corporation of America (CCA), International Design Conferences in Aspen (IDCA) are instituted to forge a creative marriage between design and industry.

✦ James K. Fogleman becomes director of design at CIBA corporation, the pharmaceutical company, and inaugurates a long tradition of inventive promotional design.

✦ John H. Johnson, editor and publisher of Johnson Publishing Co., Chicago, founds *Jet* magazine, a pocket-sized general interest weekly for the African-American population.

✦ Nikolaus Pevsner publishes *High Victorian Design.*

✦ Paul Rand designs Babo can and billboard for Babo Cleanser for B. T. Babbitt & Co., using blocks of color as the primary "image" instead of the common clichés ascribed to quotidian household products.

✦ Yusaku Kamekura, pioneer of modern graphic design in Japan, founds Japanese Advertising Artists Club in Tokyo.

✦ *Industrial Design* (*I.D.*) magazine begins publishing, Alvin Lustig designs cover and interior format.

## ADVERTISING

❧ After two years of unsuccessful attempts, William Golden designs the CBS "eye" logo based on Kurt Weihs drawing of a Pennsylvania Dutch hex sign.

❧ Hathaway Shirts ad "The Man in the Hathaway Shirt" is created by Hewitt, Ogilvy, Benson & Mather.

❧ Japan Advertising Club is founded.

❧ Peter Hawley creates Jantzen Swimsuits ad, "For Romancin' and Entrancin' . . . There's Nothing Like a Jantzen!" for Jantzen Knitting Mills, Inc.

❧ Raoul Dufy illustrates De Beers Diamonds ad for De Beers Consolidated Mines Ltd.

❧ Speedy Alka-Seltzer trademark is introduced.

Polaroid Land Camera

*Industrial Man,* his first major work on the effects of the industrial and technological age on human communications.

## POLITICS

✦ *Hochschule für Gestaltung* in Ulm, Germany, is founded by Inge Scholl and Otl Aicher in memory of family members killed by the Nazis during World War II. Max Bill becomes rector, plans curriculum and designs its buildings.

## TECHNOLOGY

✦ First direct-dial telephone call between Mayor M. Leslie Dennying of Englewood, New Jersey, and Mayor Frank P. Osborne of Alameda, California, inaugurates Bell Telephone's "no operator" service.
✦ First electric power from atomic energy is generated in Akron, Ohio.
✦ Polaroid Land Camera is produced by Edwin Land, based on his idea of an "instant" camera.
✦ The color, sequential rotating filter for television is first introduced in the United States by Peter Goldmark. CBS begins broadcasting experimental color images.

## TYPE

✦ Imre Reiner designs Reiner Script typeface.

## ARCHITECTURE

✦ F. H. K. Henrion designs the Agriculture and Country pavilions for the Festival of Britain.

## EDUCATION

✦ Appointed by Josef Albers, Alvin Lustig develops a graduate graphic design program at Yale University.

## BIRTHS AND DEATHS

Esther Bensusan Pissarro dies.
John Sloan dies.
Joseph C. Leyendecker dies.
Leslie Savan is born.
Louise Fili is born.
Michael Cronan is born.
Michele De Lucchi is born.
Piet Schreuders is born.
William Randolph Hearst, media baron, dies.

## CONSUMABLES

✦ Cable TV is launched by Zenith Radio Corporation, Chicago.
✦ Swanson and Sons Frozen Turkey TV Dinner is introduced.

## ARTS AND CULTURE

✦ First Abstract Expressionist exhibit opens at an East 9th Street Gallery, featured are Jackson Pollock, Mark Rothko, and Willem de Kooning.
✦ J. D. Salinger publishes *The Catcher in the Rye.*
✦ Marshall McLuhan publishes *The Mechanical Bride: The Folklore of*

CBS logo

# 19**52**

## GRAPHIC ARTS

✦ Adrian Frutiger becomes typeface designer and artistic manager at Deberny & Peignot, Paris.

✦ Bradbury Thompson becomes design consultant at Westvaco Corp., New York.

✦ Egbert Jacobson publishes *Seven Designers Look at Trademark Design*, a guide to contemporary developments in the art of making marks.

✦ George Lois, hired by William Golden as a designer for the CBS Television art department, designs a letterhead for the Democratic and Republican Presidential Convention coverage, with the type forming the bars of an American flag.

✦ Lester Beall moves his office from New York City to Dumbarton Farms in Connecticut.

✦ Rudolph de Harak opens design studio in New York, which carries on the traditions of Modernism.

✦ William Gaines publishes the first issue of *MAD*, a comic book that spoofs contemporary culture, including the advertising industry. It is edited by cartoonist Harvey Kurtzman.

✦ Willy Fleckhaus designs *Aufwärts* (Upwards), a German youth magazine. His emphasis is on bold type treatments that frame stark photography (this approach is further developed in his later design for *Twen* magazine).

## ADVERTISING

✦ Anacin ad slogan "Fast, Fast, Fast Relief" is created by Ted Bates & Co.

✦ Ladislav Sutnar publishes *Design for Point of Sale*, a survey of contemporary methods of in-store display.

✦ Gene Federico joins DDB, and designs the ad "She's Got to Go Out" for *Woman's Day*, a campaign intended to interest media buyers in the demographics of the magazine. The ads feature a photograph of a young (presumably married) woman engaged in various daily routines. The best-known is an exemplary visual pun, showing a woman on a bicycle, the two wheels of which are also the Os in the words GO and OUT.

✦ Ludwig Bemelmans illustrates Walker's Deluxe Bourbon ads for Hiram Walker & Sons Inc.

✦ The Advertising Research Foundation endorses A. C. Nielsen's machine-based ratings system for TV.

✦ Tony the Tiger, created by Leo Burnett Co., is introduced by Kellogg's Sugar Frosted Flakes.

## EDUCATION

✦ Henryk Tomaszewski, Polish designer, becomes a professor at L'Academie des Beaux Arts, Varsovie, until 1985.

## BIRTHS AND DEATHS

Boardman Robinson dies.

Frank Beekers is born.

Howard Chandler Christy dies.

Johanna Drucker is born.

John Atherton dies.

Katherine Dreier dies.

Lies Ros is born.

Matteo Thun is born.

Paul Eluard dies.

Rollin Kirby dies.

Gail Towey is born.

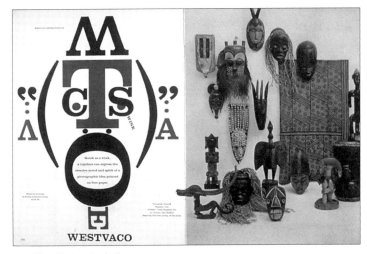

Spread from *Westvaco Inspirations*

## POLITICS

↑ FCC lifts ban on new TV stations after problems of signal interference are worked out.

## TECHNOLOGY

↟ First H-bomb explodes.

## CONSUMABLES

↑ First diet soda, No-Cal Ginger Ale, is introduced by Kirsch Beverages, Brooklyn, New York.

↑ First powdered coffee creamer, Pream, is introduced by M&R Dietetic Laboratories, Columbus, Ohio.

↑ First tranquilizer, Reserpine, is developed by British-born Robert Robinson and Swiss-born Emil Schittler.

↑ Mrs. Paul's Frozen Fish Sticks introduced.

## TYPE

✦ Hermann Zapf designs Melior typeface.

✦ Hermann Zapf designs Optima for the Stempel Foundry (through 1955).

✦ Jan Van Krimpen designs Spectrum typeface.

## ARTS AND CULTURE

♠ CBS opens its Television City production facilities in Hollywood.

♠ King George VI dies, Queen Elizabeth II is crowned in London.

♠ Henri Cartier-Bresson publishes his first important book of photographs, *The Decisive Moment.*

♠ Independent Group (artists, architects, and critics) is founded in London.

♠ Michael Ventris and John Chadwick decipher Linear B, the Creto-Mycenaean script.

♠ Samuel Beckett publishes *Waiting for Godot.*

♠ *The Holy Bible: Revised Standard Version* is among the top-selling nonfiction books of the 1950s.

DEMOCRATIC & REPUBLICAN PRESIDENTIAL CONVENTION NEWS FROM CBS TELEVISION PRESS INFORMATION ◉ 485 MADISON AVENUE NEW YORK

Letterhead by George Lois

# 19**53**

## GRAPHIC ARTS

✦ Allen Hurlburt becomes art director of *Look* until 1968, through his design breathes new life into the tired picture magazines, and makes the old *Life* magazine look passé.

✦ Edward Sorel, Reynold Ruffins, and Seymour Chwast publish the *Push Pin Almanac*, a small booklet used to promote the trio's illustration work prior to the founding (with Milton Glaser) of Push Pin Studios in New York in 1954.

✦ Ha Qiong-wen, Chinese designer for Military's Cultural Department, Beijing, gains recognition for portrayal of military heroes during Korean War and Cultural Revolution.

✦ Henry Wolf becomes art director for *Esquire*, transforms it from a collection of random spreads into a unified whole. He is given free reign to use young illustrators and photographers, often as independent features.

✦ Herbert Bayer completes his design for *World Geo-Graphic Atlas* for Container Corporation of America (CCA), a mammoth world overview that uses graphic techniques to explain shifts and transitions in the environment.

✦ Otto Storch becomes the art director at *McCall's* magazine. He combines copy and headlines with photographs into integrated spreads and further introduces the return of certain passé design forms, notably Victorian type, through 1967.

✦ A. Robert Jones becomes art director for RCA, he also starts Glad Hand Press and revives Victorian woodtypes for use in his printing.

✦ Saul Bass designs ad for *Love in the Afternoon*, a graphic of a window shade with type on it, which looks similar to a 1948 ad by Paul Rand with a window shade for Ohrbachs.

✦ Anton Stankowski designs Standard Elektrik Lorenz AG trademark.

✦ Erik Nitsche becomes design consultant for General Dynamics, creates its entire identity, and designs annual reports. Designs posters and advertisements depicting peaceful uses of nuclear power.

## ADVERTISING

❧ Bob Gage designs "The Whisper that Became a Shout" for Ohrbachs and "New York Is Eating It Up" for Levy's Bread.

❧ Camel Cigarettes ad for R. J. Reynolds Tobacco Company features John Wayne hawking for R. J. Reynolds Tobacco Company.

❧ Pablo Ferro and Fred Mogubgub, animators and commercial filmmakers, form Ferro, Mogubgub, and Schwartz, known in the industry for introducing quick-cutting and graphic effects for TV commercials.

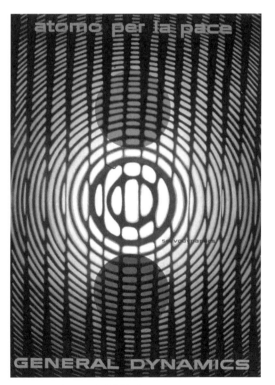

*General Dynamics* poster by Erik Nitsche

## CONSUMABLES

↗ Eggo Frozen Waffles are introduced.

## ARTS AND CULTURE

♠ Cinemascope projectors are installed in most U.S. movie theaters.

♠ Color compatible with black-and-white television is commercially introduced in the United States by National Television Systems Committee.

♠ Independent Group exhibition "Parallel of Life and Art" is presented at the London Institute of Contemporary Art.

## POLITICS

ⵏ China introduces its first Five-Year Plan for economic restructuring.

ⵏ Ethel and Julius Rosenberg, convicted for espionage, are executed.

ⵏ Korean War ends.

ⵏ Stalin dies.

## TECHNOLOGY

⚕ DNA structure is discovered.

❧ Paul Rand designs ads for Olivetti typewriters.

❧ Philip Morris Cigarettes ad features Lucille Ball.

❧ Ralph Steiner designs Air Express ad for Air Express International Corp.

❧ Richard Lindner, German-born illustrator-turned-painter, illustrates Intoxication Perfume ad for D'Orsay Sales Co.

## BIRTHS AND DEATHS

Alber Gleizes dies.
Carin Goldberg is born.
Francis Picabia dies.
John Marin dies.
Jon Savage is born.
Louise Arensberg dies.
Max Kisman is born.
Raoul Dufy dies.
Sol Hess dies.
Tom van der Haspel is born.
Vladimir Tatlin dies.
William Drenttel is born.
M. Lorraine Wild is born.
Lucille Tenazas is born.

## TYPE

♣ Adrian Frutiger designs Phoebus typeface.

♣ Paul Renner designs Topic/Steile Futura typeface (through 1955).

♣ Roger Excoffon designs Mistral typeface.

Mistral type specimen

*McCalls* magazine spread by Otto Storch

# <sup>19</sup>**54**

## GRAPHIC ARTS

✦ Alvin Lustig publishes the essay "What Is a Designer?"

✦ Hans Erni, Swiss artist and designer, designs *Atomkrieg Nein* (No to Nuclear War) poster for nuclear disarmament.

✦ Henry Luce launches *Sports Illustrated* magazine. Leo Lionni designs the dummy issue.

✦ Hermann Zapf publishes first edition of *Manuale Typographicum* (second edition in 1968).

✦ Hugh Hefner publishes the first issue of *Playboy*, originally titled *Stag Party*, with a nude pinup photo of Marilyn Monroe as its centerfold. Art Paul, a Chicago illustrator and art director is the art director. Paul designs the Playboy Bunny trademark.

✦ Nicolette Gray publishes *Nineteenth Century Ornamented Types and Title Pages*, which helps to usher in the revival of passé typefaces for contemporary applications.

✦ Norman Rockwell, the Vermeer of American illustration, is inducted into the Society of Illustrators' Hall of Fame.

✦ Push Pin Studios is founded in New York City by Seymour Chwast, Milton Glaser, and Edward Sorel, each of whom are illustrators with an interest in eclectic typography. They initiate a decorative style that serves as a counterpoint to rationalist Swiss style. (Reynold Ruffins joins the studio two years later).

✦ Robert Brownjohn designs the booklet *Watching Words Move*, in which he shows how type can be used as visual pun, using certain letters illustratively to underscore the meaning of the typeset word.

✦ Saul Bass designs his first film title sequence for *Carmen Jones*.

✦ The Comic Code Authority, founded by leading comics manufacturers, restricts violent, sexual, and political content from comic books. The manufacturers embrace this code when six states pass laws regulating the sale of magazines to minors. The Authority basically forces DC Comics, publishers of *Tales from the Crypt* and *MAD*, to cease publication. To circumvent the restrictions on content, *MAD* shifts from being a comic book to a magazine.

✦ Tom Eckersley publishes *Poster Design*, a detailed handbook on the process of poster making.

✦ U.S.S. *Nautilus* is the first atomic submarine, Erik Nitsche designs a poster, showing a huge nautilus shell with a small submarine shooting from its opening, announcing its development by General Dynamics.

✦ *Design Quarterly*, originally *Everyday Art Quarterly*, focuses on industrial design and crafts (ceases publication in 1996).

## ADVERTISING

✦ "Think Small" print ad for Volkswagen is introduced, art director, Helmut Krone at Doyle Dane Bernbach, New York. Krone is an exemplar of the "BIG IDEA" in advertising's Creative Revolution.

✦ Armin Hofmann designs logotype for the Basel Civic Theater.

✦ Bernice Fitz-Gobbon, retail advertising pioneer, former ad manager at Marshall Field's, Macy's, Gimbels, and Wanamaker, opens her own agency where numerous women copywriters get their start.

✦ CBS becomes the largest advertising medium in the world.

✦ Colonel Sanders, symbolic master of the old Southern plantation, is adopted as the trademark for Kentucky Fried Chicken.

✦ Gerald Holtom, an English textile designer, designs the symbol for the Campaign for Nuclear Disarmament (CND), England, known from then on as the "peace" symbol.

✦ Lou Dorfsman is named director of advertising and promotion for the CBS Radio Network.

✦ M&Ms ad "Melts in Your Mouth, Not in Your Hands" is created by Ted Bates & Co.

✦ New Haven Railroad logotype is designed by Herbert Matter and Norman Ives.

✦ Norman Rockwell illustrates "What Makes It Tick?" ad for Swiss Federation of Watchmakers.

✦ Paul Rand designs a full-page ad in the *New York Times* to elicit business for the Weintraub agency from the Radio Corporation of America. The ad features the "pitch" in Morse code, which, Rand knew, president David Sarnoff would understand.

Nuclear Disarmament

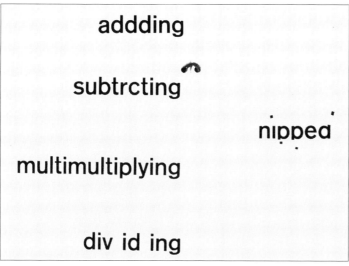

adddding

subtrcting

nipped

multimultiplying

div id ing

Pages from *Watching Words Move*

🐟 William H. Weintraub Agency falls prey to a hostile takeover, Paul Rand leaves to open his own one-person design studio with emphasis on advertising, publishing, and, ultimately, corporate design.

🐟 Winston Cigarettes "Winston Tastes Good—Like a Cigarette Should" ad is created by Wm. Esty Co.

## EDUCATION

🦅 Alexey Brodovitch is a "visiting critic" at Yale University School of Design and Architecture through 1957. He teaches publication design.

## BIRTHS AND DEATHS

André Derain dies.

Art Chantry is born.

E. McKnight Kauffer, American expatriate poster and advertising artist, dies.

Edwin Utermohlen is born.

Elizabeth Shippen Green dies.

Gerard Hadders is born.

Hannes Meyer dies.

Henri Matisse dies.

John Hersey is born.

Lyubov Sergeevna Popova dies.

Marco Zanuso Jr. is born.

Susan Kare is born.

Walter Arensberg dies.

Bud (Harold) Fisher dies.

George McManus dies.

## CONSUMABLES

🦃 Butterball Turkey is introduced.

🦃 First stereo tape recordings are made available to public by Livingston Electronic, New York.

## ARTS AND CULTURE

🦢 Daisy Mae and Li'l Abner get married.

🦢 Federico Fellini directs *La Strada*.

🦢 First airing of *Winky Dink and You*, the first "interactive" television show for children on CBS. Designer and graphic artist Harry W. Prichett Sr. and writer Edwin Brit Wyckoff developed the concept of placing a plastic film over the TV screen so that viewers could draw aspects of the cartoon in erasable crayon.

🦢 J. R. R. Tolkien publishes *The Lord of the Rings*.

🦢 *On the Waterfront* premieres.

🦢 Rudolf Arnheim publishes *Art and Visual Perception*.

## BIG BUSINESS

🏛 Ray Kroc forms first McDonald's franchise in Oak Brook, Illinois.

## INDUSTRIAL DESIGN

🛩 Ladislav Sutnar publishes *Package Design: The Force of Visual Selling*, another in his series of practical surveys on contemporary work.

🛩 Marcel Breuer designs first tubular steel furniture.

🛩 *Stile Industria* magazine is published in Italy through 1963, edited by Alberto Rosselli.

## POLITICS

🏹 McCarthy hearings begin.

🏹 U.S. Supreme Court rules against segregated schools.

## TECHNOLOGY

⚓ Dr. Jonas Salk develops the polio vaccine.

⚓ Solar battery is introduced by Bell Telephone Co.

## TYPE

🌸 Adrian Frutiger designs Univers family of type, the first large, matched family of sans-serif faces of different weights. The twenty-one Univers units have five weights and four widths and are numbered.

🌸 Georg Trump designs Trump Medieval typeface (through 1960).

🌸 Gundrun Zapf-von Hesse designs Diotima typeface.

🌸 Günter Gerhard designs Solemnis typeface, an uncial, part of the revival forms begun by Victor Hammer.

🌸 Hans (Giovanni) Mardersteig designs Dante typeface.

🌸 Hermann Zapf designs Aldus typeface.

🌸 Reynolds Stone designs Minerva typeface.

## GRAPHIC ARTS

✦ Emil Schuthess designs *Du* magazine for Conzett & Huber, Zurich. This art and culture periodical is known for its lavish use of color photography.

✦ Erik Nitsche is promoted from consultant to art director for General Dynamics Corporation.

✦ George Lewis and his New Orleans Stompers album cover is designed by Reid Miles, an early revival of the Victorian "playbill" style.

✦ Ham Fisher, creator of the comic strip "Joe Palooka," dies, artist Moe Leff continues the strip in Fisher's style.

✦ Jules Feiffer, comic-strip artist who broke down the confines of the conventional panel format, becomes cartoonist for the *Village Voice*.

✦ Leo Lionni designs the poster and catalog cover for "The Family of Man" exhibit of photographs (curator: Edward Steichen) at the Museum of Modern Art in New York, a landmark show of images that examine the customs and lives of the world's inhabitants.

✦ Lester Beall closes his New York office.

✦ Saul Bass designs the poster for Otto Preminger's *Man with the Golden Arm* and the film title sequence using a graphic, expressionist sensibility not seen before in commercial cinema.

✦ *Young Miss* magazine begins publication.

## ADVERTISING

✦ Brylcreem campaign, "A Little Dab'll Do Ya" is launched, the brainchild of Kenyon & Eckhardt.

✦ Marlboro ad introducing "The Marlboro Man" is created by Leo Burnett Co.

✦ Richards & Associates firm is founded by Stan Richards in Dallas, Texas.

✦ Shirley Polykoff becomes the lone woman copywriter for Foote, Cone & Belding, New York.

## EDUCATION

✦ Armin Hofmann, Swiss designer, conducts seminars at Yale.

✦ The Yale School of Art and Architecture, chaired by Alvin Eisenman, begins to establish itself as a link between American design and European rationalism.

## BIRTHS AND DEATHS

Albert Einstein dies.
Aldo Cibic is born.
Alvin Lustig dies.
Fernand Léger dies.
Gerard Taylor is born.
Karl Hofer dies.
Michael Mabry is born.
Mikhail Larionov dies.
Nancy Skolos is born.
Peter Saville is born.
Rudy VanderLans is born.
Steve Jobs is born.
Walter Huxley dies.
Will Ransom dies.
Yves Tanguy, French surrealist, dies.
Ham (Hammond) Fisher dies.
Warren Lehrer is born.

abcdefghijklmnopqr
ABCDEFGHIJKLMN

ABCDEFGHIJKLMNOPQRSTUVWXYZ&
abcdefghijklmnopqrstuvwxyz
$1234567890¢.,:;-!?'""–

Craw Clarendon type

## TECHNOLOGY
♠ Fiber optics are invented by Narinader Kapany.

## TYPE
♣ Ashley Havinden designs Ashley Script typeface.
♣ Freeman Craw designs Craw Clarendon typeface (through 1960).
♣ Imre Reiner designs Reiner Black typeface.
♣ Max Caflisch designs Columna typeface for the Bauer foundry.

## CONSUMABLES
➤ First transistor radio, TR-55, is launched by Sony.
➤ Tail fins appear on mid-price American cars.

## ARTS AND CULTURE
♠ Bill Haley records *Rock Around the Clock*.
♠ Independent Group begins meetings at the London Institute of Contemporary Arts to discuss the relationship between fine arts and popular culture. Its first, "Man, Machine and Motion," at the London Institute of Contemporary Art, addresses this interrelationship.
♠ Kay Thompson publishes *Eloise*, a children's book about the adventures of a little girl who lives in the Plaza Hotel, illustrated by Hilary Knight.
♠ WGBH Television, a public television station, is founded in Boston.

## INDUSTRIAL DESIGN
✦ Marlboro cigarette packet is designed by Frank Gianninoto using two trademark design elements on a white background: the logotype is in black with a heavy red "v"-shaped band placed at the top.

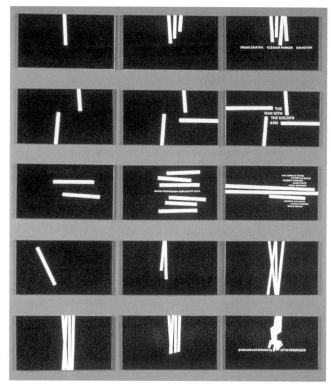

Title sequence from *Man With a Golden Arm* by Saul Bass

137

## GRAPHIC ARTS

✦ *Bon Appétite* begins publication.

✦ Edward Wright designs "This Is Tomorrow" catalog.

✦ George Tscherny, a Hungarian-born designer, starts his own freelance firm in New York City.

✦ Harvey Kurtzman edits *Trump*, published by Hugh Hefner, a satiric magazine in the *MAD* tradition. He also founds *Humbug* and *Help* magazines.

✦ Jules Feiffer creates the weekly "Feiffer" comic strip whose recurring character, Bernard Mergendeiler, is the first modern comic-strip antihero, prefiguring Woody Allen's movie persona.

✦ Ken Garland becomes the art director of *Design* magazine until 1962.

✦ Mischa Black lectures on "The Designer and the Client" at IDCA conference in Aspen. Misha Black publishes the essay "The Designer and the Client."

✦ Paul Rand illustrates *I Know a Lot of Things*, his first children's book authored by Ann Rand. He also designs book jackets for Pantheon Books' Bollingen Series through 1964.

✦ Ronald Searle illustrates Lemon Hart Rum ad "Have a Rum for Your Money" for United Rum Merchants.

✦ The Letraset company is founded in London.

✦ Willem Sandberg publishes first *experimenta typographica*, a sampler of typographic investigation.

## ADVERTISING

❧ George Him creates Schweppes Table Waters (Europe) ad for Schweppes Co., Ltd.

❧ Ladislav Sutnar designs logo and advertisements for Addo-x, a Swedish adding machine company.

❧ Lipponcott and Margulies develop Betty Crocker logo.

❧ Paul Rand becomes design consultant at IBM, appointed by Elliott Noyes, and gradually makes substantive changes in all of the packages and signs. He designs IBM slab-serifed logotype based on City typeface designed by Georg Trump.

❧ Pepsodent ad "You'll Wonder Where the Yellow Went" is created by Foote, Cone & Belding.

❧ The Complete Imbiber, promoting Gilbey's Gin, is designed by F. H. K. Henrion.

## ARCHITECTURE

⚘ CIAM (Congrés Internationaux d'Architecture Moderne), a group comprised of architects and other designers who adhere to European Modernism, dissolves.

## EDUCATION

✍ Bradbury Thompson joins the faculty of the Graphic Design program at Yale University.

✍ Louis Danziger begins teaching at the Art Center School of Design, later develops an Oral History of Design course.

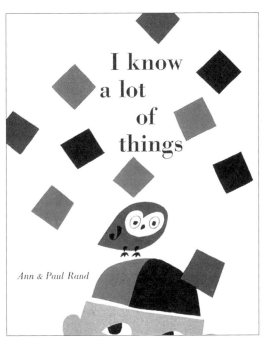

Book cover by Paul Rand

## BIRTHS AND DEATHS

Alexander Rodchenko dies.
David Carson is born.
Emil Nolde dies.
Giovanni Papini dies.
Jean Metzinger dies.
Josef Hoffmann dies.
Lyonel Feininger dies.
Paul Renner dies.
Robert Slimbach is born.
Stephen Doyle is born.
Tadeusz Trepkowski dies.
Alexander Raymond dies.

## CONSUMABLES

⊤ Fiat 600 and Nuova 500 are
introduced.
⊤ Imperial Margarine is introduced
in the United States.

## ARTS AND CULTURE

♠ Elvis Presley records "Blue Suede
Shoes."
♠ Gyorgy Kepes edits *The New
Landscape*, diverse essays relating
science and organic form to visual
arts, by Arp, Gabo, Giedion, Gropius,
Leger, and Neutra.
♠ Independent Group mounts its
exhibition "This Is Tomorrow," at the
London Institute of Contemporary
Art.
♠ Ingmar Bergman directs *The
Seventh Seal*.

## INTERIOR DESIGN

⊏ Fortunato Depero designs the
decoration and furnishing of the
Consiglio Provinciale in Trento, Italy.

## INDUSTRIAL DESIGN

✦ Charles Eames and Ray Eames
design a leather and wood lounge
chair.
✦ Gio Ponti designs 699 Superleggera
chair for Cassina.
✦ Herbert Bayer replaces Egbert
Jacobson as chairman of the
Container Corporation's department
of design.

## POLITICS

✗ Khrushchev denounces Stalin.

## TECHNOLOGY

♠ Typing correction fluid is developed
by Bette Nesmith Graham in her
garage in Dallas, Texas. It would
become "Liquid Paper," which
Nesmith will sell to Gillette in 1979.
♠ Video recorder is developed by
Ampex Co.
♠ Videotape recording makes
prerecorded commercials possible.
♠ Water slide type transfer method
developed as precursor to press-down
type.

## TYPE

♣ Paul Rand designs Westinghouse
Gothic typeface (and logotype in
1961).

Addo-x logo by Ladislav Sutnar

*Trump* magazine cover

# 19**57**

★ Theodor Seuss Geisel (Dr. Seuss) publishes *The Cat in the Hat*.
★ Virgil Finlay illustrates first science fiction cover for *Fantastic Universe*.
★ John Massey joins Container Corporation of America (CCA).

## GRAPHIC ARTS

★ AIGA holds its first package design and record cover exhibition.
★ Alan Fletcher takes job as designer at *Fortune* magazine and Time-Life corporation.
★ Andy Warhol wins the New York Art Directors Club Medal for exceptional achievement.
★ Brownjohn, Chermayeff & Geismar, a New York design firm with a "late Modernist" sensibility, is founded by Ivan Chermayeff, Thomas Geismar, and Robert Brownjohn.
★ Brownjohn, Chermayeff & Geismar design the graphics and exhibitions for American Pavilion at the 1958 Brussels World's Fair, one of their earliest commissions.
★ George Nelson publishes *Problems of Design*.
★ John Bainbridge designs posters for conducted coach tours and Underground Railway for London Transport Executive.
★ Leo Lionni writes and designs *Designs for the Printed Page* to show variations in layout methods in *Fortune* magazine.
★ Leonard Starr creates "On Stage," a soap opera comic strip with heroine Mary Perkins.
★ Paul Rand illustrates *Sparkle and Spin*, his second children's book authored by Ann Rand.
★ Richard Avedon designs his only film title sequence for *Funny Face*, the movie loosely based on his mentor, *Harper's Bazaar* art director Alexey Brodovitch.
★ *The Push Pin Monthly Graphic* publishes its first issue. The first cover is a woodcut by Seymour Chwast of an odd plant called the Devil's Apple.

## ADVERTISING

★ Clairol ad "Does She . . . or Doesn't She?" is created by Foote, Cone & Belding.
★ Greyhound ad "It's Such a Comfort to Take the Bus and Leave the Driving to Us" is created by Grey Advertising.
★ Howard Luck Gossage, advertising copywriter, forms Freeman, Mander & Gossage in San Francisco, becomes a leading force in the movement towards socially responsible advertising.
★ Mr. Clean trademark is introduced.
★ Ralph Eckerstrom designs new trademark for Container Corporation of America (CCA).
★ Stan Freberg, a satirist and advertising man, does strident spoofs of Madison Avenue's major campaigns on CBS Radio.
★ Vance Packard, advertising critic, publishes *The Hidden Persuaders*, the first investigative report on the advertising industry.

## EDUCATION

★ Anthony Froshaug teaches at Institute of Design at Ulm through 1961.
★ Tom Eckersley heads graphic design department at London College of Art and Design until 1977.

## BIRTHS AND DEATHS

Albert Bruce Rogers dies.
Alfred Tolmer dies.
Arturo Toscanini dies.
Beppe Caturegli is born.
Carlos Segura is born.
Frantisek Kupta dies.
Henry van de Velde dies.
Humphrey Bogart dies.
J. Allen St. John dies.
Jeffery Keedy is born.
Kathy Warinner is born.
Martine Bedin is born.
Nathalie Du Pasquier is born.
Neville Brody is born.
Vaughn Oliver is born.
W. A. Dwiggins dies.
Rick Poynor is born.
Henry van de Velde dies.

## INDUSTRIAL DESIGN

✦ Ettore Sottsass Jr. begins collaboration with Olivetti.

## POLITICS

✦ "Hundred Flowers" movement begins in China. Mao Tse-tung encourages intellectuals to criticize the CCP, believing the criticism would be minor. When it is not, he launches the "Antirightist" campaign, quickly turning on those who have spoken out, labeling them as rightist, and imprisoning or exiling many.

## TECHNOLOGY

✦ Soviets launch *Sputnik*, and the space age begins.
✦ Velcro is invented by George de Mistral. Velcrotex opens in Switzerland.

## CONSUMABLES

✦ Alpha-Bits cereal—the so-called Breakfast of Compositors—is introduced, featuring lightly sugared letters of the alphabet.
✦ Citroën DS is launched.
✦ First stereo disk recordings go on sale.
✦ Ford Motor Co. introduces the Edsel, one of the greatest marketing disasters of automotive history.
✦ Sweet 'N Low is introduced.

## ARTS AND CULTURE

✦ Jack Kerouac publishes *On the Road*.
✦ Township of Rovereto, Italy, finances a museum devoted to preserving and exhibiting Fortunato Depero's design and art.

## TYPE

✦ Eduard Hoffman and Max Miedinger design Neue Haas Grotesk for the HAAS type foundry in Switzerland (produced in Germany in 1961 by the D. Stempel AG typefoundry and renamed Helvetica).
✦ Univers, designed by Andrian Frutiger, is released by Deberny & Peignot (Frutiger began work on the family of faces in 1954).

Univers type specimen

## GRAPHIC ARTS

✦ Alexey Brodovitch retires as art director of *Harper's Bazaar.*

✦ Anthony Froshaug designs *Quarterly Bulletin* cover of the *Hochschule für Gestaltung,* Ulm, Germany.

✦ Bradbury Thompson begins to design Westvaco's Library of American Classics, one book a year distributed at Christmastime.

✦ Brownjohn, Chermayeff & Geismar design conceptual covers for *Pepsi-Cola World* magazine using icons of the Pepsi brand.

✦ Frank Zachary, former editor of *Portfolio,* becomes the art director of *Holiday* magazine and introduces European illustrators to the U.S. market.

✦ George Giusti designs *Holiday* magazine cover (representing England) using flat colors and three-dimensional materials.

✦ Henry Wolf leaves *Esquire* to succeed Alexey Brodovitch as art director of *Harper's Bazaar.*

✦ Herbert Spencer publishes essay "Tradition: Cliché, Prison, or Basis of Growth?"

✦ Johnny Hart creates comic strip "B. C." presenting prehistoric men who spend most of their time speculating on the world's progress and future of civilization.

✦ *New Graphic Design* (Neue Grafik) publishes its first issue. It is a magazine devoted to the Swiss style of design and typography, edited by Richard P. Lohse, Josef Müller-Brockmann, Hans Neuburg, and Carlo Vivarelli.

✦ Robert Massin becomes the art director of Editions Gallimard publishers in France.

✦ Robert Miles Runyan, a California-based corporate designer, designs the Litton Industries Annual Report.

✦ Saul Bass designs Alfred Hitchcock's *Vertigo* title sequence and an ad for Paramount Pictures Corporation.

✦ Will Burtin designs the 3-D "cell" exhibition for Upjohn pharmaceutical company, an early example of dynamic interactive design.

✦ *ULM* the journal of the Hochsule fur Gestalung is founded by Hanno Kesting (ceases publication in 1968).

## ADVERTISING

❧ Crest Toothpaste "Look, Ma! No Cavities!" ad is created by Benton & Bowles.

❧ Jane Trahey, fashion copywriter, opens Jane Trahey Associates, New York.

❧ Lester Wunderman establishes Wunderman, Ricotta & Kline advertising agency, New York.

❧ Peter Hawley creates "Betsy Bell," a trade character of a toddler with play phone, in an ad with the headline "It's Fun to Phone!" for American Telephone & Telegraph Co.

❧ The National Association of Broadcasting bans subliminal ads.

## ARCHITECTURE

❦ Ludwig Mies van der Rohe and Philip Johnson design the Seagram Building, New York, in the International style.

## EDUCATION

❧ Madsuda Tadashi founds Madsuda Tadashi Design Institute in Japan.

Cover of *Neue Grafik*

Bart van der Leck dies.
Bruce Licher is born.
Charles S. Anderson is born.
Clement Mok is born.
Giacomo Balla dies.
Jack Cole dies.
Jan van Krimpen dies.
Jean Crotti dies.
John B. Watson dies.
John Held Jr. dies.
John Newton Howitt dies.
John Sayles is born.
Keith Haring is born.
Maurice de Vlaminck dies.
Rick Valincenti is born.
Stephen M. Case is born.
Varvara Stepanova dies.
Wells Coates dies.
Frank Williard dies.

## CONSUMABLES

✛ Audiocassette player is introduced
by RCA Victor.
✛ Skateboard is introduced by Bill
Richards and his son Mark in their
Val Surf Shop in California.

## ARTS AND CULTURE

♣ Aldous Huxley publishes *Brave New
World Revisited*, an examination of
how governments can mold public
opinion through media and drugs.
♣ Vladimir Nabokov publishes *Lolita*.

## INDUSTRIAL DESIGN

✦ Arne Jacobsen designs "Egg" chair
and stool.
✦ Charles Eames designs a series of
exhibition and "communication"
projects for IBM, including the lobby
of the main headquarters in New York.
✦ Lester Beall designs interiors and
exteriors for New Haven Railroad
trains through 1960.

## POLITICS

⊁ Little Rock, Arkansas, closes
schools over desegregation.

## TECHNOLOGY

⚑ Diatype, first commercially available
photosetting system, is introduced by
Berthold.
⚑ E13B computer alphabet is
developed by Burroughs Corp.'s staff.
⚑ First heart pacemaker is inserted by
Dr. Ake Senning in Stockholm.

## TYPE

✦ Freeman Craw designs Craw
Modern typeface (through 1964).
✦ Hermann Zapf designs Optima
typeface.
✦ Roger Excoffon designs Calypso
typeface.

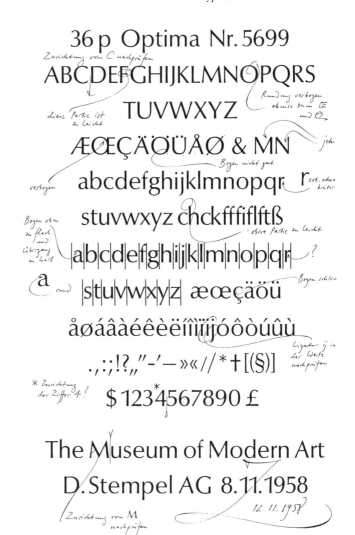

Optima type specimen

# 19**59**

## GRAPHIC ARTS

✦ *Auch Du bist liberal* (You Are too Liberal) political poster is designed by Karl Gerstner, Zurich. It shows a blurred image, in black on a bright red background, of a man, the top of his head bleeding, his right hand covering the bottom two-thirds of the poster, pointing with index finger in the manner of the 1917 *I Want You* poster by James Montgomery Flagg.

✦ *Amerika*, a Russian-language magazine, is distributed by the U.S. Information Agency in the USSR. Herb Lubalin designs and writes the issue "Carnival of the Eye," which emphasizes "concept" as the heart of American graphics.

✦ Armin Hofmann designs *Giselle* poster for Basel, Switzerland, outdoor theater in Rosenfeldpark. The vertical placement of the word "Giselle" breaks the tradition of horizontal composition.

✦ Cipe Pineles becomes the art director at *Mademoiselle* until 1961.

✦ *Communication Arts* (*CA*) magazine is founded in San Francisco, California, by Dick Coyne and Bob Blanchard. Coyne is editor and designer. Freeman Craw designs logo. It began as *The Journal of Commercial Art*, but was called *CA*.

✦ Emil Ruder publishes essay "The Typography of Order," which addresses the principle of rational simplicity in visual communications.

✦ Herb Lubalin publishes essay "What Is New American Typography?" It predicts the kinetic influence of television on contemporary typography.

✦ Ladislav Sutnar becomes the art director of *Theatre Arts* magazine until 1969.

✦ Leo Lionni authors and illustrates his first children's book, *Little Yellow and Little Blue*.

✦ Alexey Brodovitch designs Truman Capote's book *Observations*. Richard Avedon is the photographer.

✦ Paul Davis joins Push Pin Studios as an illustrator.

✦ Peter Knapp becomes the art director of *Elle*, Paris, until 1966.

✦ Saul Bass designs film title sequence for *Anatomy of a Murder*.

✦ The Composing Room publishes a series of four experimental books conceived and designed respectively by Herb Lubalin, Brownjohn, Chermayeff & Geismar, Lester Beall, and Gene Federico, edited by Aaron Burns with brief texts by Percy Seitlin, which push the conceptual limits of hot-metal composition.

✦ Wayne Fitzgerald designs the film title sequence for *Pillow Talk*.

✦ Willy Fleckhaus becomes art director for German monthly *Twen* until 1970, a periodical for sophisticated teens. His design is rooted in an emphasis on black as a background against which color photographs are framed, bold typography, and lavish double-page spreads.

✦ NASA "meatball" logo (revived in 1992) is designed by James Modarelli.

## ADVERTISING

❧ George Lois leaves Doyle Dane Bernbach to found Papert, Koenig & Lois (the agency officially opens in 1960).

❧ Maxwell House ad "Good to the Last Drop" is created by Ogilvy, Benson & Mather.

❧ Paul Rand designs Colorforms Toys trademark.

**"Nothing But Apples" by Gene Federico**

✚ Andre Francois, French illustrator
and cartoonist, designs the Christmas
box for Dutch Masters Cigars with a
flasher—Santa—who exposes cigars.

♣ Paul Rand, Charles Eames, and
Elliott Noyes begin to collaborate on
new Westinghouse Identity program.
♣ Whitney Darrow Jr. illustrates Post
Toasties, breakfast food ad for General
Foods Corp.
♣ Wrigley's Doublemint Gum jingle,
"Double Your Pleasure, Double Your
Fun," airs on the radio.

## POLITICS

✚ Charles de Gaulle becomes
president of France.
✚ Fidel Castro becomes the premier
minister of Cuba.
✚ Hawaii becomes the fiftieth state.

## TECHNOLOGY

⚶ Hovercraft is invented by
Christopher Cockerell.
⚶ IBM 401 Computer is introduced.
⚶ Microchip is invented by Kilby and
Robert Noyce.

## ARCHITECTURE

✲ Frank Lloyd Wright designs
Guggenheim Museum, New York.

## BIRTHS AND DEATHS

Ambrose Heal dies.
Bruce Mau is born.
Carol Twombly is born.
Fabien Baron is born.
Frank Lloyd Wright dies.
Georg Grosz, German satirist, dies.
Marie Reidemeister dies.
Massimo Iosa Ghini is born.
William Golden, art director of CBS
TV, dies.

## CONSUMABLES

✝ Alec Issigoni designs "Mini" car
for Morris Motors.
✝ Barbie doll is introduced.
✝ Tang is introduced.

## ARTS AND CULTURE

♨ Lou Dorfsman is named creative
director for the CBS Television
Network upon William Golden's
death.
♨ MoMA, New York, mounts its first
package design exhibit.

Barbie and Co.

"Age of the Auto" by Lester Beall

**19'60**

No one can read the future, but we know, as James has said, that 'all futures are rough.' . . . We will need every ounce of moral stamina we can find. For everything is changing, from our notion of politics to our notion of ourselves, and we are certain as we begin history's strangest metamorphosis, to undergo the torment of being forced to surrender far more than we ever realized we had accepted.

*James Baldwin, 1961*

# <sup>19</sup>**60**

## GRAPHIC ARTS

✦ Alberto Vargas's "Vargas Girls" appear in *Playboy* through 1975.

✦ Ben Shahn designs the *Stop H-bomb Tests* poster for the Committee for a Sane Nuclear Policy.

✦ Bill Slack designs *Architectural Review* through 1990.

✦ Felix Beltran, Cuban designer, becomes the art director for the Commission for Revolutionary Action, Cuba, the organization for official revolutionary propaganda.

✦ George Giusti illustrates *Holiday* magazine cover (Rome issue) depicting Romulus and Remus and the wolf. The illustration is a combination of cubistic and expressionist styles.

✦ George Tscherny designs his first poster for the School of Visual Arts (pencil behind the mold of an ear).

✦ John Berg becomes art director of CBS Columbia Records (through 1984), responsible for both designing and hiring designers who establish CBS albums as preeminent in the field.

✦ Mitsuo Katsui designs the graphic symbols for the Tokyo Olympics.

✦ Richard Gangel becomes art director of *Sports Illustrated* and introduces the practice of illustrators as visual reporters and essayists.

✦ Robert Brownjohn leaves Brownjohn Chermayeff & Geismar, the firm changes its name to Chermayeff & Geismar, New York.

✦ Rudolf de Harak designs a uniform series of book jackets for McGraw Hill, New York, using a single typeface, Akzidenz Grotesque, and symbolic, minimalist imagery.

✦ Saul Bass designs logo, poster, and film title sequence for *Exodus*, also designs the film title sequence for the movie *Psycho*.

✦ *The Trademarks of Paul Rand: A Selection* is published by George Wittenborn, Inc., New York.

✦ Tony Paladino, American advertising designer and art director, designs a logo for Alfred Hitchcock's *Psycho*.

✦ Will Burtin follows his human cell exhibition with a human "Brain" exhibition for Upjohn, where viewers are invited to walk throughout displays of the inner workings.

✦ World Design Conference is held in Tokyo, Japan.

✦ Yusaku Kamekura becomes Managing Director of the Japanese Design Center.

✦ Steff Geissbuhler is a designer for Geigy Pharmaceutical Company.

✦ *Alphabet Thesaurus, Vol. 1 & 2* is published by Photolettering, Inc. It claims the largest compilation of photo typefaces and is a prime source for the classic, conventional, and quirky types of the day.

✦ Günter Gerhard Lange begins work as Artistic Director of H. Berthold AG (to present). He develops an entire typeface program and designs Concorde and Imago typefaces.

International paper logo

## ADVERTISING

❧ American Tourister's "Gorilla" TV commercials begin, created by Doyle Dane Bernbach. The ad shows an angry gorilla violently throwing luggage around its cage, much like the typical airline baggage handlers would do.

❧ Benson & Hedges 100s "Disadvantages" ad is created by Wells, Rich, Greene, a self-effacing advertisement comically shows the problems with the new longer cigarettes.

❧ Blackglama–Great Lakes Mink "What Becomes a Legend Most?" ads are created by Jane Trahey Associates and consist of photographs of famous women who wear mink coats.

❧ Bufferin ad (with the pounding heartbeat) is created by Young & Rubicam.

❧ Chermayeff & Geismar design Chase Manhattan Bank's geometric logo and corporate identity program, which launches a trend in symbolic/abstract logo designs.

*Exodus* poster by Saul Bass

**Man and Civilization**
The Family's Search for Survival
edited by
Seymour M. Farber
Piero Mustacchi
Roger H. L. Wilson

McGraw-Hill Paperbacks

$3.25

Book cover by Rudolph DeHarak

❧ Lester Beall designs International Paper logo, a tree made from pure geometric forms, and its entire corporate identity program.

❧ Maypo cereal "I Want My Maypo" ads are created by George Lois.

❧ Paul and Ann Rand write the essay "Advertisement: Ad Vivum or Ad Hominem?" which is harshly critical of poor standards in contemporary advertising.

❧ Raymond Peynet designs Nicolas Wine's "C'est passionnant ce que vous lisez cherie? . . ." ad for Etablissements Nicolas.

❧ Right Guard ads with "Man in the Medicine Cabinet" are created by BBD&O.

❧ Roger Excoffon designs Air France campaign at U&O, a French design consultancy (continuing through 1960s).

❧ Volvo "Average Life of a Car in Sweden" ads are created by Scali, McCabe, Sloves.

❧ Wrigley's airs first Doublemint Gum TV commercial featuring the Boyd twins singing "Double Your Pleasure, Double Your Fun."

## BIRTHS AND DEATHS

Berthold Löffler dies.
Fortunato Depero dies.
James Montgomery Flagg dies.
János Mattis Teutsch dies.
Jessica Helfand is born.
Max Fleischer dies.
P. Scott Makela is born.
Vilmos Huszar dies.
Walter Dorwin Teague dies.
Walter P. Paepke dies.
Albert Camus dies.
John Covert dies.
Briget de Socio is born.
Edgar Martin dies.

## ARTS AND CULTURE

♠ "Herman Zapf, Calligrapher, Type Designer, and Typographer" exhibition is arranged and circulated by the Contemporary Arts Center, Cincinnati Art Museum (until 1961).

♠ "The Twist" is a popular dance.

♠ Fluxus movement begins. George Maciunus is the founder, along with John Cage, Ken Friedman, Dick Higgins, Ben Vautier, and Milan Knizak.

♠ Reyner Banham publishes *Theory and Design in the First Machine Age.*

♠ There are 85 million TV-set owners in the United States.

## INTERIOR DESIGN

⊏ Charles W. Moore builds Florida condominiums with "supergraphics" (huge mural-like abstract and geometric designs) by Barbara Stauffacher Solomon in the interior spaces.

## INDUSTRIAL DESIGN

⊀ Dieter Rams is named director of Braun design department.

⊀ Henry Dreyfus publishes *The Measure of Man*, a book that addresses the need for ergonomics long before it become popular to do so.

## POLITICS

⋏ John F. Kennedy is elected president of the United States.

## TECHNOLOGY

⊀ Laser technology is invented by Charles Townes, the first lasers are manufactured in the United States.

⊀ Russians decipher Mayan writing with electronic computers.

⊀ Theory of "hypertext" is developed by Ted Nelson Pharmaceutical Company.

Poster by Ben Shahn

# <sup>19</sup>**61**

## GRAPHIC ARTS

✦ Aaron Burns publishes *Typography*, which explores new developments in phototypesetting and, as type director of the Composing Room, New York, develops the first of many instructional guides.

✦ Artone ink package and logo, an Art Nouveau "A" designed by Seymour Chwast, prefigures the psychedelic interest in Art Nouveau and secessionist letterforms.

✦ Bernard Quint becomes art director of *Life* magazine.

✦ Bob Gill cofounds design firm Fletcher, Forbes and Gill, with Colin Forbes and Alan Fletcher, in London. In 1972 it evolves into Pentagram.

✦ Cipe Pineles leaves *Mademoiselle* as art director, opens her own studio.

✦ Dieter Rot, typographer and conceptual artist, publishes *Bok4A*.

✦ Ladislav Sutnar publishes *Visual Design in Action*, a monograph that details his life's work and a manifesto that calls for neo-Constructivist methods of design.

✦ Leo Lionni resigns as art director of *Fortune* magazine.

✦ Mitsuo Katsui founds design office in Tokyo.

✦ *Show* begins publication (through 1963), art director Henry Wolf.

✦ Keith Bright designs Hillside Press logo.

✦ Paul Rand designs Westinghouse and UPS (United Parcel Service) logos.

✦ Letraset's Instant Lettering dry transfer process premieres. Among some of the first type styles are Grotesque No. 9, Announce Grotesque, Gill (Bold/Medium and Bold Condensed), Sans Condensed, Egyptian Expanded, Chisel and Chisel Expanded, Venus Bold Extended and Medium Extended, Baskerville, Consort and Consort Light, Playbill, Profile, Times and Times Bold, Wide Latin, Antique No. 3, and Old English.

## ADVERTISING

✦ CBS Television network print ad "Exhilarate" is created by Lou Dorfsman/Al Amato.

✦ Hertz "Let Hertz Put You in the Driver's Seat" ad is created by Norman, Craig & Kummel.

## ARCHITECTURE

✦ Archigram architectural think tank is founded in England.

## EDUCATION

✦ National Institute of Design, India's design college, is established in the Gujarati city of Ahmadabad.

## BIRTHS AND DEATHS

Alexander Isley is born.
Bob Aufuldish is born.
Eero Saarinen dies.
Grandma Moses dies at 99.
Ian Anderson is born.
James Thurber dies.
Marius de Zayas dies.
Violet Oakley dies.
Zuzana Licko is born.

*Show* magazine cover

## POLITICS

⚡ Amnesty International is formed.

⚡ Bay of Pigs invasion fails.

⚡ Berlin Wall is constructed.

## TECHNOLOGY

⚡ Yuri Gagarin orbits Earth, and becomes the first man in space.

⚡ Alan Shepard is the first American in space.

## TYPE

✦ Freeman Craw designs Ad Lib typeface.

✦ Monotype and American Type-foundry issue Univers typeface in the United States.

## ARTS AND CULTURE

♣ "Catch-22" is coined as a phrase, based on the title of Joseph Heller's book, meaning a paradoxical, no-win situation.

♣ Alexander Liberman becomes editorial director of all Condé Nast publications worldwide.

♣ Design Institute of Baden-Württemberg in Stuttgart, Germany, sponsors exhibition of Swiss Posters (1955–1966), the first such exhibit of the Swiss style in Germany.

♣ Newton Minow, FCC chairman, lambasts TV as a "vast wasteland," on the same day Hubert Humphrey calls TV "the greatest single achievement in communication that anybody or any area of the world has ever known."

## BIG BUSINESS

🏛 Ray Kroc buys out the McDonald's Corp., headquartered in Oak Brook, Illinois.

Westinghouse logo

Book cover by Aaron Burns

# <sup>19</sup>**62**

## GRAPHIC ARTS

✦ Adrian Frutiger, type designer, opens studio with Bruno Pfäffli and André Gürtler at Arcueil, Paris.

✦ Alex Kotzky, comic-strip artist whose brilliant, sophisticated style reflects freshness, creates "Apartment 3-G" with scriptwriter Dr. Nicholas Dallis.

✦ *Amazing Stories* publishes its twenty-fifth anniversary issue using one of Frank R. Paul's last back covers.

✦ *Artforum* magazine begins publication.

✦ Bradbury Thompson edits and designs his final issue of *Westvaco Inspirations*, the house organ that he transformed into a tool for teaching designers about form and content.

✦ Burlington Industries annual report is designed by George Tscherny.

✦ *Eros* features never-before-seen nude photographs of Marilyn Monroe by Bert Stern complete with photographer's cancellation marks.

✦ Herb Lubalin redesigns the *Saturday Evening Post* in an attempt to bring the lackluster "middle American" magazine back to prominence. Photographic covers replace the emblematic Norman Rockwell illustrations, and conceptual, illustrative typography is added.

✦ Lena Horne's *Lena . . . Lovely and Alive* wins Grammy award for the best album cover, art director is Robert Jones for RCA.

✦ Martin Fox becomes editor of *Print* magazine.

✦ Maurice Binder designs the film title sequence for the James Bond thriller *Dr. No*.

✦ Norman Saunders creates *Mars Attacks* bubblegum cards for the Topps company, one of the most successful nonsports card sets in history.

✦ Paul Rand illustrates *Little 1*, a children's book authored by Ann Rand.

✦ Ralph Ginzburg publishes *Eros*, a sophisticated hardcover magazine of eroticism, and advertises through the mail with postmarks from Blueballs and Intercourse, Pennsylvania (he is arrested and imprisoned on federal charges of pandering through the mail). The art director is Herb Lubalin.

✦ Reid Miles designs Freddie Hubbard's album cover *Hub-Tones* for Blue Note.

✦ Stephen Frankfurt designs the film title sequence for *To Kill A Mockingbird* as cinematic still life of childhood objects and icons.

✦ *Sunday Times* color section is introduced in the United Kingdom.

✦ *The Jetsons* animated space-age cartoon show debuts.

✦ Walter Allner, designer and Paris editor of *Graphis*, becomes art director of *Fortune* until 1971.

## ADVERTISING

✦ Carl Ally, copywriter, leaves Papert, Koenig, Lois, and joins Amil Gargano, art director, to open Ally & Gargano, New York.

✦ David Ogilvy publishes *Confessions of an Advertising Man*.

✦ McDonald's USA golden-arches "M" is designed by Jim Schindleer.

✦ Otl Aicher designs Lufthansa German Airlines corporate identity system with Tomás Gonda, Fritz Querengásser, and Nick Roericht.

✦ Papert, Koenig, Lois becomes the first advertising agency to go public.

✦ Paul Rand designs the ABC logo, the lowercase letters modeled on Futura that exploits the series of circles.

Wolfschmidts Vodka ad by George Lois

❦ Robert Jacoby leaves Compton Advertising to join Ted Bates & Co., New York.

❦ Saul Bass designs the poster for the movie *Advise and Consent*.

❦ Salvador Dali illustrates Lenthéric 12 Perfume ad "A Portrait in Perfume" for Lenthéric Inc.

❦ Wolfschmidt Vodka print ad campaign is created by George Lois at Papert, Koenig, Lois.

## BIRTHS AND DEATHS

Barbara de Wilde is born.
Barry Deck is born.
Gabrielle Munter dies.
Gail Anderson is born.
Harrison K. McCann dies.
Jay N. Darling dies.
Marilyn Monroe dies.
Morris Louis dies.
Natalia Goncharova, Russian designer, dies.
Robert Fisher is born.
Sun Fu-xi dies
Will Bradley, Art Nouveau poster artist and typographer, dies.
Dick (Richard) Calkins dies.
Frank Kozik is born.
C. D. (clarence) russell dies.
Chen Zhi-fo dies.

## CONSUMABLES

☛ Diet Rite, Tab, and Diet Pepsi are introduced.

☛ First tab-opening drink can, invented by Ermal Clayton Fraze of Ohio, is produced by Iron City Beer, Pittsburgh. Alcoa introduces pull-top aluminum tab, eliminating the need for can openers.

☛ Polaroid instant color film is introduced.

## ARTS AND CULTURE

♨ Andy Warhol, formerly a commercial illustrator, creates his Campbell Soup cans and helps launch Pop Art.

## POLITICS

⚔ Cuban Missile Crisis occurs, but USA versus USSR military confrontation is avoided.

⚔ Zhou En-lai, Premier of China, seeks freedom for artists.

⚔ Zhou Yang, Chinese minister of culture and propaganda, calls for a more authentic picture of "middle characters," representing purity and heroic character.

## TECHNOLOGY

⚑ John Glenn becomes the first American to orbit the Earth.

⚑ Telephone and television contact is established between Europe and the United States by way of the Telstar satellite.

## TYPE

♣ Aldo Novarese designs Eurostile typeface.

ABC logo by Paul Rand

HENRY FONDA, CHARLES LAUGHTON, DON MURRAY, WALTER PIDGEON, PETER LAWFORD, GENE TIERNEY, LEW AYRES, FRANCHOT TONE, BURGESS MEREDITH, EDDIE HODGES, PAUL FORD, GEORGE GRIZZARD, INGA SWENSON SCREENPLAY WRITTEN BY WENDELL MAYES, MUSIC BY JERRY FIELDING, PHOTOGRAPHED IN PANAVISION BY SAM LEAVITT, PRODUCED AND DIRECTED BY OTTO PREMINGER, A COLUMBIA PICTURES RELEASE

*Advise & Consent* poster by Saul Bass

# 19**63**

## GRAPHIC ARTS

✦ "Cavalcade of American Comics" exhibition held in New York.

✦ Bea Feitler and Ruth Ansel become co–art directors of *Harper's Bazaar.*

✦ Before immigrating to the United States Massimo Vignelli designs covers for Sansoni Publishers in the reductive Swiss modernist idiom. Ben Rosen publishes *Type and Typography: The Designer's Type Book.*

✦ Colin Forbes designs the logo for the Designers and Art Directors Club, London.

✦ Emancipation Proclamation commemorative postage stamp is designed by Georg Olden.

✦ *Graphic Arts USA* exhibit, designed by Chermayeff & Geismar and sponsored by the U.S. Information Agency, travels to Europe and Russia. In Russia, many of the exhibit materials are surreptitiously given away to Russian designers.

✦ *Graphic Design: Visual Comparisons* is edited by Fletcher, Forbes, and Gill. The book shows the similarities in form and content of numerous visual works and objects.

✦ ICOGRADA (International Council of Graphic Design Associations) is founded.

✦ Ikko Tanaka founds Tanaka Design Studio, Tokyo.

✦ John Alcorn designs catalogs for Morgan Press, leading purveyor of revived Victorian woodtypes.

✦ Marvin Israel becomes art director at *Harper's Bazaar.*

✦ Maurice Sendak writes and illustrates the children's book *Where the Wild Things Are.*

✦ Milton Glaser designs *The White Father* book cover.

✦ *Monocle*, a satirical magazine edited by Victor Navasky and designed by Phil Gipps, makes use of numerous Victorian woodtypes and becomes an outlet for some of the finest American cartoonists and caricaturists, including David Levine, Edward Sorel, Robert Grossman, and R. O. Blechman.

✦ Pablo Picasso designs *Cannes* poster for the French National Tourist Office.

✦ Robert Freeman designs and photographs *Meet the Beatles*, his first album cover for Capital Records, Inc. Robert Massin, French typographer and designer, publishes *Exercises de Style.*

✦ Solomon Benediktovich Telingater, former Russian Constructivist typographer, receives the International Gutenberg Prize in Leipzig.

✦ *Swimmy*, a children's book about the artist as rebel, by Leo Lionni, is published.

✦ The *New York Review of Books* launches its first issue, designed by Samuel Antupit, in the wake of the New York newspaper strike.

✦ Tom Wolsley becomes art director of *Queen*, United Kingdom, until 1964.

✦ Total Design, first large multi-disciplinary design group in the Netherlands, is founded by industrial designer Frisco Kramer and graphic designers Wim Crouwel and Benno Wissing, known in Amsterdam for their precise informational design.

✦ Tom Geismar of Chermayeff & Geismar designs Mobil Corporation corporate identity system (through 1964).

✦ James Cross founds Cross Associates in Los Angeles and San Francisco.

## ADVERTISING

✦ "The Pepsi Generation" ad campaign kicks off what became known as the cola wars (Pepsi-Cola versus Coca-Cola) with Batton, Barton & Osborn as agency.

✦ Avis ad campaign "We Try Harder" begins, created by Doyle Dane Bernbach.

Graphic Arts USA exhibition

Jean Cocteau dies.
Martin Munkacsi dies.
Tristan Tzara dies.
Sylvia Plath dies.

## Consumables
⌁ Compact casette player with 3.8mm tape is introduced by Philips.

## Arts and Culture
♬ A. C. Nielsen Company ceases measuring radio audiences.
♬ First "Pop Art" show opens at the Guggenheim with Andy Warhol, Robert Rauschenberg, Jasper Johns, and Claes Oldenburg.
♬ First instant replay in television sports takes place during Army-Navy football game.
♬ Jack Paar shows clips from a London concert featuring the Beatles on his TV show. This is the first time the United States gets a glimpse of the Fab Four.
♬ Roper poll shows that 36 percent of Americans favor TV as an information source versus 24 percent favoring print media.
♬ Stanley Kubrick directs the nuclear war satire *Dr. Strangelove*, and Pablo Ferro designs his first film title sequence for *Dr. Strangelove,* using handlettering against the backdrop of refueling (symbolically copulating) aircraft.

♺ First interracial commercial for Wisk detergent plays on TV. Prior to this, African-Americans were shown only in TV commercials for products aimed exclusively at them.
♺ John Orr Young chastises his colleagues for their support of cigarette advertising in his monthly newsletter.
♺ Oscar Meyer's jingle, "I Wish I Were an Oscar Meyer Wiener," is introduced in television commercials.
♺ Political TV commercial called the "Daisy," a spot for the election of Lyndon Johnson for president, accuses his rival, Senator Barry Goldwater, of being trigger-happy with the H-bomb. The spot, created by Tony Schwartz for Doyle Dane Bernbach, shows a little girl picking petals off a daisy as the countdown towards detonation is heard on the soundtrack. It was shown only once and then pulled off the air as an offensive negative commentary.
♺ Ronald McDonald is created by McDonald's franchisee Oscar Goldstein.
♺ Saul Bass & Associates design Fuller Paints Company logo.
♺ The slogan for Wisk, "Ring Around the Collar," is written by Jim Jordan for BBD&O.

## Architecture
♱ Chestnut Hill House, designed by Robert Venturi, is one of the first postmodern buildings.

## Births and Deaths
Aldous Huxley dies.
Emily Oberman is born.
First crop of Generation X babies are born (continues through 1973).
Georges Braque dies.
J. J. P. (Jacobus Johannes Pieter) Oud dies.

## Industrial Design
✦ Henry Dreyfus designs the Polaroid Land Camera Automatic 100.
✦ Italian-born Marco Zanuso and German-born Richard Sapper collaborate on the design of the Algo I portable television set for Brionvega, one of many design classics to come from this partnership.
✦ Tom Eckersley is appointed Royal Designer for Industry.

## Politics
🕊 Free Speech movement begins at the University of California, Berkeley.
🕊 Freedom March, Washington, D.C., is the largest demonstration for civil rights ever assembled in the United States.
🕊 John F. Kennedy is assassinated by Lee Harvey Oswald, Lyndon B. Johnson becomes president.
🕊 Martin Luther King gives the "I Have a Dream" speech.
🕊 Teletype "hotline" between the White House and the Kremlin is completed.

## Technology
♆ Digital Equipment Corporation introduces the first minicomputer.
♆ Surgeon General's report links smoking to lung cancer.

*Dr. Strangelove* film title by Pablo Ferro

# <sup>19</sup>**64**

## GRAPHIC ARTS

✦ Alexey Brodovitch designs cover of *Art in America* commemorating the New York World's Fair.

✦ Art Kunkin founds and edits the *Los Angeles Free Press*, the first underground newspaper in the United States (until 1971). In the 1960s the LAFP expresses the then unpopular point of view that political scandals and economic rip-offs were happening in Washington, D.C.

✦ Brant Parker creates the comic strip "Wizard of Id," scripted by Johnny Hart.

✦ British motorway signage system is designed by Jock Kinneir and Margaret Calvert.

✦ Dugald Stermer becomes art director for *Ramparts* magazine until 1970. Stermer creates a classical format using Oxford rules and Times Roman type that is copied by the original *Rolling Stone* magazine.

✦ First Warsaw International Poster Biennial.

✦ Herbert Spencer publishes the essay "The Responsibilities of the Design Profession."

✦ Lou Dorfsman becomes design director for the entire CBS corporation. He also designs all the lettering and graphics of the New York headquarters, aka the "Black Rock," designed by the architect Eero Saarinen.

✦ Milton Glaser curates first American exhibition of the German magazine *Twen* at the School of Visual Arts, New York.

✦ Minale-Tattersfield, graphic design firm, is founded in the United Kingdom.

✦ Norman Rockwell begins illustrating for *Look* magazine.

✦ Norman Rockwell is fired by the *Saturday Evening Post* after illustrating two hundred covers, because they want to modernize their image.

✦ Op Art (radical geometric compositions) begins to influence graphic design.

✦ Pat Oliphant, editorial cartoonist, immigrates to the United States from Australia, and joins the *Denver Post*. Oliphant has a significant, modernizing influence on the appearance and approach of American editorial cartooning.

✦ Paul Davis leaves Push Pin Studios where he has introduced an illustration style that wed Folk Art and Surrealism.

✦ *Private Eye*, England's irreverent satire magazine, begins publication, featuring illustrators Ralph Steadman and Gerald Scarfe.

✦ Robert Brownjohn designs film title sequence for the James Bond thriller *Goldfinger*.

✦ Robert Massin, designer, and Henry Cohen, photographer, design a book of Eugene Ionesco's *La Cantatrice Chauve*, which uses high-contrast photography of the characters and typography used to simulate voices.

✦ Seymour Chwast designs the poster *War Is Good Business, Invest Your Son*, an early Vietnam War protest.

✦ *Surfing* magazine begins publication.

Page from *La Contatrice Chauve*

✦ Tokyo Olympics posters and logos are designed by Yusaku Kamekura.

✦ *West* magazine, the Sunday supplement of the *Los Angeles Times*, is art-directed and designed by Mike Salisbury.

✦ Armin Hofmann designs logo for the Swiss National Exhibition, Expo.

✦ Chermayeff & Geismar design American Film Institute logo.

✦ Herb Lubalin becomes partner with Ernie Smith and Alan Peckolick.

## ADVERTISING

❧ Altman/Stoller creates "Jewelry in the Golden Manner of Monet" ad for Monet Jewelers Inc.

❧ Charles Coiner retires as creative director at N. W. Ayer & Son, Philadelphia, after thirty years.

❧ Charmin toilet tissue ad "Please Don't Squeeze the Charmin" is created by Benton & Bowles.

Push Pin Graphic by Paul Davis

Cover of *Ramparts* magazine

❦ Coty lipstick print ad "Before/After," is created by Papert, Koenig, Lois, Inc.

❦ Fred Mogubgub creates first limited animation TV commercial for Ford Motors.

❦ Lester Feldman creates TV commercial of a lion walking down Wall St. for Dreyfus Fund Inc., whose logo is the king of beasts.

❦ NBC drops ban on comparative advertising.

❦ Ogilvy, Benson & Mather merges with London-based parent company Mather & Crowther to form Ogilvy & Mather.

❦ Pablo Ferro creates the Burlington Mills corporate image with fast moving, multicolored stitching animation for a television commercial campaign.

❦ Rosemarie Tissi designs advertisement for E. Lutz & Company printers, introducing a Swiss post-modern sensibility to graphic design.

❦ Talon Zipper trade ad, "Your Fly Is Open," is created by Delehanty, Kurnit & Geller.

❦ William Bernbach publishes the essay "Sometimes I Play Things I Never Heard Myself."

## ARCHITECTURE

⚊ Charles Eames and Ray Eames design IBM Pavilion at the New York World's Fair, along with the designer Debra Sussman.

## BIRTHS AND DEATHS

Austin Cooper dies.

Chip Kidd is born.

Earnest Elmo Calkins dies.

Gerrit Rietveld dies.

Giorgio Morandi dies.

Helen Lansdowne Resor dies.

Percy Lee Crosby dies.

Stanley Resor dies.

Stuart Davis dies.

Thomas M. Cleland dies.

Phil (Philip) Davies dies.

Cliff (Clifford) Sterret dies.

## CONSUMABLES

🍗 G.I. Joe, the first "action figure" doll for boys, is introduced.

🍗 Pop-Tarts are introduced.

🍗 Sir Terence Conran opens "Habitat" stores in the United Kingdom.

## ARTS AND CULTURE

♠ Beatles give their first U.S. concert.

♠ Cassius Clay wins heavyweight crown.

♠ First office fax machine, LDX, is introduced by Xerox.

♠ Marshall McLuhan publishes first edition of *Understanding Media.*

♠ *Mary Poppins* is released by Walt Disney.

♠ Mary Quant makes miniskirts popular.

♠ The New York World's Fair opens in Flushing Meadows Queens with Unisphere, the large metal globe, as its logo and centerpiece.

## INDUSTRIAL DESIGN

⚒ Container Corporation of America (CCA) establishes Center for Advanced Research in Design.

⚒ Ettore Sottsass Jr. designs Dora portable typewriter for Olivetti.

⚒ John Massey is named director of design at Container Corporation of America.

⚒ Richard C. Runyon designs packaging for Carlsberg Breweries.

## POLITICS

☈ Vietnam War escalates.

☈ Khrushchev is ousted from power.

☈ Martin Luther King wins the Nobel Peace Prize.

☈ Nelson Mandela is sentenced to life in prison. South Africa is excluded from the Olympics due to its apartheid policy.

## TECHNOLOGY

⚐ BASIC (Beginner's All-purpose System Instruction Code) is created by John Kemeny and Thomas Kurtz, Dartmouth professors of mathematics.

⚐ Electronic mouse is invented by Douglas C. Engelbart for the federal government.

## TYPE

✤ Jan Tschichold designs Sabon typeface, released by D. Stempel foundry.

Cover of *Art in America*

# ¹⁹65

## GRAPHIC ARTS

✦ Armin Hofmann publishes *Graphic Design Manual: Principles and Practice*, in which he sets down his method of rational Swiss design.

✦ Art Spiegelman becomes creative consultant for Topps Gum, Inc., later creates Wacky Packages and Garbage Pail Kids (through 1989).

✦ *Aspen*, the magazine in a box, publishes its first issue designed by Tom Courtos.

✦ Cipe Pineles becomes designer for Lincoln Center until 1970.

✦ *Dot Zero*, an architecture and design journal, is published and edited by Ralph Eckerstrom, Jay Doblin, Massimo Vignelli, and Mildred Constantine.

✦ Elton Robinson becomes art director for *Horizon*, a hardcover culture magazine.

✦ Henryk Tomaszewski designs *Cyrk* poster.

✦ International Center for the Typographic Arts opens its exhibition Typomundus 20.

✦ James McMullan, illustrator, joins Push Pin Studios in New York (leaves in 1968).

✦ Ken Deardorf becomes art director of the *Evergreen Review*, the New Left journal of art, culture, and politics.

✦ Klaus Voorman designs the Beatles' *Revolver* album using drawing and collage, leading the way to more conceptual album art.

✦ Matthew Carter arrives from London to work at Mergenthaler Linotype in Brooklyn. He is the staff type designer in the Typographic Development Division, working under Mike Parker, director of typographic development, until 1971.

✦ Neil Fujita and Robert Scudellari modernize Random House's literary imprint, the Modern Library.

✦ *Nova*, a progressive women's monthly, begins publishing (through 1975).

✦ Pablo Ferro designs title sequence for the film *The Russians Are Coming, The Russians Are Coming*.

✦ R. D. E. Oxenaar designs paper currency for the Netherlands.

✦ Richard Williams designs the film title sequence for *What's New, Pussycat?*

✦ Robert Massin designs Eugene Ionesco's *Délire è Deux*.

✦ Roy Kuhlman becomes art director of *Evergreen Review*, the left-wing art, culture, and politics magazine.

✦ *Signature* begins publication (through 1987).

✦ The Great Proletarian Cultural Revolution in China (that continues through 1976), born out of the struggle between Mao Tse-tung and President Liu Shao-qi, leads to dramatic changes in the face of Chinese graphics. Art and design revert to the more turgid Socialist Realism style that originally developed in the 1950s.

✦ The *New York Herald-Tribune*, the first newspaper to be designed like a magazine, ceases publication after newspaper strike (turns into short-lived *World Journal Tribune*).

Cover of *Aspen* magazine

## ADVERTISING

Bob Jones creates Esso gasoline ad "Put a Tiger in Your Tank!" for Humble Oil & Refining Company.
Bob Noorda, Massimo Vignelli, Jay Doblin, James K. Fogleman and Ralph Eckerstrom found Unimark design firm in Chicago, Illinois. Vignelli is director of design in Unimark's New York office.
British Rail logo is designed by Design Research Unit.
Chermayeff & Geismar design Screen Gems trademark.
Chivas Regal print ad "Give Dad an Expensive Belt" is created by Doyle Dane Bernbach.
Exxon Oil Company logo is designed by Raymond Loewy (the two XXs represent the initials used on the New York Stock Exchange when it was called Esso).
Fletcher, Forbes and Gill changes its name to Crosby, Fletcher, Forbes after Bob Gill leaves and Theo Crosby joins.
Following a string of account losses, Rosser Reeves, Ted Bates's first creative chief and promoter of advertising that offers a "unique selling proposition," resigns at age fifty-five.
Foster Grant "Who's That Behind the Foster Grants?" ad campaign is created by Geer, Dubois.
Gui Bonsiepe publishes the essay, "Visual/Verbal Rhetoric," introducing semantic theory to graphic design.
Lance Wyman begins to design the logo for the 1968 Nineteenth Olympic Games in Mexico City.
Mobil Oil's Pegasus trademark becomes secondary to new logo designed by Chermayeff & Geismar.
Newport cigarettes use an inverted boomerang logo, similar to and prefiguring the Nike Swoosh, which hasn't been designed yet.
Pillsbury Doughboy (aka Poppin' Fresh), created by Leo Burnett Co., is introduced by Pillsbury.
Saul Bass designs Continental Airlines and Celanese logos.
Siegfried Odermatt designs trademark for Union Safe Company.
The *New Yorker* and other magazines ban cigarette ads.
Volkswagen "Floating Beetle" ad is created by Doyle Dane Bernbach.
Wolff Olins, a British corporate identity firm, is founded in London.

## EDUCATION

Dietmar Winkler joins Jacqueline Casey and Ralph Coburn at the Massachusetts Institute of Technology (MIT) Design Services Department (through 1971).
Emil Ruder is a director of the Basel School of Design (until 1970).

## BIRTHS AND DEATHS

Boris Artzybasheff dies.
Carlo Carrá dies.
Charles Sheeler dies.
Fritz Helmuth Ehmcke dies.
George Vantongerioo dies.
Le Corbusier (Charles-Edourd Jeanneret) dies.
Max Ernst dies.
Pieter A. H. Hofman dies.
Théo Ballmer dies.
Winston Churchill dies.

## CONSUMABLES

Cool Whip is introduced.
Shake 'N Bake is introduced.

## ARTS AND CULTURE

Art Kane publishes "Songs of Freedom" photographs.
René Magritte becomes known to Americans through the retrospective at MoMA in 1965, and his surrealistic style begins to influence American illustration.
Richard Avedon leaves *Harper's Bazaar* to photograph for *Vogue*.
Robert Wolheim was the first person to use the word "minimalism" to describe the major art movement of the early sixties. Minimalism promoted clarity and simplicity while rejecting the ornamentation and emotional self-expression of abstract expressionism.
U.S. surgeon general mandates "Smoking Is Hazardous to Your Health" notices on cigarette packages.

## POLITICS

Anti-Vietnam demonstrations take place in the United States.
Malcolm X is assassinated in New York.

## TECHNOLOGY

Dr. Michael DeBakey implants first artificial heart during surgery.
IBM develops means of digitally storing type (basis for computer typesetting).

# 19**66**

✦ Rick Griffin, Victor Moscoso, Wes Wilson, Mouse and Kelly begin to design psychedelic posters for Bill Graham's Fillmore West and Chet Helm's Family Dog/Avalon ballroom.

## GRAPHIC ARTS

✦ *East Village Other* is founded by Allen Katzman and Walter Bowart. It introduces photomontage and collage in the style of John Heartfield, and is a wellspring for underground comic strips.

✦ *Jook Savage Art Show*, Rick Griffin's first psychedelic poster, combines an overall Indian motif, collaged steel engravings from the nineteenth century, and prototypical psychedelic lettering.

✦ Marc Chagall creates a poster for the Metropolitan Opera's opening in September 1966, for Lincoln Center for the Performing Arts and the American Federation of Arts.

✦ Massimo Vignelli (at Unimark), with Bob Noorda, designs the New York subway signage and map in 1966. The Metropolitan Transit Authority (MTA) uses the signage but rejects the map.

✦ Rick Griffin, psychedelic poster artist, opens the Berkeley Bonaparte Publishing company to produce 14" × 22" posters, many of which are inspired by turn-of-the-century advertising and 1920s tobacco tins.

✦ Tadanori Yokoo designs poster for Koshimaki Osen, using a comic-book technique of black line drawing as a means to contain flat area of process color. In this work, contemporary photographic elements are collaged together with traditional Japanese imagery.

✦ Victor Moscoso, former student of Joseph Albers at Yale University, launches his Neon Rose psychedelic poster series (through 1968), introducing vibrating colors to poster design.

## ADVERTISING

✦ George Lois creates the "Nauga," the mythical beast and trade character for Naugahyde, the synthetic leather fabric.

✦ Knoll International corporate identity designed by Unimark International, directed by Massimo Vignelli. Unimark works with Knoll until 1980.

✦ Siegfried Odermatt designs trademark for Union Safe Company.

✦ Wells, Rich, Greene is established. Mary Wells is the first woman to head a major agency.

## ARCHITECTURE

✦ *Complexity and Contradiction in Modern Architecture* is published by Robert Venturi from a series of lectures at the MoMA.

## BIRTHS AND DEATHS

Alfred P. Sloan dies.
Alvin Langdon Coburn dies.
Amédée Ozenfant dies.
André Breton dies.
Art Nelson dies.
Frank Hummert dies.
Gino Severini dies.
Jean Hans Arp dies.
Jonathan Barnbrook is born.
Maxfield Parrish dies.
Mike Mills is born.
Tony Zajkowski is born.
Egbert Jacobson dies.
Russ (Russell) Wesover dies.

Cover of the *East Village Other* by R. Crumb

## CONSUMABLES

✈ The Psychedelic Shop opens, a head shop located in the Haight-Ashbury district of San Francisco. Owned by Ron & Jay Thayland, it sells the earliest psychedelic posters.

## ARTS AND CULTURE

♣ *Visible Language*, a journal concerned with research and ideas that help define the role and properties of written language, is founded by Merald Wrolstad.

## INDUSTRIAL DESIGN

✈ Archizoom Studio is founded in Florence, Italy, by Andrea Branzi with DePas, DíUrbino, and Lomazzi. The studio's works include 1967 "Blow" (inflatable chair) and 1970 "Joe" (baseball-glove chair).

## POLITICS

✗ The Situationalists, France's anti-consumerist and anti-capitalist youth movement, is formed at Nanterre University. They will later help foment the 1968 student uprising in Paris.

Poster by Victor Moscoso

# <sup>19</sup>67

## GRAPHIC ARTS

✦ "Che Guevara" cover (and subway poster) for *Evergreen Review,* illustrated by Paul Davis, enrages Cuban exile community who bomb the offices of publisher Grove Press, New York.

✦ Alexey Brodovitch retires to France.

✦ Andy Warhol designs the Velvet Underground's album cover *The Velvet Underground & Nico* for Verve, with a banana on the front.

✦ *Art & Architecture* ceases publication.

✦ Bob Dylan's *Greatest Hits* receives a Grammy award for the best album cover, art directors John Berg and Bob Cato for Columbia.

✦ *East Village Other* publishes the *Gothic Blimp Works*, a newspaper devoted exclusively to underground comix.

✦ Edward Sorel designs the poster *Pass the Lord and Praise the Ammunition* as protest against New York Cardinal Spellman's support of the Vietnam War.

✦ Emil Ruder publishes *Typography: A Manual of Design.*

✦ Hearst publishing in New York launches *EYE*, a slick, glossy, mainstream monthly magazine designed to exploit the growing youth culture in music, fashion, sexual liberation, and drugs.

✦ Herb Lubalin designs *Mother & Child* logo for speculative magazine. The ampersand, shaped like a woman, contains the symbol of a child, a good example of Lubalin's typograms. Lettering is by Tom Carnase.

✦ Herbert Spencer's *Typographica* magazine ceases publication.

✦ A. Jacqui Morgan, illustrator, designs fantasy poster for Electric Circus, a music club in the East Village, New York.

✦ Ken Garland publishes the essay "Here Are Some Things We Must Do" questioning the role of the designer in the public sphere.

✦ *Life* magazine publishes the cover story, "The Great Poster Wave: Expendable Graphic Art Becomes America's Biggest Hang Up," about the psychedelic and "personality" poster explosion in America.

✦ The Beatles release *Sgt. Pepper's Lonely Hearts Club Band* album, cover staged and designed by Peter Blake and Jann Haworth, photography by Michael Cooper.

✦ Milton Glaser designs the "Dylan poster" based on the eclectic influences of Persian design motifs and the surrealist Marcel Duchamp's self-portrait silhouette.

✦ *OZ*, England's most famous underground newspaper, is founded by Richard Neville and Martin Sharp, and art-directed by John Goodchild.

✦ *Psychology Today* begins publication in New York.

✦ Ralph Ginzburg publishes and Herb Lubalin designs *Fact* magazine, devoted to muckraking political and social stories ignored by mainstream press. They are sued for libel by Senator Barry Goldwater for impugning his psychological health.

✦ Rick Griffin designs nineteenth-century–inspired decorative masthead for Jan Wenner's *Rolling Stone* magazine.

✦ Robert Crumb illustrates Big Brother and the Holding Company's album cover *Cheap Thrills* for CBS, art directors John Berg and Bob Cato.

✦ *Rolling Stone* begins publication in San Francisco. The first designer is Robert Williams, first art director, Robert Kingsbury.

✦ Seymour Chwast creates the "End Bad Breath" poster to protest Hanoi bombing during the Vietnam War.

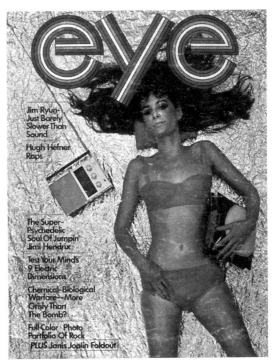

Cover of *Eye* magazine

✦ Michael Cooper designs Rolling Stones' album cover *Their Satanic Majesties Request* for Decca, a direct influence of *Sgt. Pepper*'s cover.
✦ Tomi Ungerer draws and designs "Kiss for Peace," "Eat," and other anti-Vietnam protest posters.
✦ Wayne Fitzgerald designs the film title sequence for *Bonnie and Clyde*.
✦ William S. Harvey designs The Doors' album cover *Strange Days* for Elektra.

## ADVERTISING

❧ "Cut This Out and Put It in Bed Next to Your Child" public service ad for the Urban Coalition, showing a rat, is created by Doyle Dane Bernbach and brings the horrors of poverty home to the middle class.
❧ Jay Chiat forms the advertising agency Chiat/Day, New York.
❧ Joe Sedelmaier opens Sedelmaier Film Production, Chicago, to produce commercials.
❧ Katherine McCoy works for Unimark International Co. (through 1968).
❧ Landor and Associates designs the Levi's tab logo.
❧ R. O. Blechman creates storyboard for the Alka-Seltzer "Stomach" TV commercial, which introduces his nervous line (and a talking stomach) to America.
❧ Richard Lord cofounds Lord, Geller, Federico, Einstein advertising agency, New York.
❧ William Helburn creates 100 Pipers Scotch print ad, "The Super Cowboy: We Put One Together to Show You How We Made Our Scotch" for Seagram Distillers Company.

## EDUCATION

✐ Austrian-born Hans Hollein is appointed Chair of Architecture at the Düsseldorf Academy of Arts.
✐ Muriel Cooper joins the MIT Press as its first art director. Her work in print includes over five hundred books.

## BIRTHS AND DEATHS

Ad Reinhardt dies.
Bruce Barton dies.
Carl Dair dies.
Erik Van Blokland is born.
George Salter dies.
Henry Luce dies.
Henryk Berlewi dies.
Johannes Itten dies.
Kristin Thomson is born.
László Péri dies.
René Magritte dies.
Stanley Morison, English type designer, dies.
Victor Hammer dies.

## CONSUMABLES

🌱 Gatorade is introduced.

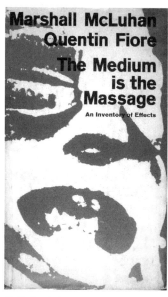

*The Medium is the Massage*

The *Dylan* poster by Milton Glaser

## ARTS AND CULTURE

♠ "Twiggy" makes her debut.
♠ Cooper Hewitt National Design Museum becomes a branch of the Smithsonian Institute.
♠ Jacques Derrida publishes *Of Grammatology*, introducing the postmodern theory of Deconstruction that a decade later would influence the course of graphic design in the academic and practical spheres.
♠ Marshall McLuhan publishes *The Medium Is the Message*, design by Quentin Fiore.

## POLITICS

🏹 Antiwar demonstration at Lincoln Memorial is attended by five hundred thousand people.
🏹 Che Guevara is executed in Bolivia.
🏹 Six-Day War is fought between Israel and Egypt.

## TECHNOLOGY

⚑ Polaroid introduces 10-sec. Film.

## TYPE

✤ Wim Crouwell, partner in Total Design, Amsterdam, designs New Alphabet. A set of letterforms suitable for CRT (cathode-ray tube) composing systems, it consists solely of horizontal and vertical lines, with each character being of equal width.

# ¹⁹**68**

## GRAPHIC ARTS

✦ Allen Hurlburt becomes director of design for Cowles Communications, Inc. until 1970.

✦ Allen Hurlburt publishes *Publication Design*, a bible for magazine art directors.

✦ Anton Stankowski designs comprehensive signage and corporate image design for the City of Berlin.

✦ *Avant Garde* is first published, edited by Ralph Ginzburg, with Herb Lubalin as art director.

✦ Chermayeff & Geismar design the posters for East Village Rock Club Electric Circus using vibrating type.

✦ George Lois designs *Esquire* magazine covers for the next eleven years. One of the most memorable depicts Muhammad Ali as Saint Sebastian, religious martyr.

✦ *Hochschule fur Gestaltung* (Institute for Design) in Ulm, Germany, closes.

✦ James Sutton and Alan Bartram publish an *Atlas of Modern Typeforms*.

✦ John Lennon and Yoko Ono design their own album cover *Unfinished Music No.1* for Apple.

✦ Massimo Vignelli designs signage for the Washington, D.C., Metro.

✦ Milton Glaser creates *Take a Trip to Lotus Land* mailing poster for Push Pin Studios.

✦ *New York Magazine* format is created by Walter Bernard and Milton Glaser.

✦ Pablo Ferro designs film title sequence and polo scene for the *Thomas Crown Affair*. It's the first time in the history of 33mm motion pictures that sixty-six images are used in one frame.

✦ Peter Murdoch (structures) and Lance Wyman (graphics), design Mexico City's 1968 Olympipic Games signage system, one of first applications of "sign theory."

✦ Rosemarie Tissi and Siegfried Odermatt share a design studio in Zurich, Switzerland. Their work marks an early departure from the traditional Swiss style.

✦ Rudolph de Harak Associates creates super graphic signage for 127 John Street in Manhattan.

✦ Ruspoli-Rodriquez designs the poster for the musical *Hair* for Nation Productions.

✦ *Screw* magazine's first issue is published by Al Goldstein and Jim Buckley, the first volley in the sexual revolution of the late sixties.

✦ The Beatles release the *White Album*, with cover design by Richard Hamilton.

✦ The *San Francisco Oracle*, edited by Allen Cohen, begins publishing in the Haight-Ashbury (until 1968). It is a beautiful "underground" publication of the sixties and continues the cultural influence of the Beat writers publishing the writings of Allen Ginsberg, Gary Snyder, Lawrence Ferlinghetti, and Michael McClure.

✦ Will Hopkins succeeds Allen Hurlburt as art director of *Look* magazine.

*Zap Comix* by R. Crumb

✦ *Zap Comix*, with strips by R. Crumb, Victor Moscoso, Rick Griffin, Spain Rodrigues, and S. Clay Wilson, premieres in San Francisco (In 1969 *Zap #3* was busted by the police for being pornographic).

## ADVERTISING

✦ Friends of the Earth's "Memo to the Fur Industry" trade ad is developed by Freeman, Mander & Gossage.

✦ Howard H. Bell becomes president of the American Advertising Federation, Washington (through 1991).

✦ Los Angeles County Human Relations Commission newspaper ad "Is Your Neighborhood All-White or All-American?" is created by Chiat/Day.

✦ Louis Dorfsman designs *Of Black America* newspaper advertisement for CBS News "Black History" series.

✦ Lynn St. John creates Hunt's Catsup ad, "If You Spent Forty Days in the Sun, You'd Be Rosy and Plump, Too," for Hunt-Wesson Foods, Inc.

✦ McDonald's USA redesigns its golden arches trademark.

✦ Mary Wells Lawrence is making $225,000 per year, the highest salary in the world—for a woman.

✦ NAB Code Authority lifts ban on advertising of feminine hygiene sprays and powders.

✦ Steve Frankfurt, Frankfurt Balkind Partners, New York, revolutionizes marketing and promotion of feature films with breakthrough campaign for *Rosemary's Baby*.

✦ Wisk detergent ad "Ring Around the Collar" is created by BBD&O.

✦ Wool Mark trademark is designed by Francesco Saroglia.

♣ Paparazzo, a term used for a freelance photographer of celebrities, is taken from the name of a character in Fellini's film *La Dolce Vita* (1959).

## INDUSTRIAL DESIGN

✦ Henry Dreyfus designs the Trimline telephone, which places all the dialing mechanism in the handset.

## POLITICS

⚔ 18 May Student Uprising in Paris gives rise to the ENSBA (École Nationale Supérieure des Beaux Arts) whose "call to arms" posters are created by Atelier Populaire, an ad hoc group of students attacking the de Gaulle Government and police.

⚔ Czechoslovakia is invaded by the USSR.

⚔ Rev. Martin Luther King Jr. is assassinated in Memphis.

⚔ Richard Nixon is elected thirty-seventh president.

⚔ Robert F. Kennedy is assassinated in Los Angeles.

## TECHNOLOGY

♣ CBS Television develops Vidifont, one of the first electronically generated typefaces for use on TV.

## EDUCATION

✎ Armin Hofmann becomes director of the Basel School of Design until 1986.

✎ Wolfgang Weingart begins teaching at the Basel School of Design, Switzerland. His teaching is based on the "positive qualities" of Swiss typography yet extends to "radically new typographic frontiers."

✎ Yale and Basel establish postgraduate studies in graphic design.

## BIRTHS AND DEATHS

A. M. Cassandre (aka Adolphe Jean-Marie Mouron) dies.

Ernst Keller, Swiss poster artist, dies.

Harold Gray dies.

John Heartfield (Helmut Herzfelde), Berlin Dada photomontagist, dies.

Kees van Dongen dies.

Marcel Duchamp dies.

Peter Arno dies.

Raymond Roker is born.

Sigfried Giedion dies.

Walt Disney dies.

Rudolph Dirks dies.

Harold Gray dies.

Upton Sinclair dies.

## TYPE

♣ Georg Trump designs Mauritius typeface.

♣ Gundrun Zapf-von Hesse designs Shakespeare typeface.

♣ Herb Lubalin and Tom Carnase create ITC Avant Garde Gothic typeface.

♣ Hermann Zapf designs Michelangelo typeface.

♣ Milton Glaser designs Baby Teeth typeface.

*Action Civique* by Attelier Populaire

## ARTS AND CULTURE

♣ *2001: A Space Odyssey* is released by MGM. The motion picture poster shows the helmeted head of one of the film's protagonists. Reflected in the visor is the great beyond.

♣ Charles and Ray Eames produce their film, *Rough Sketch of a Proposed Film Dealing with the Powers of Ten and the Relative Size of Things in the Universe* in black and white. The second version, *Powers of Ten* (1977), is more detailed and in color.

♣ MoMA, New York, mounts *Word and Image*, the first major museum poster show in the United States.

Cover of *Avant Garde* magazine

# 19**69**

## GRAPHIC ARTS

✦ "Moratorium" poster designed by Jasper Johns promoting a cessation of the bombing of Vietnam.

✦ "The South" issue of the *Push Pin Graphic*, designed by Seymour Chwast, contrasts the Old South and civil rights martyrs of the New South.

✦ Art Spiegelman becomes cartoonist and illustrator for *Cavalier, Dude, Gent,* and *Nugget* men's magazines.

✦ *Audience* magazine, a hardcover, eclectic cultural periodical, begins publication (through 1973) with art directors Seymour Chwast and Milton Glaser. It becomes an outlet for the Push Pin style of eclectic, comic, and narrative illustration.

✦ Herbert Spencer edits and designs the *Pioneers of Modern Typography*, which reintroduced the work of Europe's avant-garde typographers to a new generation of designers.

✦ *Interview* magazine is launched, art direction by Glenn O'Brien.

✦ Lawrence Ratzkin designs *The Inner City Mother Goose* by Eve Merriam, a poem in pictures that attacks urban poverty.

✦ Lorraine Schneider creates the poster "War Is Not Healthy for Children and Other Living Things," which was carried in anti-Vietnam War demonstrations organized by Another Mother for Peace.

✦ Muriel Cooper designs *Bauhaus* by Hans M. Wingier, celebrating the German design school's fiftieth anniversary.

✦ Rick Griffin designs Grateful Dead's album cover *Aoxomoxoa* for Warner Bros.

✦ Rob Roy Kelly publishes *American Wood Type*, which becomes the standard text about the Victorian era's typographic legacy.

✦ The Beatles *Yellow Submarine* film debuts, with graphics by Heinz Edelmann.

✦ The *Saturday Evening Post* ceases regular weekly publication after 148 years.

✦ *US* magazine, a paperback book–sized, alternative politics and culture journal, begins publication with Richard Goldstein as editor and Cloud Studio as designer. The paperback book becomes a curious outlet for underground publishing, heretofore relegated to tabloid newspapers and broadsheets.

## ADVERTISING

❧ F. H. K. Henrion, with Alan Parkin, publishes *Design Coordination and Corporate Image.*

❧ Hanes stocking logo is designed by the George Nelson Office.

❧ Jack Rindner creates a "dragon" sculpture made from computer circuitry for the Honeywell computers ad. Headline reads "Your Computer Is a Monster?" accompanied by slogan "The Other Computer Company: Honeywell."

❧ Levy's "You Don't Have to Be Jewish" advertising campaign designed by Bill Taubin and Doyle Dane Bernbach, uses racial and ethnic stereotypes to de-stereotype the market for deli-styled rye bread.

❧ Rudolph de Harak designs logo for Planned Parenthood–World Population.

❧ Russ Anspach, Gene Grossman, and Joel Portual found Anspach Grossman Portual, New York.

❧ Saul Bass designs AT&T (Bell) trademark, beginning a trend in globes with linear scan-line graphics.

❧ The National Urban Coalition "Let the Sunshine In" TV commercial is created by Ketchum, MacLeod & Grove.

Levy's advertisement by William Taubin

Push Pin Graphic by Seymour Chwast

## BIRTHS AND DEATHS

Beatrice Warde dies.
Ben Shahn, painter, illustrator, poster artist, dies.
Daniel R. Fitzpatrick dies.
Don Belding dies.
Howard Luck Gossage dies.
Lester Beall dies.
Ludwig Mies van der Rohe dies.
Marcello Nizzoli, Italian poster artist, dies.
Otto Dix dies.
Water Gropius dies.
W. A. (Wallace) Carlson dies.

## CONSUMABLES

➤ Charles Hall invents the modern water bed.
➤ Pringles Potato Chips are introduced.

## ARTS AND CULTURE

♬ Public Broadcasting Systems (PBS) is founded.
♬ Woodstock Music and Art Fair takes place at Yasgur's farm near Bethel, New York. Three hundred thousand attend. Arnold Skolnick designs the Woodstock '69 symbol and poster *3 Days of Peace & Music*.

## INDUSTRIAL DESIGN

✦ Ettore Sottsass Jr. designs Sistema 45 secretary's chair.
✦ Frogdesign, industrial design company, is founded by Hartmut Esslinger in Germany and later expands its offices in Altensteig, West Germany, and Japan.

## POLITICS

↗ France's de Gaulle resigns, Pompidou is elected.
↗ News reports of the My Lai massacre come out.
↗ Ronald Haeberle, an army photographer, photographs the Mai Lai massacre. In 1970 the Art Workers Coalition issues the poster *Q. And Babies? A. And Babies*. The poster uses Haeberle's color photo of dead women and children on the side of a road.

## TECHNOLOGY

↟ Apollo 11 takes off and Neil Armstrong becomes the first man on the moon.
↟ First Concorde jet flies.

## TYPE

♣ Hermann Zapf designs Textura.
♣ Wim Crouwel designs Fodor Alphabet.

Cover of *US* magazine

Cover and pages from *The Inner City Mother Goose*

1970

*predict a new breed of civilians in the next ten years! The Contented Discontents! These will be the disgruntled citizenry who are and will be content with merely complaining! They will gripe, gripe, gripe from morning until night, and yet will not do one thing themselves about it! They will gripe on the way of government, taxes, crime, sex, death costs, insurance, landlords, weather, transportations, traffic, bisexuality, homosexuality, heterosexuality, and no sexuality at all.*

The Amazing Criswell, *Your Next Ten Years*, 1969

# 19**70**

## GRAPHIC ARTS

✦ *Love* poster, an example of popularized psychedelia, is designed by Peter Max.

✦ American Airlines *Boston* poster is designed by Fred Troller Associated.

✦ Art Spiegelman develops, and Norman Saunders paints, cards that satirize brand name products for the *Wacky Packs* series for Topps Bubble Gum company.

✦ Cipe Pineles becomes director of publications for Parsons School of Design.

✦ David Edward Byrd designs poster for the musical *Follies* at the Winter Garden Theatre.

✦ David Lance Goines, a printer and calligrapher, founds St. Hieronymus Press in Berkeley, California, and starts to design and produce posters influenced by the Scottish branch of Art Nouveau.

✦ Doug Johnson and Charlie White III develop a bold new airbrush illustration style that becomes emblematic of the decade.

✦ First Earth Day, founded by Senator Gaylord Nelson (D-WI), inaugurates the recycling symbol (three arrows forming a triangle).

✦ Garry Trudeau, Yale Art School graduate, introduces the comic strip "Doonesbury."

✦ GRAPUS, an alternative French design collective is founded by former members of the Atelier Populaire: Pierre Bernard, François Miehe, and Gerard Paris-Clavel.

✦ Herman Miller's *Sweet Corn Festival* poster is designed by Stephen Frykholm/Philip Mitchell.

✦ Jacquline S. Casey designs *Stop Pollution* poster for Massachusetts Institute of Technology.

✦ Jamie Reid begins publishing his Suburban Press, an art/politics community paper in Croydon, England. Under this name he produces such artworks as subversive stickers, e.g., "Save Petrol, Burn Cars," "Keep Warm This Winter, Make Trouble."

✦ Louis Silverstein redesigns many of the *New York Times* Sunday sections, changing it from "The Old Gray Lady" to a pioneer of contemporary news and feature presentations.

✦ Paul Rand illustrates *Listen, Listen,* a children's book authored by Ann Rand.

✦ Quentin Fiore, coauthor with Marshall McLuhan of *The Medium Is the Message,* designs *Do It!* by Jerry Rubin, using cinematic effects on the printed page.

✦ Raul Martinez designs and illustrates posters in Cuba.

✦ Raymond Loewy designs U.S. Mail eagle symbol.

✦ Robert Massin publishes *Letter and Image,* which surveys ways that letterforms are used as pictures and vice versa.

✦ Roger Black designs the cover for *Amerika,* a *Parade*-like insert to go into student newspapers.

✦ Shigeo Fukuda designs graphics for Expo 70 in Osaka, Japan.

✦ *Smithsonian* magazine begins publication.

✦ Takenobu Igarashi opens design office in Tokyo.

✦ Terry Jones is the art director of London *Vanity Fair.*

✦ The *New York Times* introduces its op-ed page, which opens the newspaper to articles from outside the paper. Rejecting traditional editorial cartoons, the *Times* commissions complementary graphic commentaries from progressive American and European artists. The first art director is Louis Silverstein, followed by J. C. Suares.

✦ The *Push Pin Style* is published by Communication Arts.

Cover of *Twen* by Willi Flekhaus

✦ *Twen* magazine, designed by Rudi Flekhaus, ceases publication.

✦ International Typeface Corporation (ITC) is established by Herb Lubalin, Edward Rondthaler, and Aaron Burns, with Tom Carnase, to develop and sell new photo typefaces worldwide.

## ADVERTISING

❧ "This Bud's for You" for Budweiser is the brainchild of D'Arcy, Masius, Benton & Bowles.

❧ 7-UP's "The Uncola" ad is created by J. Walter Thompson Co.

❧ Charles and Maurice Saatchi, English brothers in their mid-twenties, open their advertising agency in London and set the industry on its ear.

❧ Cliff Freeman joins Dancer-Fitzgerald-Sample New York and gains fame for Mounds/Almond Joy with "Sometimes You Feel Like a Nut . . . Sometimes You Don't."

❧ Dannon Yogurt ads featuring 100-year-old people in Russia are created by Marsteller Inc.

❧ Howard Zieff directs "Mamma Mia" commercial for Alka-Seltzer created by Doyle Dane Bernbach agency.

❧ Mobil Oil designs and publishes op-ed advertisements to present the corporation's "editorial" points of view (or spin) on public affairs and policy.

♦ Sandgren & Murtha design Transamerica corporate identity.
♦ Sunsweet Prunes' "Today the Pits, Tomorrow the Wrinkles" slogan is written by Stan Freberg, Freberg Ltd.

### EDUCATION
✎ Gerard Unger begins teaching at the Rietveld Academy in Amsterdam.

### BIRTHS AND DEATHS
Adriano Olivetti dies.
Ben Duffy dies.
Emil Ruder dies.
Erich Heckel dies.
Jonathan Hoefler is born.
Kristen Faulkner is born.
Mark Rothko dies.
Robert Brownjohn dies.
Ruben (Rube) L. Goldberg dies.
Tobias Frere-Jones is born.
Dave Berger dies.

### CONSUMABLES
🍴 Hamburger Helper is introduced.
🍴 Orville Redenbacher Gourmet Popping Corn is introduced.

### ARTS AND CULTURE
♠ Jerry Rubin publishes *Scenarios de Revolution*, design by Quentin Fiore.
♠ Marshall McLuhan publishes *From Cliché to Archetype.*
♠ The *Push Pin Style* exhibition at the Musée des Arts Décoratifs at the Louvre features John Alcorn, Seymour Chwast, Paul Davis, Milton Glaser, and Edward Sorel.

### BIG BUSINESS
🏛 Ted Turner, president and chief operating officer of Turner Advertising Company, moves into television by acquiring an independent Atlanta UHF television station, and forms Turner Broadcasting System, Inc.

### INDUSTRIAL DESIGN
✈ Ann Ferebee publishes *A History of Design from the Victorian Era to the Present,* the first attempt at codifying a graphic design history in the context of industrial design progress.

Poster by Grapus

### POLITICS
🏹 First U.S. troops are withdrawn from Vietnam.
🏹 Kent State massacre.
🏹 War in Vietnam spreads to Laos and Cambodia.

### TECHNOLOGY
⚡ First digitized photographs are introduced.
⚡ First International direct-dial telephone call is made from New York to London.
⚡ Pocket calculator, Pocketronic Printing Calculator, is introduced by Canon Business Machines, Tokyo.

### TYPE
♣ Aldo Novarese designs Stop typeface for the Nebiolo Foundry.
♣ Herb Lubalin and Tom Carnase's Avant Garde typeface, originally designed for the *Avant Garde* magazine logo, is released by ITC.
♣ Milton Glaser designs Glaser Stencil typeface.
♣ Seymour Chwast designs Blimp typeface.
♣ Tom Carnase designs Machine typeface.

OpEd page of the *New York Times*

# 19**71**

## GRAPHIC ARTS

✦ Albe Steiner designs logo and page format for *La Sinistra*, a newspaper for the Italian Communist party.

✦ Andy Warhol designs the album cover *Sticky Fingers* for the Rolling Stones.

✦ Chermayeff & Geismar design official United States American Revolution Bicentennial Symbol.

✦ Dan Friedman designs *Typografische Monatsblatter* cover, the first expression of the New (post-Modern) Typography.

✦ David Edward Byrd designs *Jesus Christ Superstar* musical poster.

✦ Günter Gerhard Lange appointed to the Board of Directors at H. Berthold AG.

✦ Massimo and Lella Vignelli found Vignelli Associates, New York.

✦ *Money* magazine begins publication.

✦ Nicolette Gray publishes *Lettering as Drawing*.

✦ Steven Horn designs the parody of Uncle Sam *I Want You* poster titled *I Want Out* as a poster for the Committee to Unsell the War.

✦ Victor Papanek, design and environmental critic, publishes the essay "Design for the Real World."

✦ Saul Bass redesigns the Quaker Oats trademark.

## ADVERTISING

❧ Bill Backer, McCann-Erickson Worldwide, New York, creates Coca-Cola's "I'd Like to Buy the World a Coke" and "It's the Real Thing."

❧ Keep America Beautiful ad with the "crying Indian" is created for the Advertising Council by Marsteller Inc.

❧ McDonald's slogan "You Deserve a Break Today" is introduced, written by Keith Reinhard at Needham, Harper & Steers.

❧ Nike's "swoosh" logo is designed by student Carol Davidson, and bought by Nike for $35.

❧ Perdue Chicken print ad "It Takes a Tough Man to Make a Tender Chicken" is created by Scali, McCabe, Sloves.

❧ The Four A's, ANA and American Advertising Federal launch the National Advertising Board (NAB) to monitor questions of taste and social responsibility in advertising.

❧ Tobacco advertising is banned on TV.

## EDUCATION

❧ Katherine McCoy co-chairs design department at Cranbrook Academy of Art with Michael McCoy until 1998.

❧ Sheila Levrant de Bretteville creates the Women's Design Program at the California Institute of the Arts, the first course of its kind in the exploration of the relationship between feminism and design.

## BIRTHS AND DEATHS

Alexey Brodovitch dies.
Arne Jacobsen dies.
David Sarnoff dies.
Gio Ponti dies.
Igor Stravinsky dies.
Leo Burnett dies.
Raoul Hausmann dies.
Theodore Repplier dies.
Virgil Finlay dies.

Poster by Steve Horn

## CONSUMABLES

☞ Stronger warning labels on cigarette packs are demanded.

## ARTS AND CULTURE

♠ *All in the Family* debuts.

♠ David Hockney starts the "Swimming Pool" paintings.

♠ Society of Illustrators holds antiwar exhibition chaired by Alan E. Cober and Lou Meyers. It is criticized by some as coming too late in course of the Vietnam War.

♠ The *Ed Sullivan Show* ends.

## INDUSTRIAL DESIGN

✈ Ernie Smith designs Mennen Company's E (vitamin E) deodorant packaging. A lowercase sans-serif "e" is displayed prominently on the can with the character reversed out of a black square to white.

## POLITICS

✗ China is admitted to the United Nations.

✗ Twenty-sixth Amendment gives eighteen-year-olds the right to vote.

## TECHNOLOGY

♠ Intel invents the microprocessor.

## TYPE

♣ Hermann Zapf designs Zapf Civilite for Paul Hayden Duensing Foundry (to 1974).

Sketch of logo by Albe Steiner

# 19**72**

## GRAPHIC ARTS

✦ Dan Friedman designs "Wolfgang Wiengart Speaks to America" poster to announce Weingart's tour and slide presentation to eight prominent design schools.

✦ Don Matus designs New York City Ballet Stravinsky Festival poster for City Center of Music & Drama Inc.

✦ Federal Design Improvement Program for the U.S. government initiated by the National Endowment for the Arts with the active support of President Richard Nixon.

✦ *Life* magazine ceases publication (revived in the 1980s).

✦ Mervyn Kurlansky and Kenneth Grange join Crosby, Fletcher and Forbes, and the name changes to Pentagram. This same year *Pentagram: The Work of Five Designers* is published.

✦ *Ms.* magazine begins publication, founded by Pat Carbine, Gloria Steinem, and others. It is art-directed by Bea Feitler who reintroduces Victorian woodtypes as a contemporary stylistic conceit.

✦ Otl Aicher designs Munich Olympics signage.

✦ Pacific Film Archive poster is designed by David Lance Goines. His style is a revival of turn of the century Vienna Secession graphics. Robert Massin is a freelance art director for Folio publishers in France.

✦ Tadanori Yokoo, Japanese poster designer who prefigures the psychedelic movement with his wild compositions, has a one-man exhibit at MoMA, New York.

✦ Terry Jones becomes art director of *British Vogue* until 1977.

✦ Wolfgang Weingart designs covers for *Typographische Monatsblätter*, a Swiss type journal, in which he experiments with stretched out letterspacing and stepped text blocks (until 1976).

✦ Wolfgang Weingart writes "How Can One Make Swiss Typography?" which explores the essence of the Swiss style while offering alternatives to its cold rigidity.

✦ Paul Rand adds stripes to the IBM slab-serif logotype, which begins a trend in logos with scanlines. Rand's rationale is to make the otherwise heavy logo less imposing.

✦ Saul Bass designs the United Way trademark.

## ADVERTISING

❧ Jockey Underwear "Tall Man and Big Man" ads are created by Levine, Huntley, Schmidt.

❧ John Massey, director of CCA's Design and Market Research Laboratories, creates Department of Labor's institutional identity.

❧ Life cereal's "Hey, Mikey" ad is created by Doyle Dane Bernbach.

❧ NAB Code Authority lifts ban on advertising of tampons and sanitary napkins.

❧ National Advertising Board (NAB) and television networks agree to decrease TV commercial time in children's programming slots from sixteen to twelve minutes.

## ARCHITECTURE

❦ *Learning from Las Vegas* is published by Robert Venturi, Denise Scott Brown, and Steven Izenour. The book describes the study of the architecture of the Las Vegas Strip, and offers generalizations on symbolism in architecture and the iconography of urban sprawl. It inspires the "vernacular" movement in graphic design.

❦ Modernism ends, according to architecture pundit Charles Jencks, when the St. Louis Pruitt-Igoe apartment complex is demolished because it is considered a cold, inhumane place to live.

## EDUCATION

❧ Dan Friedman develops a program in visual studies at the State University of New York at Purchase (through 1975).

❧ Louis Danziger becomes director of the graphic design program at California Institute of the Arts.

❧ Michael Graves, American architect, joins faculty at Princeton University.

## BIRTHS AND DEATHS

Alréd Forbáth dies.
Andy Cruz is born.
Béla Uitz dies.
Henry Dreyfus dies.
Jeremy Dean is born.
Joseph Binder dies.
Lucian Bernhard, poster artist, dies.
Marianne Moore dies.
Neil McElroy dies.
Robert Bonfils dies.
Theodore L. Bates dies.
Will Burtin, American designer by way of Austria, dies.
Maxwell Fleischer dies.

## CONSUMABLES

↑ First video games are invented by Nolan Bushnell, engineer with Ampex.
↑ Quaker Oats 100% Natural Granola is introduced.
↑ Snapple fruit juices are introduced.
↑ The Honda Civic is launched.

## ARTS AND CULTURE

♠ Alan E. Cober publishes *The Forgotten Society*, visual essays on the mentally retarded, death row, and the aged. The book has an influence on how conceptual illustrators have addressed public issues.
♠ *Italy: The New Domestic Landscape* exhibition, New York Museum of Art, introduces America to advancements in Italian industrial and graphic design.
♠ Running Fence environmental sculpture is constructed by Christo.

## INDUSTRIAL DESIGN

↑ Jacob Jensen designs Beogram 4000 hi-fi system.

## POLITICS

↑ Five men break into Democratic Headquarters in Washington, D.C., and the Watergate scandal begins.
↑ Nixon is overwhelmingly reelected.
↑ Nixon visits China.

## TECHNOLOGY

↑ First anti-aliased digital fonts are developed by MIT.
↑ Metroset, introduced by MGD Graphic Systems (Rockwell International), allows fonts to be digitally stored as outlines.
↑ Texas Instruments produces a pocket calculator.

## TYPE

✦ Walter Tracy designs Times Europa typeface.

IBM logo (with stripes)

+ Michael Gross art-directs the *National Lampoon* cover showing a dog with a gun pointed at its head. The headline reads: "If You Don't Buy This Magazine We'll Kill This Dog."

## GRAPHIC ARTS

✦ AIGA is commissioned to design symbols for the U.S. Department of Transportation. The project chair is Thomas Geismar, with the symbols designed by Cook and Shanosky Associates of Princeton, New Jersey. The resulting symbols become the standard identifying and way-finding icons in most public places.

✦ Christopher Pullman is hired as a freelance designer for the Boston public television station WGBH.

✦ Keiji Nakazawa writes and draws "I Saw It," an autobiographical comic strip about surviving the atomic blast at Hiroshima (a year later he begins the "Gen" series—a fictional account of a boy during the same period).

✦ Michael Vanderbyl opens Vanderbyl Design in San Francisco, proponent of the California new wave style, which combines bright colors and minimalist graphic forms.

✦ National Zoo environmental graphics are designed by Wyman & Cannan.

✦ Rochelle Udell is art director at *Vogue*.

✦ Sheila Levrant de Bretteville publishes the essay "Some Aspects of Design from the Perspective of a Woman Designer," sparking concern for the earlier marginalization of women in the design field.

✦ Paul Rand designs Cummings Engine Company/US and Japan logotype.

✦ Rudolph de Harak designs the shopping bags for the Metropolitan Museum of Art, New York, which helps launch a shopping bag "art" fashion both for retail stores and museums.

## ADVERTISING

✦ American Tourister print ad "Dear American Tourister: Your Suitcase Outlasted Our House," is created by Doyle Dane Bernbach.

✦ Burger King "Have It Your Way" slogan is created by BBD&O.

✦ Charlotte Beers named senior vice president at JWT, the first female to achieve that rank in an agency.

✦ James Miho designs Champion International's "Imagination Series" of paper promotions, which are designed to entertain while selling their line of designer papers.

✦ Phil Gips and Aubrey Balkind form the design firm Gips & Balkind, New York.

✦ Robert Jacoby becomes chairman of Ted Bates & Co., New York.

✦ Wunderman, Ricotta & Kline is acquired by Young & Rubicam.

## ARCHITECTURE

✝ Charles Jencks publishes *Modern Movements in Architecture*.

## BIRTHS AND DEATHS

Ashley Haviden dies.
C. D. Crain Jr. dies.
Clara Tice dies.
James Webb Young dies.
Jaques Lipchitz dies.
Lyndon B. Johnson dies.
Pablo Picasso dies.

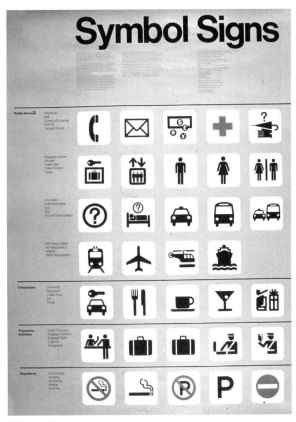

AIGA Symbol Signs

Paul Schuitema dies.
Walter Dexel dies.
Walt (Walter) Kelly dies.
Coulton Waugh dies.
Chic (Murat) Young dies.

### EDUCATION

✎ Armin Hofmann founds the Yale
University summer design program in
Brissago, Switzerland.

✎ Donis Dondis publishes the
textbook *A Primer of Visual Literacy,*
an early tract on the application of the
visual language in contemporary
society.

✎ MIT's Visible Language workshop
is cofounded by Muriel Cooper and
Nicolas Nicholas Negriponte to focus
on how computers enhance the
graphic communication process and
how high-quality graphics can
improve computer information
systems.

### CONSUMABLES

☛ The linear bar code is chosen as
the Universal Product Code.

### ARTS AND CULTURE

♣ "Art of the New York Times"
exhibition opens at the Musée des
Arts Décoratifs at the Louvre, Paris,
featuring the illustrations from the
op-ed page. It is the first time
illustration has been so honored.

♣ Earth tones mark the seventies:
rusts, oranges, browns, and the
infamous avocado green are the butt
of color jokes.

♣ Ralph Bakshi releases the
animated film *Fritz the Cat*, based
on R. Crumb's cartoon character.

### BIG BUSINESS

🏛 Federal Express Company is
founded.

### POLITICS

🏹 Arab-Israeli War.

🏹 OPEC places an embargo on oil
shipments to the United States. Oil
prices and the length of lines at gas
stations quadruple.

🏹 *Roe v. Wade* decision legalizes
abortion.

🏹 Senate Watergate Hearings begin.

### TECHNOLOGY

⚡ First commercial fax machines are
introduced.

⚡ Internet is first introduced by the
U.S. Department of Defense as a way
to integrate its research facilities and
people.

Cover of *Upper & lower case* magazine

### TYPE

✦ Berthold Wolpe designs Johnston's
Railway Type Italic.

✦ Erik Spiekermann moves from
Berlin to London, where he designs
typefaces and publishes books on
typography.

✦ *U&lc.*, the ITC house publication
cum typographic magazine is founded,
Herb Lubalin is the art director.

Cover of the *National Lampoon*

# ¹⁹**74**

✦ Saul Bass & Associates design Warner Communications trademark.
✦ Swissair trademark is designed by Karl Gerstner. The vermilion parallelogram with white cross says both "aviation" and "Switzerland."

## GRAPHIC ARTS

✦ Anthony Goldschmidt designs the film title sequence for *Young Frankenstein* as a pastiche of 1930s monster movies.
✦ Art Spiegelman and Bill Griffith cofound *Arcade Comics Revue*, an early attempt to address the intellectual aspect of underground comics.
✦ Etta Hulme joins *Fort Worth Star Telegram*, becoming the first woman editorial cartoonist on a major newspaper.
✦ Graphic Design Seminar is sponsored by National Endowment for the Arts (NEA) as part of the Federal Design Program.
✦ Jack McGregor (Jamie) Reid designs the book *Leaving the 20th Century* for Free Fall Press.
✦ Mike Salisbury redesigns *Rolling Stone* magazine.
✦ Milton Glaser leaves Push Pin Studio to found Milton Glaser, Inc. Seymour Chwast retains the name Push Pin Studio.
✦ NASA "worm" logo is designed by Danne & Blackburn (discontinued in 1992).
✦ Paula Scher designs record album covers at CBS, which has become the hothouse for innovative record packaging.
✦ Society of Scribes, Ltd. is founded in New York.
✦ The Center for Book Arts is founded in New York by Richard Minsky, the first nonprofit organization for the preservation of traditional bookmaking.
✦ John Massey designs the U.S. Department of Labor trademark and graphic standards system.

## ADVERTISING

✦ Hebrew National Beef Hot Dogs "We Answer to a Higher Authority" TV commercial is created by Scali, McCabe, Sloves.
✦ Miller Lite beer, "Tastes Great, Less Filling," ad campaign begins, conceived by McCann-Erickson Worldwide.
✦ Ragù Spaghetti Sauce "Now That's Italian!" TV commercial is created by Waring & LaRosa agency, Bob Giraldi, director.

## EDUCATION

✦ Philip B. Meggs, design educator and historian, gets an NEA grant to mount national lecture series to present his design history research to selected colleges and universities (which becomes the basis for his 1983 book *A History of Graphic Design*).

## BIRTHS AND DEATHS

Adolph Gottlieb dies.
Albe Steiner, Italian graphic designer known for his posters for *L'Unità* (Italian Communist Party newspaper), dies.
David Siqueiros dies.
First batch of Generation Next babies is born (through 1984).
George Jerome Rozen dies.
György Ruttkay dies.
Henry C. Beck dies.
Jan Tschichold, typographer, dies.
Jock Kinneir dies.
Otto Binder dies.
Otto Soglow dies.

Cover of *Arcade* magazine

## ARTS AND CULTURE

🕯 Bar codes are first used at Marsh Supermarket, Troy, Ohio.

🕯 *People* magazine, a mainstream gossip and personality weekly, begins publication.

## INDUSTRIAL DESIGN

✈ Giorgietto Giugiaro designs Volkswagen Golf, a hatchback precursor to the Rabbit.

## POLITICS

🕯 Nixon resigns on August 8, Gerald Ford becomes president and pardons Nixon on September 8.

## TECHNOLOGY

🕯 "Smart" card for storing and processing computer data is introduced.

## TYPE

❦ Ed Benguiat designs ITC Tiffany typeface.

❦ Herb Lubalin and Tony DiSpigna design Lubalin Graph typeface for ITC.

❦ Joel Kadan designs American Typewriter typeface.

❦ Tony DiSpigna and Herb Lubalin design Serif Gothic typeface.

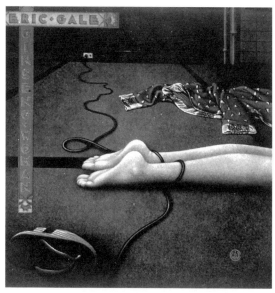

CBS album covers, illustrator, David Wilcox; art director, Paula Scher

Promotional ad for LCB&D

# 19**75**

## GRAPHIC ARTS

✦ "I ♥ NY" symbol is designed by Milton Glaser, copied by cities and businesses all over the world.

✦ *Byte* magazine begins publication.

✦ Chris Pullman art-directs the first opening title—a waving flag—sequence for PBS's Masterpiece Theater.

✦ Cipe Pineles becomes the first woman elected to the ADC Hall of Fame.

✦ Michael Schwab opens studio in San Francisco.

✦ Mike Salisbury designs *City* magazine, San Francisco. Published by movie director Francis Ford Coppola, it is an exciting mix of underground and mainstream graphic sensibilities.

✦ Paul Rand designs *Minute Man* poster for the U.S. Department of the Interior.

✦ *Punk* magazine is founded by Legs McNeil.

✦ Tadanori Yokoo designs Miles Davis album cover *Agharta* for CBS records.

✦ Victor Papanek publishes *Edugrapology—The Myths of Design and the Design of Myths,* addressing the professional and sociological role of designers.

✦ Willi Kunz designs *12 T y p o graphical Interpretations*, a book of typographical interpretations of the writings by the Canadian philosopher Marshall McLuhan.

✦ First issue of *Furore*, edited by Piet Schreuders, is a Dutch magazine about things, people, and occurrences (published irregularly).

✦ *Fine Print*, founded by Sandra Kirshbaum, is devoted to the arts of the book (ceases publication in 1990).

## ADVERTISING

✦ Paul Davis begins to design and illustrate posters for Joe Papp's New York Public Theater, launching a theater poster revival.

✦ American Express ad "Do You Know Me?" is created by Ogilvy & Mather.

✦ BMW ad "The Ultimate Driving Machine" is created by Ammirati & Puris.

✦ Bruce Crawford is made president of BBD&O Worldwide, New York (through 1983).

✦ The Federal Trade Commission Improvements Act gives the FTC power to take to court advertising agencies that violate the rules.

✦ Xerox ad "It's a Miracle" is created by Needham, Harper & Steers.

## ARCHITECTURE

✦ Charles Jencks christens the post-Modern movement in an article for the *Architecture Association Quarterly* "The Rise of Post-Modern Architecture."

## EDUCATION

✦ Thomas J. Watson Jr., president of IBM, gives the speech "Good Design is Good Business" for the Wharton School Lectures, in which he celebrates the achievements of his company and coins a phrase that is used as a mantra throughout the decade.

## BIRTHS AND DEATHS

Francis Meynell dies.
Georg Olden dies.
János Kmetty dies.
George Baker dies.

## CONSUMABLES

✦ Bic disposable razor is introduced.

✦ Famous Amos Chocolate Chip Cookies are introduced.

✦ First cereal bar, Nature Valley Granola, is introduced by General Mills.

## ARTS AND CULTURE

♣ *Gunsmoke* ends after twenty years.

## Big Business

🏛 Bill Gates and Paul Allen found Microsoft.

🏛 Home Box Office is launched by Time, Inc.

🏛 Steve Jobs and Steve Wozniak design Apple I.

## Industrial Design

✦ *The Streamlined Decade* is published, renewing interest in twenties and thirties industrial design revolution.

## Politics

✗ Khmer Rouge take Phnom Penh.

✗ Lebanese Civil War begins.

✗ South Vietnam surrenders, ending twenty-nine years of civil war.

✗ United States' involvement in Vietnam ends.

## Technology

✦ First laser phototypesetter is introduced by Monotype Corporation.

✦ First personal computer (Altair 8800) is introduced.

✦ First word processors with VDT are introduced by Wang, Vydec, Lexitron, and Linolex.

## Type

✦ Ed Benguiat designs ITC Bookman typeface.

✦ Tony Stan designs ITC Century, Cheltenham, and Garamond typefaces (Garamond adapted from a typeface by Morris F. Benton).

Cover of *City* magazine

# 19**76**

## GRAPHIC ARTS

✦ Alexander Calder designs *Under the Sun* poster for the Pennsylvania Ballet.

✦ Andrea Branzi with Alessandro Mendini and Ettore Sottsass form CDM (Design Consultancies Milan).

✦ Bruce Blackburn designs the American Bicentennial symbol.

✦ Chicago's *Chicago X* receives the Grammy award for the best album package. The art director is John Berg for Columbia.

✦ Gunter Rambow designs posters for book publisher S. Fischer-Verlag.

✦ Hipgnosis and George Hardie design Led Zeppelin's album cover *Presence* for Swan Song.

✦ Ivan Chermayeff designs poster to advertise *Upstairs, Downstairs*, the Masterpiece Theater production produced by Mobil Oil Corporation.

✦ Jonson Pederson Hinrichs & Shakery graphic design firm founded in New York.

✦ Leslie Savan publishes the essay "This Typeface Is Changing Your Life" about the widespread use of Helvetica as the official face of industry and institutions.

✦ The *New York Times* begins daily theme sections, including "Living," "Home," and "Weekend," designed by art director Louis Silverstein.

✦ *Wet* magazine, utilizing New Wave design and typography, is published in Venice, California. April Greiman and Jayme Odgers are the art directors.

✦ R. D. E. Oxenaar becomes the aesthetic advisor to the Dutch PPT.

✦ Dan Friedman designs Citibank logo while working for Anspach, Grossman, Portugal, New York.

✦ Gerald Reis founds Gerald Reis and Company, San Francisco.

## ADVERTISING

⚘ Hal Riney is hired as art director by Ogilvy & Mather, San Francisco. Within months he takes over Ogilvy & Mather and renames it Hal Riney & Partners.

⚘ NBC introduces the new "N" logo which is almost identical with (but costs considerably more than) Nebraska ETV Network's.

⚘ Supreme Court grants advertising First Amendment protection.

## ARCHITECTURE

⚑ Richard Saul Wurman, architect and designer, chairperson of the American Institute of Architects conference, coins the term "architecture of information," which he later streamlines into "Information Architecture," indicating a dichotomy between styling and understanding.

## BIRTHS AND DEATHS

Albert Kner dies.

Alexander Calder dies.

Alvar Aalto dies.

André Malraux dies.

Carl Schmidt-Rottluff dies.

Egon Schiele dies.

Hans Schleger (Zéró), British poster artist, dies.

Jerome Snyder, American illustrator/designer, dies.

Josef Albers dies.

Ladislav Sutnar, pioneer of information design, dies.

Man Ray (Emanuel Rabinovitch), creator of the Rayogramme, dies.

Rudolph Modley dies.

Sandor Bortnyik dies.

Front page of *The Home Section*

## POLITICS

ⵣ Jimmy Carter is elected 39th president of the United States.

## TECHNOLOGY

⚑ Cray 1, the first supercomputer developed by Seymour Cray, becomes the first installation at Los Alamos National Laboratory.

⚑ First fiber optics is installed in Bell Labs Product Center in Atlanta, Georgia, the prototype of a system capable of carrying 50,000 telephone calls.

⚑ NASA launches the first space shuttle.

## CONSUMABLES

⌁ Perrier is introduced.

## ARTS AND CULTURE

⚘ Grolier Club, New York (founded in 1884), a book club devoted to the aesthetics and noncommercial aspects of publishing, admits its first female member.

⚘ Punk begins in England as a style of dress, music, and graphic design.

⚘ Malcolm McLaren, impresario of punk music in England, produces and promotes the Sex Pistols, who embody the anarchic ethic, aesthetic, and pose of the punk movement.

⚘ *Signs of Life: Symbols in the American City* exhibition is organized by Venturi, Rauch and Scott Brown.

⚘ The term "Me Decade" is first applied by Tom Wolfe in the *New York* magazine, he also identifies "communicate" as one of the era's signature terms.

⚘ The United States celebrates its bicentennial by minting the bicentennial quarter.

## BIG BUSINESS

🏛 Ted Turner originates the superstation concept, TBS Superstation, by transmitting the station's signal to cable systems across the country via satellite.

## TYPE

✦ Adrian Frutiger designs Frutiger typeface.

✦ Gerard Unger designs Demos typeface.

✦ Hermann Zapf designs Zapf Book typeface.

✦ Takenobu Igarashi designed isometric, or "architectural" alphabets. Igarashi's experiments with alphabets drawn on an isometric grid evolved into three-dimensional alphabetic sculptures that Igarashi calls "architectural alphabets."

Page from *Wet* magazine

# 19**77**

## GRAPHIC ARTS

✦ Alessandro Mendini is art director of *Modo* architecture and design magazine.

✦ Centre Georges Pompidou opens, Roman Czecliwicz Cieslewicz designs identity, posters, and catalogs.

✦ Dan Perri designs the title sequence for *Star Wars*, noted for the optical effect of type that tapers off into the horizon of outer space.

✦ Frank Beekers, Lies Ros, and Rob Schroder found Wild Plakken, Dutch design firm that specializes in political work.

✦ Gert Dumbar founds Studio Dumbar in The Hague, a key proponent of antigrid design in Holland.

✦ Jeff MacNelly launches the comic strip "Shoe."

✦ Piet Schreuders, Dutch designer, publishes *Lay In—Lay Out,* a primer on the design process.

✦ Punk fanzine *Sniffin' Glue* is designed by Mark Perry in the United Kingdom. It uses handscrawled lettering for its masthead and headlines, and cut-'n'-paste typewriter type for its body text.

✦ Richard Greenberg with his brother, Robert, founds R/Greenberg Associates, a studio that specializes in film titling.

✦ Sex Pistols' *God Save the Queen* album cover is designed by Jamie Reid, who also designs *The Sex Pistols' Never Mind the Bollocks, Pretty Vacant,* and *Here's the Sex Pistols* for Virgin, in the quintessential punk cut-'n'-paste manner.

✦ *Skrien,* Dutch cinema magazine, premieres and is published until 1985.

✦ Walter Bernard redesigns, and becomes art director of *Time* magazine, giving it an orderly typographic format that frames conceptual illustration and photography.

✦ Wolfgang Weingart designs *Basel Kunstkredit* exhibition poster and ignites the postmodern aesthetic within graphic design.

✦ Rob Janoff designs Apple's apple logo for Apple Computer.

✦ Tamotsu Yagi designs graphics for Esprit Corp.

✦ The term postmodernism is first applied to the typography of April Greiman, Dan Friedman, and Willi Kunz, each influenced by Wolfgang Weingart's teaching at the Basel School of Design, Switzerland.

## ADVERTISING

✦ Michael Raab creates Xerox 9400 duplicator ad "Introducing the Xerox 9400. Will Miracles Never Cease?" for Xerox Corporation, the first in a series of print ads featuring two Roman Catholic monks using Xerox copiers.

✦ Polaroid "It's So Simple" ad is created by Doyle Dane Bernbach.

## ARCHITECTURE

✦ Charles Jencks publishes *The Language of Post-Modern Architecture.*

Cover of *Sniffin' Glue* magazine

## EDUCATION

✦ Edward Tufte, expert in information design, joins Yale University faculty.

## BIRTHS AND DEATHS

Charlie Chaplin dies.
Elvis, "the King," dies.
Fairfax Cone dies.
Hans (Giovanni) Mardersteig, printer and typographer, dies.
Misha Black dies.
Piet Zwart dies.
Robert Lowell dies.
Vladimir Nabokov dies.

Record graphics for the Sex Pistols

## POLITICS

⚔ Anwar Sadat, Egyptian president, visits Israel.

⚔ The U.S. Supreme Court decision permits lawyers to advertise.

⚔ The United States tests the "clean" neutron bomb.

## TECHNOLOGY

⚔ Apple II computer is introduced, the first personal computer with color graphics capabilities.

⚔ Hewlett Packard introduces a portable mini-computer.

## ARTS AND CULTURE

♠ Rubik's cube is patented by Erno Rubik.

♠ "Postmodern Typography: Recent American Developments" exhibition in Chicago is curated by Bill Bonnell. The exhibition includes works by Steff Geissbuhler, April Greiman, Dan Friedman, and Willi Kunz, all of whom had come to America after work or study in Switzerland.

♠ *Italian Design of the 50s* exhibition in Milan is organized by Michele DeLucchi and Andrea Branzi.

♠ *Powers of Ten: A Film Dealing with the Relative Size of Things in the Universe and the Effect of Adding Another Zero* is produced by Charles and Ray Eames. This is the color version of the *Rough Sketch* made in 1968.

♠ *Roots* TV miniseries airs.

## BIG BUSINESS

🏛 Douglas and Susie Tompkins found Esprit, the clothing manufacturer.

🏛 Rupert Murdoch, News Corp., New York, acquires the *New York Post*, and ultimately builds the world's largest media-entertainment-communications empire.

## INDUSTRIAL DESIGN

✠ The U.S. National Park Service institutes the Unigrid system, Massimo Vignelli, consulting designer; Vincent Gleason, art director; and Dennis McLaughlin, graphic designer. The Unigrid system unifies informational folders into ten broadside formats and sizes, utilizing a master grid, standardized typo-graphic and pictorial specifications, and printed on white dull-coated paper.

## TYPE

✦ David Berlow begins his career in the type industry at Mergenthaler Linotype. He designs the revivals New Century Schoolbook and New Caledonia.

✦ Ed Benguiat designs Benguiat typeface, one of the most widely used faces of the decade.

✦ Erik Spiekermann designs LoType, Block, and Berliner Grotesk typefaces for H. Berthold AG.

Poster by Wolfgang Weingart

Benguiat type specimen

## GRAPHIC ARTS

✦ April Greiman masthead for *Luxe*, based on the step (or sawtooth) rule, becomes emblematic of the new typography of the day.

✦ Art Spiegelman and Françoise Mouly found Raw Books and Graphics and publish the first issue of *Raw, the Comix Magazine for Postponed Suicides*, which takes comic strips and graphic stories to a new level of sophistication.

✦ Chris Pullman art-directs redesigned opening title—the library—sequence for PBS's *Masterpiece Theater* at WGBH.

✦ Cipe Pineles receives Award of Excellence by Society of Publication Designers.

✦ *Fetish: The Magazine of the Material World* is published and designed by Doublespace, David Sterling and Jane Kostrin, New York. It is an ambitious "zine" that looks at cultural phenomena.

✦ Keith Ablitt becomes art director of *Design* magazine, London.

✦ Louise Fili, art director for Pantheon Books (until 1989) begins her design of over two thousand book covers.

✦ Nike marathon poster is created by John Brown & Partners.

✦ Pentagram opens New York offices with Colin Forbes as director.

✦ Peter Corrison designs Rolling Stones' album cover *Some Girls* for Rolling Stones Records.

✦ R/Greenberg Associates designs the film title sequence for the first *Superman.*

✦ R. D. E. Oxenaar designs the Dutch hundred-guilder note.

✦ *Smash Hits*, English countercultural magazine, is launched.

✦ Terry Jones designs and edits *Not Another Punk Book.*

✦ The Society of Newspaper Design is founded.

✦ After a stint with Stan Richards, Woody Pirtle establishes Pirtle Design in Texas.

✦ Yusaku Kamekura is a founding member of Japanese Graphic Designers Association.

✦ Saul Bass designs a new, minimalist Girl Scout trademark.

## ADVERTISING

✦ BMW North America "The Ultimate Driving Machine" print ad is created by Ammirati & Puris.

✦ Federal Express's "When It Absolutely, Positively Has to Be There Overnight" TV commercial is created by Ally & Gargano agency and Sedelmaier Productions.

✦ Lee Iacocca leaves Ford Motor Co. to become the CEO of Chrysler Corp., Highland Park, Michigan. He becomes the most effective TV spokesman in the U.S. history.

✦ NAB Code Authority lifts ban on advertising of pregnancy test kits and "jock-itch" remedies.

# Bell Centennial
# Name & Number
# ABCDEFGHIJKLMN
# OPQRSTUVWXYZ
# 1234567890$£¢
# abcdefghijklmnop
# qrstuvwxyz.,:;-!?

Centennial type specimen

## TECHNOLOGY

♣ Adobe Systems develop Postscript.

♣ Epson introduces the dot-matrix printer.

♣ First test-tube baby, Louise Brown, is born.

## TYPE

♣ Hermann Zapf designs Zapf Dingbats.

♣ Matthew Carter designs Bell Centennial typeface, commissioned by AT&T, replacing Bell Gothic of 1938.

♣ Matthew Carter designs ITC Galliard for Mergenthaller Linotype.

## ARCHITECTURE

♈ Philip Johnson designs the postmodern AT&T building in New York City (through 1983), which looks like a Chippendale armoire.

## BIRTHS AND DEATHS

Aram Khachaturian dies.
Charles Eames dies.
Giorgio de Chirico dies.
Hannah Höch dies.
Jim Jones cult suicide in Guyana, 911 people die.
Mehemed Fehmy (M. F.) Agha dies.
Nicholas Bentley dies.
Norman Rockwell dies.
Rudolph Ruzicka dies.

## ARTS AND CULTURE

♠ A Gutenberg Bible sells for $2 million.

♠ ESPN, the twenty-four-hour sports cable network, is launched.

♠ Punk takes root in Seattle, and the music and graphics scene takes off.

♠ Showtime cable network is launched by Viacom.

## POLITICS

♐ Anwar Sadat and Menachem Begin sign Camp David Accords. Later in the year, each is awarded the Nobel Peace Prize.

Cover of first *Raw* magazine

# 19**79**

## GRAPHIC ARTS

✦ Alberto Vargas illustrates the Cars album cover *Candy-O* for Elektra.

✦ Barney Bubbles designs Ian Dury & the Blockheads' album cover *Do It Yourself* for Stitt.

✦ Birney Lettick designs *Heaven Can Wait* poster for Paramount Pictures.

✦ Condé Nast starts *Self* magazine and acquires *GQ*.

✦ *Cuisine* magazine begins publication (through 1984).

✦ David King, British graphic designer and archivist, designs the Rodchenko exhibition catalog for Museum of Art in Oxford. The layout of the exhibition reflects the simple forms utilized in Constructivism.

✦ Jayme Odgers (photographer) and April Greiman (typographer) collaborate on a recruitment poster for the California Institute of the Arts. The marriage of type and montage explore new realms of time and space in two-dimensional design.

✦ Joan Miró designs *Vogue* magazine (Paris) cover for Les Editions Condé Nast SA.

✦ Paula Scher designs *Best of Jazz* poster for Columbia Records and reintroduces Russian Constructivism to contemporary graphic design (contributing to the so-called "Retro" style, a term coined by Philip B. Meggs).

✦ R/Greenberg Associates produces film title sequence for *Alien*.

✦ Richard Hess designs Poster Exhibition poster for AIGA.

✦ Sharon Helmer Poggenpohl edits special issue of *Visual Language* on "Graphic Design Education: A Practice in Search of a Theory," which analyzes the burgeoning interest in how linguistic theory influences graphic design.

✦ Tibor Kalman with Carol Bokuniewicz and Liz Trovato found M&Co., named after Kalman's wife, Maira Kalman.

✦ Washburn College Bible is designed by Bradbury Thompson who introduces modern principles of book design, including wide margins and generous white space.

✦ Meta Design is founded in Berlin by Erik Spiekermann with Florian Fischer and Dieter Heil in London (closes 1983).

## ADVERTISING

❧ AT&T ad "Reach Out and Touch Someone" is created by N. W. Ayer & Son.

❧ Chanel TV commercial "Share the Fantasy" is created by Doyle Dane Bernbach.

❧ Charlotte Beers becomes CEO at Tatham-Laird & Kudner.

❧ Chermayeff & Geismar design National Aquarium logo.

❧ Hank Londoner creates Jordache Designer Jeans ad "the Jordache Look."

❧ Kenyon & Eckhardt, Ford's agency, switches to Chrysler.

❧ Volvo print ad "How I Bought a Volvo Wagon and Lost 1,000 Pounds of Ugly Fat" is created by Scali, McCabe, Sloves.

❧ Bill Backer opens Backer & Spielvogel.

California Institute of the Arts poster by Jamie Odgers and April Greiman

## ARCHITECTURE

Aldo Rossi designs the Teatro del Mondo in Venice, Italy.

## EDUCATION

First computer graphic design seminar is held at MIT's Visible Language workshop.

## BIRTHS AND DEATHS

Al (Alfred) Capp dies.
Daniel Starch dies.
Reynolds Stone dies.
Sonia Delaunay dies.
Xanti (Alexander) Schawinsky dies.

## CONSUMABLES

Post-It Notes are introduced by 3M.
Sony Walkman is introduced.

## ARTS AND CULTURE

Nickelodeon, the first television network for kids, is launched.

## INDUSTRIAL DESIGN

Ergonomi Design Gruppen, Sweden, is founded.
Hunter Freeman designs the New IBM Electronic 75 Typewriter ad for International Business Machines Corp.
Michael Graves designs furniture for Sunar until 1981.
Robert Venturi designs products for Alessi until 1983.

## POLITICS

Margaret Thatcher is elected British prime minister.
The U.S. Embassy in Iran is seized by revolutionaries.

## TECHNOLOGY

Compact disc is developed by Philips and Sony.
Media Lab for interdisciplinary research in new media is founded by computer graphics expert Nicholas Negroponte and Jerome Wiesner, president emeritus of MIT.
WordStar processing program is developed by Seymour Rubenstein, programmed by Rob Barnaby.

## TYPE

Adrian Frutiger designs Gypha typeface.
Hermann Zapf designs Zapf Chancery typeface.
Vic Caruso designs ITC Franklin Gothic typeface (after M. F. Benton, 1904).

## ACT OF GOD

Three-Mile Island nuclear reactor accident.

# 1980

*For hundreds of years, authors and editors have decided what to put in the packages they create for us... Now, with the new technologies, we will create our own packages, experiencing sovereignty over text . . . the accumulated impact of people exercising sovereignty over text will undoubtedly have a strong effect on the new society we are shaping.*

*John Naisbitt, 1982*

# ¹⁹80

## GRAPHIC ARTS

✦ Art Chantry designs for Seattle punk music industry (through 1990s), drawing upon the cut-'n'-paste aesthetic of the sixties underground.

✦ Art Spiegelman and Françoise Mouly publish eight large-size issues of *RAW* magazine (until 1986) that showcases a sophisticated form of comic strip or narrative visual storytelling.

✦ Bob Seger & the Silver Bullet Band's *Against the Wind* wins a Grammy award for the best album package, art-directed by Roy Kohara for Capitol.

✦ CBS records house style is developed by art directors Paula Scher, Tony Lane, Henrietta Conak, and Nancy McDonald.

✦ Dan Perri designs the film title sequence for Martin Scorsese's *Raging Bull.*

✦ Early computer illustration is created by John Hersey (through 1980s).

✦ Erik Spiekermann returns to Berlin to set up MetaDesign, which becomes Germany's largest design firm, employing more than eighty designers.

✦ First AIGA Graphic Design Leadership award is given to IBM.

✦ Gunter Rambow designs *Die Hameletmaschine* poster.

✦ Henk Elenga, Gerard Hadders, Tom van der Haspel, Helen Howard, and Rick Vermeulen found Hard Werken Design, a Dutch design collective, in Rotterdam.

✦ Johanna Drucker, design historian and educator, designs experimental books using letterpress techniques.

✦ Matthew Carter becomes typographic consultant to Her Majesty's Stationery Office (HMSO).

✦ McRay Magleby begins designing posters for Brigham Young University. They represent a complex simplicity, clean shapes, vivid color, and imaginative illustration.

✦ Mitsuo Katsui designs computer graphics (through 1980s).

✦ Neville Brody designs Cabaret Voltaire (rock group) poster, begins to make a stylistic impact by wedding Constructivist and Bauhaus concerns with geometric form and personal typographic preferences.

✦ R. O. Blechman designs "New York at Night" cover for the *New Yorker*, a visual commentary on the growing number of illuminated tops of the city's architectural landmarks.

✦ R/Greenberg Associates designs film title sequence for *Altered States.*

✦ Robert Priest becomes the art director of *Esquire* and introduces conceptual illustrators from London's Royal College of Art to American magazines.

✦ San Francisco Bay Area designers known as the Michaels—Michael Vanderbyl, Michael Manwaring, Michael Schwab, Michael Mabry, and Michael Cronin—set an aesthetic standard for West Coast practice.

✦ Sussman/Prejza, founded by Deborah Sussman and Paul Prejza in Los Angeles, specializes in environmental and graphic design.

✦ Talking Heads' *Remain in Light* album is designed by M&Co.

✦ Terry Jones launches i-D, which begins as a fashion fanzine documenting the new "street" style, and introduces "instant design," a language of spontaneous graphics.

✦ Willi Fleckhaus becomes the art director of the Sunday supplement to the *Frankfurter Allgemeine Zeitung*

✦ Wim Crouwel designs stamps for the Dutch Post Office.

✦ Wolfgang Weingart publishes his book *Projects*, based on his teaching at Basel School of Design in Switzerland.

✦ "Stars in Motion," symbol for the 1984 Los Angeles Olympics, is designed by Robert Miles Runyan Associates.

✦ Saul Bass designs Minolta logo, continuing the trend in scan-line globes which he developed with the AT&T logo.

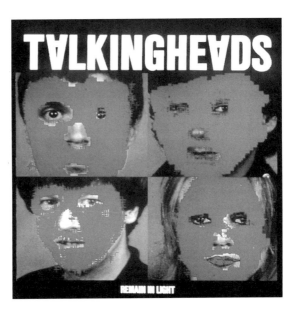

Album cover for Talking Heads by M&Co.

## ADVERTISING

♣ Burrell Communications Group, Chicago, founded by Thomas J. Burrell (b. 1939), becomes largest African-American advertising agency.

♣ Calvin Klein ads "Know what Comes between Me and My Calvins? Nothing!" are introduced, created by Calvin Klein's in-house agency.

♣ Chris Von Wangenheim creates the Maidenform Woman ad "You Never Know Where She'll Turn Up" for Maidenform Inc.

♣ U.S. Congress removes the Federal Trade Commission's power (Section 5 of the Act that allows the FTC to issue cease-and-desist orders against dishonest advertising) to stop "unfair" advertising.

## BIRTHS AND DEATHS

Jean-Paul Sartre dies.
John Lennon is murdered.
Juliette Roche dies.
Marshall McLuhan dies.
Max Miedinger dies.
Oskar Kokoschka, Viennese painter and graphic artist, dies.
Victor O. Schwab dies.

## CONSUMABLES

⚊ Cigarette sales exceed $600 billion annually.

⚊ Compact disc is introduced by Philips, Holland.

⚊ Fruit Roll-Ups are introduced.

⚊ Rollerblade skates are introduced by Scot and Brennan Olson in Bloomingdale, Minnesota.

⚊ Tandy introduces first laptop computer used primarily by journalists.

## ARTS AND CULTURE

♠ David King, British graphic designer and archivist, publishes *Stalin*, a six-volume photo-history of Stalin's regime.

♠ Jack McGregor (Jamie) Reid's graphics are purchased by Victoria and Albert Museum, London.

♠ Keith Haring begins to create "graffiti" art (through 1980s), as a student at the School of Visual Arts, New York.

## BIG BUSINESS

🏛 Apple computer goes public.

🏛 Cable News Network (CNN) is launched by Ted Turner (24-hour news channel).

🏛 MS-DOS (Microsoft Disk Operating System), originally developed by Tim Paterson, is bought by Bill Gates.

## INDUSTRIAL DESIGN

⚐ Ivan Chermayeff designs huge red *9* outdoor sculpture for 9 West 57th Street, New York.

⚐ Aldo Cibic, Austrian, with Sottsass, Thun, and Zanini, founds Sottsass Associati.

⚐ Italian-born Michele De Lucchi joins Sottsass Associati.

## POLITICS

⚐ Ronald Reagan is elected fortieth president.

⚐ Solidarity movement in Poland begins, led by Lech Walesa. Jerry Janiszewski designs Polish Solidarity Labor Union logo.

## TECHNOLOGY

⚑ dBase computer program (originally called Vulcan) is developed by Wayne Ratliff.

⚑ Intelsat V satellite relays 12,000 phone calls and two color TV channels.

## TYPE

♣ Aldo Novarese designs Novarese typeface.

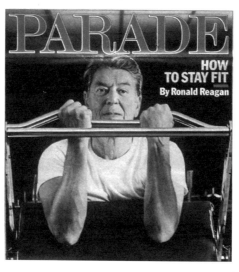

Ronald Reagan

# 19**81**

## GRAPHIC ARTS

✦ Christopher Austopchuk designs album cover for *Rachmaninoff's Piano Concerto Number 3* for CBS Records.

✦ Gary Panter designs symbol for the Screamers, a Los Angeles punk band.

✦ Grapus's Pierre Bernard designs political poster *No Neutrons, Mr. Reagan.*

✦ Lance Hidy, printmaker and book designer, designs *Support Free Nicaragua* poster.

✦ *Metropolis* magazine begins publication.

✦ Neville Brody becomes art director of the *Face* (through 1986) where he is given license to create typographic experiments, which ultimately influence the look of youth and fashion culture magazines and advertising.

✦ Page makeup systems are introduced. They use menus and mouse interface.

✦ *Print* magazine publishes its first Regional Design Annual, a signal that graphic design is now prevalent throughout the United States, not just in the major East and West Coast media capitals.

✦ The Rolling Stones' *Tattoo You* wins a Grammy award for the best album package, the art director is Peter Corriston for RS/Atlantic.

✦ Wolfgang Weingart designs *The Art of Writing* exhibition poster for *Kunstgewerbemuseum,* Zurich.

✦ ID system is developed for the Dutch PTT by Total Design and Studio Dumbar.

✦ MTV logo is designed by Frank Olinsky, Pat Gorman, and Patti Rogof of Manhattan Design, under the art direction of Fred Seibert.

✦ Texaco's revised "star" logo is designed by Anspach Grossman and Portugal.

## ADVERTISING

✦ Absolut Vodka ad "The Absolut Bottle" is created by TBWA. Based entirely on how different fine and applied artists interpret the shape of the vodka bottle (and later how different events and ideas are manifest through a metamorphosis of the bottle), this becomes the longest-running campaign in history.

✦ Fallon, McElligott, Rice, progressive Minneapolis advertising agency, is founded.

✦ Honda Motor Company *Road Scholar* poster is created by Needham, Harper & Steers.

✦ The U.S. Army ad "Be All That You Can Be" is created by N. W. Ayer & Son.

## BIRTHS AND DEATHS

Herb Lubalin dies.

Marcel Breuer dies.

Harold Foster dies.

## BIG BUSINESS

🏛 MS-DOS is refined by Bill Gates and Microsoft.

## CONSUMABLES

🏹 First 3½-inch floppy drives and disks are introduced by Sony.

🏹 First portable computer, the Osbourne I developed by Adam Osbourne, is released at a cost of $1,795. The computer weighs 24 lb. and fits under an airplane seat.

🏹 IBM introduces its first personal computer (PC) for use in the home, offices, and schools.

🏹 Lean Cuisine frozen dinners are introduced.

🏹 Pac Man mania hits.

Absolut Vodka ad

## ARTS AND CULTURE

♨ MTV, the twenty-four-hour music network debuts, and frenetic video images change the nature of commercials. Fred/Allen (Fred Seibert and Allen Goodman) is responsible for the look, feel, and positioning.

♨ Society of Typographic Art, Chicago, opens an exhibition of "Women in Design."

## INDUSTRIAL DESIGN

✦ Ettore Sottsass Jr. designs the Carlton room divider, plastic laminate on wood, a kind of cartoon version of furniture, and a quintessential example of Memphis style.

✦ Memphis Group, successor of Studio Alchymia, Milan, is founded by Ettore Sottsass Jr. The graphic design department is headed by Christopher Radl.

✦ Michael Graves designs "Plaza" dressing table and "Stanhope" bed for Memphis, named after the hotels that furniture was originally inspired by.

✦ Michael Peters Group is founded, Peters redesigns packaging and marketing for Winsor and Newton inks.

✦ Aldo Rossi designs for Alessi.

## POLITICS

☇ Anwar Sadat is assassinated.

☇ FCC deregulates radio broadcasting.

☇ Sandra Day O'Connor is appointed first woman justice of the U.S. Supreme Court.

## TECHNOLOGY

⚱ First digital type foundry (through 1992), Bitstream Inc., is founded by Matthew Carter and Mike Parker.

⚱ First Space Shuttle flight.

⚱ TCP/IP is established as standard Internet protocol by the U.S. Defense Department.

## TYPE

❧ Ed Benguiat designs Barcelonia typeface.

## ACT OF GOD

★ AIDS is recognized as epidemic.

MTV logo

Poster by Grapus

# 19**82**

## GRAPHIC ARTS

✦ VSA Partners founded by Robert Vogele, Dana Arnett, James Koval, and Curtis Schreiber in Chicago.

✦ David Berlow begins work at Bitstream Inc.

✦ *Details* magazine begins publication.

✦ Erik Spiekermann publishes his first book *Ursache & Wirkung: ein Typografischer Roman.*

✦ John Wozencroft forms Touch multimedia publishing company in London.

✦ *PC Magazine* begins publication.

✦ R/Greenberg Associates designs film title sequence for film *The World According to Garp,* featuring a flying baby that is tossed up and down on the screen. That visual is made possible by a computer process that makes the insertion of the special effect seamless.

✦ Ronn Campisi redesigns the *Boston Globe.*

✦ *USA Today* is launched by Gannett Co. Considered the fast food of journalism, it is called "Macpaper."

✦ Mutsuo Yasumura designs the Western Hemisphere globe logo, similar to Saul Bass's logos for AT&T and Minolta. *USA Today* is typeset in a regional plant via satellite command.

✦ Woody Pirtle designs "hot pepper" poster, showing a pepper sitting on a Knoll office chair, an example of playful cartoon simplicity.

✦ Anspach Grossman Portugal designs logotype for Sun Oil Company.

✦ Nickelodeon is relaunched with identity and logo created by Corey McPherson Nash, Boston.

✦ Paul Rand designs IBM rebus poster, which shows the images of an Eye, Bee, and the letter M. It was initially banned by IBM management because they feared that staff designers would take creative liberties with the logo.

✦ Vertigo Clothing Store logo is designed by April Greiman.

## ADVERTISING

✦ Apple begins a decade of aggressive ad campaigns.

✦ Dan Wieden and David Kennedy found Wieden & Kennedy, Portland, Oregon.

✦ Calvin Klein underwear ads premiere, the first of CK's provocative campaigns. They show males and females together and alone, with the CK brand on their waistband, Rochelle Udell, art director; Bruce Weber, photographer.

✦ Coca-Cola Company links "diet" to the word "coke" for the first time.

✦ Federal Express TV commercial featuring the "Fast Talker" is created by Ally & Gargano.

IBM poster by Paul Rand

✦ George Lois, Lois Pitts Gershon Pon/GGK, create the "I Want My MTV" television campaign in which Mick Jagger and other rock stars demand their MTV. The campaign's brilliance is in interlocking the famous rock personality and the network logo.

✦ IBM ad, based on Chaplin's Little Tramp character and created by Lord, Geller, Federico, and Einstein, brings into question whether it is legal to use either the real or stage identities of public figures in advertising.

✦ Perrier "Earth's First Soft Drink" print ad and TV commercial is created by Waring & LaRosa, illustrated and animated by R. O. Blechman.

## EDUCATION

✦ April Greiman becomes director of Visual Communications program at the California Institute of the Arts.

✦ Domus Academy, Milan, is founded.

✦ First MFA/Illustration program at the School of Visual Arts, New York, is founded by Marshall Arisman.

## BIRTHS AND DEATHS

Alberto Vargas dies.
Bea Feitler dies.
Bernáth Aurél dies.
Bernice Fitz-Gobbon dies.
Joyce Hall dies.
Louis Aragon dies.
Vladimir Stenberg dies.
William Bernbach dies.
John Cheever dies.

## CONSUMABLES

☂ Apple introduces Lisa, the first PC with GUI (graphical user interface).

☂ First compact disc players are launched in Japan by Philips and Sony.

☂ Home Shopping Network is launched.

☂ Lotus 1-2-3 is developed by Mitch Kapor and Jonathan Sachs. Introduced at Comdex trade show, it is the first integrated package of office functions in one program.

## ARTS AND CULTURE

♣ Disney releases *Tron*, one of the first films to use computer-generated graphics.

♣ Martha Stewart Living Omnimedia is founded—the empire begins.

♣ Maya Lin's Vietnam War Memorial is erected.

♣ Ridley Scott, TV commercial director, directs the futuristic film *Blade Runner*, based on Philip K. Dick's novel.

## BIG BUSINESS

🏛 Adobe Systems is founded in Palo Alto, California, helps launch desktop publishing. John E. Warnock, cofounder, is the firm's first chairman.

## INDUSTRIAL DESIGN

⚓ Hans Hollein designs Aircraft Carrier silver tea and coffee service for Alessi.

## TECHNOLOGY

⚑ Hewlett-Packard adopts the $3^{1}/_{2}$-inch floppy drive, the first significant company to distribute the drives for general use.

## TYPE

✦ Adrian Frutiger designs Versailles typeface.

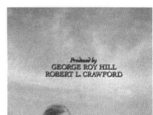

MTV advertisement by George Lois

*The World According to Garp* film title

# 19**83**

## GRAPHIC ARTS

✦ 1984 [Los Angeles] Olympic Games poster is designed by April Greiman and Jayme Odgers.

✦ *Blueprint* begins publication in England.

✦ Condé Nast revives *Vanity Fair* for which the late Bea Feitler had designed the prototype.

✦ David Carson art-directs *Transworld Skateboarding* (through 1987).

✦ Edward R. Tufte designs and publishes *The Visual Display of Quantitative Information.*

✦ First caucus on design history takes place at the College Art Association, Philadelphia.

✦ Gary Panter's comic character "Jimbo" appears on the cover of *RAW.*

✦ Keith Ablitt reformats *Design* magazine.

✦ Louise Fili designs Marguerite Duras's memoir *The Lover,* a silhouetted portrait of the author framed by an elegant, custom-designed shaded sans-serif typeface, which inspires other jacket designers to use similar letterforms.

✦ Malcolm Garrett teams up with Kasper de Graaf to launch Assorted Images.

✦ Neville Brody designs Fetish's album cover *The Last Testament for Fetish.*

✦ Pierre di Scullio publishes *Qui Résiste* (nine issues as of 1997).

✦ R/Greenberg Associates design film title sequence for *The Dead Zone.*

✦ Ron English, "guerilla" billboard artist, begins a campaign of social satire that includes such billboards as *Censorship Is Good Because* (1990), *The New World Order* (1990), *Smooth Character* (1994), and more.

✦ Rubik Studio, Budapest, is founded.

✦ Sussman/Prejza & Co. begin designing the 1984 Summer Olympics environmental graphics.

✦ Takenobu Igarashi begins a ten-year project designing his Poster Calendars, first five years for MoMA, New York City, and the next five years for the Alphabet Gallery, Tokyo (through 1993).

✦ Talking Heads' *Speaking in Tongues* wins a Grammy award for the best album package, art direction is by Robert Rauschenberg for Sire/Warner Bros.

✦ *The First Symposium on the History of Graphic Design: Coming of Age* is sponsored by the Rochester Institute of Technology and chaired by Roger Remington and Barbara Hodik.

✦ Vaughn Oliver and Nigel Grierson join the staff of British recording company 4AD and credit their work as Envelope XX (until 1987).

✦ Walter Bernard, former art director of *Time,* and Milton Glaser, cofounder of Push Pin Studios, form WBMG, New York, a magazine and newspaper design consultancy.

✦ While still studying photography at the University of California/Berkeley, before founding *Emigre* magazine, Rudy VanderLans designs a poster for the 20/20 gallery.

✦ William Longhauser designs *Postmodern* poster for an exhibition of Michael Graves's work.

✦ Dallas Zoo logo is designed by Richards, Sullivan, Brock & Associates.

✦ Milton Glaser designs the visual identity and packaging program for Grand Union supermarkets.

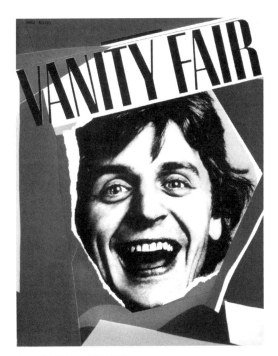

Cover of pilot issue of *Vanity Fair*

## ADVERTISING

♣ Bartles & Jaymes Wine Cooler TV commercial, featuring two elderly brothers sitting on their front porch rambling on about the cooler, introduces the tag line "We Thank You for Your Support." It is created by Ogilvy & Mather agency and the production company Pytka.

## ARCHITECTURE

✵ I. M. Pei's building of the Grand Louvre Phase II, Paris, begins.

## BIRTHS AND DEATHS

Allen Hurlburt dies.
Barney Bubbles commits suicide.
Charles Peignot dies.
Hans Neuburg dies.
Joan Miró dies.
Nikolaus Pevsner dies.
R. Buckminster Fuller dies.
Roger Excoffon dies.
Rudolph Belarski dies.
Willy Fleckhaus dies.
Alfred Andriola dies.

## CONSUMABLES

🕊 Cabbage Patch Kids are introduced.
🕊 Compaq Computer Corporation introduces the first PC clone which uses the same software as the IBM PC.
🕊 First general-interest CD-ROM product, *Grolier's Electronic Encyclopedia*, is released.
🕊 Microsoft Word is introduced by Microsoft.

Cover of *Jimbo*

## ARTS AND CULTURE

♠ *Design in America: The Cranbrook Vision, 1925–1950* exhibition is held at Detroit Institute of Arts.
♠ Final episode of *M*A*S*H*.
♠ Massimo Vignelli publishes the essay "Call for Criticism," a plea for serious critical analysis of graphic design as in other design and architecture disciplines.
♠ *Time* magazine names the computer as Man of the Year.

## INDUSTRIAL DESIGN

⚓ First M&Co. watch goes on sale.
⚓ Colorcore is launched by Formica.

## TECHNOLOGY

⚶ American and French scientists identify AIDS virus.
⚶ Cell phone network starts in the United States.
⚶ Screen interface for MacPaint is developed.

## TYPE

♣ Linotype develops Neue Helvetica, with eight weights, each with italic, extended, and condensed versions.

M&Co. clock

# 19**84**

* Daniel Pelavin designs logotype for Dr. Trout's Elixir.
* Paula Scher designs identity program for Manhattan Records based on Mondrian's *Broadway Boogie Woogie*.

## GRAPHIC ARTS

* Children's Defense Fund poster *The One on the Left Will Finish High School Before the One on the Right* is created by Fallon, McElligott.
* Dugald Stermer designs the 1984 Los Angeles Olympic Medal featuring Robert Miles Runyan's 1980 "Star in Motion" logo.
* Icons for 128k Macintosh computer are developed by Susan Kare, graphic designer, and Bill Adkinson, computer programmer.
* Joost Swarte, Dutch cartoonist, designs postage stamps for the PTT in Holland.
* National Geographic uses its first and only hologram on its cover.
* Paul Davis founds Paul Davis Studio, New York.
* Paula Scher and Terry Koppel open Koppel and Scher, New York.
* Rudy VanderLans, Zuzana Licko, Marc Susan, and Menno Meyjes found *Emigre* magazine (the name coined by Meyjes) as a tabloid featuring international artists and their art. The first printing is five hundred copies.
* Tamotsu Yagi emigrates to the United States and introduces Asian aesthetic sensibility to American design.
* *The Hot House*, a survey of Italian "New Wave" design, is published by Andrea Branzi.
* Vigon Seireeni studio is founded in California by Jay Vigon and Richard Seireeni, provides innovative graphics for the fashion industry.

## ADVERTISING

* "1984" Apple Macintosh TV commercial appears, conceived by Chiat/Day Agency, directed by Ridley Scott, and produced by Fairbanks Films.
* Bob Geldof's Band Aid single "Do They Know It's Christmas" raises 10 million pounds sterling in a matter of months, with a cover design by Peter Blake.

* Nynex logo is designed by Lippincott & Margulies.
* Reagan for President ad "It's Morning Again in America" is designed by Tuesday Team.
* *Rolling Stone* "Perception/Reality" print ad is created by Fallon, McElligott, and Rice. It attempts to position the magazine as mainstream and unhinges the perception that it is radical or underground.
* Wendy's "Where's the Beef?" TV commercial is created by Dancer Fitzgerald Sample agency, Sedelmaier Productions.

Cover of *Emigre* magazine

## EDUCATION

🙠 *Design Issues: A Journal of History, Theory, and Criticism* is founded by design historians at the School of Art and Design and the Department of Art History, University of Illinois, Chicago.

🙠 The Lubalin Study Center is established at the Cooper Union, New York. George Sadek is the director until 1992.

## BIRTHS AND DEATHS

Anthony Froshaug dies.
Herbert Matter dies.
Ray Kroc dies.
Rosser Reeves dies.
Willem Sandberg dies.

## CONSUMABLES

🕊 Apple Computer launches the Macintosh, the first successful mouse-driven computer with a graphical user interface. Macintosh screen fonts, the earliest bitmapped fonts, are designed by Susan Kare for Apple.

🕊 Chrysler launches the Minivan.

🕊 HP LaserJet, first desktop laser printer is produced by Hewlett-Packard. (Xerox developed a laser printer in 1977 but it was too expensive to produce. Canon developed a printer engine in 1983 that sold for about $1,000. Hewlett-Packard used this engine to produce the first desktop laser printer.)

🕊 Philips and Sony announce the release of the CD-ROM.

## ARTS AND CULTURE

♣ Michael Eisner becomes chairman and CEO of Walt Disney Productions.

♣ Number of host computers connected to the Internet breaks one thousand.

♣ *Utne Reader* begins publication.

♣ Walker Art Center's *Twentieth Century Poster: Design of Avant-Garde* exhibition goes on tour, becomes integral resource for historical roots of graphic design.

♣ William Gibson publishes his novel *Neuromancer* in which he coins the term "cyberspace" as "A consensual hallucination experienced daily by billions of legitimate operators in every nation. . . ." He is strongly influenced by John Shirley, who created a genre of fiction known as "cyberpunk," a dark, complex future filled with intelligent machines, computer viruses, and paranoia.

## INDUSTRIAL DESIGN

✚ Robert Venturi designs "Queen Anne" tables and chairs for Knoll.

## POLITICS

🏹 AT&T monopoly is broken up into Baby Bells.

🏹 Geraldine Ferraro is the first woman to run for vice president.

🏹 Ronald Reagan is reelected.

## TECHNOLOGY

⚔ First one-megabyte memory chip is introduced.

⚔ Internet Domain Name System (DNS) is introduced.

## TYPE

♣ Carol Twombly designs Mirarae typeface.

♣ Neville Brody designs Typeface Two.

# 19**85**

## GRAPHIC ARTS

✦ Kenneth Carbone and Leslie Smolan found Carbone Smolan Associates.

✦ Art Chantry publishes *Instant Litter: Concert Posters from Seattle Punk Culture*, the first documentary record of the decade of Punk graphics.

✦ *Design Quarterly 130* features a double issue, Wolfgang Weingart on teaching typography at the Basel School of Design, Switzerland, and Armin Hofmann on "Thoughts on the Study of Making Visual Signs" at the Basel School of Design and Yale School of Art.

✦ Design Writing Research, a design and writing partnership, is founded by J. Abbott Miller and Ellen Lupton in New York.

✦ Duffy Design Group is founded by Joe Duffy with Charles S. Anderson in Minneapolis.

✦ *Elle* (U.S.) begins publication.

✦ First issue of *MacWorld*, devoted to news about the Macintosh computer, appears.

✦ Kazumasu Nagi designs poster for the 100th anniversary of the Tokyo Prefecture.

✦ *L.A. Style* begins publication. M&Co.'s Alex Isley designs the album cover *Lost in the Stars: The Music of Kurt Weill*.

✦ *MacUser* begins publication.

✦ Massimo Vignelli's designs *Harper's Illustrated Handbook of Dogs*.

✦ Max Kisman works with Louis Rosseto on the pre-*Wired* "Language Technology" magazine and posters for the Paradiso concert hall in Amsterdam.

✦ Max Kisman, pioneer in development of digital technology for graphic design, designs Red Cross stamps for the Dutch PTT.

✦ *Newsweek* is redesigned by Roger Black.

✦ Paul Rand publishes *A Designer's Art*, his first book since *Thoughts on Design* in 1946, a collection of essays on his design process.

✦ Paula Scher designs Swatch Watch USA poster, a parody of Herbert Matter's "*Schweiz: Wirderferien-doppelte Ferien*," 1934.

✦ Regiz Pagniez becomes art director of *Elle*.

✦ Seymour Chwast becomes the director of the Push Pin Group.

✦ Shoshin Society poster series commemorating the bombing of Hiroshima, includes the work of over twenty designers and illustrators.

✦ *Spin* magazine begins publication.

✦ William Drenttel cofounds Drenttel Doyle Partners with designers Stephen Doyle and Tom Kluepfel.

✦ Words+Pictures for Business+ Culture is founded by P. Scott Makela and Laurie Haycock Makela.

✦ Zone Books, an independent press, is founded by Jonathan Crary, Hal Foster, Sanford Kwinter, Michele Feher, with designer Bruce Mau.

✦ Chermayeff & Geismar design Rockefeller Center, New York, logo.

✦ Paul Rand designs Yale University Press logo, and "eyechart" poster with Yale bulldog in place of letters.

✦ Robert Nakata, a student at Cranbook Academy, "deconstructs" the Heintz logo. This project symbolizes the launch of Deconstruction as a graphic design mannerism.

✦ *How* magazine, a magazine about graphic design business, started by R. C. Publications in New York.

✦ First issue of *Step-by-Step Graphics,* a magazine that addresses graphic designers and illustrators interested in career development.

✦ *Mediamatic*, a Dutch magazine, focuses on art and media in relation to the advances brought about by technoculture (ceases publication in 1999).

Swatch watches poster by Paula Scher

Typography by Wolfgang Weingart

## ADVERTISING

❦ VH1 is launched. Art director of identity and off-air promotion is Cheri Dorr.

❦ Bartles & Jaymes ad featuring "Frank and Ed" is developed by Hal Riney & Partners.

❦ Bill Backer sells Backer & Spielvogel to Saatchi & Saatchi for $100 million.

❦ John Hancock Financial Services "Real Life, Real Answers" TV commercial is created by Hill, Holliday, Cosmopulos agency and produced by Pytka.

## ARCHITECTURE

🕏 MIT Media Laboratory officially opens in the Wiesner Building, designed by I. M. Pei.

## BIRTHS AND DEATHS

Georg Trump dies.
Herbert Bayer dies.
Jack Tinker dies.
Marc Chagall dies.
Robert Hunter Middleton dies.
Tapio Wirkkala dies.
Tomás Gonda dies.
Chester Gould dies.

## CONSUMABLES

➤ Bill Gates introduces Windows, an operating environment with a GUI (graphical user interface).

➤ New Coke is introduced. Consumers protest, and it is quickly replaced with Classic Coke.

➤ Nintendo home entertainment system is introduced.

## ARTS AND CULTURE

♠ Aldus introduces its PageMaker program for use on the Macintosh computers, launching interest in desktop publishing.

♠ Barbara Kruger designs "alternative" billboard titled *Surveillance Is Your Busy Work.*

♠ Charles Saatchi founds his private museum in London.

♠ Christo wraps Pont Neuf, Paris.

♠ Ellen Lupton is appointed curator of the Herb Lubalin Study center of Design and Typography at the Cooper Union. Curates her first exhibit: *Herb Lubalin 1918–1981.*

♠ The term "virtual reality" is coined to describe a realistic simulation of an environment through high-speed, three-dimensional computer graphics created by using interactive software and hardware.

♠ Voyager Company, the pioneer of educational CD-ROM products, is founded by Bob Stein in New York.

## BIG BUSINESS

🏛 Steve Jobs leaves Apple Computer to found NeXT, the educational computer.

## TECHNOLOGY

⚡ Adobe Postscript, a programming language that describes the appearance of the printed page, is introduced by Adobe Systems, San Jose, California.

⚡ American TV networks begin satellite distribution to affiliates.

⚡ Stephen M. Case develops on-line services for Apple.

⚡ Synthetic text-to-speech computer pronounces 20,000 words.

## TYPE

♣ Charles Bigelow designs Lucida and Pellucida typefaces.

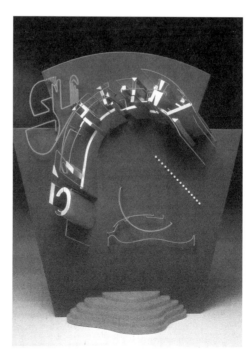

*Deconstruction*
by Robert Nakata

# ¹⁹86

## GRAPHIC ARTS

✦ April Greiman designs *Design Quarterly #133* entirely on the Macintosh computer, marking the first significant use of Macintosh tools.

✦ Carbone Smolan designs signage for the Louvre, Paris.

✦ James McMullan begins a long tenure designing illustrative posters for the theater at Lincoln Center. His first is for *House of Blue Leaves* by John Guare.

✦ Kit Hinrichs joins Pentagram, establishes San Francisco office.

✦ *MAUS Part I* by Art Spiegelman is published by Pantheon Books, New York.

✦ Max Kisman cofounds *TYP/Typografisch Papier.*

✦ Michele De Lucchi opens Studio De Lucchi.

✦ Miles Davis's *Tutu* wins Grammy award for the best album package. The art director is Eiko Ishioka for Warner Bros.

✦ R. D. E. Oxenaar designs the 250-guilder note.

✦ *Spy* magazine publishes its first issue, the original format by Stephen Doyle with art direction by Alexander Isley.

✦ The first School of Visual Arts "Modernism & Eclecticism: A History of American Graphic Design" symposium is held (director Steven Heller, codirector Richard Wilde).

✦ Tibor Kalman and Alexander Isley design poster for the first AIGA Humor Show which intentionally looks like a printer's make-ready.

✦ Walter Herdeg sells *Graphis* to Martin Pederson, the magazine office relocates from Zurich to New York City.

✦ Chermayeff & Geismar streamline the NBC Peacock.

✦ Hanna Winery label is designed by the office of Michael Manwaring.

✦ Paul Rand designs logo for Steve Job's NeXT computer company. The logo is presented to the client in a booklet designed and written by Rand that shows the evolution of his ideas.

✦ Quay & Quay Design Consultants, London, design logo for Adplates Group.

## ADVERTISING

❧ "This Is Your Brain on Drugs" series of TV commercials metaphorically, though graphically, showing the effects of narcotics, is created by Keye/Donna/Pearlstein agency and produced by Pytka.

❧ Bozell & Jacobs merges with Kenyon & Eckhardt.

❧ Burger King "Herb" campaign is a big flop.

![MAUS The Honeymoon — Chapter Two]

*Maus,* as it appeared in *RAW*

❧ California Raisins "I Heard It through the Grapevine" TV commercial is created by Foote, Cone & Belding agency and Will Vinton Productions.

❧ Needham Harper Worldwide, BBD&O International and Doyle Dane Bernbach merge to create Omnicom Group, the largest advertising agency in the world.

❧ Robert Jacoby sells Bates to Saatchi brothers for $507 million.

## BIRTHS AND DEATHS

Carlo L. Vivarelli, Swiss graphic designer, dies.
Dr. Robert Leslie dies.
Francois Truffaut dies.
Georgia O'Keeffe dies.
Henry Moore dies.
Jean Genet dies.
Paul Colin dies.
Raymond Loewy dies.

Catalog cover for Emigre Graphics

**CONSUMABLES**

- Adobe Illustrator, a vector (point)-based drawing program using Bézier curves, is introduced.
- Altys introduces Fontographer for personal computers.
- First nicotine chewing gum, Nicoret, is manufactured by Pharmacia Les Therapeutics AB in Sweden.
- Pay-per-view television is launched.

**ARTS AND CULTURE**

- Barbara Kruger designs the billboard "We Don't Need Another Hero," a commentary on gender myths and distinctions.
- David King publishes *Trotsky: A Photographic Biography*.
- Ellen Lupton, curator of the Herb Lubalin Study Center of Design and Typography, inaugurates (all in one year) an ongoing program of unique analytical exhibits, including "Meta-Metafont," which explores the early computer language for typefaces, "Global Signage: Semiotics and the Language of International Pictures," and "Massimo Vignelli: Rationalism in Graphic Design."
- *Instant Design: 1966–1986*, a retrospective of the work of Terry Jones, is staged in Tokyo, Italy, and London (through 1987).
- Keith Haring and Jenny Holzer design three untitled billboards in Vienna.
- *The Machine Age in America 1918–1941* exhibition is mounted at the Brooklyn Museum, which documents the era of Streamline design.

**INDUSTRIAL DESIGN**

- Classico pasta sauce packaging is designed by Charles S. Anderson and Haley Johnson.
- Simon Doonan joins Barneys as a window dresser, creates fantasy worlds behind glass.
- Zolo playsculpture, three-dimensional, interconnecting abstract shapes in bright postmodern colors (a PM Mr. Potato Head), is designed and marketed by Higashi Glaser Design.

**POLITICS**

- AIDS Memorial Quilt project, "The Names Project," is directed by Cleve Jones.
- Mikhail Gorbachev introduces his policies of *glasnost* and *perestroika* (openness and restructuring).

**TECHNOLOGY**

- Battery-powered vehicle (C5) is invented by Clive Sinclair.
- Programmed pacemaker is introduced by Biotronik.
- Wireless pocket-sized telephone is introduced.

**TYPE**

- Adrian Frutiger designs Centennial typeface.
- Zuzana Licko designs Oakland, Emigré, Emperor, Matrix, Modula Sans, and Universal typefaces.

Cover of *Spy* magazine

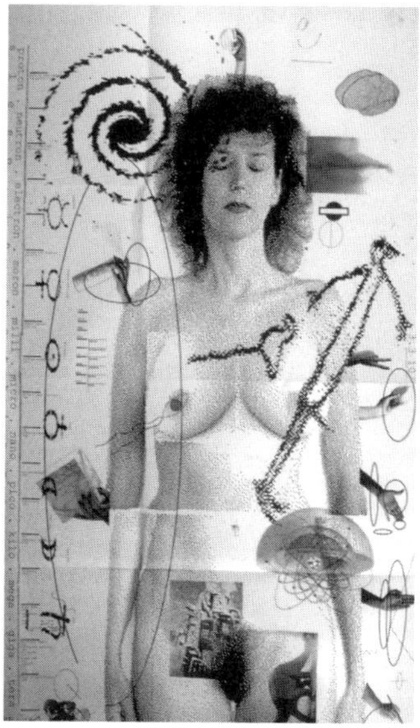

*Design Quarterly* by April Greiman

Billboard by Barbara Kruger

# 19**87**

## GRAPHIC ARTS

✦ Why Not Associates are established by Andrew Altman, David Ellis, and Howard Greenhalgh.

✦ Access Guides for cities around the world produced by Richard Saul Wurman, a series of books featuring user-friendly charts, maps, and graphs.

✦ Carol Devine Carson becomes art director at Alfred A. Knopf and hires designers Chip Kidd, Archie Ferguson, and Barbara de Wilde. Together they create a distinctive look through new typography and photographic fragmentation.

✦ Clement Mok founds Clement Mok Designs, Los Angeles.

✦ Deborah Ross and Nina Saxon design film title sequence for *Tin Men*.

✦ Edward Fella designs more than sixty posters for Detroit Focus Gallery (through 1990).

✦ Erik Spiekermann publishes *Rhyme & Reason: a Typographic Novel*, the English version of his *Ursache & Wirkung: ein Typografischer Roman*.

✦ Fred Woodward, formerly of *Texas Monthly* and *Regardie's*, becomes art director of *Rolling Stone*. Gail Anderson becomes deputy art director.

✦ Lorraine Louie, book designer, designs "Vintage Contemporaries" paperback book series (through 1980s) and, using pastel colors and undulating decorative shapes, creates a visual code for baby boomers: "yuppiebacks" paperback novels.

✦ Neville Brody becomes the art director of *Arena* (through 1990). In this magazine he seeks to cool down the frenzy of contemporary design by concentrating on a minimal, nondecorative typography, and this develops into a more expressive, painterly approach.

✦ Neville Brody opens his own London studio.

✦ *Pacific Wave: California Graphic Design* is published with cover design by John Hersey.

✦ Paul Peter Piech, designer, and Gustavo Espinosa, Columbian photographer, collaborate on the posters for Amnesty International's "Abolish Torture" exhibition.

✦ Paul Rand is awarded the Florence Prize for Visual Communication. He is the first recipient in the field of graphic design.

✦ R/Greenberg Associates designs film title sequence for *The Untouchables*.

✦ Robbie Conal, a painter and designer, initiates guerrilla-style posters protesting Reagan and Bush.

✦ Roger Black forms Roger Black Incorporated and designs newspapers and magazines internationally.

✦ Sub Pop Records is founded in Seattle by Bruce Pavitt and Jonathan Poneman, with art director Art Chantry.

✦ *Visible Language* publishes a special issue on "The Avant Garde and the Text," edited by Stephen Foster.

## ADVERTISING

♪ "Lying Joe Isuzu" TV commercial for Isuzu automobiles is created by Jerry Della Femina, McNamee WCRS, Inc. agency, Travisano DeGiacomo Films, production.

♪ American Express "Membership Has Its Privileges" print ad is created by Ogilvy & Mather.

♪ Cliff Freeman creates Little Caesars' "Pizza! Pizza!" TV commercial.

♪ KRON-TV, San Francisco, is the first major-market station to air a condom commercial.

♪ Martin Sorrell WPP Group, London, stuns world with his $566 million "hostile" takeover of J. Walter Thompson Co.

♪ NYNEX Yellow Pages TV commercial is created by Chiat/Day agency and Koetz & Company, production company.

♪ Restaurant Florent identity and advertising, designed by M&Co., introduces raw vernacular elements.

Poster by Robbie Conal

✣ Saatchi & Saatchi merges Backer & Spielvogel with Bates to form Backer Spielvogel Bates.

✣ *Reklama* (advertising) magazine is published in Moscow with a cover that is a parody of El Lissitzky's well known, yet culturally out of favor, "reading" poster.

## BIRTHS AND DEATHS
André Masson dies.
Andy Warhol dies.
Merald Wrolstad, founding editor of *Visible Language*, dies.
Walter M. Baumhofer dies.

## CONSUMABLES
☂ Campbell's Special Request soups are introduced.

☂ HyperCard, designed by Apple engineer William Atkinson, is introduced, a system tool that simplifies development of in-house applications.

☂ Snapple iced tea is introduced.

## ARTS AND CULTURE
♠ A. C. Nielsen introduces "people meter," replacing its diary system.

♠ Black Monday. The stock market drops 22.6 percent.

♠ Cable industry is deregulated by the U.S. government.

♠ Cartoon Art Museum is established, with an endowment from Charles M. Schulz, in San Francisco.

♠ Van Gogh *Irises* sells for $49 billion.

## BIG BUSINESS
🏛 Rupert Murdoch launches Fox Broadcasting Co.

## INDUSTRIAL DESIGN
⚘ Ralph Lauren Chaps packaging, in which vintage stock images are the key visual elements, is designed by the Duffy Design Group.

## TECHNOLOGY
⚡ Digital audiotape is introduced.

⚡ Genetic fingerprinting is introduced, discovered by Dr. Alec J. Jeffreys of Leicester University, England.

Most of the minuscule forms were antici
Most of the minuscule forms wer
Most of the minuscule for
Most of the minuscule f
Most of the minuscu
Most of the minus
Most of the min
Most of the minuscule forms were anticipat
Most of the minuscule forms were a
Most of the minuscule forms

Stone type family specimen

## TYPE
❦ Matthew Carter designs Charter typeface.

❦ Summer Stone designs ITC Bodoni.

❦ Sumner Stone design Stone Family of type.

Advertisement for Restaurant Florent by M&Co.

Cover of *Reklama* magazine

# 19**88**

## GRAPHIC ARTS

✦ Alexander Isley opens his own studio, Alex Isley Design, New York.

✦ April Greiman designs the cover for *Workspirit,* the Vitra Design Journal.

✦ *Beach Culture* magazine, designed by David Carson, becomes a showcase for his typographic experiments which are based, in part, on Macintosh constraints and effects.

✦ Gran Fury, anti-AIDS activist design collective, designs "Kissing Doesn't Kill" which is posted on the sides of buses.

✦ Gunter Rambow, designer/photographer, and Michael van de Sand, photographer, create theater poster for *Sudafrikanisches Roulette.*

✦ Juan Gatti designs the film title sequence for *Women on the Verge of a Nervous Breakdown.*

✦ John Wozencroft with Neville Brody publishes a treatise on the evils of corporate design culture in the *Guardian,* London.

✦ M&Co. creates type-driven video for the Talking Heads' *(Nothing But) Flowers,* in which the lyrics appear on the screen and move both in sync with the tune and the meaning of the lyric.

✦ Museum of Modern Art "Modern Poster" exhibition poster is designed by April Greiman.

✦ Patrick Coyne succeeds his father, Richard Coyne, as editor of *Communication Arts* magazine (*CA*).

✦ Sharon Helmer Poggenpohl assumes the editorship of *Visual Language.*

✦ Tibor Kalman is guest editor for a special issue of *ID* magazine dedicated to the new wave in graphic design in which all the designer/writers design their own pages.

✦ Vaughn Oliver launches his own studio, called v23, in London.

✦ Woody Pirtle joins Pentagram New York.

✦ Il Fornaio Bakery identity is designed by Michael Mabry Design, influenced by art deco Italian posters.

✦ Javier Mariscal designs Cobi mascot for the Barcelona Olympics.

## ADVERTISING

✦ Saul Bass designs the new YWCA trademark.

✦ Madonna's Pepsi-Cola commercial is pulled by BBD&O after one airing due to controversy over the "Like a Prayer" music video.

✦ Motel 6 ad "We'll Leave a Light on for You" is created by the Richards Group.

✦ Nike ad "Just Do It" with Michael Jordan is created by Wieden & Kennedy.

✦ Steuben Glass "The Clearest Form of Expression" print ad is created by Doyle Graf Mabley.

✦ WPP acquires the Ogilvy Group for $864 million, the highest price ever paid for an agency.

## BIRTHS AND DEATHS

Alec Issigonis dies.

Charles Addams dies.

Gerd Arntz dies.

Ray Eames dies.

Richard P. Lohse dies.

Wieland Herzfelde dies.

Milton Caniff dies.

## CONSUMABLES

✦ Canon Color Laser Copier is introduced.

✦ Video Walkman is developed by Sony.

**Cover of *Beach Culture* by David Carson**

## ARTS AND CULTURE

♠ CDs outsell vinyl records.

♠ China has eight hundred advertising agencies (in 1979 there were ten).

♠ Keith Haring designs the billboard "Crack Is Wack."

♠ MoMA mounts Deconstructivist Architecture exhibition.

♠ Neil Young's "This Note's for You" is banned by MTV and later that year is awarded best video by MTV.

♠ Neville Brody is given a ten-year retrospective at the Victoria and Albert Museum, London.

♠ Ninety-eight percent of households in the United States have TV sets.

## BIG BUSINESS

🏛 McDonald's plans to open twenty outlets in Moscow.

🏛 PepsiCo signs a deal to open two Pizza Huts in Moscow.

🏛 Time Inc. and Warner Communications merge (worth $14 billion).

## POLITICS

🏃 First world conference on AIDS is held.

🏃 George Bush is elected forty-first president.

🏃 Guerrilla Girls launch an ongoing campaign against inequity in the art world, which includes the billboard, *First They Want to Take Away a Woman's Right to Choose, Now They Are Censoring Art.*

## TECHNOLOGY

⚡ First computer morphing is introduced by Industrial Light & Magic in the film *Willow.*

## TYPE

♣ Zuzana Licko designs Modula Serif typeface.

**WOMEN IN AMERICA EARN ONLY 2/3 OF WHAT MEN DO. WOMEN ARTISTS EARN ONLY 1/3 OF WHAT MEN ARTISTS DO.**

A PUBLIC SERVICE MESSAGE FROM **GUERILLA GIRLS** CONSCIENCE OF THE ART WORLD

Advertisement by the Guerilla Girls

Spread from *Beach Culture*

# 19**89**

## GRAPHIC ARTS

✦ "Typography as Discourse" poster for Cranbrook Academy of Art is designed by Allen Hori.

✦ AIGA National Conference, "Dangerous Ideas," cochaired by Tibor Kalman and Milton Glaser, is the first design conference to address issues of social responsibility.

✦ Bathhouse Theatre, Seattle, poster for *Macbeth* is designed by Art Chantry, one of a series of posters Chantry designed for the Seattle cultural scene that exemplifies the grunge sensibility.

✦ Cao Jie, Chinese book designer, is awarded the gold medal for book design from the International Book Fair in Leipzig.

✦ David Bowie's *Sound + Vision* wins Grammy award for the best album package, art director, Roger Gorman for RyKodisc.

✦ *Emigre No.10* marks the shift from a cultural to a graphic design journal.

✦ Grapus designs a poster for the Human Rights Exhibition for the Bicentenary of the French Revolution.

✦ Lee Clow becomes art director of TBWA/Chiat/ Day, Playa del Rey, California.

✦ Louise Fili opens Louise Fili Ltd., New York.

✦ Marlene McCarty and Tibor Kalman/M&Co. design "Mirth" postcard, which uses type and words in place of objects.

✦ Neville Brody, working with Weiden and Kennedy agency, designs "Just Slam It" campaign for Nike.

✦ Philippe Apeloig designs *L'age typographique* (The Age of Typography) poster.

✦ Richard Eckersley designs *Telephone Book: Technology, Schizophrenia, Electric Speech* by Avital Ronell, an eccentric look at technology and its relation to the philosophy that defines the twentieth century. His design typographically underscores the quirks and fancy of the author's writing style.

✦ The Society of Typographic Arts changes its name to the American Center for Design.

## ADVERTISING

⚞ Calvin Klein introduces all-nude Obsession Perfume ads.

⚞ Eveready Energizer introduces the Energizer Bunny in its "Still Going" TV commercials created by Chiat/Day/Mojo agency and Coppos Films.

⚞ Nike introduces its "Bo Diddley" TV commercial, first of the "Bo Knows" campaign created by Wieden & Kennedy agency and Pytka.

⚞ Oliviero Toscani and Benetton attack global problems through Benetton ad campaign which eschews promoting its product line in favor of journalistic images of war, famine, and AIDS.

⚞ Reebok "Bungee" TV commercial is created by Chiat/Day/Mojo agency and Plu Productions.

⚞ Saturn ad "A Different Kind of Company. A Different Kind of Car" is created by Hal Riney & Partners.

## BIRTHS AND DEATHS

Berthold Wolpe dies.
Charles T. Coiner dies.
Edward Bawden dies.
Finn Juhl dies.
Jay Doblin dies.
Jean Carlu dies.
Marion Harper Jr. dies.
Norman Saunders dies.
Salvador Dali dies.

## CONSUMABLES

🕇 Sony camcorder is introduced.

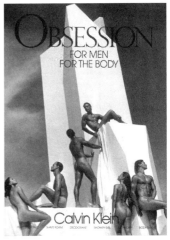

Obession advertisement

United Colors of Benetton Advertisement by Oliviero Toscani

## ARTS AND CULTURE

♠ *Adbusters* magazine is founded by Kalle Lasn to expose and satirize dubious practices in mass advertising through the process of "culture-jamming."

♠ Barbara Kruger designs *Untitled* (*Your Body Is a Battleground*) for use in the women's rights march on Washington, D.C.

♠ Charles S. Anderson leaves the Duffy Design Group and founds Charles S. Anderson Design Company, Minneapolis, Minnesota, and creates the CSA Archive to market his huge collection of vintage stock art.

♠ Pacific Link, fiber-optic cable company, opens.

♠ Walker Art Center, Minneapolis, mounts "Graphic Design in America: A Visual Language History," curated by Mildred Friedman, the first major retrospective exhibition of graphic design in a significant American art museum.

♠ Adobe Systems Inc. invites designers and illustrators to its headquarters in Palo Alto to beta-test its new imaging software tentatively named Photoshop. *Print* magazine calls the event "Camp Adobe."

## BIG BUSINESS

🏛 Dutch PPT is privatized.

🏛 Bill Gates buys the world's largest photo archive (The Bettmann Archive from Otto Bettmann).

## POLITICS

⚡ Berlin Wall is demolished, signaling the collapse of Eastern European Communist regimes.

⚡ Sixteen magazines around the world take part in the "Fax for Freedom" (a protest by fax supporting the Tiananmen Square protesters).

## TECHNOLOGY

⚡ Tim Berners Lee, a researcher at CERN, conceives Hypertext.

## TYPE

✦ Carol Twombly designs Trajan, Lithos, and Charlemagne typefaces for Adobe.

✦ David Berlow cofounds the Font Bureau Inc. with Roger Black.

✦ Erik Van Blockland and Just van Rossum found LettError, Holland, a virtual type foundry, and introduce their animated character "Typoman."

✦ FontShop is founded in Berlin by Erik and Joan Spiekermann.

✦ Gerard Unger designs Cyrano typeface.

✦ Jeffery Keedy designs Keedy Sans typeface.

✦ Max Kisman works in Barcelona designing typefaces for FontShop International and FUSE (through 1992).

✦ Otl Aicher designs Rotis typeface.

✦ Robert Slimbach designs Adobe Garamond and Adobe Garamond Bold typefaces for Adobe.

✦ Zuzana Licko designs Lunatix and Senator typefaces and, with Rudy VanderLans, Oblong and Variex typefaces.

Poster by Barabara Kruger

# 1990

*We can only stand pessimism for so long. The lift, when it comes—maybe starting in 1992, will take us to this new phase of the socioquake. You'll see the consumer psyche veer toward hope. You'll feel the mood rise. We'll be buying, yes, but buying carefully with a new awareness that buying is a political act having ramifications all the way up the chain of life. After the lift, conviction will replace caution.*

**Faith Popcorn, 1991**

## GRAPHIC ARTS

✦ Adobe releases Photoshop, the computer imaging program which allows designers a wide range of photographic options.

✦ Erik Spiekermann begins Meta Design Phase III design studio in Germany.

✦ FontShop International is founded in Berlin by Erik Spiekermann and Neville Brody.

✦ Fabien Baron redesigns *Interview* magazine using bold gothic typefaces with major-scale changes.

✦ Irma Boom, progressive Dutch designer and former designer for the Government Printing Office, opens firm in Amsterdam.

✦ John Wozencroft and Neville Brody start the FUSE project, a digital magazine of type and typography. Wozencroft is editor.

✦ Neville Brody opens FontWorks with Stuart Jensen.

✦ *Octavo*, a magazine of typography and graphic design, is launched by the British design firm 8vo.

✦ P. Scott Makela designs *Cranbrook Design: The New Discourse* poster.

✦ Paul Rand designs the Benjamin Franklin's 200th Anniversary poster, *Celebrating 200 years of his Genius.*

✦ Peter Saville, known for his progressive record album covers, joins Pentagram UK and resigns a year later.

✦ R/Greenberg Associates produces opening film title sequence for *Bonfire of the Vanities.*

✦ *RAW*, edited by Art Spiegelman and Françoise Mouly, is reissued as three digest-size magazines with new content published by Penguin Books (until 1991).

✦ Richard Saul Wurman publishes the *US Road Atlas*, his series of Access Guides mark a new user friendliness towards information design (or, as Wurman has dubbed it, "information architecture").

✦ Rick Poynor founds *EYE* magazine, the London-based magazine of progressive graphic design practice, theory, and history, designed by Stephen Coates.

✦ Robert Newman becomes art director at *Entertainment Weekly.*

✦ Robert Newman becomes art director of *Details.*

✦ Theodor Seuss Geisel (Dr. Seuss) publishes his last book, *Oh the Places You'll Go.*

✦ Tibor Kalman, founder of M&Co., becomes design director of *Interview* magazine, replacing Fabien Baron.

✦ Time Warner's first annual report titled "Why" is designed by Kent Hunter at Gips Balkind. It marks the introduction of post-Modern typographic and pictorial vocabulary to business publications.

✦ Time Warner cable's "eye-ear" logo is designed by Steff Geissbuhler, partner at Chermayeff & Geismar.

*RAW*, paperback edition

## ADVERTISING

❧ Why Not Associates design billboards for Smirnoff Vodka UK, introducing the New Wave to mainstream advertising agency, Young & Rubicam.

## EDUCATION

✒ Sheila Levrant DeBretteville, graphic design and public art activist, becomes chairperson of the graphic design graduate program at the School of Art at Yale University, replacing Alvin Eisenman.

## BIRTHS AND DEATHS

Dick Coyne, dies.

Erté (Roman de Tirtoff), art deco illustrator, dies.

F. H. K. Henrion dies.

Keith Haring dies.

William Paley dies.

## ARTS AND CULTURE

♠ Barbara Kruger's "I Shop Therefore I Am" billboard is exhibited at the Kölnischer Kunstrerein, Cologne.

♠ Edward R. Tufte writes, designs, and self-publishes *Envisioning Information* and sells thousands from his garage through a few well-placed advertisements.

♠ Perry Farrel creates Lollapalooza tour, a celebration of alternative music.

♠ The first McDonald's opens in Moscow.

♠ *The Simpsons*, created by Matt Groening, first airs as short segments on the *Tracy Ullman Show.*

↗ South African dissident Nelson Mandela is freed after twenty-seven-and-a-half years of imprisonment.
↗ Soviet Communists power base weakens and the old guard is forced to allow other political parties to exist.

## INDUSTRIAL DESIGN

↗ Philippe Starck designs "Juicy Salif" lemon squeezer for Alessi.

## POLITICS

↗ Children's Television Act passes, regulates children's programs and advertising. The groundwork is laid by Peggy Charren, Action for Children's Television, Boston.
↗ Reunification of East and West Germany.

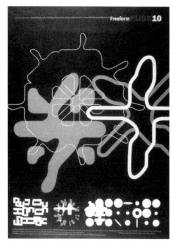

Fuse poster

## TECHNOLOGY

↑ Canon Optic still-video camera records single-frame images onto a floppy disk.

## TYPE

✦ Arcadia typeface is designed by Neville Brody.
✦ Barry Deck designs Template Gothic typeface, distributed through Emigre Fonts. Based on stencil lettering that he saw on a sign in a laundromat, it becomes the emblematic typeface of the decade.
✦ Bob Aufuldish and Kathy Warinner, Web designers, compile fontBoy interactive type catalog (through 1990s).
✦ Carlos Segura designs Dingura typeface for T-26.
✦ Carol Twombly designs Adobe Caslon typeface for Adobe Systems.

✦ Eric van Blokland and Just van Russum, design a so-called self-degrading digital typeface (one that digitally changes from keystroke to keystroke), Beowolf for the FontShop.
✦ ITC Officina typeface is designed by Erik Spiekermann.
✦ Jonathan Barnbrook designs Spindly Bastard typeface.
✦ Manusans typeface is designed by Jeffery Keedy for Emigre Fonts.
✦ P. Scott Makela designs Dead History typeface for Emigre Fonts.
✦ Smokebomb, a digital type foundry, is founded by Nancy Mazzei and Brian Kelly in Brooklyn, New York.
✦ Sumner Stone, formerly type director at Adobe Systems, opens his own type foundry in Palo Alto, California.
✦ Zuzana Licko designs Citizen, Elektrix, Totally Gothic, Totally Glyphic, and Triplex (italic by John Downer) typefaces.

TEMPLATE GOTHIC / REGULAR & BOLD $65

a A b B c C d D e E f F g G h H i I j J k K l L m
M n N o O p P q Q r R s S t T u U v V w W x X y Y
z Z 0 1 2 3 4 5 6 7 8 9 ! ? № ℗ $ & * { } " "
a A b B c C d D e E f F g G h H i I j J k K l I
m M n N o O p P q Q r R s S t T u U v V w W x X
y Y z Z 0 1 2 3 4 5 6 7 8 9 ! ? № ℗ $ & * { } " "

P9yEG

Template Gothic type specimen

Cover of *Octavo* magazine

# ¹⁹91

## GRAPHIC ARTS

✴ Art Chantry designs COCA Season Poster (*The Night Gallery*), which introduces an ersatz industrial catalog style to the already vernacular-based grunge style.

✴ David B. Greenberger publishes zine, the *Duplex Planet*.

✴ *Emigre No.19* "Starting From Zero" issue addresses editor Rudy VanderLans' question: "Does all experimentation in graphic design eventually lead to the simplification of graphic design?" The entire issue is set in one sans-serif typeface—Template Gothic—and text is set flush left, ragged right.

✴ First issue of *Purple*, a youth culture magazine based in Paris, is art-directed by Christophe Bunnquell.

✴ Grapus, the French left-wing design collective that began as Atelier Populair, disbands; members start their own design firms.

✴ Josh Abelon publishes zine, the *Elana Rosa Veiga Torres Newsletter for This World and Beyond*.

✴ Michael Bierut leaves Massimo Vignelli, where he is vice president, and becomes a partner of Pentagram New York.

✴ Michael Mabry designs *Colour* poster for AIGA New York, based on Russian Constructivist palette of colors and forms.

✴ Paula Scher closes Koppel and Scher and joins Pentagram New York.

✴ Plazm Media Collective (includes *Plazm* magazine, Plazm Fonts, Plazm Design Group) is created in Portland, Oregon.

✴ Randy Balsmeyer and Kim Everett design film title sequence for Spike Lee's *Jungle Fever*.

✴ ReVerb, a graphic design studio, is founded in Los Angeles by Lorraine Wild, Whitney Lowe, Somi Kim, Susan Parr, and Lisa Nugent.

✴ Rick Poynor and Edward Booth-Clibborn coedit *Typography Now!* the benchmark collection of "new typography" in the postmodern and deconstructive aesthetic sensibility.

✴ Robert Fisher designs Nirvana's album cover *Nevermind* for Geffen records.

✴ Saul Bass creates the opening titles for Martin Scorsese's *Cape Fear*.

✴ Susanna Sloat publishes zine, *Manhatan Slow Lane* zine, New York.

✴ Tibor Kalman becomes the founding editor of Benetton's *Colors* magazine with photographer Oliviero Toscani (two years later closes M&Co. and moves the magazine to Rome).

✴ Paul Rand designs IDEO Design land Morningstar Investment Advisers logos.

✴ Rick Valicenti designs "Esse," a Gilbert Paper Co. promotion piece, a wild agglomeration of type and color.

✴ Premier issue of *Colors*, a magazine that takes a jaundiced view of war, religion, race, travel, and shopping, founded by Oliviero Toscani and edited by Tibor Kalman.

## ADVERTISING

✴ The *Village Voice* subscription ad "Hell, No, I Don't Want Your Stupid Newspaper" is created by Mad Dogs & Englishmen.

## ARCHITECTURE

✴ Frank Gehry's Guggenheim, Bilboa, Spain, begins construction.

## BIRTHS AND DEATHS

Aaron Burns dies.
Cipe Pineles dies.
Jacqueline S. Casey dies.
Otl Aicher dies.
Richard Hess dies.
Rick Griffin dies in a motorcycle accident.

## CONSUMABLES

✴ Color Classic is introduced by Macintosh, predating the 1998 colorful iMac design.

✴ Windows 3.0 is introduced by Microsoft.

AIDS poster by Gran Fury

## ARTS AND CULTURE

♠ Douglas Coupland publishes *Generation X.*

♠ The loop of red ribbon becomes the visual icon for AIDS. The international symbol of AIDS awareness is first seen on television at the New York 1991 Tony Awards.

♠ VCR, the fastest selling domestic appliance in history, is found in three out of four U.S. households.

## BIG BUSINESS

🏛 Stephen M. Case's work for Apple's on-line services becomes America Online, Dulles, Virginia.

🏛 Ted Turner acquires Hanna-Barbera Cartoons, including their three thousand–episode library, distribution rights, and production facility.

## POLITICS

🏹 AIDS activist group ACT UP launches AIDS Coalition to Unleash Power campaign in Denver, Colorado.

🏹 South Africa ends apartheid.

## TECHNOLOGY

⚓ Apple releases QuickTime media format.

⚓ Morphing by computer is fully exploited in James Cameron's *Terminator 2: Judgment Day.*

⚓ Tim Berners Lee and CERN (the European Laboratory for Particle Physics) release the World Wide Web program.

## TYPE

✤ Erik Spiekermann designs FF Meta typeface for FontShop International.

✤ Erik van Blokland designs FF Erikrighthand typeface for FontShop.

✤ Frank Heine designs Remedy Double typeface for Emigre Fonts (becomes one of the most commonly used digital faces in the mainstream).

✤ Jeffery Keedy designs Hard Times typeface.

✤ Miles Newlyn designs Democratica Bold typeface for Emigre Fonts.

✤ Neville Brody designs Six and Seven typefaces.

✤ Sumner Stone designs Print typeface for *Print* magazine.

✤ Zuzana Licko designs Journal typeface.

Remedy type specimen

# 19**92**

## GRAPHIC ARTS

✦ Alexander Branczyk, cofounder of xplicit ffm, based in Frankfurt, becomes art director of the techno-house magazine *Frontpage*.

✦ Art Spiegelman wins a Pulitzer Prize for *Maus: A Survivor's Tale*. The comic-strip book about his father's life in Nazi Europe began in 1976 as a comic strip. The first book was published in 1986, with part two released in 1991.

✦ Cathy Guisewite receives the Reuben, NCS Cartoonist of the Year award, for her comic strip "Cathy."

✦ Fabien Baron redesigns *Harper's Bazaar*.

✦ Max Kisman begins association with the Dutch graphic design collective Wild Plakken.

✦ Meta Design opens offices in San Francisco.

✦ Mike Mills, skateboard designer, designs CD cover for Deee-Lite's "I Had a Dream" album.

✦ Nicholas Callaway publishes Madonna's *Sex* book designed by Fabien Baron with metal covers and spiral binding wrapped in a silver plastic bag—it sells like hotcakes.

✦ Tina Brown, former editor of the *Tattler* (London) and *Vanity Fair* (New York) becomes editor of the *New Yorker* and begins to make shifts in editorial and art/design policy.

✦ *Greatis*, Russian design and advertising journal published by the Greatis studio in Moscow (ceases publication in 1994).

✦ Micro Ilic introduces typographic pictures—type set and contoured to be read as images, to the *New York Times* Op-Ed page.

## ADVERTISING

✦ Harley-Davidson print ad "It's Not Too Late to Run Away," is created by Carmichael Lynch, an attempt to snare the middle-aged baby boomer with an invitation to the open road.

✦ Knoll stationery standards are developed by Chermayeff & Geismar.

✦ Women's Action Coalition logo is designed by Bethany Johns and Marlene McCarty in New York.

✦ Woody Pirtle designs logo for Fineline Features.

## EDUCATION

✦ John Wozencroft begins teaching at Central St. Martin's School of Art and Design in London and develops a new course for BA in Graphic Design.

## BIRTHS AND DEATHS

Armando Testa dies.
Dom Sylvester Houédard dies.
Emerson Foote dies.
Max Huber dies.

## ARTS AND CULTURE

♪ CNN goes online.

♪ Jean Armour Polly coins the phrase "surfing the Net."

♪ Michelangelo, a computer virus, threatens to infect computers around the world.

♪ Ted Turner launches the Cartoon Network, the world's first twenty-four-hour, all-animation television service.

## POLITICS

↗ Bill Clinton is elected president of the United States.

## TECHNOLOGY

↑ Videophone 2500 introduced by AT&T.

CRACKhouse

AaBbCcDdEeFfGgHhIiJjKkLlMm
NnOoPpQqRrSsTtUuVvWwXxYyZz
0123456789!@#$%^&*()

BRICKHOUSE

AaBbCcDdEeFfGgHhIiJjKkLl
MmNnOoPpQqRrSsTtUuVvWwXx
YyZz0123456789!@#$%^&*()

HOUSEBROKEN

ABCDEFGHIJKLM
NOPQRSTUVWXYZ
0123456789

House Industries type specimens

## TYPE

❧ Andy Cruz designs Roughhouse digital typeface for House Industries.

❧ Erik Spiekermann designs FF Meta, a humanistic sans-serif typeface family (FontShop International).

❧ Jonathan Hoefler designs Didot typeface designed for redesign of *Harper's Bazaar* by Fabien Baron, and Ziggurat family for *Rolling Stone* magazine.

❧ Just van Rossum designs FF Karton typeface.

❧ Myriad Multiple Master typeface—the first multiple master typeface for Adobe Systems—is designed by Robert Slimbach and Carol Twombly, Robert Slimbach designs Poetica typeface.

❧ Sumner Stone designs EndsMeansMends typeface.

❧ Tobias Frere-Jones designs Garage Gothic, based on letterforms used on garage receipts, typeface for FontBureau, Cambridge, Massachusetts.

# HALOGEN LIGHTS
BOLD

## Antifreeze with a cool, minty flavor!
REGULAR

## Metal buckets chock full of nuts and bolts
BOLD

# PIPE WRENCH
BLACK

## Professional & Reliable
BOLD

# MERCHANTS
REGULAR

52 OFFICES CONVENIENTLY LOCATED IN THE TRI-STATE AREA
REGULAR

## Factories and Workrooms
BLACK

# HIGHWAY ROADBLOCK
BOLD

Garage Gothic was derived from numbered tickets given at parking garages. "Irregular contours and rough alignments found on the lettering were retained, albeit restrained" says designer Tobias Frere-Jones. Tickets from other garages suggested a pair of heavier weights, which he formed into the Garage Gothic series; FB 1992.

ABCDEFGHIJKLMNOPQRSTUVWXYZabcdefghijklmnopqrstuvwxyzßffffifflfifl¶$$£¥#ƒ0123456789‰‰¢°=‹·›'"/¿?¡!&
{/}[\]{|}*-‚„‚‹›«»‹›""‚·‗•‡†@®©℗™√♦áàâäãåæçéèêëíìîïñóòôöõøœúùûüÿÁÀÂÄÃÅÆÇÉÈÊËÍÌÎÏÑÓÒÔÖÕØŒÚÙÛÜY

**Garage Gothic type specimen**

# 19**93**

★ Federal Express (FedEx) logo is redesigned by Lindon Gray Leader, Landor Associates.
★ Sagmeister Inc. studio, founded in New York by Stefan Sagmeister, specializes in CD packaging design.

## GRAPHIC ARTS

★ Chip Kidd's dinosaur illustration is used in the logo for Steven Spielberg's thriller *Jurassic Park.*
★ David Carson is the founding designer of *Ray Gun* magazine, which becomes the clarion of both the new music and the new digital typography.
★ Edward Fella designs the poster *Keep the Irregularities Inconsistent.*
★ Gary Koepke begins as *Vibe* magazine design director.
★ House Industries begins, with the original partners of Brand Design Company Wilmington, Delaware.
★ Jane Metcalfe and Louis Rossetto launch *Wired* magazine with John Plunket and Barbara Kuhn as design directors.
★ Lucas de Groot joins MetaDesign, Berlin.
★ Number Seventeen, a New York design studio specializing in on-air TV graphics, is founded by Emily Oberman, formerly of M&Co., and Bonnie Siegler.
★ Paul Rand writes *Design Form and Chaos* published by Yale University Press, New Haven & London, which includes critiques on the chaotic appearance of postmodern graphic design. Critics react to what they perceive as a reactionary attack on younger designers.
★ Saul and Elaine Bass design title sequence for Martin Scorsese's *The Age of Innocence.*
★ Chicago Board of Trade annual report is designed by VSA Partners, Inc., Chicago, notable for its use of "talking" type characterized by scale and color changes to simulate voices.
★ Earth Technology annual report designed by Rigsby Design, Houston, Texas.

## ADVERTISING

❧ Healthtex print ad "You've Got 23 Seconds to Get Your Two-Year-Old from the Sandbox to the Potty. Go" is designed by the Martin Agency.
❧ Nike TV commercial "Barkley of Seville," featuring the basketball star Charles Barkley in an ironic operatic setting, is created by Wieden & Kennedy agency, produced by Pytka.
❧ Paul Rand designs *50 Years of the Warsaw Ghetto Uprising* newspaper ad for Holocaust Remembrance Day using candles to represent the Jews who perished.

## BIRTHS AND DEATHS

Reid Miles dies.
Thomas J. Watson Jr dies.
Harvey Kurtzman dies.

## CONSUMABLES

➤ Consumers buy corals, soft yellows, and yellow-greens. Effects such as pearlescent, iridescent, holographic, and metallic are changing the future of color.
➤ Harvest Burger is introduced.
➤ Progresso Healthy Classics soups are introduced.
➤ SnackWell's cookies and crackers are introduced.

## ARTS AND CULTURE

♣ Bill Clinton and Al Gore get their own e-mail addresses.
♣ The Internet has five million online users worldwide.
♣ *Time* magazine goes online.

Fellaparts dingbat specimen

## TECHNOLOGY

⚡ Mosaic is released (first graphics-supporting Web browser), developed by Marc Abdreessen, Eric Bina, and the National Center for Super-computing Applications (NCSA).

⚡ V-chip is introduced.

## TYPE

❦ Carter and Cone Type Foundry is founded in Cambridge, Massachusetts, and releases Mantinia and Sophia typefaces designed by Matthew Carter.

❦ Edward Fella designs Fella Parts, a collection of abstract designs used as dingbats, for Emigre Fonts.

❦ GarageFonts is founded in Del Mar, California, by David Carson, Betsy Kopshina, and Norbert Schultz.

❦ Jonathan Hoefler designs typefaces Ziggurat & Leviathan for Hoefler Type Foundry, New York.

❦ Neville Brody designs Autosuggestion, an experimental typeface published in *Fuse 9*.

❦ Prototype, digital type foundry, is founded by Charles Wilkin, owner of Automatic Art and Design, in Columbus, Ohio.

❦ Shift, a digital type foundry, is founded by Joshua Distler in San Francisco, California.

❦ Tobias Frere-Jones designs Interstate typeface based on the type used on roadway signs for FontBureau.

Cover and pages from *Ray Gun* by David Carson

# <sup>19</sup>94

Racism poster by James Victore

## GRAPHIC ARTS

✦ Adams Morioka Inc. is founded by Sean Adams and Noreen Morioka.

✦ Art Chantry designs "Kustom Kulture" poster.

✦ *Blam,* first CD-ROM experimental magazine, Eric Swenson and Keith Seward editors, is published by the Voyager Co.

✦ *Blender,* online magazine, is started by Felix Dennis in England.

✦ Hard Werken merges with Ten Cate Bergmans design office to form Inzio communications firm, Amsterdam.

✦ Max Kisman designs for the World Wide Web servers of Dutch progressive public television broadcasting station VPRO-digital and for *HotWired.*

✦ *Maximumrocknroll,* one of many punk zines, is published.

✦ Milton Glaser creates OLD/NEW poster for the School of Visual Arts, where he begins to use narrative texts in a hypertext manner.

✦ Nutrition Facts Label, designed by Burkey Belser, is used on all American food products.

✦ *Racism* poster is designed by James Victore in response to a television feeding frenzy over African-American–Jewish racial conflict in Brooklyn, New York.

✦ Rodney Alan Greenblat designs the graphics for Dazzeloids, CD-ROM for Voyager, New York, a pioneering and visionary, interactive virtual fantasy world.

✦ Tribute to the music of Bob Wills and the Texas Playboys, *Asleep at the Wheel*, wins Grammy award for the best recording package, art director, Buddy Jackson for Liberty.

✦ *Zed* "The Politics of Design" issue is the first design journal to include a CD-ROM.

✦ "Flyer Mania" begins, the enthusiasm for dance party flyers advertising clubs in the United States and Europe.

## ADVERTISING

✦ California Fluid Milk Processor Advisory Board "Got Milk?" TV commercial is created by the agency Goodby, Silverstein & Partners, and the production company Propaganda Films.

✦ Dewar's print ad "You Thought Girls Were Yucky Once, Too" is created by Leo Burnett Company.

✦ The Public Theater identity is redesigned by Pentagram partner Paula Scher, she introduces a vocabulary of "street forms," including old woodtypes and show-card graphics.

✦ William Burroughs is featured in an advertisement for Swag Snowboard Apparel.

## BIRTHS AND DEATHS

Arnold Varga dies.
Ed Cleary dies.
Max Bill dies.
Muriel Cooper dies.
Paul Delvaux dies.
Richard Nixon dies.
Theo Crosby dies.
Theodor Geisel, Dr. Seuss, dies.

## CONSUMABLES

✦ Fruitopia drinks are introduced.

## ARTS AND CULTURE

✦ *Doors of Perception 1,* the first international multimedia conference, takes place in Holland.

✦ First online bank, First Virtual, opens.

Rave flyer

Terry Zwigoff directs the film *Crumb*, about the life of underground cartoonist R. Crumb, launching a sixties subterranean artist as mainstream cult hero.

The *New York Times* goes online. The design director is Ron Louie.

*Wired* magazine goes online with *HotWired*.

World Wide Web Consortium (W3C) is formed.

## BIG BUSINESS

Adobe Systems buys Aldus, the manufacturer of PageMaker.

Amazon.com is founded.

Marc Andressen and Jim Clark form Mosaic Communications Corporation (now Netscape).

Yahoo! is launched by David Filo and Jerry Yang.

## POLITICS

Nelson Mandela is elected president of South Africa.

## TYPE

Alexander Branczyk and Thomas Nagel start publishing their experimental font collection, Face2Face, featuring more than one hundred fonts that challenge possibilities of legibility and PostScript.

Carter and Cone Type issues Big Caslon CC.

Ed Benguiat designs ITC Edwardian Script regular for International Typeface Corporation.

Edwin Utermohlen designs Big Ed and Hey Stupid digital typefaces.

Elliot Earls designs Heimlich Maneuver, Penal Code, and Klieglight typefaces for his Apollo Program type foundry.

Heike Nehl, Sibylle Schlaich, and Heidi Specker at Moniteurs, Berlin, design typefaces for *1000 clubzine*, Front Page, and *Sense*.

Jeremy Dean designs Crackhouse digital typeface for House Industries.

Jonathan Barnbrook designs Exocet typeface, named after the guided missile used by British armed forces in their attacks on Argentina during the Falkland War.

Kristen Faulkner designs Housemaid digital typeface.

Neville Brody proposes "a new typographic brutalism" exemplified by his Freeform font.

Tobias Frere-Jones designs Nobel typeface from a 1929 design by Sjoerd Henrik de Roos, Amsterdam.

Zuzana Licko designs Whirligigs typeface for Emigre Fonts.

Rave flyer

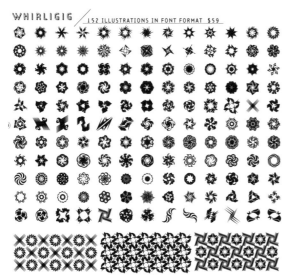

Whrligig dingbat specimen

* Paul Rand designs USSB logotype for early satellite television service, his last logo design.

## ADVERTISING

* ESPN Sports print ad "This Is SportsCenter" is created by Wieden & Kennedy and introduces the sophisticated postmodern design language to sports.
* Little Caesar's Pizza "Training Camp" TV commercial is created by Cliff Freeman & Partners, agency, Propaganda Films, production.
* Maurice and Charles Saatchi leave their agency, as shares plunge 30 percent.
* Saatchi & Saatchi reemerge as newly created Cordiant.
* TBWA and Chiat/Day merge.

## ARCHITECTURE

* Mario Botta designs the San Francisco, California, Museum of Modern Art (SF MoMA).
* United States Holocaust Memorial Museum is designed by Ralph Applebaum Associates.

## GRAPHIC ARTS

* Aaron Rat publishes the zine *Tard Nation.*
* April Greiman designs the Nineteenth Amendment Postage Stamp for the U.S. Postal Service.
* Balsmeyer and Everett design the title sequence for Spike Lee's *Clockers.*
* *Emigre* magazine shrinks its size from tabloid to standard magazine, and its content becomes more critical and theoretical.
* *Factsheet Five,* the zine that chronicles all zines, states that the World Wide Web is "a new definition for zines."
* Garry Trudeau receives the Reuben, NCS Cartoonist of the Year award, for "Doonesbury."
* Kyle Cooper designs title sequence for the movie *Seven,* which introduces scratchy, layered, postmodern typography to film-title design.
* Max Kisman receives audience award at the Design Prize of the City of Rotterdam for his television graphics and animation.
* Paul White designs Bjork's album cover *Post for One Little Indian.*
* Paula Scher's *Bring in da Noise, Bring in da Funk* poster revives a vernacular street poster sensibility.
* Razorfish Studios is founded to specialize in Web design.
* *Salon,* the digizine, premiers with interface designed by Mignon Khargie.
* *Slate,* one of the first successful online magazines, is launched.
* VizAbility CD-ROM is designed by MetaDesign.
* Landor Associates designs the Document Company Xerox trademark.

## BIRTHS AND DEATHS

Bradbury Thompson dies.
Dan Friedman dies.
Ollie Harrington dies.
Walter Herdeg dies.
Walter Landor dies.
Ira Herbert dies.

## ARTS AND CULTURE

* Anthon Beek, Dutch designer, has major retrospective at the Herb Lubalin Study Center of Design and Typography, curated by Ellen Lupton.
* Disney Online is launched, founded by Jake Winebaum, art-directed by Adam Breivis.
* Internet encompasses more than seven million computers and tens of millions users worldwide.
* Laurie Anderson's *Puppet Motel* and Art Spiegelman's *Maus: A Survivor's Tale* are published on CD-ROM by Voyager.

Postage stamp by April Greiman

*Se7en* film titles by Kyle Cooper

♣ Nickelodeon Online is launched on America Online. David Vogler is creative director and executive producer.

## BIG BUSINESS
🏛 Microsoft releases Windows 95.
🏛 Netscape goes public.

## POLITICS
⚐ National Labor Committee (NLC), a New York–based Greenpeace-styled anticorporate advocacy group, is founded by Charles Kernaghan.

## TECHNOLOGY
⚑ Sun Microsystems introduces HOT Java Web browser and the Java programming language.
⚑ *Toy Story* is released, the first full-length feature film created by Pixar Studios entirely by computer animation.

## TYPE
❧ Bob Aulfuldish starts fontBoy digital foundry.
❧ Jonathan Hoefler designs HTF Fetish No. 126 typeface (through 1996).
❧ Lucas de Groot designs Jesus Loves You typeface.
❧ Matthew Carter designs Walker font typeface as the proprietary face of the Walker Art Center in Minneapolis.
❧ Teal Triggs cofounds with Liz McQuiston the Women's Design Research Unit (WD+RU). Projects include the "conceptual typeface" for FUSE, Pussy Galore.
❧ Zuzana Licko designs Soda typeface.

Nickelodeon America Online screen by David Vogler (© Nickelodeon)

Pussy Galore type specimen

# 19**96**

## GRAPHIC ARTS

✦ Cipe Pineles is given, post-humously, AIGA medal for Lifetime Achievement.

✦ Clement Mok Designs becomes Studio Archetype, "information architecture" firm in Los Angeles.

✦ David Byrne's *Feelings* and Lou Reed's *Set the Twilight Reeling* CD packagings are designed by Sagmeister, Inc., with a sophisticated *art brut* sensibility.

✦ Golden Gate National Parks Association posters are designed by Michael Schwab.

✦ Imaginary Forces, a design firm specializing in film title sequences and TV on-air graphics, is founded by Kyle Cooper and Peter Frankfurt in Los Angeles, California. Kyle Cooper/Imaginary Forces designs the film title sequence for *Twister* in which the type flies over the screen as if caught in a tornado.

✦ Martin Neumier founds *Critique*, a journal of design criticism based in Palo Alto, California.

✦ Paul Rand produces *From Lascaux to Brooklyn*, his last monograph, published by Yale University Press, New Haven.

✦ Peter Girardi and John Carlin found Funny Garbage, a design firm specializing in new media and print.

✦ FG designs CDs for Voyager and Web sites for Cartoon Network, Nike, Luka Bop, and others.

✦ Austrian designer Robert Kalina designs first series of euro banknotes for the new European Union (EU) (through 1997).

✦ *Wallpaper*\* magazine comes to America from England as the lifestyle magazine of Generation Next, designed with a neo-Modern simplicity.

✦ Rational Software annual report, Cahan & Associates, is one of many the firm has produced that challenge the conventionality of annual reports through use of handlettering and fragmented photography.

✦ J. Abbott Miller publishes *Dimensional Typography*, a study of the shape of letters in virtual environments, and ignites interest in experimental, amorphic letters.

## ADVERTISING

⚘ Anheuser-Busch Budweiser Beer "Clydesdales" TV commercial is created by DDB Needham, agency, and Propaganda Films, production.

⚘ Jason Kedgely and Tomato design title sequence for Danny Boyle's film adaptation of Irvine Welsh's novel *Trainspotting*.

⚘ Polaroid "See What Develops" print ad is created by Goodby, Silverstein & Partners.

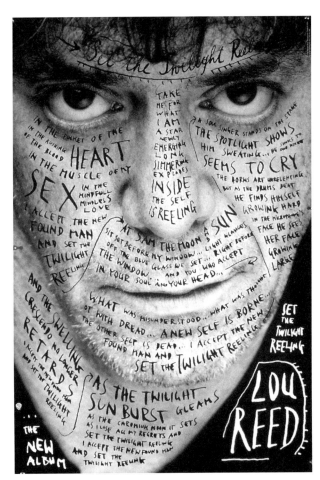

Lou Reed poster by Stefan Sagmeister

🏛 Microsoft releases Internet Explorer 3.0.

🏛 Steve Jobs returns to Apple Computers as chief executive.

## POLITICS

🏹 Bill Clinton is reelected president of the United States.

🏹 President Clinton signs the Telecommunications Act that impacts Internet communications, part of which is Title V, Communications Decency Act.

## EDUCATION

🖎 Katherine McCoy leaves Cranbrook after twenty-three years as co-chair, with Michael McCoy, of the design department.

## BIRTHS AND DEATHS

Josef Müller-Brockmann dies.
Paul Rand dies.
Ralph Eckerstrom dies.
Saul Bass dies.
Vance Packard dies.
Jerry (Jerome) Siegel dies.

## CONSUMABLES

🍟 Lay's Baked Potato Crisps are introduced.

🍟 Palm Pilot goes on the market.

## ARTS AND CULTURE

🎨 International Museum of Cartoon Art is established in Boca Raton, Florida. It is the only museum of its kind, with representation from over fifty countries.

🎨 Number of Internet hosts reaches 12.8 million.

🎨 *Mixing Messages: Graphic Design in Contemporary Culture* exhibit is on display at Cooper Hewitt, Ellen Lupton is curator.

🎨 Senegalese online, the first Internet Café, presents artworks by a group of twenty artists, writers, and musicians, produced by Metiscana.

🎨 Voyager publishes Rick Prelinger's *Our Secret Century: New Media as Historical Intervention* (a twelve-part CD-ROM).

Viscosity type specimen

## TECHNOLOGY

⚡ *NOVA Online* producer, Liesl Clark, from WGBH public television in Boston, sets out for Mount Everest to create *NOVA*'s first-ever "online adventure." The mission documents the making of an IMAX feature film on Everest by the IMAX filmmaking team. (A second expedition in 1997—also by Clark and crew—marked the beginning of real media e-mail through a satellite phone, allowing a Web site to be built and modified daily from Everest. This expedition was the foray into true Web and television convergence for WGBH, Boston.)

⚡ Web TV is introduced.

## TYPE

✦ Gary Hustwit founds Exploding Font Company.

✦ Kathy Warinner and Bob Aufuldish design Viscosity typeface.

✦ Univers Revolved typeface designed by Ji Boyl Lee.

# 19**97**

## Graphic Arts

✦ AIGA mounts "The Greening of Design" competition exhibition focusing on the use of recyclable materials and renewable resources.

✦ Bureau's Marlene McCarty and Donald Moffett design the film title sequence for *The Ice Storm*.

✦ David Carson designs *Blue*, a travel magazine for Generation X, Generation Next, and whomever else is interested.

✦ Edward R. Tufte writes, designs, and publishes *Visual Explanations: Images & Quantities, Evidence and Narrative* and *Visual and Statistical Thinking: Display of Evidence for Decision-Making*.

✦ Emigre Fonts announce their own version of the Bodoni typeface through a poster designed by Massimo Vignelli, with the headline, "It's Their Bodoni."

✦ *Jungle*, a magazine about progressive design and typography, is published in South Korea.

✦ Kemistry, London design firm, is founded by a group of broadcast designers.

✦ Meta Design becomes Germany's largest design company.

✦ *Powers of Ten Interactive (the Eames Process)* is written and designed by Eames Demetrios, and distributed by Pyramid Media.

✦ Rick Poynor, founding editor of *EYE*, resigns after seven years to further pursue his own writing.

✦ *Rock and Roll Hall of Fame and Museum Rock Facts* handbook is designed by Michael Bierut, Pentagram New York, who also designs the interior graphics of the museum designed by I. M. Pei.

✦ Stefan Sagmeister designs *Jambalaya* poster, otherwise known as the "headless chicken poster," for the AIGA biennial conference in New Orleans. The poster is noteworthy for the illustration of a headless chicken and the handwritten (often full of typos) listing of the conference's contents.

✦ Tadanori Yokoo receives Mainchi Art Award, Tokyo.

✦ The Colorado chapter of the AIGA publishes *43 Literacy Posters* featuring work by Kit Hinrichs, Bob Aufuldish, Jilly Simmons, Paula Scher, Michael Mabry, Max Kisman, and others.

✦ The *New York Times* publishes news sections in full color for the first time (after gradually introducing color into its feature sections over the preceding four years).

✦ Tucker Viemeister joins Razorfish as executive vice president of research and development.

✦ Turner Classic Movies Director of the Month title sequence is designed by R/Greenberg Associates.

✦ Yee Haw Industries, a design firm, is founded in Knoxville, Tennessee, by Julie Belcher and Kevin Bradley; their work is influenced by primitive signboards.

Literacy poster, designer, John Bielenberg; photographer, Paul Franz-Moore

🏛 Philip Morris experiences "Marlboro Friday," as shares in the company plunge 23 percent.

## POLITICS

🏃 Communications Decency Act is declared unconstitutional in the case of *Reno vs. ACLU*. (Plaintiffs are persons associated with computer and/or communications industries who publish or post material on the Internet. They challenge two provisions of the CDA directed at Internet communications that might be deemed "indecent" or "patently offensive" for minors, on the grounds that those provisions infringe upon the rights protected by the First Amendment and the Due Process Clause of the Fifth Amendment.)

🏃 National Labor Committee (NLC) organizes rally in New York City called "The Holiday Season of Conscience" using reconfigured, mainstream corporate and product logos as weapons in the war against over-commercialization.

## TYPE

✦ Massimo Vignelli and Emigre Fonts collaborate on Filosofia typeface.

## ADVERTISING

🎣 Cordiant spins off Saatchi & Saatchi and Bates Worldwide into separate companies.

🎣 Mars, Inc. Snickers "Not Going Anywhere for a While?" TV commercial is created by BBD&O, agency, and @radical.media, production company.

🎣 WPP combines the media operation of JWT and O&M to form the Alliance, the largest U.S. media buyer with more than $2 billion billing.

## EDUCATION

✂ First MFA/Design program at the School of Visual Arts, New York, is founded (chairperson Steven Heller).

## BIRTHS AND DEATHS

Abram Games dies.
Nicolette Gray dies.
Tom Eckersley dies.

## CONSUMABLES

🌱 Tamagotchi, the virtual pet, is introduced.

## ARTS AND CULTURE

♫ Negativland, the band that coined the term "culture jamming," releases an anti-pop album called *Dispepsi* including disfigured Pepsi jingles.

Poster by Yee Haw Industries

# ¹⁹98

New Volkswagen Beetle logo (based on three half circles forming the shape of the new Beetle) is introduced.

## GRAPHIC ARTS

✦ Angus Hyland, Pentagram UK, designs modern-looking, conceptual paperback covers for all the books of the Bible.

✦ Garson Yu of Yu + Co designs the film title sequence for *Among Giants*.

✦ Hideki Nakajima designs the Japanese *Cut* magazine using eclectic typographical materials.

✦ *Life* magazine hires Paul Ritter (formerly of *Colors*) as art director.

✦ Madonna's *Ray of Light* wins Grammy award for the best recording package, art director, Kevin Reagen for Maverick/Warner Bros.

✦ Milton Glaser, Walter Bernard, and Mirko Ilic design film title sequence for Nora Ephron's movie *You've Got Mail*. The sequence is created entirely on a Silicon Valley computer system.

✦ Stefan Sagmeister designs a David Byrne doll for the cover of his album *Feelings*.

✦ The official symbol or glyph for the Euro design is based on the Greek Epsilon.

✦ John Maeda designs the interactive *Tap, Type, Write*, CD-ROM for Digitalogue Co. which pays tribute to the typewriter in the digital realm.

✦ After a three-year hiatus, Tibor Kalman founds new firm called Baby (later reverts to name M&Co.).

✦ *Tibor Kalman: Perverse Optimist*, edited by Peter Hall and designed by Michael Bierut, is published.

✦ *Zap #14* published, continuing a thirty-year run of pioneer underground comix, edited by Victor Moscoso, Spain Rodrigues, S. Clay Wilson, and others.

## ADVERTISING

♫ Apple Computer, Inc., "Think Different" ad campaign consists of posters featuring Pablo Picasso and, eventually, many other geniuses. TBWA Chiat/Day is the creator.

♫ Camel Cigarettes' Joe Camel the "Smooth Character" advertising campaign is forced to cease because it is perceived as appealing to teenagers.

♫ Swiss Army Brands print ad "The Swiss Never Begin Sentences with 'If I only had a . . .'" is the work of Mullen Advertising.

♫ The Wells advertising agency closes.

## BIRTHS AND DEATHS

Alan E. Cober dies.
Victor Papanek dies.
Pierre Boulat dies.
Bob Kane dies.
Shirley Polykoff dies.

## CONSUMABLES

✵ Electronic postal stamps become available from the U.S. Postal Service's Web site.

✵ Frito-Lay's WOW! chips are introduced.

## ARTS AND CULTURE

♨ Dogs become fashionable in books and advertising. Over fifty canine models are employed to sell everything from cigarettes (Benson & Hedges) to soup (Campbell's) to carpets (Einstein Moomjy).

♨ *South Park*, a limited-action animation and dystopian *Peanuts*, premiers on Comedy Central.

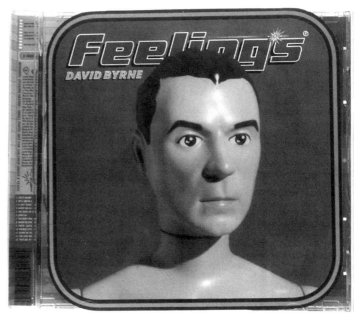

David Byrne album design by Stefan Sagmeister

## BIG BUSINESS

🏛 America Online acquires Netscape Communications Corporation in a stock transaction of $4.2 billion.

🏛 Interpublic combines Western International Media with Initiative Media in Paris to create the world's largest media management shop with $10 billion in billings.

## INDUSTRIAL DESIGN

✛ Apple releases the iMac, marketed on its user-friendliness and multiple color casing options, this launches the computer as fetish item.

✛ Michael Graves introduces a line of products at Target discount stores.

## POLITICS

🏃 Cigarette makers and state attorneys general draft a $206 billion deal that curbs marketing and settles lawsuits to recover Medicaid costs.

🏃 News of President Clinton's affair with White House intern Monica Lewinsky breaks over the Internet. The House of Representatives approve two articles of impeachment against President Clinton.

🏃 The Digital Millennium Copyright Act ("The Act") is created to extend and clarify the copyright protection (offered in the copyright law of 1978) for creative works online. It is enacted to implement two copyright treaties: the World Intellectual Property Organization Copyright Treaty and the World Intellectual Property Organization Performances and Phonograms Treaty, which were finalized in Geneva two years earlier.

## TECHNOLOGY

⚡ Motorola introduces the i Den i1000 Plus digital cell phone with two-way radio, alpha-numeric pager, e-mail, fax, and two-way messaging with access to the Web.

## TYPE

✦ Barry Deck designs Eunuverse, "a hybrid of a Eunuch and Univers," for *Ray Gun*.

*Zap Comix* No. 14

# 19**99**

## GRAPHIC ARTS

✦ Art Spiegelman creates "41 Shots, 10 Cents" cover for the *New Yorker*, a critique on the New York police shooting the unarmed Amadou Diallo forty-one times. Off-duty police officers stage a protest demonstration in front of the *New Yorker*'s offices.

✦ *Emigre* and five other design magazines in the United States and England publish the "First Thing Manifesto 2000," calling for greater awareness of the role designers play in promoting corrupt corporations.

✦ John Maeda publishes his book *Design by Numbers,* in which he explores the nexus of programming and design.

✦ Peter Max, who popularized pseudo-psychedelic art in the sixties, designs the largest rock 'n' roll stage set in history for Woodstock '99.

✦ Stefan Sagmeister is the art director and Hjalti Karlsson codesigner of *Your Action World* by David Byrne, a book of photographs, epigrams, and cultural sightings, with rubber cover and plastic carrying case.

✦ *U&lc* magazine, founded by Herb Lubalin, ceases publication. International Typeface Corporation, which published it, is absorbed by the Letraset Corporation.

✦ Eric Adigard designs the book *Architecture Must Burn* uses a collection of kinetic illustrations.

## ADVERTISING

⚓ McCann-Erickson (250 offices worldwide) celebrates its ninety-eighth birthday.

⚓ Graham Routhenwaite creates illustrations for Levi's ads, reintroducing illustration to advertising after it has long been second to photography.

## EDUCATION

✒ David Crow, lecturer in graphic design at University College Salford, starts an M.A. program in Environmental Graphics in Manchester, England.

## BIRTHS AND DEATHS

Gene Federico dies.
Leo Lionni dies.
P. Scott Makela dies at age 36.
Saul Steinberg dies.
Tibor Kalman, founder of M&Co. and "Bad Boy of graphic design," dies at age 49.
Carl Ally dies.
Clifford Baldowski dies.
Hugh Haynie dies.

## CONSUMABLES

✈ Computers are owned by half of all U.S. households.

✈ Power Macintosh G4 is introduced by Apple.

✈ World's first Person-to-Person Gift Exchange Service goes online.

✈ Larry Flynt, publisher of *Hustler* magazine, develops a branded product line. "I'm really very, very disappointed that I didn't move into the retail business years ago, because I never realized the marketing power of the *Hustler* name and logo."

Page from *Architecture Must Burn* by Eric Adigard

## INDUSTRIAL DESIGN

✈ Inflate, producer of inflatable plastic household items, has an exhibition at the Victoria and Albert Museum, London.

## POLITICS

🏃 Member nations in the European Union (EU) officially adopt the euro as its common currency on January 1.

🏃 "Buy Nothing Day," November 26, becomes a day of anticonsumer actions in Times Square, New York.

🏃 The Digital Millennium Copyright Act is passed by Congress.

🏃 Business Leaders for Sensible Priorities (BLSP) founded by Ben Cohen of Ben and Jerry's ice-cream fame, launches grass-roots bus tour to win back funding for education from defense department appropriations. Graphics designed by Sefan Sagmeister.

## ARTS AND CULTURE

♠ Philip Morris–owned Altoids Mints brand spends $250,000 to buy works by twenty emerging artists for its *Curiously Strong Collection*, a travelling art collection that echoes the Altoids' slogan "Curiously Strong Mints."

♠ *Sensation*, Charles Saatchi's collection of young British artists, comes to the Brooklyn Museum of Art, stirring significant public controversy and New York City mayor's protest over certain "sacrilegious" pieces.

## BIG BUSINESS

🏛 Martha Stewart Living Omnimedia issues IPO, and her key employees get rich.

🏛 Charges are brought against Microsoft under the Sherman Anti-Trust Act, and Microsoft is branded a monopoly by U.S. District Judge Thomas Penfield Jackson from his findings (November 5).

🏛 R. R. Donnelley & Sons Company becomes the largest commercial printer in the United States, run by its 26,000 employees.

🏛 Ted Turner merges his media company with Time Warner to create a $17 billion conglomerate.

Page from *Architecture Must Burn*

Business Leaders for Sensible Priorities cups

2000

*The Kinko's, Starbucks, and Blockbuster clerks buy their uniforms of khakis and white or blue shirts at the Gap; the "Hi! Welcome to the Gap!" greeting cheer is fueled by Starbucks double espressos; the résumés that got them the jobs were designed at Kinko's on friendly Macs, in Helvetica 12-point on Microsoft Word. One imagines that everyone shows up for work smelling of CK One . . . their faces freshly scrubbed with Body Shop Blue Corn Mask, before leaving apartments furnished with Ikea self-assembled bookcases and coffee tables.*

*Naomi Klein, 1999*

# 20**00**

## GRAPHIC ARTS

✦ AIGA opens its CG2000 show in its newly designed headquarters on lower Fifth Avenue, New York.

✦ First Things First manifesto fosters many debates on the efficiency of social responsibility in design.

✦ HEARx Ltd. and Time Magazine form marketing partnership to focus on the "Over Fifty" population with the introduction of the first large-print newsweekly.

✦ International Typeface Corporation (ITC) introduces *U&lc Online*, the first issue since the twenty-six-year-old type and graphics magazine publication announced that the print version would no longer be available after the October 1999, No. 2, Vol. 26 issue.

✦ Kinko's launches Online Poster and Calendar Site, custom-designed poster, calendar, and banner printing over the Internet.

✦ *Life* magazine, founded in 1936, folds (for the second time, first was in 1972) after fifty-seven years.

✦ Massimo and Lela Vignelli close office and move business into their home in New York City.

✦ Olivero Toscani, leaves Benetton and becomes creative director of *Talk* magazine.

✦ Bruce Mau writes and designs *Life Style*, a 500-plus-page manifesto/biography that combines issues of life and work.

✦ Razorfish, Inc., the digital solutions provider, extends its core offering by joining forces with Audio House, a United Kingdom–based provider of audio for digital and traditional media companies.

✦ Razorfish's San Francisco office designs Web interfaces and systems for DoubleTwist. Their digital solutions will bring enhanced processing power and scientific rigor to all who are interested in genetic research.

✦ April Greiman joins Pentagram as a partner.

✦ Chaz Maviyane-Davies designs posters protesting human rights abuses in Zimbabwe.

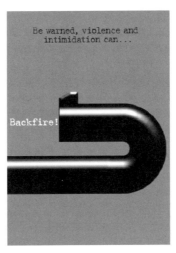

Poster by Chaz Maviyane-Davies

## ADVERTISING

❦ Creative Media Group (CMG) designs one of the top two hundred business-to-business Web sites, ranking highest in Net Marketing 200's Publishing Category, according to Advertising Age's *Business Marketing* magazine.

❦ BP, "Beyond Petroleum," ad campaign created by the Brand Integration Group (B.I.G.) of Oglivy, New York.

## BIRTHS AND DEATHS

Bob Gage dies.
Bill Segal dies.
Charles M. Schulz dies.
Edward Gorey dies.
Tony Arefin dies

## ARTS AND CULTURE

♠ Charles M. Schulz retires Charlie Brown after fifty years. The last daily appears on Jan. 3, 2000, and the last Sunday strip on Feb. 13, a few hours after Charles's death.

♠ Adobe Systems Incorporated and Adobe Systems Co., Ltd., announce the Japanese version of Adobe InDesign, an innovative, new page-layout software with the most extensive support for Japanese text and typography since the advent of desktop publishing.

♠ Space Imaging's CARTERRA, first high-resolution satellite images of the Earth, are available for sale.

♠ Chee Pearlman resigns as editor of *I.D.* magazine. Chris Mount assumes the post.

♠ *Nest* magazine awarded National Magazine Award for "Overall Excellence."

♠ The recipients of the First National Design Awards are announced.

* Agfa Monotype acquires International Typeface Corporation (ITC).
* GarageFonts introduces two hundred new fonts including Benderhead by Brian Sooy, Cruz Grafica by Ray Cruz, Flurry by Peter Kin-Fan Lo, and pictographic fonts, Media Icons by Chris Wiener and Muscles by Roberto Brunetti and Pierluigi Portolano. The new releases span the globe, with designers from four continents.
* House Industry's releases House 3009 typeface featuring five futuristic styles.
* HTF Hoefler Text, originally designed for Apple Computer's TrueType GX system (and appearing as part of the Macintosh Operating System), the HTF Hoefler Text family of types, is now available for the first time in PostScript.

Poster by Chaz Maviyane-Davies

* International Typeface Corporation (ITC) releases three new font families, two by designer Jochen Schuss and the third by Galapagos Design's George Ryan.
* Porchez Typofonderie designs Parisine and Parisine Plus typefaces, the six-weight family includes three sub-families—Clair, Standard, and Sombre, as well as small caps, issued by International Typeface Corporation (ITC).
* The Font Bureau releases its twenty-fourth retail font pack, which comprises two new families designed by Cyrus Highsmith (Dispatch) and Andy Stockley (Spira).

* Wolfgang Weingart publishes *Typography*, a 480-page monograph about his life's typographic work.
* Nillenium designed by Chester for Thirstype.

### BIG BUSINESS
🏛 Michael Lynton is named president of AOL International.

Nillennium-Light

Nillennium-LightItalic

Nillennium-Medium

Nillennium-MediumItalic

**Nillennium-Bold**

*Nillennium-BoldItalic*

**Nillennium-Heavy**

**Nillennium-HeavyItalic**

Nillennium type specimen

## 1900-2000 BIRTHS AND DEATH DATES (ALPHABETICAL)

*This is a selection of artists, designers, and cultural figures who have had an impact on the visual culture.*

**A**

Alvar Aalto 1898–1976
Al Achenbaum b. 1925
Charles Addams 1912–1988
Mehemed Fehmy (M. F.) Agha 1896–1978
Otl Aicher 1922–1991
Josef Albers 1888–1976
Carl Ally 1924–1999
Carl Anderson 1865–1948
Charles S. Anderson b. 1958
Gail Anderson b. 1962
Ian Anderson b. 1961
Alfred Andriola 1912–1983
Ruth Ansel b. 1938
Guillaume Apollinaire 1880–1918
Louis Aragon 1897–1982
Louise Arensberg 1897–1953
Walter Arensberg 1878–1954
Roone Arledge b. 1931
Rudolf Arnheim b. 1904
Peter Arno 1904–1968
Gerd Arntz 1900–1988
Jean Hans Arp 1887–1966
Boris Artzybasheff 1899–1965
Charles R. Ashbee 1863–1942
John Atherton 1900–1952
Bob Aufuldish b. 1961
Bernáth Aurél 1895–1982
Georges Auriol 1863–1939
Richard Avedon b. 1923
N. W. Ayer 1847–1928

**B**

Bill Backer b. 1926
George Baker 1915–1975
Leon N. Bakst 1866–1924
Clifford Baldowski 1918–1999
Hugo Ball 1886–1927
Giacomo Balla 1871–1958
Théo Ballmer 1902–1965
Jonathan Barnbrook b. 1966
Fabien Baron b. 1959

Bruce Barton 1886–1967
Saul Bass 1920–1996
Theodore L. Bates 1901–1972
Walter M. Baumhofer 1904–1987
Herbert Bayer 1900–1985
Aubrey Beardsley 1872–1890
Lester Beall 1903–1969
C. C. (Charles Clarence) Beck b. 1910
Henry C. Beck b. 1903–1974
Samuel Beckett b. 1906
Martine Bedin b. 1957
Anthon Beeke b. 1940
Frank Beekers b. 1952
Charlotte Beers b. 1935
Peter Behrens 1868–1940
Rudolph Belarski 1900–1983
Don Belding 1897–1969
Nicholas Bentley 1907–1978
Linn Boyd Benton 1844–1932
Morris Fuller (M. F.) Benton 1872–1948
John Berg b. 1932
Dave Berger 1908–1970
Henri Bergson 1859–1941
Henryk Berlewi 1894–1967
Pierre Bernard b. 1942
William Bernbach 1911–1982
Lucian Bernhard 1883–1972
Leonard Bernstein 1918–1990
Charles Bigelow b. 1945
Max Bill 1908–1994
Joseph Binder 1898–1972
Otto Binder 1911–1974
Misha Black 1910–1977
R. O. Blechman b. 1930
Herbert L. Block b. 1909
Umberto Boccioni 1882–1916
Robert Bonfils 1886–1972
Pierre Bonnard 1867–1947
Gui Bonsiepe b. 1934
Sandor Bortnyik 1893–1976
Pierre Boulat 1925–1998

Will Bradley 1868–1962
Andrea Branzi b. 1938
Georges Braque 1882–1963
André Breton 1896–1966
Marcel Breuer 1902–1981
Clare Briggs 1875–1930
Alexey Brodovitch 1898–1971
Neville Brody b. 1957
Robert Brownjohn 1925–1970
Leo Burnett 1892–1971
Aaron Burns 1922–1991
Thomas J. Burrell b. 1939
Will Burtin 1908–1972
Ernie (Ernest) Bushmiller b. 1905

**C**

Max Caflisch b. 1916
Alexander Calder 1898–1976
Earnest Elmo Calkins 1868–1964
Dick (Richard) Calkins 1895–1962
Margaret Calvert b. ca. 1935
Milton Caniff 1907–1988
Al (Alfred) Capp 1909–1979
W. A. (Wallace) Carlson 1894–1969
Jean Carlu 1900–1989
Tom Carnase b. 1939
Carlo Carrá 1881–1965
Carol Devine Carson b. 1944
David Carson b. 1956
Matthew Carter b. 1937
Stephen M. Case b. 1958
Jacqueline S. Casey 1927–1991
A. M. (Adolphe Jean-Marie Mouron) Cassandre 1901–1968
Beppe Caturegli b. 1957
Marc Chagall 1887–1985
Art Chantry b. 1954
Charlie Chaplin 1889–1977
Warren Chappell b. 1904
John Cheever 1912–1982
Ivan Chermayeff b. 1932
Jay Chiat b. 1931
Hans Christiansen 1866–1945

Howard Chandler Christy 1873–1952
Seymour Chwast b. 1931
Aldo Cibic b. 1955
Ed Cleary 1949–1994
Thomas M. Cleland 1880–1964
Chuck Close b. 1940
Lee Clow b. 1942
Wells Coates 1895–1958
T. J. Cobden-Sanderson 1840–1922
Alan E. Cober 1936–1998
Alvin Langdon Coburn 1882–1966
Ralph Coburn b. 1923
Jean Cocteau 1889–1963
Fré Cohen 1903–1943
Charles T. Coiner 1898–1989
Jack Cole 1914–1958
Paul Colin 1892–1986
Elizabeth Colwell 1881-*unknown*
Fairfax Cone 1903–1977
Paul Conrad b. 1924
Austin Cooper 1890–1964
Muriel Cooper 1925–1994
Oswald B. Cooper 1879–1940
Le Corbusier (Charles-Edourd
    Jeanneret) 1887–1965
John Covert 1882–1960
C. D. Crain Jr. 1885–1973
Walter Crane 1845–1915
Freeman Godfrey Craw b. 1917
Bruce Crawford b. 1929
Seymour Cray b. 1925
Michael Cronin b. 1951
Percy Lee Crosby 1891–1964
Theo Crosby 1925–1994
Jean Crotti 1878–1958
Wim Crouwel b. 1928
Robert Crumb b. 1943
Andy Cruz b. 1972
John Steuart Curry 1897–1946
Cyrus H. K. Curtis 1850–1933

**D**

Carl Dair 1912–1967
Salvador Dali 1904–1989
Louis Danziger b. 1923
Jay N. Darling 1876–1962
Paul Davis b. 1938
Phil (Philip) Davis 1906–1964
Stuart Davis 1894–1964
Jeremy Dean b. 1972
Billy (William) De Beck 1890–1942
Sheila Levrant de Bretteville b. 1940
Giorgio de Chirico 1888–1978
Barry Deck b. 1962

Viktor Nikolaevich Deni 1893–1946
Edgar Degas 1834–1917
Rudolf de Harak b. 1924
Robert Delaunay 1885–1941
Jerry Della Femina b. 1936
Roger de La Fresnaye 1885–1925
Michele De Lucchi b. 1951
Paul Delvaux 1897–1994
Charles Demuth 1883–1935
Fortunato Depero 1892–1960
André Derain 1880–1954
Briget de Socio b. 1960
Henri de Toulouse-Lautrec
    1864–1901
Maurice de Vlaminck 1876–1958
Barbara de Wilde b. 1962
Walter Dexel 1890–1973
Marius de Zayas 1880–1961
Sergei Diaghilev 1872 –1929
Rudolph Dirks 1877–1968
Walt Disney 1901–1968
Tony DiSpigna b. 1943
Otto Dix 1891–1969
Jay Doblin 1920–1989
Dick Dooijes b. 1909
Lou Dorfsman b. 1918
Tad (Thomas Aloysious) Dorgan
    1877–1929
Arthur G. Dove 1880–1946
Stephen Doyle b. 1956
Grace Gebbie Drayton 1887–1931
Katherine Dreier 1877–1952
William Drenttel b. 1953
Henry Dreyfus 1904–1972
Johanna Drucker b. 1952
Marcel Duchamp 1887–1968
Ben Duffy 1902–1970
Joe Duffy b. 1949
Raoul Dufy 1887–1953
Gert Dumbar b. 1940
Nathalie Du Pasquier b. 1957
Phil Dusenberry b. 1936
W. A. Dwiggins 1880–1957

**E**

Charles Eames 1907–1978
Ray Eames 1912–1988
Richard Eckersey b. 1941
Tom Eckersley 1914–1997
Ralph Eckerstrom c. 1922–1996
Otto Eckmann 1865–1902
Fritz Helmuth Ehmcke 1878–1965
Hanno H. J. Ehses b. 1943
Michael Eisner b. 1942

Henk Elenga b. 1947
Paul Eluard 1895–1952
Hans Rudi Erdt 1883–1918
Max Ernst 1891–1965
Erté (Roman de Tirtoff) 1892–1990
Joseph Michael Essex b. 1947
Hartmut Esslinger b. 1945
Roger Excoffon 1910–1983

**F**

Kristen Faulkner b. 1970
Gene Federico 1918–1999
Jules Feiffer b. 1929
Lyonel Feininger 1871–1956
Bea Feitler 1938–1982
Edward Fella b. 1938
Louise Fili b. 1951
Virgil Finlay 1914–1971
Bud (Harold) Fisher 1885–1954
Carl Fisher b. 1924
Ham (Hammond) Fisher 1900–1955
Robert Fisher b. 1962
Bernice Fitz-Gobbon 1894–1982
Daniel R. Fitzpatrick 1891–1969
James Montgomery Flagg 1877–1960
Willy Fleckhaus 1925–1983
Maxwell Fleischer 1888–1972
Alan Fletcher b. 1931
Jerzy Flisak b. 1930
Jim Flora b. 1914
James K. Fogleman b. 1919
Emerson Foote 1906–1992
Mary Hallock Foote 1847–1938
Alréd Forbáth 1897–1972
Colin Forbes b. 1928
Henry Ford 1863–1947
Harold Foster 1892–1981
Steve Frankfurt b. 1931
Stan Freberg b. 1926
F. H. K. (Henri Kay Frederick)
    Henrion 1914–1990
Gene Frederico b. 1919
Cliff Freeman b. 1941
Tobias Frere-Jones b. 1970
Dan Friedman 1945–1995
Anthony Froshaug 1920–1984
Adrian Frutiger b. 1928
Shigeo Fukuda b. 1932
R. Buckminster Fuller 1895–1983
Sun Fu-xi 1898–1962

**G**

Abram Games 1914–1997
Bob Gage 1921–2000

Aleksei Gan 1893–1942

Amil Gargano b. 1933

Ken Garland b. 1929

Antonio Gaudi 1852–1926

Paul Gauguin 1848–1903

Philip Geier b. 1935

Theodor Seuss Geisel 1904–1994

Thomas Geismar b. 1931

Steff Geissbuhler b. 1942

Jean Genet 1910–1986

Günter Gerhard b. 1921

Karl Gerstner b. 1930

Charles Dana Gibson 1867–1944

Sigfried Giedion 1888–1968

Bob Gill b. 1931

Arthur Eric Rowton Gill 1882–1940

Julius Gipkens 1883–*unknown*

George Giusti b. 1908

Milton Glaser b. 1929

Alber Gleizes 1881–1953

David Lance Goines b. 1945

Carin Goldberg b. 1953

Ruben (Rube) L. Goldberg
    1883–1970

William Golden 1911–1959

Morton Goldsholl b. 1911

Natalia Goncharova 1881–1962

Tomás Gonda 1926–1985

Bertram G. Goodhue 1869–1924

Edward Gorey 1925–2000

Pat Gorman b. 1947

Howard Luck Gossage 1917–1969

Adolph Gottlieb 1903–1974

Frederic W. Goudy 1865–1947

Chester Gould 1900–1985

Michael Graves b. 1934

Harold Gray 1894–1968

Nicolette Gray 1911–1997

Elizabeth Shippen Green 1871–1954

Richard Greenberg b. 1947

Robert Greenberg b. 1949

April Greiman b. 1948

Rick Griffin 1944–1991

Juan Gris 1887–1927

Water Gropius 1883–1969

George Grosz 1893–1959

Hector Guimard 1867–1942

George Guisti b. 1908


**H**

Gerard Hadders b.1954

Joyce Hall 1891–1982

Victor Hammer 1882–1967

Tom van der Haspel b. 1953

Keith Haring 1958–1990

Marion Harper Jr. 1916–1989

Ollie Harrington 1912–1995

Johnny Hart b. 1931

Raoul Hausmann 1886–1971

Ashley Haviden 1903–1973

Hugh Haynie 1927–1999

Ambrose Heal 1872–1959

William Randolph Hearst 1863–1951

Erich Heckel 1883–1970

John Held Jr. 1889–1958

Jessica Helfand b. 1960

Steven Heller b. 1950

Ira Herbert 1927–1995

Walter Herdeg b. 1908–1995

George Herriman 1880–1944

John Hersey b. 1954

John Heartfield (Helmut Herzfelde)
    1891–1968

Wieland Herzfelde 1896–1988

Richard Hess 1934–1991

Sol Hess 1886–1953

Ken Hiebert b. 1930

Al Hirschfeld b. 1903

Hannah Höch 1889–1978

Jonathan Hoefler b. 1970

Karl Hofer 1878–1955

Josef Hoffmann 1870–1956

Armin Hofmann b. 1920

Burne Hogarth b. 1911

Ludwig Hohlwein 1874–1949

Hans Hollein b. 1934

Bill (William) Holman b. 1903

Kris Holmes b. 1950

Arno Holz 1863–1929

Claude C. Hopkins 1866–1932

John Newton Howitt 1885–1958

Elbert Hubbard 1856–1915

Max Huber 1919–1992

Frank Hummert 1879–1966

Allen Hurlburt 1910–1983

Vilmos Huszar 1884–1960

Walter Huxley 1890–1955


**I**

Lee Iacocca b. 1924

Takenobu Igarashi b. 1944

Massimo Iosa Ghini b. 1959

Alexander Isley b. 1961

Alec Issigonis 1906–1988

Johannes Itten 1888–1967


**J**

Arne Jacobsen 1902–1971

Egbert Jacobson 1890–1966

Robert Jacoby b. 1928

Charles Jencks b. 1939

Jacob Jensen b. 1926

Cao Jie b.1931

Steve Jobs b. 1955

Henry Lewis Johnson 1867–1937

John H. Johnson b. 1918

Philip Johnson b. 1906

Edward Johnston 1872–1944

Finn Juhl 1912–1989

Qian Jun-tao b. 1906


**K**

Charles W. Kahles 1878–1931

Tibor Kalman 1949–1999

Yusaku Kamekura b. 1915

Wassily Kandinsky 1866–1944

Art Kane b. 1925

Bob Kane 1916–1998

Shiro Karamata b. 1937

Susan Kare b.1954

Mitsuo Katsui b.1931

E. McKnight Kauffer 1890–1954

Jeffery Keedy b. 1957

Ernst Keller 1891–1968

Walt (Walter) Kelly 1913–1973

David Kennedy b. 1940

John E. Kennedy 1864–1928

Gyorgy Kepes b. 1906

Harry Graf Kessler

Hank (Henry) Ketchum b. 1920

Aram Khachaturian 1903–1978

Chip Kidd b. 1964

Günther Kieser b.1930

David King b. 1943

Jock Kinneir 1917–1974

Rollin Kirby 1875–1952

Ernst Ludwig Kirchner 1880–1938

Max Kisman b. 1953

Paul Klee 1879–1940

Gustav Klimt 1862–1918

Julius Klinger 1872–1950

Gustav Klutsis 1895–1938*

János Kmetty 1889–1975

Albert Kner 1899–1976

Harold H. Knerr 1883–1949

Rudolf Koch 1876–1934

Oskar Kokoschka 1886–1980

Terry Koppel b. 1950

Frank Kozik b. 1962

Ray Kroc 1902–1984

*See Klutsis entry in Politics section of 1938, p. 99.

Willi Kunz b. 1943
Frantisek Kupta 1871–1957
Harvey Kurtzman 1924- 1993

**L**

József Nemes Lampérth 1891–1924
Walter Landor 1913–1995
Tolbert Lanston 1844–1913
Mikhail Larionov 1881–1955
Henri de Toulouse-Lautrec
    1864–1901
J. L Mathieu Lauwericks 1864–1932
Wells Lawrence b. 1918
Alfred Leete 1882–1933
Fernand Léger 1881–1955
Warren Lehrer b. 1955
Jan Lenica b. 1928
Dr. Robert Leslie 1885–1986
David Levine b. 1926
Joseph C. Leyendecker 1874–1951
Alexander Liberman b. 1912
Bruce Licher b. 1958
Zuzana Licko b. 1961
Leo Lionni 1910–1999
Jaques Lipchitz 1891–1973
Li Qun b. 1912
El (Lazar Markovich) Lissitzky
    1890–1941
Raymond Loewy 1893–1986
Berthold Löffler 1874–1960
Richard P. Lohse 1902–1988
George Lois b. 1931
William Longhauser b. 1947
Adolf Loos 1870–1933
Richard Lord b. 1926
Morris Louis 1912–1962
Robert Lowell 1917–1977
Herb Lubalin 1918–1981
Henry Luce 1898–1967
Alvin Lustig 1915–1955

**M**

Michael Mabry b. 1955
August Macke 1887–1914
Arthur H. Mackmurdo 1851–1942
Theodore F. MacManus 1872–1940
Jeff MacNelly b. 1947
René Magritte 1898–1967
P. Scott Makela 1960–1999
Kazimir Malevich 1878–1935
Stéphane Mallarmé 1842–1898
André Malraux 1901–1976
Michael Manwaring b. 1942
Franz Marc 1880–1916

Hans (Giovanni) Mardersteig
    1892–1977
John Marin 1870–1953
Filippo Tommaso Marinetti
    1876–1944
Javier Mariscal b. 1950
David Stone Martin b. 1916
Edgar Martin 1898–1960
John Massey b. 1931
Robert Massin b. 1925
André Masson 1896–1987
Henri Matisse 1869–1954
Herbert Matter 1907–1984
Bruce Mau b. 1959
Bill (William) Mauldin b. 1921
Peter Max b. 1937
Vladimir Vladimirovich Mayakovskiy
    1893–1930
Hy Mayer b. 1917
Harrison K. McCann 1880–1962
Winsor "Silas" McCay c. 1871–1936
John McConnell b. 1939
Katherine McCoy 1945
John T. McCutcheon 1870–1949
Neil McElroy 1904–1972
James H. McGraw Sr. 1860–1948
Marshall McLuhan 1911–1980
George McManus 1884–1954
James McMullan b. 1934
Douglas C. McMurtrie 1888–1944
George Melly b. 1926
Gian Carlo Menotti b. 1911
Ottmar Mergenthaler 1854–1899
Jean Metzinger 1883–1956
Hannes Meyer 1889–1954
Francis Meynell 1891–1975
Robert Hunter Middleton 1898–1985
Max Miedinger 1910–1980
François Miehe b. 1942
Ludwig Mies van der Rohe
    1886–1969
Reid Miles 1927–1993
Mike Mills b. 1966
Joan Miró 1893–1983
Rudolph Modley 1906–1976
László Moholy-Nagy 1895–1946
Clement Mok b. 1958
Farkas Molnar 1897–1945
Piet Mondrian 1872–1944
Claude Monet 1840–1926
Dmitrii Stakhievich Moor 1883–1946
Charles W. Moore b. 1925
Henry Moore 1898–1986
Marianne Moore 1897–1972

Giorgio Morandi 1890–1964
Stanley Morison 1889–1967
Talwin Morris 1865–1911
William Morris 1834–1896
Victor Moscoso b. 1936
Koloman Moser 1868–1918
Zack (Zachery) Mosley b. 1906
Robert Motherwell b. 1915
Jean-Marie Mouron 1901–1968
Alphonse Mucha 1869–1939
Josef Müller-Brockmann 1914–1996
Martin Munkacsi 1896–1963
Gabrielle Munter 1877–1962
Peter Murdoch b. 1940
Rupert Murdoch b. 1931
John Cullen Murphy b. 1919
Herman Muthesius 1861–1928

**N**

Vladimir Nabokov 1899–1977
Kazumasa Nagai b. 1929
Condé Nast 1873–1942
Thomas Nast 1840–1902
Art Nelson 1907–1966
Hans Neuburg 1904–1983
Otto Neurath 1882–1945
Peter Newell 1862–1924
William Nicholson 1872–1949
Erik Nitsche b. 1908
Marcello Nizzoli 1895–1969
Kenneth Noland b. 1924
Emil Nolde 1867–1956

**O**

Violet Oakley 1874–1961
Emily Oberman b. 1963
Thomas Ockerse b. 1940
Jayme Odgers b. 1939
Siegfried Odermatt b. 1926
David Ogilvy 1911–1999
Georgia O'Keeffe 1897–1986
Joseph Maria Olbrich 1867–1908
Georg Olden 1920–1975
Claes Oldenberg b. 1929
Frank Olinsky b. 1950
Vaughn Oliver b. 1957
Adriano Olivetti 1901–1970
Rose O'Neill 1874–1944
Frederic Burr Opper 1857–1937
Emmanuel Orazi 1860–1934
José Orozco 1883–1949
J. J. P. (Jacobus Johannes Pieter) Oud
    1890–1963
Richard Outcault 1863–1928

Michael Ovitz b. 1946
R. D. E. Oxenaar b. 1929
Amédée Ozenfant 1886–1966

**P**

Vance Packard 1914–1996
Walter P. Paepke 1896–1960
William Paley 1901–1990
Victor Papanek 1925–1998
Giovanni Papini 1881–1956
Gerard Paris-Clavel b. 1943
Brant Parker b. 1920
Mike Parker b. 1929
Maxfield Parrish 1870–1966
Art Paul b. 1925
Harry Peach 1874–1936
Charles Peignot 1897–1983
Georges Peignot 1872–1914
Irving Penn b. 1917
László Péri 1889–1967
Nikolaus Pevsner 1902–1983
Francis Picabia 1878–1953
Pablo Picasso 1881–1973
Frank Pick 1878–1941
Maurice Pillard-Verneuil 1869–1942
Cipe Pineles 1911–1991
Giovanni Pintori b. 1912
Woody Pirtle b. 1943
Camille Pissarro 1830–1903
Esther Bensusan Pissarro 1870–1951
Lucien Pissarro 1863–1944
Sharon Helmer Poggenpohl b. 1943
Shirley Polykoff 1908–1998
Gio Ponti 1881–1971
Lyubov Sergeevna Popova 1889–1954
John E. Powers 1837–1919
Rick Poynor b. 1957
Christopher Pullman b. 1941

**Q**

Ha Qiong-wen b. 1925
Qian Jun-tao b. 1906

**R**

Barbara Radice b. 1943
Gunter Rambow b. 1938
Paul Rand 1914–1996
Will Ransom 1878–1955
Robert Rauschenberg b. 1925
Man Ray (Emanuel Rabinovitch) 1890–1976
Alexander Raymond 1909–1956
Ethel Reed 1876–1898
Rosser Reeves 1910–1984

Jack McGregor (Jamie) Reid b. 1947
Marie Reidemeister 1898–1959
Keith Reinhard b. 1935
Ad Reinhardt 1913–1967
Frederick Remington 1861–1909
Paul Renner 1878–1956
Theodore Repplier 1889–1971
Helen Lansdowne Resor 1886–1964
Stanley Resor 1879–1964
Louis Rhead 1857–1926
Silas Rhodes b. 1915
Gerrit Rietveld 1888–1964
Hal Riney b. 1932
Boardman Robinson 1876–1952
Phyllis K. Robinson b. 1921
Juliette Roche 1884–1980
Norman Rockwell 1894–1978
Alexander Rodchenko 1891–1956
Albert Bruce Rogers 1870–1957
Raymond Roker b. 1968
Alfred Roller 1864–1935
Edward Rondthaler b. 1905
Lies Ros b. 1952
James Rosenquist b. 1933
Allen Rosenshine b.1939
Samuel Rosenstock 1896–1945
George Jerome Rozen 1895–1974
Emil Ruder 1914–1970
Reynolds Ruffins b. 1930
C. D. (Clarence) Russell 1895–1963
Luigi Russolo 1885–1947
György Ruttkay 1898–1974
Rudolph Ruzicka 1883–1978

**S**

Eero Saarinen 1910–1961
Charles Saatchi b. 1943
Maurice Saatchi b. 1946
George Sadek b. 1928
Gordon Salchow b. 1940
Mike Salisbury b. 1941
George Salter 1897–1967
Willem Sandberg 1897–1984
Antonio Sant'Elia 1888–1916
David Sarnoff 1891–1971
Jean-Paul Sartre 1905–1980
Koichi Sato b. 1944
Josef Sattler 1867–1931
Norman Saunders 1907–1989
Jon Savage b. 1953
Leslie Savan b.1951
Peter Saville b. 1955
John Sayles b. 1958
Christian Schad b. 1918

Morton Livingston Schamberg 1881–1918
Xanti (Alexander) Schawinsky 1904–1979
Paula Scher b. 1948
Egon Schiele 1890–1976
Hans Schleger (Zéró) 1898–1976
Oskar Schlemmer 1888–1943
Stafan Schlesinger 1896–1944
Joost Schmidt 1893–1948
Carl Schmidt-Rottluff 1884–1976
Piet Schreuders b. 1951
Rob Schroder b. 1950
Paul Schuitema 1897–1973
Charles M. Schulz 1922–2000
Victor O. Schwab 1898–1980
Kurt Schwitters 1887–1948
Douglass G. A. Scott b. 1947
Joe Sedelmaier b. 1933
George Segal b. 1924
Elzie Segar 1894–1938
Carlos Segura b. 1957
Gino Severini 1883–1966
Ben Shahn 1898–1969
Lu Shao-fei b. 1903
Charles Sheeler 1883–1965
Peter Shire b. 1947
Joe Shuster 1914–1992
Jerry (Jerome) Siegel 1914–1996
Len Sirowitz b. 1932
David Siqueiros 1896–1974
Nancy Skolos b. 1955
Robert Slimbach b. 1956
Alfred Sloan 1875–1966
John Sloan 1871–1951
John Smale b. 1927
Sidney Smith 1877–1935
Otto Soglow 1900–1975
Barbara Stauffacher Solomon b. 1932
Susan Sontag b. 1933
Edward Sorel b. 1930
Martin Sorrell b. 1945
Ettore Sottsass Jr. b. 1917
George James Sowden b. 1942
Herbert Spencer b.1924
Erik Spiekermann b.1947
J. Allen St. John 1872–1957
Anton Stankowski b. 1906
Frank Stanton b. 1908
Daniel Starch 1983–1979
Franciszek Starowicjski b. 1930
Leonard Starr b. 1925
Saul Steinberg 1914–1999
Albe Steiner 1913–1974

Alex Steinweiss b. 1916
Joseph Stella 1877–1946
Georgy Stenberg 1900–1933
Vladimir Stenberg 1900–1982
Varvara Stepanova 1894–1958
Alice Barber Stephens 1858–1932
Dugald Stermer b. 1936
Bert Stern b. 1929
Cliff (Clifford) Sterrett 1883–1964
Florine Stettheimer 1871–1944
Gustav Stickley 1858–1942
Reynolds Stone 1909–1979
Sumner Stone b. 1945
Otto Storch b. 1913
Pat (Patrick) Sullivan 1888–1933
Deborah Sussman b. 1931
Ladislav Sutnar 1897–1976
Waldemar Swierzy b. 1931

**T**

Madsuda Tadashi b. 1922
Ikko Tanaka b. 1930
Yves Tanguy 1900–1955
Vladimir Tatlin 1885–1953
Gerard Taylor b. 1955
Walter Dorwin Teague 1883–1960
Karel Teige 1900–1950
Lucille Tenazas b. 1953
Armando Testa 1917–1992
János Mattis Teutsch 1884–1960
Bradbury Thompson 1911–1995
J. Walter Thompson 1847–1928
Kristin Thomson b. 1967
Matteo Thun b. 1952
James Thurber 1894–1961
Clara Tice 1888–1973
Louis Comfort Tiffany 1848–1933
Lajos Tihanyi 1885–1938
Jack Tinker 1906–1985
Rosemarie Tissi b. 1937
Alfred Tolmer 1876–1957
Henryk Tomaszewski b. 1914
Gael Towey b. 1952
Walter Tracy b. 1914
Howard Allen Trafton 1897–1946
Jane Trahey b. 1923
Tadeusz Trepkowski 1914–1956

Garry Trudeau b. 1948
Georg Trump 1896–1985
George Tscherny b. 1924
Jan Tschichold 1902–1974
Carol Twombly b. 1959
Tristan Tzara 1896–1963

**U**

Béla Uitz 1887–1972
Masanori Umeda b. 1941
Gerard Unger b. 1942
Daniel Berkeley Updike 1860–1941
Edwin Utermohlen b. 1954

**V**

Rick Valincenti b. 1958
Erick Van Blokland b. 1967
Théo van Doesburg 1883–1931
Kees van Dongen 1877–1968
Henry van de Velde 1863–1957
Michael Vanderbyl b. 1947
Rudy VanderLans b. 1955
Bart van der Leck 1876–1958
Jan van Krimpen 1892–1958
Arnold Varga 1926–1994
Alberto Vargas 1896–1982
Robert Venturi b. 1925
Gustave Verbeck 1867–1937
Rick Vermeulen b. 1950
Massimo Vignelli b. 1931
Sam Vitt b. 1926
Carlo L. Vivarelli 1919–1986
Charles A. Voight 1887–1947
Baroness Elsa von Freytag-
    Loringhoven 1874–1927
Alexei von Jawlensky 1864–1941
Count Ferdinand von Zeppelin
    1838–1917

**W**

Emery Walker 1851–1933
Beatrice Warde 1900–1969
Andy Warhol 1928–1987
Kathy Warinner b. 1957
John B. Watson 1878–1958
Thomas J. Watson Jr. 1914–1993
Coulton Waugh 1896–1973

Sylvester L. Weaver b. 1908
Qin Wei b. 1911
Wolfgang Weingart b. 1941
Emil Rudolf Weiss 1875–1943
Hendrik N. Werkman 1882–1945
Russ (Russell) Westover 1886–1966
Dan Wieden b. 1945
Lorraine Wild b. 1953
Al Williamson b. 1931
Frank Williard 1893–1958
Robert Wesley "Wes" Wilson b. 1937
Dietmar Winkler b. 1938
Tapio Wirkkala 1915–1985
Henry Wolf b. 1925
Berthold Wolpe 1905–1989
Fred Woodward b. 1953
Frank Lloyd Wright 1867–1959
Lester Wunderman b. 1920
Richard Saul Wurman b. 1936
N. C. Wyeth 1882–1945
Lance Wyman b. 1937

**X**

Lu Xun 1881–1936

**Y**

Chitfu Y b. 1943
Tadanori Yokoo b. 1936
Art Young 1866–1943
 Chic (Murat) Young 1901–1973
James Webb Young 1886–1973
Gu Yuan b. 1919

**Z**

Barry Zaid b. 1939
Tony Zajkowski b. 1966
Marco Zanini b. 1954
Marco Zanuso b. 1916
Marco Zanuso Jr. b. 1954
Hermann Zapf b. 1918
Gundrun Zapf-von Hesse b. 1918
Eva Zeisel b. 1906
Cai Zhen-hau b. 1912
Chen Zhi-fo 1898–1962
Ai Zhong-xin b. 1915
Howard Zieff b. 1943
Piet Zwart 1885–1977

## I. AIGA MEDAL AND DESIGN LEADERSHIP AWARD RECIPIENTS

### AIGA Medal

1920 Norman T. A. Munder
1922 Daniel Berkeley Updike
1924 John C. Agar
1924 Stephen H. Horgan
1925 Bruce Rogers
1926 Burton Emmett
1927 Timothy Cole
1927 Frederic W. Goudy
1929 William A. Dwiggins
1930 Henry Watson Kent
1931 Dard Hunter
1932 Porter Garnett
1934 Henry Lewis Bullen
1935 Rudolph Ruzicka
1935 J. Thompson Willing
1939 William A. Kittredge
1940 Thomas M. Cleland
1941 Carl Purington Rollins
1942 Edwin and Robert Grabhorn
1944 Edward Epstean
1945 Frederic G. Melcher
1946 Stanley Morison
1947 Elmer Adler
1948 Lawrence C. Wroth
1950 Earnest Elmo Calkins
1950 Alfred A. Knopf
1951 Harry L. Gage
1952 Joseph Blumenthal
1953 George Macy
1954 Will Bradley
1954 Jan Tschichold
1955 P. J. Conkwright
1956 Ray Nash
1957 Dr. M. F. Agha
1958 Ben Shahn
1959 May Massee
1960 Walter Paepcke
1961 Paul A. Bennett
1962 Wilhelm Sandberg
1963 Saul Steinberg
1964 Josef Albers
1965 Leonard Baskin
1966 Paul Rand
1967 Romana Javitz
1968 Dr. Giovanni Mardersteig
1969 Dr. Robert R. Leslie
1970 Herbert Bayer
1971 Will Burtin
1972 Milton Glaser

1973 Richard Avedon
1973 Allen Hurlburt
1973 Philip Johnson
1974 Robert Rauschenberg
1975 Bradbury Thompson
1976 Henry Wolf,
1976 Jerome Snyder
1977 Charles and Ray Eames
1978 Lou Dorfsman
1979 Ivan Chermayeff and Thomas Geismar
1980 Herb Lubalin
1981 Saul Bass
1982 Massimo and Lella Vignelli
1983 Herbert Matter
1984 Leo Lionni
1985 Seymour Chwast
1986 Walter Herdeg
1987 Alexey Brodovitch
1987 Gene Federico
1988 William Golden
1988 George Tscherny
1989 Paul Davis
1989 Bea Feitler
1990 Alvin Eisenman
1990 Frank Zachary
1991 Colin Forbes
1991 E. McKnight Kauffer
1992 Rudolph de Harak
1992 George Nelson
1992 Lester Beall
1993 Alvin Lustig
1993 Tomoko Miho
1994 Muriel Cooper
1994 John Massey
1995 Matthew Carter
1995 Stan Richards
1995 Ladislav Sutnar
1996 Cipe Pineles
1996 George Lois
1997 Lucian Bernhard
1997 Zuzana Licko and Rudy VanderLans
1998 Louis Danziger
1998 April Greiman
1999 Steven Heller
1999 Tibor Kalman
1999 Katherine McCoy

### AIGA Design Leadership Award

1980 IBM Corporation
1981 Massachusetts Institute of Technology
1982 Container Corporation of America
1982 Cummins Engine Company, Inc.
1984 Herman Miller, Inc.
1985 WGBH Educational Foundation
1986 Esprit
1987 Walker Art Center
1988 The New York Times
1989 Apple and Adobe Systems
1990 The National Park Service
1991 MTV
1991 Olivetti, 1991
1991 Sesame Street, Children's Television Workshop
1993 Nike, Inc.
1998 Champion International Corporation
1999 Knopf

## II. ART DIRECTORS CLUB OF NEW YORK HALL OF FAME LAUREATES

1972 M. F. Agha
      Lester Beall
      Alexey Brodovitch
      A. M. Cassandre
      Rene Clark
      Robert Gage
      William Golden
      Paul Rand
1973 Charles Coiner
      Paul Smith
      Jack Tinker
1974 Will Burtin
      Leo Lionni
1975 Gordon Aymar
      Herbert Bayer
      Cipe Pineles Burtin
      Heyworth Campbell
      Alexander Liberman
      László Moholy-Nagy
1976 E. McKnight Kauffer
      Herbert Mayer
1977 Saul Bass
      Herb Lubalin
      Bradbury Thompson
1978 Thomas M. Cleland
      Lou Dorfsman
      Allen Hurlburt

George Lois
1979 W. A. Diggins
George Giusti
Milton Glaser
Helmut Krone
Willem Sandberg
Ladislav Sutnar
Jan Tschichold
1980 Gene Federico
Otto Storch
Henry Wolf
1981 Lucian Bernhard
Ivan Chermayeff
Gyorgy Kepes
George Krikorian
William Taubin
1982 Richard Avedon
Amil Gatgano
Jerome Snyder
Massimo Vignelli
1983 Aaron Burns
Seymour Chwast
Steve Frankfurt
1984 Charles Eames
Wallace Elton
Sam Scali
Louis Silverstein
1985 Art Kane
Len Sirowitz
Charles Tudor
1986 Walt Disney
Roy Grace
Alvin Lustig
Arthur Paul
1987 Willy Fleckhaus
Shigeo Fukuda
Steve Horn
Tony Palladino
1988 Ben Shahn
Bert Steinhauser
Mike Tesch
1989 Rudolph deHarak
Raymond Loewy
1990 Lee Clow
Reba Sochis
Frank Zachary
1991 Bea Feitler
Bob Gill
Bob Giraldi
Richard Hess
1992 Eiko Ishioka
Rick Levine
Onofrio Paccione
Gordon Parks

1993 Leo Burnett
Yusaku Kamekura
Robert Wilvers
Howard Zieff
1994 Alan Fletcher
Norman Rockwell
Rochelle Udell
Andy Warhol
1995 Robert Brownjohn
Paul Davis
Roy Kuhlman
Jay Maisel
1996 Bill McCaffery
Erik Nitsche
Arnold Varga
Fred Woodward
1997 Allan Beaver
Sheila Metzner
B. Martin Pedersen
George Tscherny
1998 Tom Geismar
Chuck Jones
Paula Scher
Alex Steinweiss
1999 R. O. Blechman
Stan Richards
Richard Wilde
Annie Leibovitz
2000 Pablo Ferro
Tadanori Yokoo
Joe Sedelmaier
Ed Benguiat

### Special Educators Award

1983 Bell Bernbach
1987 Leon Friend
1988 Silas Rhodes
1989 Hershel Levit
1990 Robert Weaver
1991 Jim Henson
1996 Steven Heller
1998 Red Burns

### III. SOCIETY OF ILLUSTRATORS NEW YORK HALL OF FAME LAUREATES

*elected posthumously*

1958 Norman Rockwell
1959 Dean Cornwell
1960 Harold Von Schmidt
1961 Floyd Davis
1962 Edward Wilson
1963 Walter Biggs
1964 Arthur William Brown

1965 Al Parker
1966 Al Dorne
1967 Robert Fawcett
1968 Peter Helck
1969 Austin Briggs
1970 Rube Goldberg
1971 Stevan Dohanos
1972 Ray Prohaska
1973 Jon Whitcomb
1974 Tom Lovell
1974 Charles Dana Gibson*
1974 N. C. Wyeth*
1975 Bernie Fuchs
1975 Maxfield Parrish*
1975 Howard Pyle*
1976 John Falter
1976 Winslow Homer
1976 Harvey Dunn
1977 Robert Peak
1977 Wallace Morgan*
1977 J. C. Leyendecker*
1978 Coby Whitmore
1978 Norman Price*
1978 Frederick Remington*
1979 Ben Stahl
1979 Edwin Austin Abbey*
1979 Lorraine Fox
1980 Saul Tepper
1980 Howard Chandler Christy*
1980 James Montgomery Flagg*
1981 Stan Galli
1981 Frederic R. Gruger*
1981 John Gannam*
1982 John Clymer
1982 Henry P. Raleigh*
1982 Eric (Carl) Erickson*
1983 Mark English
1983 Noel Sickles*
1983 Franklin Booth*
1984 Neysa Moran McMein*
1984 John LaGatta*
1984 James Williamson*
1985 Charles Marion Russell*
1985 Arthur Burdett Frost*
1985 Robert Weaver
1986 Rockwell Kent
1986 Al Hirshfeld
1987 Haddom Sundbloom*
1987 Maurice Sendak
1988 Rene Bouche*
1988 Pruett Carter*
1988 Robert T. McCall
1989 Erté
1989 John Held Jr.*

| 1989 | Arthur Ignatius Keller* | 1994 | Elizabeth Shippen Green* | 1997 | Joe DeMers* |
|------|------------------------|------|-------------------------|------|-------------|
| 1990 | Burt Silverman | 1994 | Ben Shahn* | 1997 | Maynard Dixon* |
| 1990 | Robert Riggs* | 1995 | James Avati | 1997 | Harrison Fisher* |
| 1990 | Morton Roberts* | 1995 | McClelland Barclay* | 1998 | Robert M. Cunningham |
| 1991 | Donald Teague | 1995 | Joseph Clement Coll* | 1998 | Frank Frazetta |
| 1991 | Jessie Willcox Smith* | 1995 | Frank E. Schoonover* | 1998 | Boris Artzybasheff* |
| 1991 | William A. Smith* | 1996 | Herb Tauss | 1998 | Kerr Eby* |
| 1992 | Joe Bowler | 1996 | Anton Otto Fisher* | 1998 | Edward Penfield* |
| 1992 | Edwin A. Georgi* | 1996 | Windsor McCay* | 1998 | Martha Sawyers* |
| 1992 | Dorothy Hood* | 1996 | Violet Oakley* | 1999 | Andrew Loomis |
| 1993 | Robert McGinnis | 1996 | Mead Schaeffer | 1999 | Rose O'Neill |
| 1993 | Thomas Nast* | 1997 | Diane and Leo Dillon | 1999 | Adolph Treidler |
| 1993 | Coles Phillips* | 1997 | Frank McCarthy | 1999 | Mitchell Hooks |
| 1994 | Harry Anderson | 1997 | Chesley Bonestell* | 1999 | Stanley Meltzoff |

# SIGNIFICANT YEARS IN AMERICAN ADVERTISING

## ADVERTISING CAMPAIGNS

1929 Coca-Cola, "The Pause That Refreshes," D'Arcy Co.

1948 DeBeers, "A Diamond Is Forever," N. W. Ayer & Son.

1955 Marlboro, The Marlboro Man, Leo Burnett Co.

1957 Clairol, "Does She . . . or Doesn't She?," Foote, Cone & Belding.

1959 Volkswagen, "Think Small," Doyle Dane Bernbach.

1963 Avis, "We Try Harder," Doyle Dane Bernbach.

1971 McDonald's, "You Deserve a Break Today," Needham, Harper & Steers.

1974 Miller Lite beer, "Tastes Great, Less Filling," McCann-Erickson Worldwide.

1981 Absolut Vodka, The Absolut Bottle, TBWA.

1988 Nike, "Just Do It," Wieden & Kennedy.

## ADVERTISING SLOGANS

1912 "When It Rains It Pours" (Morton Salt)

1929 "The Pause That Refreshes" (Coca-Cola)

1933 "Breakfast of Champions" (Wheaties)

1948 "A Diamond Is Forever" (DeBeers)

1957 "Does She . . . or Doesn't She?" (Clairol)

1959 "Good to the Last Drop" (Maxwell House)

1963 "We Try Harder" (Avis)

1974 "Tastes Great, Less Filling" (Miller Lite)

1988 "Just Do It" (Nike)

1984 "Where's the Beef?" (Wendy's)

## ADVERTISING JINGLES

1931 "Mmm, Mmm, Good" (Campbell's Soup)

1959 "Double Your Pleasure, Double Your Fun" (Wrigley's Doublemint gum)

1947 "Pepsi Cola Hits the Spot" (Pepsi Cola)

1948 "See the USA in Your Chevrolet" (GM)

1955 "A Little Dab'll Do Ya" (Brylcreem)

1954 "Winston tastes Good Like a Cigarette Should" (Winston)

1963 "I Wish I Were an Oscar Meyer Wiener" (Oscar Meyer)

1970 "It's the Real Thing" (Coca Cola)

1971 "You Deserve a Break Today" (McDonald's)

1981 "Be All That You Can Be" (U.S. Army)

## ADVERTISING ICONS

1893 Aunt Jemima (Aunt Jemima pancake mixes and syrup)

1893 The Michelin Man "Bibendum" (Michelin tires)

1925 The Jolly Green Giant (Green Giant vegetables)

1938 Elsie [the Cow] (Borden dairy products)

1921 Betty Crocker (Betty Crocker food products)

1952 Tony the Tiger (Kellogg's Sugar Frosted Flakes)

1955 The Marlboro Man (Marlboro cigarettes)

1963 Ronald McDonald (McDonald's restaurants)

1965 The Pillsbury Doughboy (Assorted Pillsbury foods)

1989 The Energizer Bunny (Eveready Energizer batteries)

# BIBLIOGRAPHY

## BOOKS

Ackland-Snow, Nicola, and others. *The Art of the Club Flyer*. London: Thames and Hudson, 1996.

Adams, Steven. *The Arts & Crafts Movement*. Secaucus, NJ: Chartwell Books, Inc., 1987.

Becker, Stephen. *Comic Art in America*. New York: Simon and Schuster, Inc., 1959.

Bierut, Michael, and others, ed. *Looking Closer: Critical Writings on Graphic Design*. New York: Allworth Press, 1994.

Bierut, Michael, and others, ed. *Looking Closer III: Classic Writings on Graphic Design*. New York: Allworth Press, 1999.

Bilski, Emily D. *Berlin Metropolis, Jews and the New Culture, 1890–1918*. Berkeley, Los Angeles, London: University of California Press, 1999.

Bird, William L. Jr. *Better Living: Advertising, Media, and the New Vocabulary of Business Leadership 1935–1955*. Evanston, Illinois: Northwestern University Press, 1999.

Blackwell, Lewis, contributor. *The End of Print: The Graphic Design of David Carson*. San Francisco: Chronicle Books, 1996.

Cabarga, Leslie. *Progressive German Graphics, 1900–1937*. San Francisco: Chronicle Books, 1994.

Chernevich, Elena. *Soviet Commercial Design of the Twenties*. New York: Abbeville Press, 1987.

Clever, James. *A History of Graphic Art*. Ilkley, West Yorkshire, England: Scolar Press Limited, 1977.

Collins, Michael. *Towards Post Modernism: Decorative Arts and Design Since 1851*. Boston: Little, Brown and Co., 1987.

Couperie, Pierre, and others. *A History of the Comic Strip*. New York: Crown Publishers, Inc. 1968.

Craig, James and Bruce Barton. *Thirty Centuries of Graphic Design*. New York: Watson-Guptill Publications, 1987.

DeNoon, Christopher. *Posters of the WPA*. Los Angeles: Wheatley Press, 1987.

Dluhosch, Eric and Rotislav Svácha, eds. *Karel Teige 1900–1951: L'enfant Terrible of the Czech Modernist Avant-Garde*. Cambridge, London: MIT Press, 1999.

Dormer, Peter. *Design Since 1945*. New York: Thames and Hudson, Inc., 1993.

Duncombe, Stephen. *Notes from Underground: Zines and the Politics of Alternative Culture*. London, New York: Verso, 1997.

Fabre, Maurice. *A History of Communications*. New York: Hawthorn Books, Inc., 1963.

Friedman, Mildred. *Graphic Design in America: A Visual Language History*. Minneapolis: Walker Art Center. New York: Harry N. Abrams, Inc., 1989.

Gonzáles, Julio. *Lajos Kassák*. Budapest: IVAM Centre, 1999.

Heller, Steven and Julie Lasky. *Borrowed Design: Use and Abuse of Historical Form*. New York: Van Notrand Reinhold, 1993.

Heller, Steven and Karen Pomeroy. *Design Literacy: Understanding Graphic Design*. New York: Allworth Press, 1997.

Heller, Steven. *Design Literacy (continued): Understanding Graphic Design*. New York: Allworth Press, 1999.

Heller, Steven. *Paul Rand*. London: Phaidon Press Ltd., 1999.

Heller, Steven and Louise Fili. *Typology: Type Design from the Victorian Era to the Digital Age*. San Francisco: Chronicle Books, 1999.

Heller, Steven and Anne Fink. *Faces on the Edge: Type in the Digital Age*. New York: Van Nostrand Reinhold, 1997.

Hekett, John. *Industrial Design*. New York: Thames and Hudson, Inc., 1993.

Hiesinger, Kathryn B. and George H. Marcus. *Landmarks of Twentieth-Century Design: An Illustrated Handbook*. New York: Abbeville Press Publishers, 1993.

Hillebrand, Henri, ed. *Graphic Designers in Europe/3*. New York: Universe Books, 1973.

Hillebrand, Henri, ed. *Graphic Designers in the US/2*. New York: Universe Books, 1971.

Hollis, Richard. *Graphic Design: A Concise History*. London: Thames and Hudson, Ltd., 1994.

Holme, Bryan. *Advertising: Reflections of a Century*. New York: Viking Press, 1982.

Hornung, Clarence P. and Fridolf Johnson. *200 Years of American Graphic Art*. New York: George Braziller, 1976.

Horsham, Michael. *20s & 30s Style*. London: Chartwell Books, Inc., 1989.

Labuz, Ronald. *Contemporary Graphic Design*. New York: Van Nostrand Reinhold, 1991.

Lesser, Robert. *Pulp Art*. New York: Gramercy Books, 1997.

Lewis, John. *The Twentieth Century Book*. London: Studio Vista Limited, 1967.

Lionni, Leo. *Between Worlds: The Autobiography of Leo*

*Lionni.* New York: Alfred A. Knopf, 1997.

Lupton, Ellen and Abbot Miller. *Design, Writing Research: Writing on Graphic Design.* London: Phaidon Press Limited, 1999.

Marchand, Roland. *Creating the Corporate Soul: The Rise of Public Relations and Corporate Imagery in American Big Business.* Berkeley, Los Angeles, London: University of California Press, 1998.

Martin, Diana. *Graphic Design: Inspirations and Motivations.* Cincinnati: Northlight Books, 1995.

McAlhone, Beryl, and others. *A Smile in the Mind: Witty Thinking in Graphic Design.* London: Phaidon Press Ltd., 1998.

McDermott, Catherine. *Design Museum Book of Twentieth Century Design.* Woodstock, NY: Overlook Press, 1998.

Meggs, Philip B. *A History of Graphic Design,* First Edition. New York: Van Nostrand Reinhold, 1983.

Meggs, Philip B. *A History of Graphic Design,* Second Edition. New York: Van Nostrand Reinhold, 1992.

Meggs, Philip B. *A History of Graphic Design,* Third Edition. New York: John Wiley & Sons, 1998.

Meggs Philip B. *6 Chapters in Design: Bass, Chermayeff, Glaser, Rand, Tanaka, Tomaszewski.* San Francisco: Chronicle Books, 1997.

Miller, J. Abbot. *Dimensional Typography: Case Studies on the Shape of Letters,* A Kiosk Report. Princeton: Princeton Architectural Press, 1996.

Minick, Scott and Jiao Ping. *Chinese Graphic Design in the Twentieth Century, 1870–1920.* New York: Van Nostrand Reinhold, 1990.

Müller-Brockmann, Josef. *A History of Visual Communications.* Teufen, Switzerland: Verlag Arthur Niggli, New York: Visual Communication Books, Hastings House, 1971.

Parry, Linda, ed. *William Morris.* New York: Harry N. Abrams, Inc., 1996.

Reed, Walt and Roger. *The Illustrator in America: 1890–1980.* New York: Madison Square Press, Inc., 1984.

Steranko, James. *The Steranko History of Comics.* Reading: Supergraphics, 1972.

Thomson, Ellen M. *The Origins of Graphic Design in America.* New Haven & London: Yale University Press, 1997.

Thorgerson, Storm and Aubrey Powell. *100 Best Album Covers.* London, New York, Sydney: DK Publishing, Inc., 1999.

Wrede, Stuart. *The Modern Poster.* New York: Little, Brown and Company, 1988.

Whitford, Frank, ed. *The Bauhaus: Masters and Students by Themselves.* Woodstock, NY: Overlook Press, 1993.

## PERIODICALS

*Advertising Age: The Advertising Century* Special Issue. 1999.

*Graphic Design and Advertising: Timeline.* Communication Arts. Vol. 41, No. 1, pp 80–95, 1999.

Spiegelman, Art. "Comix 101: Forms Stretched to Their Limits." *The New Yorker.* April 19, pp. 77–85, 1999.

## EXHIBITION BOOKS, ANNUALS, PROMOTIONAL MATERIAL, NEWSLETTERS

Albrecht, Donald, and others, essayist. *The Work of Charles and Ray Eames: A Legacy of Invention.* New York: Harry N. Abrams, Inc., 1997.

American Institute of Graphic Arts. *Graphic Design USA: 16 The Annual of the AIGA.* New York: Watson-Guptill Publishing, 1995.

Groninger Museum. *Memphis 1981–1988.* Milan: Como Sud, 1990.

Lupton, Ellen. *Mixing Messages: Graphic Design in Contemporary Culture.* New York: Cooper-Hewitt National Design Museum, Smithsonian Institution, and Princeton Architectural Press, 1996.

Naumann, Francis M. and Beth Venn. *Making Mischief: Dada Invades New York.* New York: Whitney Museum of American Art, 1996.

Spiegelman, Art. *Comix, Essays, Graphics and Scraps.* New York: La Centrale dell'Arte/Raw Books, 1998.

*Graphis Design Annual 1998* and *1999.* New York: Watson-Guptill Publications, Inc.

Heller, Steven, ed. *Design & Style-7, Bauhaus 1919–1933.* Cohoes, NY: Mohawk Paper Company, distributors, 1989.

*American Design Century.* Cloquet, MN: Potlatch Corp., distributors, 1999.

*Apple Media Arts.* vol. 2, no. 1, 1999.

## REFERENCE BOOKS AND ENCYCLOPEDIAS

Dormer, Peter. "Introduction." *The Illustrated Dictionary of Twentieth Century Designers.* New York: Mallard Press, 1991.

Crystal, David. *The Cambridge Factfinder.* New York: Cambridge University Press, 1993.

Julier, Guy. *The Thames and Hudson Encyclopedia of 20th Century Design and Designers.* London: Thames and Hudson, Ltd., 1993.

Katz, Ephraim. *The Film Encyclopedia.* New York: Harper Perennial, 1994.

Pile, John. *Dictionary of 20th Century Design.* New York: Roundtable Press, Inc., 1990.

Wallechinsky, David. *The People's Almanac Presents the 20th Century.* New York: Little, Brown and Co., 1995.

*1995 Information Please Almanac Atlas & Yearbook.* New York: Houghton Mifflin Co., 1995.

## WORLD WIDE WEB

Harvey, R. C. "R. C. Harvey Nominates the Century's Top U.S. Editorial Cartoonists." *The Detroit News.* www.detnews.com/AAEC/winter99/harvey/harvey.htm

"Comic Art and Graffix Gallery." *Virtual Museum and Encyclopedia.* www.comic-art/index2.htm

"Timeline of Computer History." *The Computer Museum History Center.* www.computerhistory.org/timeline/

Brown, David E. Brown. "Punk is Not Dead." *Metropolis Insites*, July 1998. www.metropolismag.com

*Communication Arts.* www.commarts.com

*Cooper Hewitt National Design Museum.* www.si.edu/ndm

*Counterspace.* www.studiomotiv.com/counterspace

*Rochester Institute of Technology Design Archive.* http://design.rit.edu/timeline.html

*Émigré.* www.emigre.com

*Fuse 95.* www.fontshop.de/fuse95/fusetalk

*Graphis.* www.graphis.com/main.EN.html

*The Herb Lubalin Study Center for Design and Typography.* www.cooper.edu/art/lubalin

Lange, Alexandra. *The Bookmaker.* www.design.rit.edu/timeline.html

*National Cartoon Society.* www.reuben.org/nsc_history.asp

*Museum of Modern Art.* www.moma.org

*Print magazine.* www.printmag.com/home/index.html

*Razorfish studios.* www.rsub.com/about.html

*Razorfish Studios.* TypoGRAPHIC. www.typographic.razorfish.com

*Society of Illustrators.* www.societyillustrators.org/permanent_collection

*Scudiero, Maurizio. The Italian Futurist Book.* Colophon Gallery. www.colophon.com/gallery/futurism/index.html

*Typereview.* www.typereview.com

*Typographic.* www.TYPOgraphic.com

*U&lc Online.* www.esselte.com/itc/ulc/index.html

*Yahoo News.* www.dailynews.yahoo.com

# INDEX

## A

Aalto, Alvar, 79, 182
Abstract Expressionism, 129, 159
Achenbaum, Al, 71
Addams, Charles, 208
Advertising Clubs of America, 40
Advertising Code, 38
A. G. Hyde & Sons, 48
Agha, Mehemed Fehmy (M. F.), 110, 187
Aicher, Otl, 65, 126, 129, 152, 174, 216
Albers, Josef, 61, 73, 94, 127, 129, 160, 182
Alex Isley Design, 208
Ally, Carl, 152
Ally & Gargano, 152, 186
American Association of Advertising Agencies, 52
American Institute of Graphic Arts (AIGA), 26, 46
Ammirati & Puris, 180, 186
Analytical Cubism, 34
Anderson, Carl, 72
Anderson, Charles S., 143, 202, 205, 211
Anderson, Gail, 153, 206
Anderson, Ian, 150
Ansel, Ruth, 98, 154
Apollinaire, Guillaume, 53–54, 55
Aragon, Louis, 56, 197
Arensberg, Louise, 47, 133
Arensberg, Walter, 47
Arnheim, Rudolf, 25, 135
Arno, Peter, 25, 165
Arntz, Gerd, 208
Arp, Jean Hans, 47, 51, 139, 159
Art Deco, 68, 70–71, 82, 83, 88, 99, 214
  European, 60
Art Nouveau, 4, 7, 10, 16, 20, 26, 38, 40, 46, 109, 150, 153, 170
  Dutch, 30
Artzybasheff, Boris, 159
Ashbee, Charles R., 4, 20, 109

Ashcan School, 33
Associated Advertising Clubs of America, 24, 40, 46
Associated Advertising Clubs of the World, 46
Association of American Advertisers, 13
Association of National Advertisers, 13, 46
Atherton, John, 110, 130
Aufuldish, Bob, 150, 215, 225, 228
Aurél, Bernáth, 57, 197
Auriol, Georges, 6, 100
Avedon, Richard, 67, 114, 140, 144, 159
Ayer, N. W., 77, 188

## B

Backer, Bill, 73, 172, 188, 203
Backer & Spielvogel, 188
Backer Spielvogel Bates, 207
Baker, George, 108
Bakst, Leon N, 69
Baldowski, Clifford, 55
Ball, Hugo, 51, 53, 74
Balla, Giacomo, 38, 48, 143
Ballmer, Théo, 21, 159
Barnbrook, Jonathan, 159, 215, 223
Baron, Fabian, 145, 214, 218
Barton, Bruce, 54, 69, 163
Barton, Durstine & Osborn, 72, 76
Barton, Ralph, 84
Bass, Saul, 61, 116, 132, 134, 136, 142, 144, 148, 153, 159, 166, 172, 174, 186, 192, 196, 208, 216, 220, 227
Bates, Theodore L., 18, 92, 104–105, 159, 175
Bates Worldwide, 229
Batten, Barton, Durstine & Osborn (BBD&O), 76, 83, 104, 116, 149, 155, 164, 176, 180, 204, 208, 229
Batton, Barton & Osborn, 154
Bauhaus, 56, 60–62, 64–67, 69, 70–

74, 76, 83, 89, 96–97, 99, 104, 192
  Manifesto, 56
Baumhofer, Walter M., 25, 88, 207
Bayer, Herbert, 66, 70, 71, 72–73, 76, 82, 90, 92, 97, 98, 101, 117, 120, 132, 139, 203
Beall, Lester, 22, 92, 96, 112, 130, 136, 143, 144, 149, 167
Beck, C. C., 104
Beck, Henry C., 22, 88, 178
Bedin, Martine, 140
Beeke, Anthon, 105, 224
Beekers, Frank, 130, 184
Beers, Charlotte, 92, 188
Behrens, Peter, 5, 16, 17, 19, 22, 30–31, 33, 35, 38, 45, 105
Belding, Don, 167
Bentley, Nicholas, 30, 187
Benton & Bowles, 92, 105, 142, 156
Benton, Linn Boyd, 87
Benton, Morris Fuller (M. F.), 23, 29, 31, 33, 45, 47, 53, 61, 79, 83, 120
Berg, John, 87, 148, 162, 182
Bergson, Henri, 107
Berlarski, Rudolph, 199
Berlewi, Henryk, 69, 163
Bernard, Pierre, 109, 170, 194
Bernard, Walter, 164, 230
Bernbach, William, (Bill), 41, 122, 157, 197
Bernhard, Lucian, 26, 38, 40, 42, 48, 64, 77, 118, 127, 175
Bigelow, Charles, 114, 203
Bill, Max, 33, 74, 84, 108, 129, 222
Binder, Joseph, 66, 86, 92, 100, 104, 106, 112, 175
Black, Misha, 111, 138, 184
Black, Roger, 202, 206, 211
Blackburn, Bruce, 182
Blackett & Sample, 74
Blackett-Sample-Hummert, 74, 83
Blechman, R. O., 100, 126, 154, 163, 192, 196
Block, Herbert L., 34, 126
Blue Rider, 61, 65. *See also Der Bluer*

*Reiter*

Boccioni, Umberto, 38
Bonfils, Robert, 175
Bonnard, Pierre, 118
Bonsiepe, Gui, 91, 159
Bortnyik, Sandor, 71
Boulat, Pierre, 71, 115
Bozell & Jacobs, 62
Bradley, Will, 23, 24, 30, 38, 54, 70,
    153
Branzi, Andrea, 98, 161, 182, 185
Braque, Georges, 34, 155
Breton, André, 56, 63, 69, 159
Breuer, Marcel, 21, 61, 71, 73, 77, 93,
    135, 194
Briggs, Clare, 24
Brodovitch, Alexey, 82, 90, 106, 122,
    135, 140, 142, 144, 156, 162, 172
Brody, Neville, 140, 192, 194, 198,
    201, 206, 208–210, 214–215, 217,
    221, 223
Brownjohn, Chermayeff & Geismar,
    140, 142, 144, 148
Brownjohn, Robert, 71, 134, 140, 148,
    156, 171
Burnett, Leo, 92, 172
Burns, Aaron, 65, 150, 170, 216
Burrell, Thomas J., 100, 193
Burtin, Will, 33, 98, 114, 122, 127,
    142, 148, 175


**C**

Caflisch, Max, 50, 110
Calder, Alexander, 182
Calkins, Dick (Richard), 78
Calkins, Earnest Elmo, 21, 94, 157
Calkins & Holden, 21
Calvert, Margaret, 156
Caniff, Milton, 90, 108, 118
Capp, Al (Alfred), 34, 90, 189
Carlu, Jean, 82, 86, 101, 106, 108, 210
Carnase, Tom, 100, 162, 165, 170,
    171
Carrá, Carlo, 38, 52, 159

Carson, Carol Devine, 206
Carson, David, 139, 198, 208, 220,
    221, 228
Carter, Matthew, 97, 158, 192, 207,
    225
Case, Stephen M., 143
Casey, Jacqueline S., 74, 127, 170, 216
Cassandre, A.M.(Adolphe Jean–Marie
    Mouron), 66, 77, 84, 86, 90, 92,
    95, 97, 100, 165
Cassatt, Mary, 73
Caturegli, Beppe, 140
Chagall, Marc, 160, 203
Chantry, Art, 135, 192, 210, 216, 222
Chaplin, Charlie, 44, 95, 105, 184
Chappell, Warren, 25, 64, 99, 105
Charles S. Anderson Design Com-
    pany, 211
Chermayeff & Geismar, 148, 154,
    156, 159, 164, 172, 188, 202, 204,
    214, 218
Chermayeff, Ivan, 87, 140, 182, 193
Chiat, Jay, 84, 163
Chiat/Day, 163, 164, 200, 206, 224
Chiat/Day/Mojo, 210
Christiansen, Hans, 13, 114
Christy, Howard Chandler, 130
Chwast, Seymour, 84, 132, 134, 140,
    150, 156, 166, 171, 178, 202
Cibic, Aldo, 136, 193
Circle of Hungarian Activists, 49
Cleary, Ed, 122, 222
Cleland, T. M., 21, 53, 76, 82, 104,
    157
Cliff Freeman & Partners, 224
Close, Chuck, 105
Clow, Lee, 109, 210
Coates, Wells, 143
Cobden–Sanderson, T. J., 65
Cober, Alan E., 94, 175, 230
Coburn, Alvin Langdon, 44, 52, 159
Coburn, Ralph, 127, 159
Cocteau, Jean, 40, 155
Cohen, Fré, 22, 110
Cohen, Henry, 156

Coiner, Charles T., 94, 156, 210
Cole, Jack, 47, 106, 143
Coles Phillips, 62
Colin, Paul, 70, 86, 204
Colwell, Elizabeth, 44, 51
Conde Nast, 110, 117, 151, 188, 198
Cone, Fairfax, 22, 184
Constructivism, 63–64, 65, 66, 70, 82,
    192
    Russian, 64
    Movement, 56
Cook and Shanosky Associates, 176
Cooper, Austin, 66, 68, 82, 157
Cooper, Muriel, 71, 163, 166, 177,
    222
Cooper, Oswald Bruce., 57, 60, 63,
    77, 105
Le Corbusier. *See* Le Corbusier
Cordiant, 224, 229
Crain, C. D. Jr., 82, 176
Crain Communications, 82
Crane, Walter, 48
Craw, Freeman, 143–144, 151
Craw, Freeman Godfrey, 52
Crawford, Bruce, 78, 180
Cray, Seymour, 71, 183
Cronin, Michael, 129, 192
Crosby, Fletcher, Forbes, 159, 174
Crosby, Percy Lee, 60, 157
Crosby, Theo, 71, 159, 222
Crotti, Jean, 143
Crouwel, Wim, 77, 163, 167, 192
Crumb, Robert, 110, 162, 164, 177,
    223
Cruz, Andy, 219
Cubism, 38, 148
    Czech, 41
    Synthetic, 45
Curry, John Steuart, 116
Curtis, Cyrus H. K., 38, 89


**D**

Dada, 51, 52, 56, 63–64, 65, 67, 90,
    165

Berlin, 55, 57, 61
New York, 53
Dair, Carl, 42, 163
Dali, Salvador, 25, 85, 95, 117, 120, 153, 210
Daniel Starch & Staff, 28
Danne & Blackburn, 178
Danzinger, Louis, 67, 122, 138, 174
D'Arcy, MacManus, Benton & Bowles, 91
D'Arcy, Masius, Benton & Bowles, 170
Darling, Jay N., 50, 153
Davis, Paul, 98, 144, 156, 162, 171, 180, 200
Davis, Phil (Philip), 90
Davis, Stuart, 157
De Beck, Billy (William), 56
de Bretteville, Sheila Levrant, 105, 172, 176, 214
de Chirico, Giorgio, 47, 52, 67, 187
de Harak, Rudolph, 130, 148, 164, 166, 176
de La Fresnaye, Roger, 71
De Lucchi, Michele, 129, 193, 204
*De Stijl*, 52, 63
de Wilde, Barbara, 153
de Zayas, Marius, 45, 150
Dean, Jeremy, 175, 223
Deck, Barry, 215, 231
Deco, 64
Deconstructionism, 163, 202, 209
Degenerate Art, 97
Delaunay, Robert, 107
Delehanty, Kurnit & Geller, 157
Della Femina, Jerry, 94
DeLucchi, Michele, 185
Delvaux, Paul, 222
Demuth, Charles, 92
Deni, Viktor Nikolaevich, 54, 86, 116
Depero, Fortunato, 40, 46, 48–49, 68, 70, 74, 76, 78, 84, 88, 127, 141, 149
*Der Bluer Reiter*, 41. *See also* Blue Rider
Derain, André, 135

Design and Industries Association, 48
Design Research Unit, 159
Deutsche Werkbund, 30
*Devetsil* Group, 61
Dexel, Walter, 76, 176
Diaghilev, Sergei, 40, 78
Dirks, Rudolph, 44, 122
Disney, Walt, 18, 65, 84, 97, 105, 157, 165
DiSpigna, Tony, 110, 179
Dix, Otto, 167
Doblin, Jay, 61, 158, 159, 210
Dooijes, Dick, 34, 121
Dorfsman, Lou, 55, 100, 104, 110, 116, 134, 145, 150, 156, 164
Dove, Arthur G., 116
Doyle, Stephen, 139, 202
Doyle Dane Bernbach, 122, 148, 154–155, 158–159, 163, 171, 174, 176, 188, 204
Doyle Graf Mabley, 208
Drayton, Grace Gebbie, 60, 84
Dreier, Katherine, 61, 130
Drenttel, William, 133, 202
Dreyfuss, Henry, 25, 97, 105, 149, 155, 165, 175
Drucker, Johanna, 130, 192
Du Pasquier, Nathalie, 140
Duchamp, Marcel, 41, 45, 52–53, 55, 61–62, 104, 162, 165
Duffy, Ben, 116, 171
Duffy, Joe, 122, 202
Duffy, Raoul, 128, 133
Duffy Design Group, 202, 207, 211
Dumbar, Gert, 105, 184
Dumm, Edwina, 50
Dusenberry, Phil, 94
Dwiggins, W. A., 5, 64, 79, 93, 99, 106, 140

**E**
Eames, Charles, 30, 92, 106, 109, 111, 127, 139, 143, 145, 157, 165, 185, 187

Eames, Ray, 42, 106, 111, 127, 139, 157, 165, 185, 208
Eckersey, Richard, 107, 210
Eckersley, Tom, 47, 110, 134, 140, 155, 229
Eckerstrom, Ralph, 65, 140, 158, 159, 227
Eckmann, Otto, 17, 21
Ehmcke, Fritz Helmuth, 34, 159
Eisner, Michael, 109, 201
Elementarism, 68
Elenga, Henk, 118, 192
Eluard, Paul, 130
Erdt, Hans Rudi, 40, 50, 55
Ernst, Max, 47, 63, 90, 159
Erté, (Roman de Tirtoff), 68, 214
Essex, Joseph Michael, 118
Esslinger, Hartmut, 167
Excoffon, Roger, 38, 133, 143, 149, 199
Expressionism, 27, 38, 41, 64, 148
German, 61

**F**
Fallon, McElligott, Rice, 194, 200
Faulkner, Kristen, 171
Fauve Movement, 13
Federico, Gene, 55, 116, 118, 130, 144, 232
Feiffer, Jules, 78, 136, 138
Feininger, Lyonel, 28, 55–56, 139
Feitler, Bea, 98, 154, 174, 197, 198
Fella, Edward, 98, 206, 220, 221
Fili, Louise, 129, 186, 198, 210
Finlay, Virgil, 47, 140, 172
Fisher, Bud (Harold), 30, 32
Fisher, Carl, 69
Fisher, Ham (Hammond), 82, 136
Fisher, Robert, 153, 216
Fitz-Gobbon, Bernice, 134, 197
Fitzpatrick, Daniel R., 44, 167
Flagg, James Montgomery, 144, 149
Fleckhaus, Willy, 71, 130, 144, 192, 199

Fleischer, Maxwell, 77, 149
Fletcher, Alan, 84, 140, 150
Fletcher, Forbes & Gill, 154, 159
Flisak, Jerzy, 83
Fogleman, James K., 128, 159
Folk Art, 156
Foote, Cone & Belding, 83, 112, 136, 138, 140, 204
Foote, Emerson, 28, 218
Foote, Mary Hallock, 98
Forbáth, Alréd, 175
Forbes, Colin, 77, 150, 154, 186
Ford, Henry, 118
Foster, Harold, 78, 94, 96
Frankfurt, Stephen, 84,152,164
Frankfurt Balkind Partners, 164
Freberg, Stan, 73, 140, 171
Freberg Ltd., 171
Frederico, Gene, 232
Frederick, Otto, 77
Freeman, Cliff, 170, 206
Freeman, Mander & Gossage, 140, 164
Frere-Jones, Tobias, 171, 221, 223
Friedman, Dan, 172, 174, 182, 184, 185, 224
Frogdesign, 167
Froshaug, Anthony, 61, 140, 142, 201
Frutiger, Adrian, 77, 130, 133, 135, 141, 152, 189, 197, 205
Fukuda, Shigeo, 87, 170
Fuller, Buckminster R., 76, 122, 199
Furtiger, Adrian, 183
Futurism, 27, 34, 47, 49, 56, 68, 70, 74, 127
Fu-Xi, Sun, 71, 153


**G**

Gage, Bob, 62, 122, 132, 236
Games, Abram, 47, 108, 120, 229
Gan, Aleksei, 62, 64, 109
Gargano, Amil, 89, 152
Garland, Ken, 78, 122, 138, 162
Gaudi, Antonio, 73

Gauguin, Paul, 17, 22
Geisel, Theodor Seuss (Dr. Seuss), 25, 126, 140, 214, 222
Geismar, Thomas, 84, 140, 154, 176
Geissbuhler, Steff, 109, 148, 185, 214
Genet, Jean, 38
Geometric Formalism, 38
Georg Jensen Workshop, 26
George Batten Co., 76
George Batten Newspaper Advertising Agency, 5
Gerhard, Günter, 148
German Workshop, 24
Gerstner, Karl, 144, 178
Gibson, Charles Dana, 16, 48, 52, 112
Giedion, Sigfried, 120, 139, 165
Gill, Arthur Eric Rowton, 77, 79, 105
Gill, Bob, 84, 150, 159
Gipkens, Julius, 52
Giusti, George, 33, 100, 109, 142, 148
Glaser, Milton, 78, 126, 132, 134, 154, 156, 162, 164, 165, 166, 171, 178, 180, 198, 210, 222, 230
Gleizes, Alber, 133
Goines, David Lance, 114, 174
Goldberg, Carin, 133
Goldberg, Ruben (Rube) L., 16, 30, 133, 171
Golden, William, 41, 96, 104, 120, 128, 145
Goldsholl, Morton, 41, 126
Goncharova, Natalia, 153
Gonda, Tomás, 73, 203
Goodhue, Bertram G., 68
Gorey, Edward, 71, 236
Gorman, Pat, 118, 194
Gossage, Howard Luck, 52, 140, 167
Gottlieb, Adolph, 22, 178
Goudy, Frederic W., 5, 8–9, 11, 13, 19, 23, 33, 41, 46, 48, 49, 51, 55, 57, 60, 62, 67, 69, 73, 74, 77, 79, 83, 94, 95, 100, 104, 116, 117, 118
Gould, Chester, 84
"graffiti" art, 193
Graves, Michael, 91, 174, 189, 195,

198, 231
Gray, Eileen, 77
Gray, Harold, 68, 165
Gray, Milner, 111
Gray, Nicolette, 41, 98, 134, 172, 229
Green, Elizabeth Shippen, 60, 135
Greenberg, Richard, 118, 184
Greenberg, Robert, 184
Greiman, April, 120, 182, 184, 185, 186, 188, 196, 198, 204, 208, 224, 236
Grey Advertising, 118, 140
Griffin, Rick, 112, 160, 162, 164, 166, 216
Gris, Juan, 18, 43, 75
Gropius, Walter, 40, 47, 55, 56, 62, 66–67, 67, 69, 70–71, 72, 73, 76, 90, 97, 139, 167
Grossman, Robert, 154
Grosz, George, 50, 52, 55, 62
Guimard, Hector, 109


**H**

Hadders, Gerald, 135, 192
Hal Riney & Partners, 182
Hall, Joyce, 112, 197
Hammer, Victor, 71, 82, 111, 163
Haring, Keith, 143, 193, 209, 214
Harper, Marion Jr., 50, 210
Harrington, Ollie, 42, 92, 224
Hart, Johnny, 142, 156
Hausmann, Raoul, 52, 82, 172
Haviden, Ashley, 22, 83, 128, 137, 176
Heal, Ambrose, 145
Hearst, William Randolph, 42, 44, 48, 129, 162
Heartfield, John (Helmut Herzfelde), 50, 52, 55, 62, 66, 74, 86, 89, 90, 160, 165
Heckel, Eric, 27, 171
Held, John Jr., 70, 143
Helfand, Jessica, 149
Herbert, Ira, 74
Herdeg, Walter, 82, 112, 204, 224

Herriman, George, 40, 44

Hersey, John, 135, 192, 206

Herzfelde, Wieland, 52, 62, 208

Hess, Richard, 91, 188, 216

Hess, Sol, 39, 61, 133

Hewitt, Ogilvy, Benson & Mather, 120, 128

Hinrichs, Kit, 228

Hirschfeld, Al, 22, 64

Höch, Hannah, 52, 57, 82, 187

Hoefler, Jonathan, 171, 219, 221, 225

Hofer, Karl, 136

Hofmann, Armin, 61, 118, 134, 136, 144, 156, 158, 165, 177, 202

Hoffmann, Josef, 11, 22, 26, 139

Hofman, Pieter A.H., 159

Hogarth, Burne, 94

Hohlwein, Ludwig, 32, 40, 46, 94, 122

Hollein, Hans, 163, 197

Holman, Bill (William), 92

Holmes, Kris, 127

Holz, Arno, 78

Hopkins, Claude C., 30, 87

Howitt, John Newton, 78, 143

Hubbard, Elbert, 8, 18, 48

Huber, Max, 120, 126, 218

Hummert, Frank, 74, 97, 159

Hurlburt, Allen, 38, 116, 128, 132, 164, 199

Huszar, Vilmos, 52, 149

Huxley, Walter, 93, 136

**I**

Igarashi, Takenobu, 112, 170, 183, 198

Isley, Alexander, 150, 202, 204, 208

Issigonis, Alec, 28, 145, 208

Itten, Johannes, 163

**J**

J. Walter Thompson Company, 13, 32, 40, 42, 68, 86, 170, 206

Jacobsen, Arne, 21, 143, 172

Jacobson, Egbert, 95, 130, 139, 160

Jacoby, Robert, 77, 153, 176, 204

Jane Trahey Associates, 142

Jansen, Gustav B., 94

Jencks, Charles, 100, 174, 176

Jensen, Jacob, 73, 175

Jie, Cao, 210

Jobs, Steve, 136

John Brown & Partners, 186

Johnson, Egbert, 159

Johnson, Henry Lewis, 11, 22, 26, 40, 97

Johnson, John H., 108, 114, 128

Johnson, Philip, 28, 187

Johnston, Edward, 22, 47, 51, 54, 77, 112

Juhl, Finn, 42, 123, 210

Jun–tao, Qian, 28, 82

**K**

Kahles, Charles W., 22, 28

Kalman, Tibor, 122, 188, 204, 208, 210, 214, 216, 230, 232

Kamekura, Yusaku, 48, 126, 128, 148, 156, 186

Kandinsky, Wassily, 18, 38, 41, 55, 65, 72, 112

Kane, Art, 71, 159

Karamata, Shiro, 97

Kare, Susan, 135, 200, 201

Katsui, Mitsuo, 84, 148, 150, 192

Kauffer, Edward McKnight, 42, 46, 54, 68, 88, 96, 104, 128, 135

Keedy, Jeffery, 211, 215

Keller, Ernst, 54, 165

Kelly, Walt (Walter), 122

Kennedy, David, 105, 196

Kepes, Gyorgy, 28, 96, 114, 139

Kessler, Harry Graf, 44

Ketcham, Hank (Henry), 128

Khachaturian, Aram, 22, 187

Kidd, Chip, 157, 220

Kieser, Gunther, 83

King, David, 188, 193, 205

Kinneir, Jock, 52, 156, 178

Kirby, Rollin, 130

Kirchner, Ernst Ludwig, 27, 54, 98

Kisman, Max, 133, 202, 211, 218, 222, 224, 228

Klee, Paul, 41, 61, 69, 72, 105

Klimt, Gustav, 11, 55

Klinger, Julius, 52, 127

Klutsis, Gustav, 67, 76, 78, 99, 109

Kmetty, János, 180

Kner, Albert 105, 182

Knerr, Harold H., 122

Koch, Rudolf, 39, 41, 65, 77, 91, 93

Kokoschka, Oskar, 52, 98, 193

Koppel, Terry, 127, 200

Koppel and Scher, 200, 216

Kroc, Ray, 21, 201

*Kunstlervereinigung,* 34

Kunz, Willi, 110, 180, 184, 185

Kupta, Frantisek, 140

Kurtzman, Harvey, 138

**L**

Lambert & Feasley, 66

Lampérth, Jóozsef Nemes, 50, 61, 69

Landor, Walter, 44, 106, 224

Landor and Associates, 106, 163

Lang, Fisher & Stashower, 104

Larionov, Michael, 136

Lautrec. *See* Toulouse-Lautrec

Lauwericks, J.L. Mathieu, 24, 87

Lawrence, Wells, 55

Le Corbusier, (Charles-Edourd Jeanneret), 55, 60, 71, 74, 77, 118, 120, 159

Leete, Alfred, 48, 89

Léger, Fernand, 56, 87, 101, 104, 136, 139

Lenica, Jan, 77

Leo Burnett Co., 92, 130, 136, 159, 222

Levine, David, 73, 154

Levine, Huntley, Schmidt, 174

Leyendecker, F. X., 64

Leyendecker, Joseph, 52, 129

Liberman, Alexander, 42, 96, 106, 112, 151

Licko, Zuzana, 150, 200, 205, 209, 211, 215, 217, 223, 225

Lintas, Lever International Advertising Services, 76

Lionni, Leo, 38, 88, 100, 118, 122, 126, 136, 140, 144, 150, 154, 232

Lipchitz, Jaques, 176

Lissitzky, El, (Lazar Markovich), 54, 56, 60, 62, 63–64, 66, 69, 70, 71, 72, 73–74, 76, 78, 79, 82, 107, 207

Löeffler, Berthold, 149

Loewy, Raymond, 91, 104, 159, 170, 204

Loffler, Berthold, 30

Lohse, Richard P., 21, 208

Lois, George, 84, 130, 144, 149, 153, 160, 164, 196

Longhauser, William, 118, 198

Loos, Adolf, 28, 89

Lord, Geller, Federico, Einstein, 163

Lord, Richard, 73, 163

Lord & Thomas, 30, 60

Louis, Morris, 42, 153

Lowell, Robert, 52, 184

Lubalin, Herb, 55, 104, 144, 152, 156, 162, 164, 165, 171, 177, 179, 194, 201, 203, 205, 224, 232

Luce, Henry, 67, 82, 94, 134, 163

Lustig, Alvin, 48, 104, 114, 121, 122, 126, 127, 129, 134, 136


**M**

Mabry, Michael, 136, 192, 216, 228

Macke, August, 41, 47

Mackmurdo, Arthur H., 109

MacManus, John & Adams, 91

MacManus, Theodore F., 48, 74, 91, 105

MacNelly, Jeff, 184

Magritte, René, 104, 159, 163

Makela, Laurie Haycock, 202

Makela, P. Scott, 149, 202, 214, 215, 232

Malevich, Kasimir, 45, 56, 92

Malraux, André, 182

Manwaring, Michael, 109, 192, 204

Marc, Franz, 41, 50

Mardersteig, Hans (Giovanni), 135, 184

Marin, John, 133

Marinetti, Filippo Tommaso, 34, 38, 43, 45, 47, 49, 83, 90, 112

Mariscal, Javier, 127

Marsteller, Inc., 172

Martin, David Stone, 50

Martin, Edgar, 68

Massey, John, 84, 140, 157, 174, 178

Massin, Robert, 71, 142, 154, 156, 158, 170, 174

Masson, André, 207

Matisse, Henri, 120, 135

Matter, Herbert, 87, 90, 92, 94, 100, 101, 111, 117, 121, 134, 201

Mau, Bruce, 145, 202, 236

Mauldin, Bill (William), 62

Max, Peter, 97, 170, 232

Maxwell Sackheim & Co., 118

Mayakovsky, Vladimir Vladimirovich, 55, 57, 66, 74, 83

McCann, Harrison King, 42, 83, 153

McCann–Erickson Worldwide, 83, 72, 178, 232

McCay, Winsor "Silas," 22, 34, 94

McConnell, John, 100

McCoy, Katherine, 114, 163, 172, 227

McCutcheon, John T., 20, 122

McDougall, Walt, 4

McElroy, Neil, 25, 110, 175

McGraw, James H. Sr., 94, 120

McLuhan, Marshall, 41, 129, 157, 163, 170, 171, 180, 193

McManus, George, 42, 114

McMullan, James, 91, 158, 204

McMurtrie, Douglas Crawford, 65, 67, 74, 77–78, 96, 112

Memphis Group, 195

Memphis Style, 195

Menotti, Gian Carlo, 41

Meyer, Adolf, 62

Meyer, Hannes, 76, 135

Meynell, Francis, 66, 180

Middleton, Robert Hunter, 69, 75, 79, 83, 85, 95, 105, 203

Miedinger, Max, 141, 193

Miehe, François, 109, 170

Mies van der Rohe, Ludwig, 142, 167

Miles, Reid, 74, 136, 152, 220

Mills, Mike, 159, 218

Milton Glaser, Inc., 178

Minale-Tatersfield, 156

Minimalism, 159

Miró, Joan, 71, 188, 199

Modernism, ix, 47, 90, 97, 140, 174

Modley, Rudolph, 28, 182

Moholy-Nagy, László, 61, 62–63, 66–67, 71, 72, 74, 76, 97, 116

Mok, Clement, 143, 206, 226

Molnar, Farkas, 63, 114

Mondrian, Piet, 38, 52, 53, 97, 112, 200

Moor, Dmitrii Stakhievich, 28, 82, 84, 116

Moore, Charles W., 71, 149

Moore, Henry, 204

Moore, Marianne, 175

Morandi, Girogio, 157

Morison, Stanley, 65, 79, 87

Morris, Talwin, 7, 41

Morris, William, 5

Morrison, Stanley, 163

Moscoso, Victor, 94, 160, 164

Moser, Koloman, 11, 13, 20, 22, 55

Mosley, Zack (Zackery), 88

Motherwell, Robert, 48

Mouron, Adolphe Jean-Marie, 66

Mucha, Alphonse, 18, 28, 100

Müller-Brockmann, Josef, 227

Munkacsi, Martin, 155

Munter, Gabrielle, 41, 153

Murdoch, Peter, 105, 164

Murdoch, Rupert, 84, 185, 207

Murphy, John Cullen, 120
Muthesius, Herman, 24, 30, 77


**N**

N. W. Ayer & Son, 6, 12, 13, 16
Nabokov, Vladimir, 143, 184
Nagai, Kazumasa, 78, 202
Nast, Condé, 109
Nast, Thomas, 21
National Advertising Board (NAB), 172, 174, 186
National Outdoor Advertising Bureau, 50
Needham, Harper & Steers, 172, 180, 194
Needham Harper Worldwide, 204
Nelson, Art, 30, 159
Neo–constructivism, 150
Neuburg, Hans, 25, 142, 199
Neurath, Otto, 70, 94, 96, 104, 114
"New Wave," 200
Newell, Peter, 32, 40, 42, 69
Nicholson, William, 122
Nitsche, Erik, 33, 78, 90, 132, 136
Nizzoli, Marcello, 167
Noland, Kenneth, 69
Nolde, Emil, 139
Nonobjective art, 38, 45
Norman, Craig & Kummel, 122, 150
Noyes, Elliott, 145
N. W. Ayer & Son, 42, 62, 118, 120, 156, 194


**O**

Oakley, Violet, 60, 150
Oberman, Emily, 155
Odermatt, Siegfried, 73, 126, 159, 160, 164
Odgers, Jayme, 100, 182, 188, 198
Ogilvy, Benson & Mather, 144
Ogilvy, David, 41, 152
Ogilvy & Mather, 157, 180, 182, 199, 206

Ogilvy Group, 208
O'Keeffe, Georgia, 53, 204
Olbrich, Joseph Maria, 11, 33
Olden, Georg, 61, 114, 154, 180
Oldenberg, Claes, 78, 155
Olinsky, Frank, 127, 194
Oliver, Vaughn, 140, 208
Olivetti, Adriano, 18, 98, 171
Omega Workshop, 45
Omnicom Group, 204
O'Neill, Rose, 112
Op Art, 156
Orazi, Emmanuel, 26, 91
Orozco, José, 122
Oud, J. J. P. (Jacobus Johannes Pieter), 52, 69, 155
Outcault, Richard, 20
Outdoor Advertising Association, 46, 70
Outdoor Advertising Association of America, 70
Ovitz, Michael, 116
Oxenaar, R. D. E., 78, 158, 182, 186, 204
Ozenfant, Amédée, 55, 60, 159


**P**

Packard, Vance, 47, 140, 227
Paepke, Walter P., 73, 128, 149
Paley, William, 18
Papanek, Victor, 71, 172, 180, 230
Papert, Koenig & Lois, 144, 152–153, 157
Papini, Giovanni, 44, 139
Paris-Clavel, Gerard, 110, 170
Parker, Brant, 156
Parker, Mike, 78, 158
Parrish, Maxfield, 38, 64, 159
Paul, Art, 71, 134
Paul Davis Studio, 200
Peach, Harry, 94
Peignot, Charles, 97, 199
Peignot, Georges, 47
Penn, Irving, 52

Pentagram, 174, 186, 204, 208, 214, 216, 222, 228, 230, 236
Péri, László, 64, 163
Pevsner, Nikolaus, 21, 94, 128, 199
Picabia, Francis, 53, 60, 69, 133
Picasso, Pablo, 18, 31, 34, 97, 154, 176
Pick, Frank, 32, 107
Pickering, Willian, 4
Pineles, Cipe, 41, 86, 90, 100, 108, 118, 120, 126, 144, 150, 158, 170, 180, 186, 216, 226
Pintori, Giovanni, 42, 95, 126
Pirtle, Woody, 110, 186, 196, 208, 218
Pissarro, Camille, 22
Pissarro, Esther Bensusan, 22, 129
Pissarro, Lucien, 22, 112
Pollock, Jackson, 42, 110, 129
Polykoff, Shirley, 33, 136
Ponti, Gio, 139, 172
Pop Art, 153
Popova, Lyubov Sergeevna, 65, 135
Poppenpohl, Sharon Helmer, 188, 208
Poster Advertising Association, 70
Postmodernism, ix, 126, 184
Powers, John E., 16
Poynor, Rick, 214, 228
Productivism, 61
Progressive Movement of China, 82
Pullman, Christopher, 107, 176, 180, 186
Purism, 55, 60
Push Pin Studio, 158, 164, 178, 198, 202


**Q**

Qiong-wen, Ha, 71, 132
Qian Jun-tao, 28


**R**

Radice, Barbara, 110
Rambow, Gunter, 98, 182, 192, 208
Rand, Ann, 149, 152, 170

Rand, Paul, 47, 64, 90, 92, 94, 96, 98, 106, 109, 110, 113, 114, 116, 118, 126, 127, 128, 132–133, 134, 138, 139, 140, 144–145, 149, 150, 152, 170, 174, 176, 180, 196, 202, 204, 206, 214, 216, 220, 224, 226, 227

Ransom, Will, 55, 136

Rauschenberg, Robert, 71, 155, 198

Ray, Man, (Emanuel Rabinovitch), 49, 53, 56, 61, 62, 63, 79, 92, 101, 104, 182

Raymond, Alexander, 90

Rayonism, 43

Reed, Ethel, 9

Reeves, Rosser, 38, 104, 159, 201

Reid, Jack McGregor (Jamie), 118, 178, 193

Reidemeister, Marie, 104, 145

Reinhard, Keith, 172

Reinhardt, Ad, 44, 163

Reiss Advertising, 104

Remington, Frederick, 34

Renner, Paul, 75, 133, 139

Repplier, Theodore (Ted), 110, 116, 172

Resor, Helen Lansdowne, 32, 157

Resor, Stanley, 32, 50, 68, 157

R/Greenberg Associates, 184, 186, 188, 192, 196, 198, 206, 214, 228

Rhead, Louis, 73

Rhodes, Silas, 48, 118

Richards & Associates, 136

Rietveld, Gerrit, 53, 69, 91, 157

Riney, Hal, 87, 182

Robinson, Boardman, 130

Robinson, Phyllis K., 62, 122

Roche, Juliette, 193

Rockwell, Norman, 50, 68, 134, 152, 156, 187

Rodchenko, Alexander, 52, 56, 60, 61, 62, 63–64, 66, 68, 71, 79, 82, 139, 188

Rogers, Albert Bruce, 19, 26, 47, 49, 76, 79, 140

Roker, Raymond, 165

Roller, Alfred, 20, 92

Rondthaler, Edward, 26, 94, 170

Ros, Lies, 130, 184

Rosenquist, James, 89

Rosenstock, Samuel, 114

Rothko, Mark, 171

Rowell, George, P., 7

Rozen, George Jerome, 86, 92, 122, 178

Ruder, Emil, 47, 118, 144, 162, 171

Ruffins, Reynolds, 83, 132, 134

Runyon, Richard C., 157

Russian Constructivism, 47

Russian Suprematist Movement, 45

Russolo, Luigi, 38, 118

Ruttkay, György, 178

Ruzicka, Rudolph, 64, 101, 187


**S**

Saarinen, Eero, 38, 150, 156

Saatchi, Charles, 110, 170, 203–204, 224, 233

Saatchi, Maurice, 116, 170, 203–204, 224

Saatchi & Saatchi, 203, 207, 224, 229

Sadek, George, 77

Salisbury, Mike, 107, 156, 178, 180

Salter, George, 97, 163

Sandberg, Willem, 138, 201

Sandgren & Murtha, 171

Sant'Elia, Antonio, 50

Sarnoff, David, 172

Sartre, Jean-Paul, 26, 193

Sato, Koichi, 112

Sattler, Josef, 84

Saul Bass & Associates, 155, 178

Saunders, Norman, 92, 152, 210

Savage, Jon, 133

Savan, Leslie, 129, 182

Saville, Peter, 136, 214

Sayles, John, 143

Scali, McCabe, Sloves, 149, 172, 188

Schad, Christian, 55

Schamberg, Morton Livingston, 55

Schawinsky, Xanti (Alexander), 25, 88, 92, 94, 100

Scher, Paula, 120, 178, 188, 192, 200, 202, 216, 222, 224, 228

Schleger, Hans, 182

Schlemmer, Oskar, 60, 63, 64, 65, 67, 110

Schlesinger, Stafan, 112, 121

Schmidt, Joost, 66, 68, 71, 72, 76, 120

Schmidt-Rottluff, Carl, 182

Schreuders, Piet, 129, 180, 184

Schroder, Rob, 184

Schuitema, Paul, 60, 176

Schulz, Charles M., 65, 126, 236

Schwab, Victor O., 52, 193

Schwitters, Kurt, 68, 70, 74, 120

Secession
    Austrian, 12
    Neue, 38
    Vienna, 11, 20, 22, 24, 46, 174

Sedelmaier, Joe, 89, 163

Sedelmaier Productions, 186

Segal, Bill, 236

Segal, George, 69

Segar, Elzie, 56, 78, 98

Segura, Carlos, 215

Severini, Gino, 38, 159

Shahn, Ben, 110, 122, 148, 167

Shanghai Style, 60

Shao–fei, Lu, 22, 82

Sheeler, Charles, 53, 159

Shire, Peter, 118

Sirowitz, Len, 87

Skolos, Nancy, 136

Slimbach, Robert, 139, 219

Sloan, Alfred, 159

Sloan, John, 38, 42, 129

Smale, John, 74

Smith, Sidney, 56, 64

Soglow, Otto, 70

Sontag, Susan, 89

Sorel, Edward, 83, 132, 134, 154, 162, 171

Sorrell, Martin, 114, 206

Sottsass, Ettore Jr., 52, 141, 157, 167,

182, 193, 195
Sottsass Associates, 193
Sowden, George James, 109
Spencer, Herbert, 69, 156, 162, 166
Spiekermann, Erik, 118, 177, 185, 196, 206, 214, 215, 217, 219
St. John, J. Allen, 51, 52, 140
Stankowski, Anton, 28, 132, 164
Stanton, Frank, 33
Starch, Daniel, 28, 189
Starck, Philippe, 215
Starowicjski, Franciszek, 83
Starr, Leonard, 140
Steinberg, Saul, 114, 126, 232
Steiner, Albe, 44, 172, 178
Steinweiss, Alex, 50, 120
Stella, Joseph, 116
Stenberg, Georgy, 64, 71, 77, 89
Stenberg, Vladimir, 64, 71, 77, 197
Stepanova, Varvara, 60, 62, 66, 74, 143
Stephens, Alice Barber, 87
Stermer, Dugald, 94, 156, 200
Stern, Bert, 152
Sterrett, Cliff (Clifford), 20, 42
Stickley, Gustav, 18, 27, 109
Stile Libertt, 20
Stone, Reynolds, 34, 135, 189
Stone, Sumner, 114, 207, 215, 217, 219
Storch, Otto, 44, 132
Studio Alchymia, 195
Studio Boggeri, 88
Studio De Lucchi, 204
Sullivan, Pat (Patrick), 62
Suprematism, 63
  Russian, 64
Surrealism, 47, 53, 63, 65, 69, 71, 92, 109, 136, 156, 159
Sussman, Deborah, 84, 157, 192
Sutnar, Ladislav, 84, 86, 100, 106, 112, 126, 130, 135, 138, 144, 150, 182
Swarte, Joost, 200
Swierzy, Waldemar, 8

**T**

Tadashi, Madsuda, 65, 142
Tanaka, Ikko, 83, 154
Tanguy, Yves, 136
Tatlin, Vladimir, 63, 133
Taylor, Gerald, 136
Teague, Walter Dorwin, 100, 149
Ted Bates & Co., 130, 134, 153
Teige, Karel, 60, 66, 72, 73, 76, 88, 92, 127
Testa, Armando, 52, 127, 218
Teutsch, János Mattis, 149
Thompson, Bradbury, 41, 100, 108, 112, 115, 127, 130, 138, 142, 152, 188, 224
Thompson, J. Walter, 50, 77
Thompson, Kristin, 163
Thun, Matteo, 130, 193
Thurber, James, 106, 150
Tice, Clara, 176
Tiffany, Louis C., 4, 89
Tihanyi, Lajos, 89, 98
Tinker, Jack, 28, 203
Tissi, Rosemarie, 97, 157, 164
Tolmer, Alfred, 84, 140
Toulouse-Lautrec, Henri de, 6, 18
Tomaszewski, Henryk, 47, 126, 130, 158
Tracy, Walter, 47, 175
Trafton, Howard Allen, 89, 95, 116
Trahey, Jane, 142, 148
Trepkowski, Tadeusz, 47, 139
Trudeau, Gary, 170, 224
Trump, Georg, 83, 91, 135, 138, 165, 203
Tscherny, George, 69, 138, 148, 152
Tschichold, Jan, 21, 66, 70, 72, 76, 83, 84, 85, 87, 88, 89, 92, 118, 157, 178
Twombly, Carol, 145, 201, 211, 215, 219
Tzara, Tristan, 51, 52, 60, 155

**U**

Uitz, Béla, 175
Umeda, Masanori, 107
Unger, Gerard, 109, 171, 183, 211
Unimark International Co., 159, 160, 163
Union of Artists, 52
Updike, Daniel Berkeley, 5, 26, 107
Utermohlen, Edwin, 135, 223

**V**

Valincenti, Rich, 143
Van Blokland, Erick, 163, 211, 215, 217
van de Velde, Henry, 46, 140
van der Leck, Bart, 50, 52, 55, 61, 143
van Doesburg, Théo, 52, 54, 62, 64, 68, 70, 72, 83, 84
van Dongen, Kees, 165
van Krimpen, Jan, 61, 71, 85, 131, 143
Vanderbyl, Michael, 118, 176, 192
Vanderbyl Design, 176
VanderLans, Rudy, 136, 198, 200, 211, 216
Varga, Arnold, 73, 222
Velde, Henry van de, 32
Venturi, Robert, 155, 160, 174, 183, 189
Verbeck, Gustave, 22
Vermeulen, Rick, 127
Vienna Workshops, 22
Vignelli, Massimo, 84, 154, 158, 159, 160, 164, 172, 185, 199, 202, 205, 216, 228, 229, 236
Vignelli Associates, 172
Vitt, Sam, 73
Vivarelli, Carlo L., 122, 204
Voight, Charles A., 54
von Freytag-Loringhoven, Elsa, 74
von Jawlensky, Alexei, 107
Vorticism, 47

**W**

Walker, Emery, 26
Warde, Beatrice, 86, 167
Warhol, Andy, 77, 140, 153, 155, 162, 172, 207
Warinner, Kathy, 140, 215, 227
Washburn Crosby Co., 62
Watson, John B., 143
Watson, Thomas J. Jr., 47, 180, 220
W.B.Doner & Co., 127
Weaver, Sylvester L., 33
Wei, Qin, 41, 99
Weingart, Wolfgang, 107, 165, 174, 184, 192, 194, 202, 237
Weiss, Emil Rudolf, 45, 73, 79, 110
Werkman, Hendrik N., 66, 115
Westover, Russ (Russell), 54, 62
Wieden, Dan, 196
Wieden & Kennedy, 196, 208, 210, 220, 224
Wild, M. Lorraine, 133
William Weintraub Advertising, 106
Williard, Frank, 66
Wilson, Robert Wesley "Wes," 97

Wirkkala, Tapio, 48
Wm. Esty Co., 135
Wolf, Henry, 132, 142, 150
Wolpe, Berthold, 26, 85, 87, 99, 177, 210
Woodward, Fred, 206
Wright, Frank Lloyd, 18, 21, 26, 32, 34, 43, 51, 145
Wunderman, Lester, 61, 118, 142
Wunderman, Ricotta & Kline, 142
Wurman, Richard Saul, 94, 182, 206, 214
Wyman, Lance, 97, 159, 164

**X**

Xun, Lu, 61, 94

**Y**

Y, Chitfu, 110
Yokoo, Tadanori, 94, 160, 174, 180, 228
Young, Art, 20, 38, 55, 110

Young, James Webb, 42, 116, 176
Young, Murat (Chic), 82
Young & Rubicam, 66, 72, 86, 109, 110, 148, 176, 214

**Z**

Zaid, Barry, 100
Zajkowski, Tony, 159
Zanini, Marco, 193
Zanuso, Marco Jr., 135
Zapf, Hermann, 55, 123, 127, 131, 134, 143, 149, 165, 167, 173, 183, 187, 189
Zapf-von Hesse, Gundrun, 55, 135, 165
Zeisel, Eva, 28
Zepplin, Count Ferdinand von, 17
Zhen-hau, Cai, 42
Zhi-fo, Chen, 69, 82
Zhong-xin, Ai, 48, 106
Zieff, Howard, 171
Zwart, Piet, 93, 184

## BOOKS FROM ALLWORTH PRESS

**Graphic Design and Reading: Explorations of an Uneasy Relationship**
*edited by Gunnar Swanson* (softcover, 6¹/₂ × 9⁷/₈, 240 pages, $19.95)

**Design Connoisseur: An Eclectic Collection of Imagery and Type**
*by Steven Heller* (softcover, 7¹/₂ × 9³/₈, 208 pages, $19.95)

**Design Literacy (continued): Understanding Graphic Design**
*by Steven Heller* (softcover, 6³/₄ × 10, 296 pages, $19.95)

**Design Literacy: Understanding Graphic Design**
*by Steven Heller and Karen Pomeroy* (softcover, 6³/₄ × 10, 288 pages, $19.95)

**Design Culture: An Anthology of Writing from the AIGA Journal of Graphic Design**
*edited by Steven Heller and Marie Finamore* (softcover, 6³/₄ × 10, 320 pages, $19.95)

**Looking Closer 3: Classic Writings on Graphic Design**
*edited by Michael Bierut, Jessica Helfand, Steven Heller, and Rick Poynor* (softcover, 6³/₄ × 10, 304 pages, $18.95)

**Looking Closer 2: Critical Writings on Graphic Design**
*edited by Michael Bierut, William Drenttel, Steven Heller, and DK Holland*
(softcover, 6³/₄ × 10, 288 pages, $18.95)

**Looking Closer: Critical Writings on Graphic Design**
*edited by Michael Bierut, William Drenttel, Steven Heller, and DK Holland*
(softcover, 6³/₄ × 10, 256 pages, $18.95)

**Design Dialogues** *by Steven Heller and Elinor Pettit* (softcover, 6³/₄ × 10, 272 pages, $18.95)

**The Swastika: Symbol Beyond Redemption?**
*by Steven Heller* (hardcover, 6¹/₂ × 9¹/₂, 176 pages, $21.95)

**Sex Appeal: The Art of Allure in Graphic and Advertising Design**
*by Steven Heller* (softcover, 6³/₄ × 10, 288 pages, $18.95)

**AIGA Professional Practices in Graphic Design**
*The American Institute of Graphic Arts, edited by Tad Crawford* (softcover, 6³/₄ × 10, 320 pages, $24.95)

**Business and Legal Forms for Graphic Designers**
*by Tad Crawford and Eva Doman Bruck* (softcover, 8¹/₂ × 11, 240 pages, includes CD-ROM, $24.95)

Please write to request our free catalog. To order by credit card, call 1-800-491-2808 or send a check or money order to Allworth Press, 10 East 23rd Street, Suite 510, New York, NY 10010. Include $5 for shipping and handling for the first book ordered and $1 for each additional book. Ten dollars plus $1 for each additional book if ordering from Canada. New York State residents must add sales tax.

To see our complete catalog on the World Wide Web, or to order online, you can find us at *www.allworth.com*.